BORN AGAIN, AGAIN

BORN AGAIN, AGAIN

That time I fell down a rabbit hole and spent twenty-two years as a
Bible thumping, tongue speaking, Gospel preaching,
Born Again Christian. And then I woke up.

෴

Kathy Martens

WWW.KACKYBIRDPRESS.COM

KACKYBIRD PRESS
HATCHED IN SACRAMENTO CALIFORNIA
WWW.KACKYBIRDPRESS.COM

Library of Congress Control Number:2019910586

ISBN: PB: 978-1-7333687-0-4; eBook: 978-1-7333687-1-1

Published by Kackybird Press
Printed in the United States of America
Design by Kathy Martens

Author photo by Cat Gwynn | www.catgwynn.com

To find out more about the author please visit:
www.kathymartens.com

PROLOGUE

xii

BORN

1

BORN AGAIN (PART I)

30

BORN AGAIN (PART II)

72

BORN AGAIN (PART III)

264

BORN AGAIN, AGAIN

354

THAT GIRL'S GOTTA LOTTA NERVANA

366

EPILOGUE

374

WITH ALL MY HEART, THANK YOU

375

AUTHOR BIO

376

To Mike, Em, and Tim: my North.

"The soul is the perceiver and revealer of truth."
~Ralph Waldo Emerson

PROLOGUE

PROLOGUE

"What can wash away my sin?
Nothing but the blood of Jesus;
What can make me whole again?
Nothing but the blood of Jesus."

THE FAMILIAR WORDS OF THE OLD hymn—now set to electric guitars—swirl around us as we make our way through the tunnel. Words that have been a source of consolation and home for me these last two-plus decades. They pulse, rhythmic and modern, atop a voice made for rock-n-roll: like broken plate glass, smooth and crystalline on the surface, jagged and cutting on the edges. She sings:

"Oh! precious is the flow

That makes me white as snow;

No other fount I know,

Nothing but the blood of Jesus . . ."

I try to focus on the words; I picture it: a fount of blood. I find no comfort in the message in this moment; it feels violent, paradoxical, distant. And it's nearly drowned by the other voices. Moaning and wailing, bursts of cackling laughter, streams of comingled gibberish and coherent prayers murmured and shouted, all echo and bounce off the strains of the music. A cacophony.

The voices are familiar, people I know and love. The walls of the *fire tunnel*, as it is called, are my brothers and sisters in Christ, standing shoulder to shoulder along the breadth of the altar. Their hands and declarations brush and bludgeon us as we, the recipients of their ministry, walk through this gauntlet of prayer. I know this is meant to be a blessing—why do I rue this exercise?

As we move slowly through, like a string of prisoners walking the green mile, the activity around us grows toward chaos. Many of those praying over us are becoming increasingly fervent, frenzied, fomenting like so many monkeys on the brink of complete pandemonium.

My eyes barely open, I stumble into Fran—very wide Fran—who has stopped in front of me and is doubled over, bobbing her torso up and down and yelling, "Ho!" She repeats her cry with each bob, "Ho-oh-oh-oh!" Her bottom seems to expand with every deep bow.

She finally drops to her hands and knees, continuing her circuit at a crawl. The dozen or so people ahead of us move forward in various states of staggering and weaving, a queue of drunken sailors. Three bodies ahead of me, Brenda crumples in a faint and is gently caught and carried off to the side, the tunnel wall parting to allow her to be transported to a spot on the floor. Many other bodies are strewn there, *slain in the Spirit*, each covered with a small shimmery *modesty blanket*.

Carefully I proceed, hands held out in front of me palms up, like I'm carrying an invisible tray of something precious and breakable, a ring bearer transporting the promise of true love. Hands reach from the sides of the tunnel of bodies and rest gently on my hands, my head, my shoulders. Some of them quake as if full of electricity. I'm jostled now and then by someone on the sideline losing their balance and oozing into me as if to invite me into the inebriation.

"Get her, Lord!" they shout.

"Fire! Holy Fire! Fill her!" The prayers are intense, insistent. They rise up and fill the air like Southern heat, close and thick and sticky. It's hard to breathe in here.

I'm willing to receive whatever the Spirit wants to impart to me, but the hullabaloo around me is distracting. I know the expectation is for some kind of manifestation: a quiver, a twitch, a full body shake, an invisible punch in the gut, an eruption of Holy laughter, but I'm just not feeling it.

Instead, each beat of my heart is sending a gush of irritation that seeps through my system, transforming into anger as it surges up to the top of my skull trying to bash its way to freedom.

I make my way to the end of the tunnel. Finally, air. I'm suddenly swept with a deep and terrible tiredness. The tray I've been carrying weighs a thousand pounds. I let my arms drop. I want to keep walking, out the door, to our car, and into the sunset. But we're in so deep.

When did my faith start being such a heavy a burden? How did something that was once a refuge to me become so much work?

How the heck did I get here?

BORN

BORN

"I could tell you my adventures—beginning from this morning," said Alice a little timidly; "but it's no use going back to yesterday, because I was a different person then." - Alice's Adventures in Wonderland

IT ALL STARTED HERE (Or, be careful what you pray for.)

I LIE NEXT TO MY HUSBAND, WHO is managing to sleep like a baby despite all of the resounding noise inside my head. My pounding heart threatens to pummel its way through my rib cage. My left-brain stacks one scenario on top of another at such a ridiculous rate I fear if it goes on much longer, I'm going to crash my hard drive.

Eternity with God or a career in film? Eternity with God or fame and wealth? Eternity with God or friends, margaritas, and dirty jokes? What will I choose? Heaven or Hell? What will it be? Questions and fears pluck at the strings of my mind, a dissonant and disquieting duet.

My chest and upper lip feel slick and clammy. I'm nauseous, muscles clamped down tight. I want to unzip and crawl out of my skin.

Then with no premeditation, I pray. With all my being. "God, please," I breathe, "Please."

Hot tears make their way down my cheeks, pool at the base of my throat.

Up 'til now everything had been fine. I was on my way. I was rolling along: a newlywed, a first year student at performing arts school, wholly immersed in my passion, learning the sacred craft; exploring my feelings, my sensuality, my potty mouth. I had discovered my *To Be*—that's actor speak for how to *stop acting* and *to be* in the moment—and had my sights fully set on my future at the podium where I would stand holding my little Golden Man, thanking my director, my fellow actors, and members of the Academy. Then I met Patricia. Patricia knew Jesus. She was an absolute anomaly in that den of iniquity called acting school. She didn't even cuss. We became fast friends.

We were an unlikely pair, Patricia and I. She was quiet and kind. She was unassuming and gentle. She was straight and narrow. I was intense, opinionated, sexually explicit in my humor, had a take-charge way of operating, and the mouth of a sailor. I'll never know why she was interested in me as a friend. You might think, since she was a devout Christian, her motivation was to make sure I got saved, but she never once preached at me. She never once suggested I bow my head, close my eyes, and receive Jesus as my Lord and Savior. She accepted me exactly as I was.

Perhaps the reason I was so drawn to her was that she loved me, in all my heathen splendor, and it made me want to be a better person. And I did genuinely try to be better. When I was in her presence, my colorful expletives were always appended with an apology. "Fuck! Sorry." "Goddamit! Sorry." To which Patricia would invariable respond with a shrug, a little smile, and a soft, "It's okay." Even delicious gossip was beginning to leave an acrid taste on my tongue. Behavioral convictions began to haunt me, whereas before they were easily ignored or unnoticed entirely.

There was something about the way she simply lived her faith—with such authenticity—that drew me in. As I witnessed her quiet devotion, my own longing for something that real, that intensely intimate, began to become too much to bear. The deep ache in my gut to apprehend *the truth* was very disturbing to me. So I started asking her questions.

"So, what is the deal with Christianity? Do I have to be a missionary? 'Cuz I hate bugs." "Will I go to hell if I don't believe in Jesus?" "Do I have to give up my Sunday mornings?" "What about cussing?" "I suppose smoking weed is totally out." "Do I have to go around the neighborhood knocking on doors and handing out pamphlets?" "Oh God, will I have to give up all my friends?" "Will they give *me* up?" "Sex, can I still have sex?" "I mean *good* sex?"

I was tripping so badly because I'd known this guy in my college theatre days, Heinrick, and he was also Born Again. He was a nice enough fellow, but would often create giant holes in the conversation with random wild-eyed giggling and constant religious comments. He rambled about the Lord with a slight lisp, and his sudden verbal ejaculations had a way of making people clench. We would be going over blocking for a scene and the director would say, "Cross left," and Heinrick would say, "Jesus bore the croth for your thinth," or "Pick up your croth and follow me." *Oh God. Would I become like Heinrick?*

I don't recall how Patricia answered all of my insane questioning, except for one explanation that has never left me.

We were sitting together on the cool strip of lawn that bordered the front of the arched entrance to the performing arts school where we were classmates. I could hear the distant *tink-scritch, tink-tink-tink,* of steel on steel as students in the fencing class battled it out in the inner quad of the school campus.

Patricia was running a yellow highlighter along her lines inside her copy of *Bus Stop*.

"I guess I'm just always aware of His presence," she said.

"Like, you mean, all the time?" I asked.

"Pretty much," she said.

I pictured Jesus sitting in Patricia's comfy wicker chair holding her My Little Pony cushion while she and her boyfriend get it on in her—wait a minute—*Ohhhhhh, now I see why the no sex/fondling/kissing before marriage thing is so big. But what about after marriage? Does the Lord hang out in the boudoir then too? Gaaaah! Jeeez, I don't know . . .*

"Does He talk to you?" I pressed.

She ran her thumb tips over the cuticles of her lovely slender nails. She had been a hand model at one time. "Sort of. I guess it just comes naturally to me—imagining Him beside me in every situation. Guiding me. Helping me to make the right choices. I'm just always aware of His presence, and His love for me."

Now I envisioned a sepia toned, soft-focused Robert Powell in his course woolen robe and long flowing hair sitting in the passenger seat of Patricia's Honda Accord, gently advising her, "Turn right on Sepulveda, beloved daughter," all the while looking at her with those piercing cerulean eyes, enraptured with her beauty and sending waves of adoration and unconditional love into her soul.

When I was coming out of my tweens I was curiously attracted to Robert Powell. His huge face consumed the front of the TV guide section of the Sunday *Chronicle*, heralding the coming of *Jesus of Nazareth*. He gazed at me kindly with sad, knowing eyes, his earthy shawl lightly covering his long oiled hair. I kept that edition in my room for a long time and studied the face of the man people called Savior. Those blue eyes penetrated me deeply. I secretly wanted him. Through my teens I kinda had a thing for guys that looked like Jesus, but I also liked guys who smelled nice and those things, sadly, seldom went together.

My family wasn't Christian, per se. That is, we didn't attend church when I was growing up. In fact, for a long time I thought God's last name was Dammit. Religion was never a topic of discussion that I was aware of. As a young child I did often, however, contemplate the idea of God and was drawn to the mystery man Jesus. I had friends who were churchgoers who seemed to know who Jesus was. Our neighbors across the street were Mormon, and they always seemed to be headed to church. They invited me to go with them once (they had a daughter my age, eight or nine) but I didn't want to because they also had a nineteen-year-old son who was a Dwarf, and I was terrified of his miniature size. He was also kind of an asshole and just plain mean, but I remember thinking that Jesus might want me to try to see his heart and be nice to him. I didn't go over there often.

On the rare occasion that I went to church with some friend for Easter or something, I always felt pretty certain that God *was*, and that somehow I was connected to Him. I was always confused, though, by the fact that there were so many opinions about exactly *who* God was and what made Him happy and sad. Stories of following Him seemed to come with one price tag or another, and that was enough to keep me safely on my heathen path. I even heard once about a guy passing through town who'd been traipsing around the country in a robe, dragging a huge wooden cross on his back. That was way out of my price range, but I admired his passion.

I think what fascinated me in actuality was the *idea* of Jesus. I was taken with the notion that there might truly be a wise and wonderful person who judged no one and who would hug me and tell me how much I was loved. I recall wondering if I would ever have the ability to look into someone else's heart and feel the same kind of love that I hoped Jesus would feel if he looked into mine. I wanted very much to be like that.

Patricia was like that.

In the weeks that followed my conversation with Patricia, I pondered her answers, and my spiritual quest began to take on a new urgency. It became an agonizing maze of confusing images, maddening questions and dark, twisted fears. This strange need to settle on what it was that I believed seemed to be escalating for no reason that I could put my finger on. I would lay awake at night, my mind swirling with scenes of starving African children, street corner soapboxes, and a new wardrobe of high-necked frocks and knee socks.

And now, here I am, experiencing another late night foray into the Twilight Zone, all of my frantic ruminations sending me into what would be known decades later as a panic attack.

"Please help me," I pray. "Help me to know if you're real. Show me if Jesus is the deal and if I'm supposed to follow Him. Please, God . . ." My prayers melt into the kind of crying I remember as a child, coming up from deep inside my guts, except I try to suppress my moans so I won't wake Mike. Wracking, silent sobs. Hot coursing tears.

Suddenly, with the swiftness of a sudden summer breeze, the most surprising sense of calm washes over me. My tears abate abruptly. I'm aware of some other presence. A sweet heaviness descends from the top of my head and runs down my entire body like dense, warm, melting honey; all my convulsed muscles relax and melt into the bed. I'm wrapped in a soft blanket of love so strong that it holds me fast, like a parent holding a flailing child to keep her from injuring herself. I weep some more, but this time it feels more akin to joy; and then, I sleep. Like a baby.

I wake the next day relieved by the absence of impending insanity. In fact, I feel pretty damn good. *So what the heck was all that? Was that God?*

Was it Jesus? I'm not sure, but I feel a deep sense that I have a friend on the other side, at least. And it appears they like me a lot.

I lie in bed listening to the gentle slapping of water coming from the shower, a cheerful rhythm behind Mike's quiet singing: *I wanna sing you a love song, I wanna rock you in my arms all night long . . .*

FOUNDATIONAL IMPRINTS (Or, maybe it all started here . . .)

I was born into a middle-class white family. My picturesque suburban homeland was comfortably arranged in tidy patterns of streets and cul-de-sacs lined with well-appointed single-family tract homes in pastel hues. And there was, of course, one sore thumb marring the landscape. Everything on that lot was grayscale and peeling. Thorny brambles hugged the sad house closely and reached to the roof, which was crowned with its own perpetual storm system. Shady characters of unknown origin inhabited it, including a teenage boy with one very large orthopedic shoe. Other than that, our neighborhood was all Sprouse-Reitz Five & Dime and ice cream trucks.

Being the youngest with a chasm of age between my two siblings and myself—they're ten and twelve years older—I was, in effect, an only child (my mom said I was a delightful and very welcome oops). Consequently, I spent most of my time by myself. My sister and brother moved out of the house by the time I was eight, and my parents both worked. My house key dangled around my neck from a little ball chain; I wore my dog-tag with a soldierly courage and perhaps even a bit of pride at being thought mature enough to be home alone after school.

In some ways, hanging out with myself so much as a kid might have been what I really preferred. Or, I suppose, it could have been the cause of all my odd peculiarities. Solitude can be a wonderful breeding ground for imagination, and I ended up with a highly active one that gave me many long hours (and subsequent years) of very creative play.

My parents were decent folk. They worked hard and provided well. We did some normal stuff like camping, birthday parties with cake and presents, Christmas with trimmed trees, and family visits to gramma and grampa's house. My parents were also fairly social, throwing parties with bee-hived women and crew cut men in attendance, cheese fondue, and mom wowing the crowd with Rachmaninoff and boogie-woogie on the piano. And there was plenty of alcohol. Plenty.

My childhood recollections of my dad: tall, thin and dashing, broad smile, copious curly black hair, neatly coifed in short perfect waves, Old Spice. He was like a movie star, a demi-god to me. I was his spaniel, following him around, happily engrossed in his every move.

Watching him shave was a ritual I loved. His electric razor buzzed cheerfully, changing pitch as it glided over the curves and dimples of his jaw and chin. I would endeavor to contort my face along with him. He would reach over and run the vibrating shaver heads over my smooth little girl skin. I had no idea the cap was on. He would splash the sweet and spicy aftershave into both hands and rub them together briskly; then with quick, graceful movements, he'd apply the cooling elixir to his cheeks, his chin, his neck. He'd rub his hands smartly together again, and then one quick pat for my cheeks too. "Howz'at my little Kacky Bird," he'd say laughing and smiling. I'd touch his freshly shaved face; soft and smooth and smelling like adventure.

I wanted to be like my dad. When we worked together outside in the yard, I liked to take off my shirt like he did. I'd put it in my back pocket, just like him. When I played house with the neighbor kids across the street, I always wanted to be the dad. They didn't want to play house with me anymore because I said that my shirt must be off and tucked in my back pocket. That's how dads do it. Don't they know that? Dumb girls.

My mom: a beauty; thin, flat stomach, slender legs; brown hair like rich chocolate, sometimes heaped on her head like piles of dark clouds, sometimes pulled tight and shiny, in a long, smooth ponytail, her smile sweet, like springtime sunshine. Her soft brown eyes—round like a doe—would look into mine, relaxed and safe. She was mostly gentle and kind, but sometimes I could hear her voice, upset, shouting, harsh, in the late hours when she and Dad would fight.

And music. Oh how she played her music. She made our piano sing. The melodies of Chopin, Beethoven, Bach, Rachmaninoff would wind their way up the stairs and into my bedroom. I knew the names because they'd lived in our house from before I was born. For hours she'd play. Pianissimo. Forte. I wanted to be like my mom, but she and our piano had a special understanding that I would never know, so I would try to be like her in this way: I'd try to be kind.

My father worked in computers; my mother, in our restaurant. They bought the pizza parlor when I was quite young. Maybe five. Maybe younger. We spent many hours there, surrounded by the aromas of yeasty dough, tomato sauce, garlic, and spicy sausage. Beer. It was my second home. My mom also spent many hours in her office in our house. Adding machine, ashtray, butts, large books with many columns of numbers. Her fingers would fly over the keys just like on our piano. Adding. Subtracting. She was often very busy, but I could find things to do.

My parents separated and then divorced before I hit double digits. The lead-in to their separation was raw and angry and full of hurtful words, better left to drift into the forgotten. These memories were tucked deeply away, quietly running the background programs that underpinned my operating system over the years that followed. There's a clear division of my recollection of my parents before and after that event—like a story in two parts—but with a lot of missing pieces.

I didn't see my dad very much once he no longer lived in our house. He moved to Indiana for work shortly thereafter, and didn't return to California until I was nearly out of my teens. It was just my mom and me for many years and I spent most nights sleeping in her bed. We snuggled like a pair of spoons and I often fell asleep trying to match the rhythm of her breathing. She would hold my hand. Squeeze, squeeze, squeeze, meant: I, love, you.

I have only isolated and fleeting memories of my siblings living at home. My sister, the eldest, was a strong presence for the few years of recollection I have of her there. She was very tall and willowy, and carried herself like an Amazon queen. Her long brown mane reached right to her spectacular tush. In fact, her hair was so long, she used empty beer cans as curlers. She could command a room with her quietly fierce energy and long sexy legs. Although it wouldn't have been conceived of in the late sixties (well, except for in some very B sci-fi movies), I had an innate sense that she might rule the world one day and that she would do so with a firm but kind hand.

My sister was at once loving and terrifying. I'd lie in her lap, and her tummy would tell me secrets: "Erierierieirierrrrr. Oyoyoyyoyieeeeririr. Weeeeouyoioioi." She'd play her guitar and sing her haunting renditions of *Because* and *Puff the Magic Dragon*. Oh the melodic tapestries she would weave around me like warm wispy blankets. But God forbid I should chew my potato chips with the gleeful abandon with which they were meant to be chewed—then it was "OFF WITH HER HEAD!" All she had to do was utter a quiet, "Kathy," which meant, "Thou shalt not crunch thy potato chips! Thou shalt suck on them before chewing, until they are good and mushy and quiet, lest I raise mine right arm and smite thee with the pox!" She can still do the same thing today with a glance over the tops of her granny glasses.

Her wedding was like a magical fairy tale. It was there that I learned that she was indeed, a Queen of the faeries and not of the great warrior goddesses as I had previously surmised. The planning, the provisions that were being gathered, clandestine meetings and frequent comings and goings of the queen's entourage began to bring my secret lineage into the light.

When The Day finally arrived, I awoke with my tummy in an uproar, feeling weak and woozy. Everyone was bustling and buzzing in an intense frenzy and all I could do was try to stay out of the way. Being of the royal line, I was admitted into the inner chamber of the attending faeries, where we all donned our spider silk gowns and flower tiaras.

As Handmaiden to the Queen, I was given the sacred task of distributing the crafty blossom, love-in-idleness, to each of the worshippers in the Mitrópoli, preparing the way for Her Majesty. I was so nervous, and sick as a dog in my peachy satin raiment. I was hoping with all my heart not to barf upon it and ruin its shimmery loveliness.

Of course, being a young princess myself, I performed my task with great skill and grace, my feet nary touching the earth as I floated down the aisle scattering petals and handing out posies to the devoted. The only blot on the ethereal event: the tripping of the groom as he made his way down the white carpet to where his ushers awaited his arrival and where he would receive his beloved Sovereign Lady. There was but a momentary hushed gasp from the assemblage, but no one gave thought to what meaning this little stumble might hold in the stars. Just a little falter; perhaps a slight wrinkle in the runner, a miscalculated shoe size, but surely no omen to bring worry to the joy of the day. Surely not.

The great wedding feast followed at our home, our ordinary house having been transformed into a worthy setting. Our backyard patio and doughboy pool were arrayed fittingly like Titania's bower. Miles of silk ivy and exotic flowers entwined themselves around every fixed object. The many tentacled pool sweep was the Kraken—its wriggling arms wrangled and harnessed into a playful fountain—throwing rainbows into the air from the center of the Queen's mirrored forest pool. Dazzling melon balls and lobster tails and ever-flowing champagne abounded. The day was as a dream to me and over in a blink.

As she ran through showers of rice to get into the honeymoon getaway car, we marveled that my sister had transmuted into Aphrodite, decked in velvet indigo hot pants and knee high blue suede go-go boots. Her waist-long brown hair flowed behind her as she made her way through her adoring subjects and into her sunset. I felt no joy in her blessed event; I was losing an anchor and a guardian angel. Without her, my brother would be free to torture me at will.

☙

Oh brother. My brother. He didn't mean any of it to be mean, I'm sure, but what he called fun, was the stuff of psycho thrillers and *Inner Sanctum* episodes. Well, I guess one man's fun is another's nightmare. The subconscious plantings of my brother's twisted antics (that were somehow presented as "babysitting") were I'm sure, among the seeds of fear that ultimately drove me to the arms of sweet Jesus.

Here are a few excerpts from Little Kacky's Shop of Horrors:

The young girl, so innocently trusting, prattled on about Baby Bear and Goldilocks, as her loving older brother tucked her into her snuggly warm bed.

"Sweet dreams," he cooed. Just the tiniest twist at the corner of his grin. He made his way down the hall, promising to turn on the bathroom light as a beacon of hope and guardian against ghouls and ghosts.

She shimmied her way deep into the enveloping softness and safety of the covers, far from the edge, where she'd been told that boney fingers and creeping things could gain entry. All was quiet. All was drifting into the drowsy, dreamy land of Mr. Sandman. Then from the darkness it began. Just a single chord at first. Then another more dissonant one, a half-step higher. From the recesses of the dark house, the piano—which regularly purred with happy harmonies at the masterful stroke of her beloved mother—seethed with the music of impending doom. Two ominous chords played again and again with increasing tempo and ferocity until they were crashing together in an insane cacophony of demented music mixed with the screams of a terrified and traumatized girl-child. And the laugh. That demonic laugh. It came closer, moving toward the bedroom of the frozen tot.

Then in popped the familiar giggling face of the "babysitter." He asked, "You okay?" He chuckled as he wandered off to the family room to watch Night Gallery. "G'night!"

⁂

Little girl in bed. Alone upstairs. Dark night. A scraping scuffling noise approached outside her window.

Two story house. *What could get up on the roof?* reasoned her five-year old mind.

Footsteps crunched on the dry shake shingles outside the dormer. Closer. A hag's scratchy voice crooned, "Kaaaaaaathyyyyyy."

The petrified girl dared a glance at the dark glass. Suddenly a ghostly white hand smacked against the thin barrier with a sickening slap, twitching and grasping, palm pressed flat against the pane, fingers wriggling, reaching for her, squirming, coming to get her.

That familiar giggle again. Just the babysitter.

⁂

Little Kackybird, as her papa so lovingly called her, sat alone, contentedly eating her snack of cheddar cheese squares at the sunny kitchen table. She liked to use colorful toothpicks to pick up each buttery block and pop it into her mouth. Then a big swig of milk to wash it all down, just like dad did with his homemade brew and chunks of Swiss. Papa usually drank his beer out of heavy glass-bottomed pewter steins that were big enough to fit Kacky's entire head into; but she was happy with her little glass jelly jar. No one could make cheese and beer sound as good as dad. Like a Viking of old, he'd take a big bite of cheese, a frothy quaff of ale, and with cheeks bulging would pronounce with great joy, "Zjatcha gud hunga cheej, Kackybird!" She practiced hard to get the slurppy words out without the contents of her mouth dribbling down her shirt. It was an art.

On this particular bright spring day, the birds sang outside the wide window that looked onto the shimmering blue lake (doughboy pool). Mamma was busy doing her Saturday chores. The men were out rabbit hunting, so it was a very pleasant afternoon with just the girls at home.

Without warning, up into the window popped the mangled head of a bunny piked on a bloody stick. Shrieking violins scratched out pulsing notes as the disembodied head danced and bobbed before the swooning child. Little Thumper's lifeless eyes lolled at Little Kacky pleading "Save me from this nefarious bastard!" From just below the window ledge the triumphant hunter-brother jumped up, laughing, "We're back!"

My brother had issues of his own. I have memories of him running through the house, our red-faced father hot on his tail, yelling, cussing, and threatening life and limb. The odd thing was, I also remember my brother laughing then too. Seems that whatever pain he would have to endure as recompense for whatever he did was well worth it for the fun of seeing my dad come unhinged.

Call him demented and sadistic; call him fun loving and puckish—whatever he may have been—my brother always marched to his own drummer. But, he has long since forsaken his Schadenfreude and, oddly enough, given his heart to Jesus.

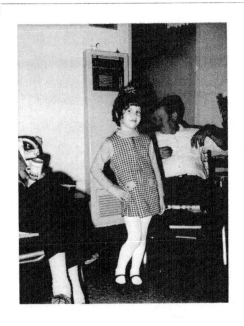

A STAR IS BORN.

A STAR IS BORN

I decided quite young that no matter who or what God was, I was going to be a famous actor. Or a rock star. Perhaps I gravitated toward the arts as a way to bring some of my imaginary worlds into this one. And perhaps, as a way to find some sense of connection, some sense that I wasn't alone.

I was first exposed to theatre when I was probably five or six. I watched, transfixed, as my sister stood onstage in a high school production of which she was the star. I was instantly and strangely drawn to this dark art. And I adored the movies. I remember vividly my sister taking me to see my first film on the big screen. We went to the drive-in to behold *The Golden Voyage of Sinbad*. Pure bedazzlement. The chick with the eye on her palm and the crazy possessed Shiva statues freaked me out, but other than that I was solidly captivated.

When I was a bit older, my mom took me to my first grown up movie: The Sting. I was smitten. It wasn't so much the sexiness or the violence—although that was alluring to me—it was more the intrigue, the wonderful characters, the art direction. And the story. All the world went away for a minute. All I could think was, *I want to do that*. I wanted to be a part of creating something so magical and entrancing that it held the audience in rapt wonder. In bed at night, lying very flat and still, I was able to transform into a one-dimensional version of myself immortalized on a giant movie poster.

I was equally drawn to music. Yep, demon Hollywood was working in sync with the fiend Rock-n-Roll to woo my virgin soul into the pit. By age twelve, I had already headlined at many a coliseum, backed up by Peter Frampton, wailing at the top of my voice into my hairbrush. At thirteen, a friend introduced me to a girl who introduced me to some guys who were looking for a female vocalist for their rock band. Of course I was wicked impressive at the tryout with my big belty voice and rockin' giant hair. They signed me at once. We did a total of one gig downtown at the annual summer arts festival in the park. Then, sadly, we broke up. Summer was over, and it was time for us to move on with starting back to school and all.

And then it happened. When I was fourteen, a notice appeared in the newspaper. The local community theatre was holding auditions for their summer production of *Sugar* (the musical version of the film *Some Like it Hot*, which starred Marilyn Monroe)—and I knew it was my destiny. Should I dare to try? It was yes or die. But this was a whole new world for me. What do I do? What should I sing for my audition piece? Well, of course: "Desperado" by The Eagles would be perfect. I hadn't heard of Hammerstein, Sondheim, or Schwartz yet, but I walked into that audition room and wowed that unsuspecting panel of theatre people with my gutsy rock-n-roll ballad. Luckily, I had enough savvy to leave my hairbrush in the car.

In a manner of speaking, it was during my first curtain call that I was born again. I swept onstage with the rest of the chorus girls at the end of our first performance of *Sugar*, and the thunderous applause of the crowd was nothing less than heavenly intoxication. I had been baptized into the Sacred Church of the Insatiable Thespian, and there was no turning back. After that there wasn't a show I didn't audition for and play a part in for many years.

I don't recall thinking much about God during that time, except perhaps during my second production, *Godspell*. I guess you could say that it was my first Bible study. I learned some of the parables and cried genuine tears when Jesus wiped the grease paint from each of our faces, saying goodbye to his beloved disciples just before his betrayal and subsequent crucifixion. Every night as we writhed and wailed during our clown Jesus' metaphorical death, I felt a profound sense of sorrow, guilt, and deep anguish; and again, cried big crocodile tears. This experience was another taste of the crack that is acting—the zone where you touch the soul of a character—and for those of us with the weakness, it is a forever addiction.

Addiction was a path I could have easily taken. It runs in my family. Looking back on some of my addictive tendencies, I can venture to say that it may have been some kind of extraterrestrial intervention that brought the arts and specifically theatre into my world. Life could be too damn painful for me, and because I was just plain curious, some of the things I went to for comfort could have led down the slippery slope to AA or NA.

When I was in seventh grade, I got busted for smoking pot. The actual smoking part started in sixth grade—I got high for the first time with a friend's dad. My mom and my stepdad (yes, she remarried—another scary story altogether) decided that I must have been bored with school. The solution? Why of course, bypass eighth grade and bump me up to high school, where more mature kids and greater academic challenge would surround me. From my mouth: "Yes! Bring on the algebra!" In my head: *Yes! Easier access to weed!*

And other interesting substances.

I'm not going to lie to you; I tried it all. Well not *all*. Luckily, most of the really bad stuff was not available or affordable to me, but what I could get I dibble-dabble-di-doobied in.

There were a couple of times that being high got scary. Like the time my friend Sammy and I decided it would be really smart to drop acid at an amusement park. When I got tired of my feet appearing to be about a half mile down below my knees, seeing the whole world through a fish eye lens, and experiencing intermittent deafness, I said, "Okay, I'm done now." But the Evil Buzz said, "No, no you're not-ot-ot-ot . . . we're going to do this for several more hoursssss . . . " I don't recall that we went on any rides that day. We didn't need to.

Despite my curiosity, I also had a predilection for being fearful which was probably a blessing in disguise. I was afraid of getting too high, afraid of getting brain damage, afraid of becoming a strung-out junkie, of being busted, of failing algebra, of being a *really* bad girl, of waking up with some guy I'd never met, of vomiting or being vomited on—all ingredients for a beautiful, holy recipe to keep me from turning forever to the Dark Side.

As providence would have it, pretending to be someone else was much more fun for me, so Sam Shepard, Richard Rogers, and Constantin Stanislavsky became benign addictions I could live with.

෴

I really should thank my (ex) stepdad for the bright idea of promoting me from seventh grade straight into high school. (I have little else to thank him for—oh, except requiring me to learn to change a tire and check my oil before I could get my license.) The part of the intervention I'm glad for was his encouragement during high school to sign up for concurrent classes at the local college (to keep me *really* busy, dontcha know). I'm sure he was thinking psychology or auto shop. What did I take? Why, drama classes of course.

Oh, and also ballet, jazz, modern, and tap. Of course, I fell in love with the Dance. Here was another drug that got deep into my cells. It awakened some distant past-life muscle memory that exploded with joy in this new-found movement.

My teacher was a tough African American woman with no tolerance for slackers or crybabies. Ms. Evelyn was in her forties and though her middle had caught up with her edges, she was lithe and dense, with a back end like two solid volleyballs lashed together with steel tape. Built like a Mack, moved like Pavlova. She had two daughters in the class who were destined for the professional ballet. They moved like silk and leapt like gazelles, chins held high, dancing in a stratosphere that I would never achieve. There were quite a few advanced dancers in class, all of whom where patient and kind to me, some became my dear friends. There were a few actors there as well, trying to round out their skills for theatre. I was one of those.

I worked hard in Ms. Evelyn's class. I wanted to move like a gazelle too, but for all my long limbs and thin frame, when I looked in that wide mirror that spanned the dance room, I always looked more like a giraffe—a little stiff and gangly. Their grand jetés looked like upside down T's. Mine looked like upside down Y's. I didn't have a lot of stretch. Oh how I wished my mom had started me at nine. Perhaps I would have bypassed the ganja for a tutu. Nonetheless, I pushed myself relentlessly, ever hopeful that one day I would somehow be good enough to call myself a dancer.

One day, somewhere around my third year of dance classes, I was in a rehearsal for a recital. I was struggling mightily with a piece of choreography; I botched every double jazz turn in the piece. Every time. Anger rose up out of my bowels, and I hollered and cussed and bawled like a petulant little kid.

"Step outside with me please, Miss Kathy." Ms. Evelyn was cool as a cucumber. A frozen one.

We stepped into the cold cement breezeway outside the classroom door. The frigid atmosphere blasted my hot, sweaty muscles. Ms. Evelyn didn't flinch.

"Uuuuuugh! I'm sorry! I'm just so frustrated!" I said, hugging myself against the frosty evening air.

"Sh." Ms. Evelyn silenced me with a sound.

"I like you, Miss Kathy. But if you want to be in my company, you have got to get a hold of your temper. You need to relax and realize that you will never be a professional dancer. You may as well cut yourself some slack and just enjoy the class. Don't cheat yourself out of that."

I no longer felt the cold. Only numbness. Her voice seemed muffled and far away, but her eyes shined like two black marbles. I had a sudden revelation that I worshipped this fierce woman who was breaking my heart.

I knew she spoke true, but even so, I carried that wound with me for many, many years, right next to the little dancer that lived in my soul.

WUV . . . TWOOO WUV . . .

I was a fourteen-year-old boy when I met my soulmate. We met at a cast party for the musical Oliver, in which I played the Artful Dodger. The fact that they cast a sixteen year-old girl in the role wasn't for a lack of young boys who would have killed me for the part. (I had some legitimate suspicions and fear of my understudy, a cheeky smartass nerd-boy who ". . . should'a had the part—besides everyone knows she only got it because she knows the director.") But the truth is I totally nailed the audition—in full costume, complete with vintage naval formal wool tailcoat and antique beaver skin top hat. And Cockney dialect? Look out Depp. It also helped that I had no boobs at the time.

Meanwhile, back at the cast party. Where I met Mike? You remember, the soulmate? Since it was the afterparty for the *Oliver* dress rehearsal and I was costumed as a boy, my future honey-bun saw me and, well, he didn't really notice me, being not gay at all. He was also dating my girlfriend. It wasn't until we did a college production of *Don't Drink the Water* together that he noticed me. In that one he played a gay chef and I played a nymphomaniac. Perhaps we should move on to the wedding.

Mike and I lived together for a couple of years before we entered into holy matrimony. I don't know if it was still considered holy since we'd already done the deed: you know, shared the bath soap and farted in front of each other and the like. We did make an earnest attempt at abstinence for the last month before the wedding. I think we made it for about four days. We tried, we really did, though I'm not sure why. At any rate Mike's brother, who was a pastor, performed our beautiful ceremony with great relief, finally making an honest man out of his philandering brother.

Our wedding took place under the willows, beyond the Faerie Queen's bower, on a lovely mid-summer afternoon. My handmaidens were white and yellow daisies, stark and lovely against the green and blue of the grass and sky. My father's hands shook a little as he held mine tightly—I thought perhaps he wouldn't let go. We waited in the wings for the music to begin.

With its shimmering ethereal tones, the Fender Rhodes tinkled out the opening notes, and then the lover stepped forward. Microphone in hand, the exceedingly tall and handsome Prince of the Grove fix'd his eyes on his Beloved and began his love song.

"There's a wren in the willow wood, flies so high and sings so good . . ."

Yes folks, my lover sang to me as I floated down the aisle. Not a dry eye in the house—or park, as it were. Mike is an exceptionally gifted songwriter and musician. He's also a marvelous actor. He's a fantastic writer. But people let me tell you, this guy's singing voice? Like that of a god. I mean really ladies—and fellas too for that matter—when those magical pipes send forth that velvety voice, you wanna rip off your bra and scream out his name. So, my wedding? Truly the stuff of faerie tales and great love stories.

GURUS SCHMURUS

The only outward expression of anything remotely religious for Mike and I during our early years together was a production of *Jesus Christ Superstar* (guess who played Jesus—no, not me silly, Mike—I told you, the guy can sing).

At one point, however, we did spend a few weeks exploring the realm of the spirit with a couple we met randomly at a little hometown street fair.

Peter and Mara came up from Santa Cruz to hang in the area for a while. They were probably only a few years older than we were, but had somehow gotten stuck in the 60s.

At first glance, I thought Peter was a yuppie. He dressed simply: short-sleeved polo shirt, khaki slacks, penny loafers. He was soft-spoken and clean-cut.

Mara, on the other hand, let her armpit hair flow in all its glory. Braless, bouncing free under her baby-doll tank top, flowy skirt, gorilla legs, she had it all going on.

Modern-day flower children, they spoke to us of love, peace, communal living, and the cosmic consciousness. They told us how they'd asked the Universe to lead them to where they should go in order to help bring love and good karma to the consumerism-riddled masses. Then they opened up a map, closed their eyes, pointed to an arbitrary spot, and low and behold, we were the lucky winners!

Peter was so meek and kind that he somehow charmed us into letting the two of them crash at our place. They took nothing for the journey except a staff—no bread, no bag, no money in their belts. They wore sandals but brought no extra tunic (okay, I exaggerate, but you get the idea: *we* bought the groceries).

The first few days were interesting. It felt so grownup-like and spiritual to take in these wayfaring gurus. We sat at their feet and learned about how to be enlightened. We put crystals around our apartment, ate black beans and some kind of nasty miso soup, and learned to trust God by leaving our door unlocked (my mom had a conniption over that concept). It was all new and strange and altogether unlike us.

By day, the duo bummed around town, chatting with people on the street, preaching their New Age Gospel. I'm not sure how he pulled it off, but Peter managed to book a couple of workshops for spiritual seekers at a local church. I attended one of them; a handful of curious pilgrims showed up. We sat on the floor and Peter delivered his mystical message, but I never could figure out exactly what that was. We sat in quiet meditation for much of it.

While Peter was the gentle lamb, Mara was the bossy lion. She had more of a militant approach.

One evening, a couple weeks in, we gathered together in our sparse living room for a time of meditation. The lighting was dim with a number of candles lit. The shadows from the flames flickered on the walls, casting long, dancing teardrops. Mike had taken out his guitar and was strumming a soft tune; it was one of the love songs he'd written, melodic and soothing. Peter preferred the carpet to the couch where Mara sat. I also sat on the floor, at Mara's feet.

"Giving foot massages is an excellent way to demonstrate a humble and giving heart," she said, holding out her foot; she had recently given us a teaching on how important it was to learn servant-hood. I wasn't sure if this was a request or what, but nonetheless, I began massaging her foot . . . like this was normal for me. The whole moment was sitting a little sideways, but hey, they were the gurus—and our guests.

Peter softly hummed to Mike's tune. After a little while Mara folded her legs into Lotus position and said, "Peter and I would like to make an invitation."

I would like to go wash my hands, I thought. I tried to make it a point to not touch my face.

"We're so excited about your receptivity to the ways of Spirit," she continued. "We think you would love life back at Spirit Farm in Santa Cruz." She smiled broadly.

"Wha—farm? Like . . . live on a farm?" I said.

"You mean the commune," Mike said.

"We'd like you to consider joining," Peter said. His gaze was soft and kind. His smile was so honest, one of his front teeth was slightly darker than the other.

"One requirement, though," Mara added, "would be committing to a life of celibacy."

Sound of brakes screeching.

"Uh . . ." I said.

"Yeah, I don't know about that," Mike said. He bugged his eyes out at me.

"Don't think we're much interested in that," I said.

Peter looked at Mara, shrugged his shoulders. Mara's claws came out.

"Wow. Really," she said, her head cocked to the left, right eyebrow raised. "I thought you guys were interested in growing spiritually."

"I . . . I am. I'm interested in . . . that, but . . . no sex?" I said.

"Wow, I can't believe this. After spending so much time with you guys, teaching you. You acted like you were into it—and now you're putting the brakes on." Her cheeks flushing, she started gathering her few belongings into her knapsack.

I was thinking she was going to storm right out the door, but Peter laid a gentle hand on her back. "Mara. Let's give them some room to think about it. Sleep on it."

"We appreciate the offer," Mike said, looking at me, eyebrows like question marks, "but I don't—"

"Yeah, sleep on it," I said, smiling. I would sooner invite a serial killer in to tea than be rude.

Mike and I bumped and stumbled over each other making our way to our room.

Lying in bed face-to-face in the dark, the soft amber glow of the clock radio faintly lit Mike's face. "Holy cow," he whispered.

"Oh my God," I said. We giggled without sound for a moment.

"I'm done with this . . . really Kath," he said.

"I know. Me too."

I don't remember if we had sex that night, but, probably.

First thing in the morning, they were out the door. We thanked them for their love and wisdom, and breathed a great sigh of relief as we waved goodbye.

"That was so weird," Mike said.

"You gotta draw the line somewhere," I said.

That bizarre little interlude curbed our spiritual hunger for some time.

HOLLYWOOD HERE WE COME!

The following summer we were rehearsing for a production of *The Wizard of Oz*— Mike played the Scarecrow to my Dorothy—when a friend of mine inspired me to take my love of theatre to a new level.

"Performing arts school, huh?" Mike said.

"Yeah. In L.A.," I said.

"Marie says it's a legit school?" Mike said.

"It's a three year program. Well, two years, and a third year that's a full on Production Company. Marie loves it."

"How much is it?"

"Don't know. A lot probably, but it's fully accredited and I can get student loans and probably even a little extra to help us move, maybe."

"L.A. You ready for that? It's a long way from Kansas."

"I really want to do this."

"Well, I guess professional careers as actors aren't gonna happen for us here in Podunk, California," Mike said. "You think Marie has room on her couch?"

Marie and I had known each other since we were young teenagers. I did my first show, *Sugar*, with her. We played two of the girls in Sugar's hot girl-band The Syncopators. She was a year or so older than I—I think she was sixteen, but somehow to me she seemed like she was thirty. She exuded a womanly maturity and a palpable sexuality that I greatly admired at fourteen. Marie was also what was referred to as "a triple threat," meaning she could sing, dance, and act. She'd been dancing and performing since she could walk, and was trained in just about every form of dance: ballet, jazz, tap, ballroom.

I, being absolutely green to theatre, knew no one in the *Sugar* cast (I think I was the youngest member). At the first rehearsal, she took me under her wing and made me feel like I was part of the in-crowd. The music director walked around all of the chorus people holding a stack of booklets.

"Here are your librettos," he said, passing them out with great care like they were rare Carthusian manuscripts. "Lose it, and it'll cost you fifty bucks."

We had just finished a fifteen-minute vocal warm up doing exercises that I had never heard. Luckily, I'd had three years of piano, so I was able to fumble my way through the scales well enough. My hands shook as I took my music from the maestro; I'd never sung harmony parts before.

"Sopranos please stand here, mezzos here, altos there. We'll start with number seven, please, *Sun on My Face*. Take a quick look at your parts, and we'll take it from the top in five minutes."

Five minutes! I looked at my music, heart pounding. I knew those lines and shapes; they meant something, but I couldn't remember. The group of sopranos across from us altos had already figured out the first three bars and sounded like a chorus of angelic beings. I wanted to cry and run away. I took a deep breath and remembered, *oh yes, lines; these are the treble, that's bass; and three dots, that's a triad. Alto is on the bottom. Oh God, five dots . . . which one is mine?*

Marie scooted in next to me. "Hey, I'm Marie," she said. I looked at her. She was so pretty. My face felt all bunchy. She flashed a dimply smile at me. We tried to work out the notes together based on what was floating over from the friggin' know-it-alls. Marie got it quickly too, but friendliness billowed off of her. I felt my shoulders drop, my chest relax. As I became more focused, it seemed that I found the notes naturally too. Having her full, velvety voice right next to my ear helped keep me on track. We nailed the first three bars and the director called for quiet. Marie smiled at me again. I stifled a silly giggle that did a little back flip and wiggled its way down to my belly. I was fourteen going on four. It was gonna be a fun ride.

When the star of the show—our Marilyn—got up to sing, my heart dropped. This girl couldn't sing her way out of a pickle jar. What was the director thinking? This part was made for Marie. Sugar was standing here beside me. Over here guys! In the chorus!

Marie just had that thing about her: a Monroe kind of magic. I didn't know it until later shows, because we only had like, one line each, but she also came fully loaded with some powerful acting chops underneath the gorgeous.

Our friendship grew through the subsequent years, we did many shows together, shared a rowdy group of theatre friends, she even sang at our wedding. Not long after I began junior college, Marie moved to Los Angeles to attend acting school. After her first year she told me that it was the most amazing thing she'd ever experienced. That up to that point, she hadn't understood what acting really was—that there was so much more to know.

I couldn't imagine what it was that I'd been missing, but whatever it was she was learning, whatever mysteries they were revealing to her down there in actor land, I wanted some of that. Marie was someone I highly respected and admired. I was sure she would someday land among the stars and I wanted on *that* train.

༺༒༻

My Academy audition was held in a meeting room at a big hotel in downtown San Francisco. I sat on the floor like a pound puppy that had been hit by a car. My right arm frozen across my mid-section at a right angle, ensconced in a twenty-pound plaster cast.

"I am your spaniel; and, Demetrius, the more you beat me, I will fawn on you . . ."

I'd rehearsed this monologue a hundred times. The movement I had in my head for the scene, however, was fairly impeded by the monstrous appendage dangling from my shoulder.

"Your wrongs do set a scandal on my sex, we cannot fight for love as men may do; we should be wooed and were not made to woo. I'll follow thee and make a heaven of hell, to die upon the hand I love so well." I sort of scooted around in pursuit of my fair Demetrius, more like a three-legged toad than a loyal doggie.

"That was fine. Thank you," said one of the heads seated in front of me, stopping me before I could crawl all the way up to their feet. I sat back on my haunches and looked up at the moderators for the audition. They sat four abreast at a long table at the head of the cold, sparsely furnished room. They each had stacks of stapled papers and headshots in front of them. The glare from the high afternoon sun illuminated the bank of large windows behind their heads, casting them partially in shadowy silhouette. That coupled with the fact that I was still on the floor made me feel like a tourist sitting at the base of Mt. Rushmore with the massive statues talking down at me.

"How did you break your arm?" the female of the quartet asked.

I fumbled my way to my feet. "I should have my cast off in a few more weeks," I said.

They waited for my answer. "Oh, I fell during a dance number in a production of *They're Playing Our Song*," I said. I raised my stump before them.

The four heads turned back and forth to each other, torsos leaning forward and then back slightly to see around each other. It seemed like they were smiling, but my eyes were all wonky.

"You'll hear back from the admissions committee in about six weeks," Thomas Jefferson said.

And that was that. "Well, thank you very much," I said. I started to reach out my begrimed plaster claw, then thought better of it and gave a feeble wave of my left hand.

I made my way out into the blinding light of day. My eyes ratcheted my pupils down to pinholes. It made me feel like my feet weren't quite touching the ground, although that might also have been because I hadn't breathed for the twelve minutes of my audition.

I gingerly descended the long cement staircase to the street; it wouldn't do to take a tumble down the three flights and break the rest of the bones in my body.

Six weeks later, I got the envelope. The powers that be had decided: I was in. So my hubby and I, dreams and loan papers in hand, loaded up the Civic and moved to Beverleeeeee . . . Pasadena, that is . . . And there, in the land of swimmin' pools and movie stars, I began studying at The American Academy of Dramatic Arts.

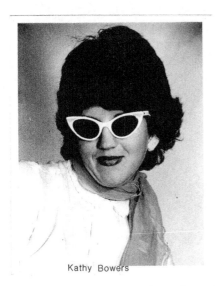

Kathy Bowers

Michael J. Martens

GREASE (IS THE WORD)

CAN YOU GUESS?

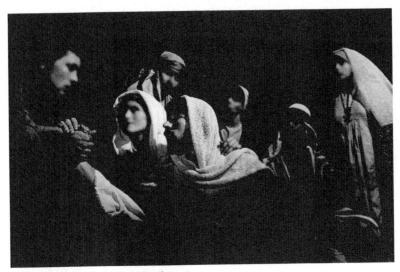

JESUS CHRIST SUPERSTAR

I ADMIT IT. I WAS A MIME.

BORN AGAIN
(PART I)

BORN AGAIN (PART I)

A WHOLE NEW WORLD

WHEN MARIE SAID THAT ACTING SCHOOL was an amazing thing, I didn't fully conceive of the life-changing journey upon which I was about to embark. When I count the milestones, my time at the Academy was, without a doubt, one of the most deeply impactful experiences of my life.

I'm sure it was partly due to the nature of the immersion experience; we all ate, drank, slept, laughed, cried, sweated, and pooped the craft of acting. We buffeted our bodies together in dance class and pulled every muscle together in fencing class. We learned the nuances of strange and wonderful dialects and practiced the subtle beauty of iambic pentameter and rhyming couplets. Together, we all discovered that, the thing we'd been doing before? *That* was not acting. That was something else. A cheap counterfeit. We were now walking on hallowed ground, being knit into a great legacy. We were being inducted into the holy ranks of the Keepers of the Divine Secret, the True Practitioners of the Sacred Art, the Circle of Truth Tellers.

The first thing we had to learn was how to stop acting.

We had to remove our masks in order to be worthy of donning new ones. We had to get naked so that we could clothe ourselves in the truth of the characters whose story we were telling. Our own personal truth had to be accessible so that we could express theirs. We had to learn to be real before we could learn to pretend. I must stop now. I'm coming dangerously close to sharing too much of the Deep Magic. You'll have to shell out your own damn cash if you want to know more.

I have heard it wrongly stated that, "Those who can't do, teach." What a load of horse apples. Not to say that there aren't teachers who need to find another line of work. Our professors at the Academy, however, were all (well mostly all) working actors, incredible artists, and highly skilled instructors. My first acting teacher was no exception and will always have a special place in my heart.

To look at Ms. Mary, you would never suspect that such massive power could reside in so diminutive a vessel. Five-foot-nothing wrapped around a passionate gift for teaching that could fill a universe. It filled mine anyway, for the short semester I was graced with her tutelage.

Every session of her class was revelation upon revelation for me. I devoured her lectures and hung on her every word of individual instruction during my scene work. She challenged every untruthful moment and drove me to tears more than once as she pushed me past my own self-imposed limitations. It was in her classes that I learned respect for acting and began my lifelong love affair with the craft.

She went on weaving her spells for thirty-some years after that, forever ruining each unsuspecting young fledgling that came waltzing into class thinking they knew a little something about acting. Ms. Mary only recently retired from teaching, and now, in her late sixties, is enjoying a successful second act to her acting career.

THE INVITATION

I'm not sure if it was the will of some cosmic casting director in the sky, or because he had some kind of savior complex, or because the man could rock Gethsemane and a loincloth, but toward the end of my first year at school, Mike was cast as Jesus, again, in a second production of Jesus Christ Superstar at a small theatre in Burbank.

I wanted badly to do the show too, but I was in the middle of first year exam plays at the Academy and therefore still technically in school and not allowed to audition for any extracurricular theatre. It's a damn shame too, because I was born to play the Magdalene, and besides, that chick only got the part because she knew the director.

I did, however, cheat the school rules a little because I took the job as spot operator on the production (without pay of course). It was a cool opportunity, as the lighting designer had worked on shows for the Beatles and had a fab Liverpudlian dialect.

I must confess that I also didn't trust the bombshell playing the divine Ms. M though—she was a little too convincing as she cradled my honey's head in her lap, stroked his fevered brow and crooned, "Everything's alright, yes, everything's fine." She had bounteous Farrah Fawcett hair and a fine ass, and I didn't like it one bit. Holy hell, how was I ever going to make it through seeing Mike do an actual love scene? But I don't have a jealous bone in my body . . .

During rehearsals for JCS, I met Cindy. She was a member of the chorus and she was a Born Again Jew. As in, a Christian Jew. I didn't know there was such a thing.

Cindy was tall and olive skinned, and had giant, curly hair—like me. She was fun and goofy and easy to get to know. She had an amazing singing voice and great passion for theatre. Cindy was also uninhibited about sharing her faith. She wasn't pushy, but she wasn't afraid to talk about it. She was kind and loving like my other Born Again friend, Patricia, but not so prim; in fact, she was a smidge on the wild side. I liked that. So, there was some hope; a person like me could be saved and still retain some personality. (Not saying that Patricia didn't have personality, she just tended to color neatly inside the lines.)

My new friend lived alone in a tiny rented one-room cottage that was behind a larger home in a cute suburban area of LA. I would drive out to her place from time to time. We'd go out to lunch or hang in her mini-pad and talk for hours. We talked a lot about God and Jesus. Cindy never made me feel stupid as I voiced my myriad questions about Christianity. She knew the Bible well and could explain the plan of salvation simply and clearly. She never asked me to bow my head and close my eyes and confess, and I felt safe to explore the Christian religion without a compulsion to make some kind of commitment. The more we talked, the greater my spiritual hunger became, until it was pushing its way up from the depths of my darkness like a pale, starving sapling searching for the light of the sun.

 C/3

Mike was raised a Lutheran. You could set your clock by the Martens family church attendance. Their rather sizable clutch, all spit-spot and neatly combed would file smartly into their pews, and with this, the pastor knew that it was alright to begin. It was during these inspiring sermons that Mike's eldest brother dreamed of a flock of his own, and Mike just dreamed while dozing on Dad's shoulder. Mike's parents were good Christian people. They loved their kids and lived their lives with integrity. I don't know the exact reason they left the church when Mike was fifteen, something about church politics, money, and building projects. In the end, they decided that the family would feel much closer to God while water skiing on the weekends. Mike shed only tears of joy over that decision.

Despite my curiosity about Christianity, becoming a churchgoer at the height of my almost adulthood was about as far off my radar as it could be. I was twenty-one for God's sake. Life was supposed to be about throwing myself headlong into my craft, partying, meeting producers at Hollywood cocktail soirées, networking, and you know, *really living*. Yes, I was entertaining all kinds of disturbing considerations about becoming a Christian, but a regular Sunday-go-to-meeting kind of gal? I couldn't wrap my imagination around that one. It was part of the equation I didn't want to think about.

"I'm going to be singing a solo in church this Sunday. You wanna come hear me?"

Cindy is always no pressure and cool. Hmmm. Go to church? The idea makes me feel a little like I'm standing on ice in hard-soled shoes. Well, maybe we could think of it more like going to a concert. Was this making some kind of commitment? Will I have to stand up and say my name and confess that I'm a sinner? *Okay, just breathe. She asked you to come hear her sing, not offer up your firstborn.*

"Sure, why not," I say.

Later that evening:

"Church?" Mike says. "Meh."

"Just to hear Cindy sing," I say.

"I don't like it when you commit me to stuff without asking me. Besides, Cindy's *your* friend," he says.

"You used to go to church," I say.

He is quiet for a bit.

"I guess it's fine. But please ask me first next time."

I figured he'd be fine with it. It's not like he was a complete heathen. Note to self: ask him first next time.

❧

It's a disorienting thing to be up early on a Sunday morning. My circadian rhythm is all confused and a little put out. I'm not a coffee drinker (as of yet), but can see that church people must certainly be. I sort of float through getting ready and taking the half-hour drive to the church as if I'm not inside my own body.

The church stands on the corner of the quaint little village, glinting white in the sun. A vast concrete staircase leads up to its striated columns and dark walnut doors. Like a great white in a small pond, it dwarfs the lesser structures that share the neighborhood. Across the street and down the block a bit, a pocket-sized little chapel with a lonely steeple looks on, blushing in the shadow of such a stately and superior edifice of God.

Mike and I pull into the parking lot and sit for a moment before approaching, considering whether or not a fast break for home might be in order. But we gather our aplomb and set our faces toward the castle in the sky. As we approach the steps, a friendly older gentleman dressed smartly in dark slacks, button down shirt and tie greets us. I wonder if we've perhaps underdressed. Jeeves doesn't turn his nose up at us however; he welcomes us warmly and directs us, not up the staircase, but around the corner to the basement door. *Oh, I guess this is where they send the under-dressers.*

I find it a little odd that the services are being held down in the underbelly of the monster. (We later find out that the main sanctuary—a word that is new to me and a little mysterious and cool—is under renovation.)

Folding chairs lined up in neat rows serve as makeshift pews. Off-white acoustical tiles create the low ceiling overhead; the floor is covered in large, gold-flecked linoleum squares. Here too are many columns, but these are of the serf class, their only job being to undergird the massive hierarchy above. There's a small dark stage built into the wall at the far end of the room. In front of this, stand a few skirted tables and a lectern serving as a provisional altar—a humble and frankly disappointing display in comparison to what the outside of this splendid house of God promised. Nonetheless, I feel comfortable in the more unassuming environment, which brings some relief to my apprehension over venturing into this uncharted water.

The pastor is already up front, and things seem to be underway as we head to a couple of empty seats as near to the exit sign as possible. Cindy catches our eye, waving us to come sit by her.

"That's Pastor Terry," she whispers. "He's totally awesome."

The pastor is an average guy, a bit short on hair, with a kind face. He looks somewhat out of place in the long white robe with its lengthy, flowing collar. *Ah, that must be his phylactery,* I conjecture to myself. I had heard that term in a line from *Godspell*—Jesus had said something about the priests in their flowing phylacteries, and I figure maybe this is one of those. He greets his flock with a gentle voice and charming smile. I feel at once that this is a guy I can probably trust, and heck, maybe even like.

I don't recall what Cindy sang. I know it was gorgeous and undoubtedly something by Amy Grant. I can't say I remember what the sermon was about either. I do remember, however, that aside from the hymn parts, I was kind of liking church, if this was indeed what church was like. It didn't feel threatening at all, and it was a kick watching the tiny old woman in the chair in front of us slowly leaning to the right as she took her morning nap.

After the service, the congregants all work together, clearing the chairs and bringing out the folding tables for—lucky us—potluck Sunday. I feel like a dork because I didn't bring anything to share, but I'm starving. I spent the last half hour of the sermon contemplating my navel as the aroma of reheated taco casserole began swirling its way under my nose from the adjacent kitchen. So out comes everyone's pot-lucky best, and despite my instinct to want to run away from any kind of socializing, we decide to stay and partake of the free fare. Cindy introduces us to Pastor Terry. He's shed his holy garments and is now dressed like a normal person—slacks, short sleeved button-down, all in muted, earthy colors. He's warm, engaging, and seems unpretentious and genuine. *Yep, I like this guy.* We meet his wife and two daughters; they're a real nice family.

Mike and I are quiet as we pull out of the parking lot and head for home. I finally speak up. "I kind of enjoyed that."

"Yeah. It was nice," Mike says.

"Cindy sounded good," I say.

"Yeah."

"Maybe we could visit again sometime," I say.

The car is full of hush. My head is not. *Well, that was actually pretty cool. I think I could maybe get into this church thing. I mean, why not? Of course, it would mean getting up early every Sunday. Crap. That'll be hard. But will they try to run my life? Will I have to start going to Bible studies and women's groups and all that shit too? I suppose I'll have to start watching my garbage mouth. Ugh. EVERY Sunday? Hm. I wonder if I could get a solo like Cindy. Maybe a duet. I wonder if they ever do any theatre down on that stage. I hate tuna casserole. Warm creamy tuna . . . just gross. The taco thing was okay though.*

Mike interrupts, "I had a weird experience once a few years ago. It was before I met you, actually. I haven't thought about it for a long time. I was having trouble sleeping one night, so I was just laying in bed kind of like meditating or something, or I guess maybe I was praying. All of a sudden this heavy force came down on top of me and pinned me to the bed."

"Was it God?"

"I don't know what it was," he says. He's quiet for a second. "I tried to wiggle free, but I couldn't move."

"Were you scared?"

"Not at all. I don't know how to describe it. It felt like . . . like total acceptance and love and safety. Like all the good things you can think of. I don't know how to describe it."

"Did it talk to you?" I say.

"There were no words, no direction, nothing like that. Just love I guess."

"That is weird," I say.

We're quiet for a bit. He says, "Yeah, I guess I wouldn't mind going again."

I've always been an all or nothing kind of gal. I jump into stuff with both feet. Sometimes that works out for me—depending on what the stuff is. So it was decided. We would give this church-going thing a go.

 confidence

For some reason the sermon this particular Sunday draws me in like the Enterprise in a tractor beam. I can feel it pulling at my heart, so I throw on my reverse thrusters and dig in my heels. I try and try to resist the tugging, but with each point of his message, Pastor Terry's words bring a deeper sense of conviction. Not that it's in any way heavy-handed. In fact, it is like he is, gentle and reassuring. But underneath the delivery, there's clearly a magical power beckoning me to make some kind of decision. For so long, I've been perched atop a narrow fence, frantically bobbing, swaying, and flailing my arms for balance, trying to get my spiritual footing. I feel my heartbeat increase and amplify inside my chest. The edge of a cliff looms. Suddenly he's done with his message, and the words I've been dreading come forth.

"Now, with every head bowed and every eye closed, I'd like to give an invitation to discipleship." The chugging in my ears nearly drowns out his mild voice. "If anyone here would like to come forward, repent of their sins, and receive Jesus Christ as their Lord and Savior, now is the time."

Without thought or hesitation I stand up. As if propelled by some unseen force, I step out into the aisle, water welling up in my eyes, my feet carrying me forward without my mind's permission.

When I'm a few steps away from the welcoming, but somewhat surprised Pastor Terry, I walk through my curtain of tears and throw myself into his outstretched hands—the very arms of Jesus—with a cathartic moaning sob, and hang on him there, weeping like a child. I can feel him stiffen up a bit at this unexpected response, and somehow I can also feel every eye in the room behind me gawking at this unprecedented display. Apparently having the invitation accepted, much less with such enthusiasm, is not the normal fare here. I come up from the pastor's soggy shoulder looking a bit like Alice Cooper or maybe Tammy Faye Baker. Someone nearby presses a tissue into my hand. I don't care that the wet spot left by my eyes upon his royal robe has a bit of a shiny trail left by my snotty nose. Years and years of pent-up fears, swirling questions, and deep longings are being released and are flowing out of my face from every orifice, and I don't even care.

All of the mental and emotional gymnastics I had been going through concerning my spiritual quandary had been a constant slow leak in my energy bucket. That day I laid my burden at the foot of the cross. Though I didn't feel all that different, I did feel somehow lighter, like something of a load had been lifted. So now I was saved. Praise the Lord, hallelujah, amen. Now I could focus my energy on getting to know my newfound friend, Jesus.

For a little while, anyway.

Turns out that this small step took me onto a path leading directly through a brand new jungle—The Great Forest of Churchy Doctrine. Here,

I would replace my worries and fears about who God was with new and improved ones about how to please Him and how to gain the approval of the Community of His believers. But this was still blissfully unknown to me. For the moment, I could simply bask like a child in the glowing love of the Lord. For the moment, it was just Him and me.

☾

The envelope was thick: a very good sign. "On behalf of the faculty of The American Academy of Dramatic Arts, we congratulate you on being selected to return for the Second Year Program."

Having duly noted (and judged) the great and not-so-great levels of talent in the first year class, I felt honored and relieved to have made the cut. I was, and still am in many ways, a Jekyll & Hyde when it comes to believing in my own gifts. Depending on whether it's raining or shining, whether I am ovulating, menstruating, copulating, or master—well, you get the idea—my belief in myself and my abilities can be like quicksilver in the barometer.

Needless to say, I was ecstatic and conciliated that my envelope was not skinny. Skinny meant that there was no need for all of the paperwork that was included in the invite letter package that we all longed and hoped for. So it was confirmed, I had something—perhaps only the ability to pay—but it was something. Does anyone else in my age bracket still have student loan payments?

THE REAL DEAL: 100% NATURAL, NO ARTIFICIAL COLORS OR FLAVORS ADDED

As a newborn baby Christian, all I could think about was how hungry I was, how much I craved all the pure, wholesome milk of God's Word that I could get. I began to devour the Scriptures, and looked forward to Pastor Terry's Sunday messages. Cindy was an avid follower of a few T.V. preachers—*PTL (Praise the Lord)* was a favorite show of hers—and I tried tuning in from time-to-time, but frankly it was a little over the top for me. When I first laid eyes on Tammy Faye doing her Alice Cooper thing, I felt a little embarrassed at the prospect that these were now my people. I'd seen bits of some of these shows before and had participated heartily in casting my fair share of disparaging commentaries, but I mean, wouldn't you? If you were me? Now, however, I knew in my heart that I wasn't supposed to judge what seemed like some of the worst acting I'd ever seen; I was supposed to love them and try to see their hearts through all of the bad Roman décor, diamond bracelets, giant eyelashes, and running mascara. Don't know if I ever got there.

All I wanted was to know and understand what the Bible said and what it meant for me. I wanted my Christianity to be authentic, like it was for the early disciples. I wanted Jesus to speak to me the way I knew He spoke to Patricia and Cindy, the way that must be possible for me now that I had finally said yes and committed my life to serving Him.

Serving Jesus. I was learning to love Him (though I must confess that he still looked a lot like Robert Powell in my mind), but how could I serve Him? That was a big question for me. What should that look like? I flashed back on some of the scenarios I obsessed over back in my early spiritual wrestling days: missionary to a foreign land, door-to-door sales, street corner soapboxing. A bit of fear peeped its nasty head in to say hi. No, Jesus loved and accepted me as I was. He wouldn't call me to do something I absolutely abhorred and call it service, would He? There must be something He had prepared for me; I trusted that at the proper time, He would show me. I hoped that it might somehow involve my love for the arts rather than large flying insects or sandwich boards and megaphones.

☙

My frame was not hidden from you when I was made in the secret place, when I was woven together in the depths of the earth. Your eyes saw my unformed body; all the days ordained for me were written in your book before one of them came to be. ~Psalm 139: 15-16

The long, hot, smoggy days of late summer were dragging into the long, hot, smoggy days of early fall and school was just around the corner. I wondered if my newfound faith would change things for me there. I couldn't imagine that it should be a problem, I was still me and I was still as passionate as ever for my craft and for my impending career in theatre and film. I hadn't given much deep thought to the impact my devotion to the Lord might soon have on my dreams, my relationships, or on my work.

Speaking of work, yeah, you know, the day job. Mike had agreed to pick up most of the financial slack while I attended school, but I still needed to work so we didn't completely drown. Early on in relocating to beautiful sunny Los Angeles, I landed part-time employment as an assistant in a medical lab. Every afternoon I spent two hours driving to and from our main client to pick up blood. I had early classes, so by the time I was rolling back into Pasadena from my run, I was mighty sleepy. I eventually had my routine down so well that I could time the drive back to the lab to perfectly coincide with a red light at the end of the 110 Freeway as it dumped into South Pasadena. I would come to a stop, throw my car into park and instantly fall sound asleep as I waited for the thirty-second light. As soon as I sensed the cars around me starting to move, I would snap awake, refreshed and ready to finish my workday. I would head back to the lab with my specimens, write up some paperwork, make some blood slides, draw off serum from the centrifuge tubes, and then clean the lab. After doing this for my whole first year of school—same thing, every day—I could do it with my eyes closed. With no one there to bug me, I could also go over lines, character bios, and scene beats while I performed my duties. And now, I could think about last Sunday's sermon and memorize Bible verses too. Fantastic!

Oh, did I mention that the place where I picked up all our specimens was an abortion clinic? I knew that Jesus and I were going to have some stuff to work out.

There was a man who often stood on the street corner in front of the clinic. He wore a long ratty overcoat, had short disheveled hair, and a few days stubble. He looked sad and angry and carried a large sign with a huge picture of a bloody fetus pasted on it. His placard was warped and peely from exposure to the weather and much use. He didn't rant and rave; he spoke quietly with some of the women coming and going from the clinic, handing them Bible tracts and pamphlets about abortion. I always dropped my head and sped past him and tried not to look closely at the gruesome reminder on that big poster that he held up for the ladies. I had things to do and places to be and certainly didn't care to get into a debate about the rightness or wrongness of abortion. I didn't have the time or energy to think about it, and I had always been way too careful to ever have to cross that bridge of decision myself. Should I ever come upon that bridge, heaven forbid, I had no idea at that time what my choice might be, but I didn't feel inclined to judge or deny someone else theirs.

The clinic was always jammed with people. In the back of my mind I marveled at the sheer numbers—and I mean every day—of women there for *treatment*; but again, I couldn't bring it to the front of my consciousness. The issue was too big, too messy, and too volatile for me to face. I had dreams and goals, and this job was helping me to get there; I wasn't about to undermine my good fortune in landing it with a morality dilemma.

There was a small area that I had to pass through on my way into the back of the clinic where the blood and urine samples awaited my pick-up. It was like a small kitchen, with stainless steel counters and a huge double sink. There was often a staff person working in there as I went through, the blood on her gloves and sides of the sink telling me that I didn't want to look around too much and to move through as quickly as possible. I couldn't think about what was in the ice chests that were filled with little plastic containers like the ones that liver comes in at the grocery store. Something the color of brick swirled beneath the cloudy white plastic lids. Thankfully those specimens were on their way to somewhere that wasn't my lab. I kept my eyes forward and completed my mission swiftly and without thought.

For the first year on the job I was able to successfully detach from any moral issues and maintain a middle of the road opinion on abortion, because it would never be *my* issue. Although my church wasn't particularly vocal about the subject, I knew that The Church In General had a definite stance on it, and I was becoming more and more aware that in time I was going to have to square with this and pick a side.

And now, Jesus is taking the ride downtown with me. He's walking with me past all of the girls packed into the waiting room like crayons. Surely they aren't all here for abortions, right? I mean, surely some of them are just here for medical services. But every day I write up twenty or thirty lab slips, all for abortions. He's walking with me through the little kitchen where they sort through the wreckage too. I wonder about all these babies. Potential people. Will I one day be standing on the sidewalk holding a sign? Yep, I had a lot to think about.

This was to be my first real taste of the war of the worlds—and there was a whole feast awaiting me. If the real deal was what I was truly looking for, there would be many aspects of my life that would not hold up in the Holy Light of Day.

TAKE ME TO THE WATER, DIP ME IN THE RIVER

I began to feel a deep conviction that if I was serious about my new-found faith, it was my duty to make some kind of public declaration of it (as if accosting the pastor and smearing my bodily fluids and mascara on him wasn't enough of a display). In keeping with my *both oars in* mentality, I was determined to take this thing all the way and do it right.

Pastor Terry suggested that it would be an appropriate thing for me to be baptized. Well, that sounded cool. I always thought baptism was pretty much for babies, but I also knew from *Godspell* that the early disciples of John the Baptist headed out to the Jordan to be washed, so how cool would it be to follow their radical example and take the plunge? I imagined Pastor Terry sporting a large Afro, rainbow suspenders, bright orange Keds, dipping a sponge in an old metal bucket and squeezing that cleansing water over my head; then the whole congregation bursting into a rousing full choral number of "Prepare Ye the Way of the Lord," dancing on buckets and running through the aisles (this would not have been unheard of had it been in the Pentecostal Church—plenty of fun stories ahead).

I was thrilled to find out that the new sanctuary was going to be all sparkling and shiny new in time for my big day and that I would be able to be dunked in the big people tank right there in the Holy of Holies. I'm sure the church building fund must have been monumental, because the work done inside was nothing less than pure artistry. The Council of the Church Revitalization Committee wisely chose a master painter, a Michelangelo of craftsmen, to come in and create marble where there was none, burled wood, crown molding, and beams where before there was mere fir and plaster. Intersecting fissures that glistened with rivulets of gold spread out across the enclosed balustrade, emulating great slabs of marble that ran up the curving stairs to the balcony in the clouds. Pillars that previously stood there, embarrassed and exposed in their pallid, bare skin, now shone like smooth stone. It was like walking into a courtyard of Olympus. Only this was the Inner Sanctum of the One True God. Every majestic detail appeared as natural and as breathtakingly beautiful as the real material out of which it pretended to be fashioned. It was at once reality and illusion. Art imitating Heaven.

And ohhh the organ! I'd been in a couple of big churches before, but I'd forgotten about the big-ass organs! Ours was no exception. The pipes were set into the walls at the front like a gargantuan pan flute, a row of giant brassy soldiers ready to sing, and when they did, they raised the roof. When I first heard those suckers blast out *Praise God From Whom All Blessings Flow,* I thought my heart was going to stop or my spleen explode from the pounding sound waves. It was crazy huge and sexy. I loved and hated all that big noise. It was like the voice of God when He's feeling his testosterone. I also found it rather comical to note that the man behind the curtain was none other than little tiny Ethyl The Church Lady in her pillbox and Sunday frock, playing her heart out for the King of Kings.

I'm standing alone in the small dressing closet that is tucked behind the vast baptismal. It's a little musty inside, the tight space muffling all sound and stealing all breath. But it's also womb-like and oddly comforting. The nice church lady has given me a thin, white cotton gown to wear, much like the kind in the hospital, but not to be worn open in the back. Since I'm going to be submerged in water, it's obvious that I am to remove my clothing first. *Damn. Didn't wear a bra today.* I guess just my panties will have to do. I stand there for a moment in my nakedness. It seems apropos. I slip on my simple gown. I begin to sweat.

Out in the sanctuary sits a handful of my new church family: Cora and Bob (an elderly couple who had become surrogate grand parents to us), Cindy, the youth pastor and his wife, all gathered to show their love and support as I take this life-changing step. The only other person I've invited is Mike's eldest brother (the pastor who married us); he has driven quite a ways to be here as a witness to my commitment. I didn't tell any of my family or non-Christian friends I'm doing this; they'd probably think I've slipped a cog. They'd think I was becoming some kind of religious zealot. What was I going to do, send out invitations? Please join me as I, a fully-grown adult, get baptized. No, this is perfect. An intimate gathering for an intimate moment.

The grandeur of the altar is even grander as the great curtain has been parted to reveal the baptismal. It stands higher than the altar itself, but the pool-sized font is sunken into the floor and spans the entire width of the reredos. The devoted enters from one side, and the pastor enters from the opposite. It makes for great ceremony and spectacle—a real-life passion play unfolding on a magnificent stage.

A light tap on the dressing room door signals that it's time. I open the door. The nice lady gives me a comforting smile and motions to the short cloth wrap that hangs on a hook behind me. Like Tom Hanks, she accompanies me on the short walk to the wings, only the floor isn't green. There is no sound in the sanctuary. No great fanfare. Not even a whisper or a cough. *Maybe nobody showed up*, I think. It matters not; once again, it's me and Jesus. A small set of steps leads up to the platform. The Church Lady takes my wrap. I take each step: one, two, three. I peer down into the font and see, to my chagrin, a floating stratum of scummy film on the mirrored surface of my enchanted pool. In the aftermath of the months of construction and plastering, no one thought to clean out the tub, and now I stand here, preparing to go swimming in the sludge. My only hope is that the layer of flotsam will part for us by the shear holiness of the moment.

Pastor Terry stands across from me. He smiles, his eyes twinkle, and I forget all about the cesspool between us. He beckons for me to come to him. To my surprise, there's a submerged ramp for me to enter by, making our revealing to the audience magical, as if we gradually descend into the depths. Like a robed druid and a virginal maiden, we glide into the water and meet in the center where he takes my hands. The pastor looks into my eyes with reassurance and comfort and gives me a moment to take a deep breath before we turn to face those gathered for the occasion. All twelve of them.

Then he begins to speak. For the first time, I notice that the water is barely tepid. I hope he'll keep it brief, but this, alas, is not usually his style. Though pastor Terry is always interesting and relevant in his sermons, he isn't typically concerned with their length.

"Kathy," Pastor Terry says. He looks at me with those big brown doe eyes.

"We, your new family in Christ, are here today to bear witness to and celebrate your decision to be baptized as a new disciple of Christ. Today, you are making the public declaration that you are His, from head to toe, and that your life is no longer your own."

Okay, I like the idea of being His. The my 'life no longer my own' part I can't wrap my head around yet, but go on . . .

"As you pass under the water, so you die with Him and arise as a new creature in Christ."

Love the metaphor. Submerging is like dying. Coming up from the water is like being born new, fresh and squeaky clean. Love it, go on . . .

"Through His blood, you are made clean, forgiven of all of your sin. Through the washing of the water of baptism, you are set apart for his service . . .*

K, no need to panic here, he didn't say anything about foreign missions or bicycle tours, just service. Getting a bit nippy in here now Pastor, maybe could you pick up the pace a smidge?

". . . and empowered by the Holy Spirit for living a life pleasing to God and for service to your fellow man."

Empowerment sounds good—and more than anything I want to please God . . .

I feel Pastor Terry squeeze my hand, which I don't remember being a signal of any kind that we've discussed, but before I know it we're doing for real what we practiced yesterday. The prayer for shortness and sweetness is apparently paying off.

I hear the words, "I baptize you in the name of the Father, and of the Son, and of the Holy Ghost."

No time to think. No time to swim away. I assume the position with adept movements as if I've done this many times. Crossing my arms over my chest while pinching my nose closed with my right hand, I take a deep breath, and at once, like a graceful tango dancer, Pastor Terry shifts behind me, supporting me behind my shoulders and around the front of my waist, and dips me backwards into the pool. As the water closes over me, I gaze into the face of Antonio Banderas smiling down at me from behind his Zoro mask, a red rose clenched between his teeth. And in the twinkling of an eye, I'm coming up out of the cold water, taking in a big gulp of the air of Heaven and once again, weeping like someone who's just won the grand prize. I feel inclined to giggle manically as well, but just stand there, dripping and crying and grinning. Pastor Terry looks like a triumphant dad watching his four-year-old ride her tricycle for the first time. I am filled with love. Filled with exuberance, with joy and then suddenly with the great awareness that I'm standing here, in the spotlight, with a white sheet clinging to my very chilly breasts.

I can think of nothing better to do than to throw my arms around pastor, yet again, in a big ridiculous hug. He laughs and seems genuinely full of joy for me, for my happy day. The audience claps. They're getting used to my theatrics and are clearly pleased to have the entertainment. Pastor Terry gently pries me off of his chest, turns me around with a patient smile, and I wade my way through the gathering pond scum to my stage right exit.

There is no ethereal music, no dove descending from on high, no great shaft of light through massive white clouds. There isn't even a potluck. I go back to my tiny dressing room, dry off, and get dressed. I make my appearance out front to say thanks to a couple of well-wishing stragglers, then we all go our separate ways, and that is that.

Afterward, Mike and I go out to lunch with his big brother (his treat, as usual). Mike gives me a beautiful Bible bound in dusty rose-stained leather that I still own to this day; the cover, now scuffed, faded, and worn; the pages filled with highlights, underlining, and margin notes. It's been read cover to cover numerous times. Well, okay, I probably only read *Kings* once—but let me tell you, once is enough. Mike's brother gave me a sweet little "Precious Moments" figurine to commemorate my big plunge. It was of an adorable huge-eyed little girl being baptized in a big old wooden barrel by an adorable huge-eyed little boy dressed in an oversized pastor's robe; an adorable huge-eyed puppy playfully watches the ceremony. I put it on a shelf next to the huge-eyed bride and groom figurine he gave us for our wedding.

SCENES AND REVELATIONS

I read somewhere that the only seasons in Los Angeles are fire, flood, riot and earthquake, but I knew that fall must have officially arrived because the early morning temperature was dropping into the low seventies. The trees in Southern California never get the memo, so they don't remember to don their orangey-gold coats. The seasons kind of slide from warm to warmer to warm again, ebbing and flowing like the steady traffic jams, often parking altogether in the middle of hot.

For those of us returning to the Academy, this was a special fall: the beginning of second year studies at AADA. Time for the real deal, the meat, the hardcore craft. I was excited about the classes, the teachers, the depth of the work, and the theatre camaraderie—like no other that I have encountered—that would build through our shared experience. Here we would dive deeply into our psyches, allow ourselves to be naked and vulnerable, buffet our bodies until we cried from the pain, and entrust our very souls to our revered instructors. It was heaven.

☙

I sit in the solitary chair, facing the rest of the class. Here we are, together again at last; the disciples of His Righteousness, our acting professor, Peter Henry, separated at birth from Jack Nicholson.

"So, Ms. Martens," Dr. Henry says, "Share with us how you spent your summer."

I know he's looking for something along the lines of, "Well, I bared my breasts in a blackbox production of Equus." Or, "I lay naked on a block of ice to have a sense memory of death." Or, "I spent three weeks in Griffith Park as a bag lady." My pits start their effusion.

"Well, actually, I . . . I um . . . well, I . . ." My palms and inner thighs join my armpits in their issuance. "Well, I was . . . born again. I became a Christian."

Silence.

The Godfather doesn't stir, he only sits there, gazing at me, arms crossed, chin resting on fist. Then his eyebrows do a slow arc upwards as his face cracks into a huge grin. He sits up, nodding and looking around at my classmates (who are dumbfounded). His gaze snaps back to me, his countenance now transforming to that of The Grand Inquisitor.

"Born again," he slowly croaks. He purses his lips out as if he's about to blow me a kiss. "Born again."

Silence again. For like, an hour.

"So, do you think your . . . conversion, will get in the way of the work?" He levels his furrowed brow at me.

"No." I answer with all the confidence I can muster. I wonder if there are sweat circles growing at my crotch. "I don't know why it would," I add, cocking my head.

He nods his head again, those pursed, pokey-outey lips again. "Good. Who's next?"

Feeling a bit out of body, I float back to my seat among my stunned and addlepated peers—each of whom has a great thought bubble over-head that reads, *WTF?!* No one dares jump right up. How the hell do you follow that?

Needless to say, I left ol' Peter Henry with plenty of food for thought on what kind of characters he would assign me to play that semester.

☙

I sit in the hot seat, once again, facing the class—I've just finished my monologue from *Night Mother*. Dr. Henry levels his gaze at me, eyes squinted so as to cut into my soul.

"I'm thinking a scene from *The Maids* would be good for you to work on," he pronounces, seemingly prescribing the cure for my newfound religion.

He studies me without a word, and then says, "Yes, Genet would be good for you." His face erupts into that Nicholson grin once again as he sits up tall, nodding and looking around at the rest of the class as if to say, "Huh? Yes? Obviously, right? Perfect, right?"

Jean Genet's juicy play is about two housemaids, Solange and Claire, who, while their despised Madame is out of the house, love to role-play as evil mistress and naughty maid. They construct elaborate sadomasochistic rituals involving the symbolic demise of their master. The play is loosely based on the infamous Papin sisters who brutally murdered their employer and her daughter in France in the thirties.

I don't think Peter Henry was trying to be mean or disrespectful. He was there to be a mentor, a guide, to help me dive deeply into my inhibitions and to deliver me from them. Or else he was a twisted sonofabitch who liked to see me squirm. Either way, I wasn't going to let fear or constraint keep me from doing the work—and I wasn't going to let him win.

I'm paired with Trina. She isn't my first choice, but it doesn't matter. Only the work matters. The following week, we're scheduled to go up with our scene. Henry lets us get all the way through it the first time. When we finish, we sit facing our peers. He sits, as always, among them, contemplating us. He looks around at the group, nodding, then directs his focus back to us.

"Do it again."

We start the scene again. A few lines in, he stops us. "Claire, get down on the floor," he commands. I obey.

"Solange sit in the chair," he says. My partner moves without question to the chair.

"Clair, crawl to Madame, and sit at her feet." I do so. "Now caress the Madame's feet." Without thought or hesitation, I reach out and gently pet Trina's foot.

"Give her a nice massage," he urges.

I pick up her foot. She does not have particularly nice feet. They're clean enough, but very dry and cracked and calloused. She's in desperate need of some cuticle work. I gently and lovingly massage her foot, her ankle, her calf.

"Kiss her foot." A little hesitation on my part. I'm sure he didn't notice it. I bring her foot to my face and tenderly stroke it with my cheek. I kiss it. I let go of my fear. Her foot becomes my beloved. My sweet freak.

"Suck on her toes," he fairly whispers.

Yes, yes I did.

My passionate actress-self is unfettered and wild. My inner-child-Christian is hyperventilating and passing out. Nevertheless on I go.

"Okay, now start the scene."

Mercifully we move into the scene and finish it, admittedly, with much more freedom and abandon than the first go-around.

Something inside me shifted a little that day. I don't know if I gained a little deeper understanding of lesbians, a greater capacity for non-judgment, a smidge more sexual freedom, or a lifelong commitment to keeping my toes well groomed, but something broke a little loose. It may just have been one of my screws, but I most certainly gained a bit more favor with the maestro. He understood that I was serious about the craft.

KINSHASA HERE WE COME! OR NOT . . .

On any given Sunday at our church if you sat in the back of the house, you would look out over a sea of white and blue. This was because the congregation of the church was made up of, in large part, seniors. Looking back now, there were probably a fair share of folks who were the age I am now (middle). The youth pastor and his wife had a little girl, so they were probably in their early thirties, but being a twenty-something whippersnapper, they all seemed pretty old to me. Other than Cindy, I don't recall anyone else of college age.

We often sat behind Ruth, a sweet little dozing granny; we got such joy out of seeing her do her weekly slow lean to the right. We made bets on whether she would finally fold all the way horizontal, or if she would stop at about twenty-two degrees. Sunday mornings started to feel a bit like a family gathering. Most of the folks were full of warm hugs and chitchat and it was rather comforting having a whole new gaggle of grandparents and older aunties and uncles. I hadn't spent much time with my own extended family since my very early childhood; they were spread out and not particularly close to one another. Family get-togethers were rare, especially once my nuclear one blew apart.

One couple in particular took a special liking to Mike and me. They always made sure we were properly lavished with jolly greetings and hugs, and soon adopted us and invited us home for lunch.

Cora and Bob's home is tucked away in an old, well-kempt neighborhood close to the church. We miss it on the first pass, but as we turn around I catch the number on the curb.

"There it is," I say, pointing.

We pull into the spacious semi-circular driveway. The house is a single story in the Frank Lloyd Wright style, boxy and flat-roofed with wide, low eaves and an extended carport. It appears to be suspended in the mid nineteen-fifties. Old-growth persimmon, magnolia, and oak trees surround it closely so it's shady and cool. It looks like a place where many meals have been and continue to be spread before gatherings of grown children and grandchildren at Thanksgiving and Christmas.

The garage is open and their car is neatly parked inside. Mike pulls into the connected carport, and we get out. I'm excited to be visiting our new friends and feel a twinge of first date nerves, but I'm hungry, and the aroma of something warm and yeasty has already made its way out to welcome us.

Bob opens the door beaming a sunny smile and invites us in. The home is cheery but quiet; the interior well appointed some thirty years ago, doesn't appear timeworn.

Cora's merry voice rings out from the kitchen, "Make yourself at home, young ones, lunch is on its way!"

Bob sweeps us through the entryway and down a few steps to the dining room and the simply set table. The wall-to-wall windows look out onto the considerable backyard that I had suspected was hidden there, much more open than the front and allowed to run a little on the jungle wild side. Cora comes bubbling into the room, a large wooden salad bowl in her hands.

"Hellooooo, young ones! Well, praise the Lord and happy Sunday!" she says, her voice like chimes.

I'm in love. Cora is about as close to being anyone and everyone's gramma as she could be. Her tiny frame and sprightly step belie her human descent and point more toward faerie blood. Her short white curls are combed out into a frisky Betty White bob—she's classy but not stuffy. It's plain to see that she was a hottie in her day. She exudes a contagious joie de vivre that draws people into her orbit like a tractor beam.

"You sit right down, I'll be back in a jiffy with the soup," she warbles.

"Homemade," Bob says. He winks and nods with pride.

In the center of the long table, a sturdy grapevine basket is brimming with warm freshly baked rolls. How can she do this? How can she be home from church for less than an hour and have fresh-baked rolls and home-made soup? I marvel. I want to be just like her when I grow up. Cora rejoins us at the table, gracefully spreading her napkin in her lap. I have already done so, and silently thank my grandma for teaching me table etiquette.

Always bring your fork to your mouth, not your mouth to your fork," my grandmother's voice echoes in my mind. *"Take your elbows off the table,"* she reminds. *"Chew with your mouth closed,"* she adds, my personal favorite, and *"First, put your butter on your bread plate, then you may butter your bread one bite at a time."* Her gentle but firm voice would guide me into Good Manners Heaven today.

At Bob's subtle prompting, we bow our heads and fold our hands.

"Heavenly Father, we give thanks for the bounty we are about to receive. Bless us this day, and thank you for our guests, dear Mike and Kathy, may you bless and keep them."

My innards feel warm and full as I imprint this image—"bounty"—onto my heart as being the defining attribute of a life lived for God.

We sit in the den for dessert and tea. Cora puts out a small plate of shortbread cookies each of which holds a dollop of apricot jam in its center. They're sublime and melt in our mouths.

"I suppose I have lured you here under false pretenses today," Cora confesses. Her eyes are actually twinkling. I swear it. She wants me to head up a bake sale for the Sunday school fund? She has a multi-level marketing opportunity she wants to share with us? She's really with the mob and is part of a money laundering operation run through the church finance committee? She has my full attention.

"Before I share with you, let's all stand up and get our blood moving after that wonderful lunch!" she says. With gleeful effervescence, she jumps to her feet.

I'm confused but follow her lead obediently.

"Let's shake off the afternoon sleepies with some light calisthenics," she fairly sings. She throws her arms out exclaiming, "Arm circles!"

We all coalesce into synchronized rhythm with stupid grins on our faces; her enthusiasm is so contagious. A few sets of cross crawls, overhead stretches, and toe touches (I think she can bend the deepest), and our heart rates are sufficiently raised, our digestion adequately aided.

Cora opens her presentation with, "Well, I'd like to start with a short video."

It's Amway. I knew it!

She pops the VHS cassette into the player and after the picture finishes tracking and steadies, the narrator begins telling us the extraordinary story of Clarence Jordan, Millard Fuller, and *The Cotton Patch Gospels*.

The movie is brief (my prayer of brevity is getting finely tuned and powerful) and inspiring. It introduces us to two radical men of God who truly live out their faith in a way that strikes me to the core.

In the early 1960s, Millard Fuller was a brilliant young businessman and lawyer who was a self-made multi-millionaire by the age of twenty-nine. Unfortunately all work and no play made the wifey a grumpy girl. She finally drew the proverbial line in the sand of his unending work hours and relentless pursuit of the green. Mr. Fuller quickly realized his folly and the emptiness of riches (oh I should love to try such emptiness, just for a minute) and he and the missus decided to give away all their stuff and dedicate their lives and their great wealth to helping the poor build low-cost, simple homes using interest-free loans. Thus was born Habitat for Humanity.

Radical. High impact. Life changing. I love this kind of shi—stuff.

Anyway, the Fullers and Habitat went on to eventually build over

500,000 houses, sheltering 2.5 million people worldwide.

I'm floored. Here is my fairytale version of what it means to be a Christian, being lived out in real-time right in my own world. Cora claps her hands and grins broadly.

"Hurrah for Millard and Linda Fuller! Hurrah for Habitat!"

We all join in, sheepishly applauding with the Cheerleader for Humanity.

"I have a book for you to read," Cora says. She presses into my hands a crisp new paperback entitled *Love in the Mortar Joints*, by Millard Fuller.

"I want you to read the amazing story of how Habitat was born. I think you'll find it very inspiring."

"I already do," I say. And I mean it. "I can't wait to read it."

∽

I devoured the book and was, of course, immediately struck with a deep conviction that I was being called to Africa. My greatest dread was upon me. Foreign missions. Latrines. Bugs. Oh why, my Lord, *why?* The more I read, the stronger the feeling became. I finally decided that perhaps the possibility of taking a short-term trip to Zaire to participate firsthand in a building project didn't sound so horrifying. In fact, the more I thought about it, the more my passion and sense of adventure welled up. I could picture myself there, swinging a hammer and mixing mortar.

I read parts of the book to Mike. He was sweet and patient with me as I shared my enthusiasm for this amazing ministry. He thought that what was being done for the poor was admirable but, "Africa, Kathy? Us? Are you stoned?" He wasn't convinced.

We spent several days talking about it.

I argued that we should trust God and take a step of faith. I could write a letter to Millard Fuller, explain what I was sensing, and see if he felt that God might be leading us to go to Kinshasa. Mike finally conceded. I don't think he was any more convinced at that point that it was something he was interested in doing; he was just tired of going around on it. Deep down, I don't know that I was sure I was cut out of the right material either; you know, bugs and dirt and all. But, it was fun to fantasize about our safari for the Lord. So, I sat down and wrote the letter.

☙

Between school, homework, and work-work, I was one busy bee. A month passed and the letter to Millard Fuller still stood on the kitchen table, propped up on the homemade Popsicle stick napkin holder I had made at church craft night. As more and more of my energies were directed toward my studies, the intensity I had felt about sailing off to Africa waned a bit. I was still super excited about the good work of Habitat, but now my thoughts about it were often accompanied by a large side order of anxiety and guilt. Why was I dragging my feet on this? Why hadn't I mailed the letter? I felt like I was letting the Lord down. He called me to action, and I was hesitating, clinging to comfort and selfish desires. This was my first big test of faith, and I was failing.

We sat with Cora and Bob at one of our frequent after-church potlucks. As we chatted and ate, and I babbled on to Cora about the deep conviction that reading *Love In the Mortar Joints* brought to my heart. She smiled sweetly as she listened intently.

"I don't know. I was so sure that God wanted us to go to Kinshasa, but now that we've taken a step, I feel kinda frozen and scared."

"Well, Kathy, have you considered that you're not getting a green light from the Lord because He's got something He needs you to do *here*?" She smiles, her eyebrows raised.

A flood of relief sweeps over me as I realize that she's graciously about to present us with an out.

"You've got to trust that He's speaking to you through your heart. I'm sure that He's mightily pleased with your enthusiasm and willingness to serve. But you came to Los Angeles with a dream in mind and have set yourself on that path. He's seen to it that your needs have been met. I think that if you're patient and continue to wait upon Him, He'll show you a way that you may be of help right here and still stay true to your dreams."

My heart nearly bursts with gratitude, and tears well up as I reach for a hug. "Thank you, Cora," I sob. "I want so much to do something. I think the work Millard is doing is awesome and important, and I want to be a part of it somehow."

Cora smiles her dear sweet smile and hands me a tissue. "I've come to find that Jesus is a good shepherd and is gentle with his sheep. I think you'll know what you need to do when the time is right. Then, whatever it is, it'll *feel* right."

As Mike and I drive home, the sense of relief is palpable in the car. We crank up the radio and belt at the top of our lungs with Duran Duran and U2 and Queen. We laugh and make silly small talk. Mike cracks his usual corny jokes and I my dirty ones. Our little cottage greets us happily as we park in the carport. The world seems ever so much lighter when it isn't perched on our shoulders. I pick up the letter from the kitchen table as we head for the bedroom for a little Sunday Afternoon Delight. I start to toss it in the wastebasket but stop short and slip it into my desk drawer instead. Just in case.

IT'S SHOWTIME FOLKS!

"I have an idea, " I announce.

"You? An idea? Unheard of," Mike says. He sets down the book he's reading.

"I know how we can be involved with Habitat without being missionaries in Africa."

"Yeah?" he says. He looks cautiously optimistic.

"I'm going to produce and direct a production of *Godspell* to raise money for Habitat!"

You and what army? my inner critic chides.

"That sounds very ambitious," Mike says.

"We can keep it real streamline—super low budget. We could ask the church to help fund it and ask for donations from the congregation too." My heart is pounding and my pits are doing their nervous rain dance. "If we did it next summer, I would have like nine months for pre-production, fund raising, and planning."

Mike sits there, arms crossed, holding his chin with one hand, his right index finger pressed against his lips—his version of The Thinker. "Well, that actually sounds kinda cool. Let's talk to Pastor Terry about it. See what he thinks."

This is perfect! This feels right—just like Cora said. No bugs, no camping in the dirt, no porridge—just actors and audiences. God is awesome!

We schedule a meeting with Pastor Terry for the following Sunday after church. He invites us to have lunch with him and his family at his house. I cannot contain my enthusiasm and spill my whole plan with nary a breath for anyone else's edgewise words. He listens, grinning and nodding.

"That sounds like a fantastic idea, Kathy."

His teenage daughter Megan sits nearby. "Yeah, cool!"

"I'll bring the idea before the Board and see what kind of response we get."

A few days later I get a call from pastor saying that he's arranged a little meeting with the board, the elders and deacons, and myself. It's my chance to share my idea and see if I can convince them to support my most worthy cause. He has set it for two weeks hence, so I have time to put together my pitch. Game on.

By the time my meeting comes, I've assembled a comprehensive presentation, complete with a Habitat storyboard filled with compelling pictures of happily housed African families, charts, graphs and the like. I've written a business plan with financial projections, a production calendar, and plan of action. I'm as ready as any CFO preparing to meet with an investor group.

I make the drive to the church alone, as Mike is pulling a Saturday shift (he's now working in the credit card fraud division at Bank of America; apparently criminals don't take the weekends off). Cindy won't be there either, she's got something else gong on. I'm on my own for this one.

Now, I experience pre-show jitters like most actors. It's not generally a big problem; I simply do some relaxation exercises, get centered, and go on when the lights come up. I get lost in the character and the action, and all is well. This presentation, however, is a different animal altogether.

I get down to the basement multi-purpose room early, set up my boards, get my notes arranged on the podium, and then chat with pastor Terry for a few minutes. My normal butterflies are doing their aerial ballet inside my tummy, but I know that I know my stuff, and I'm prepared to wow 'em.

Pastor gives me a lovely introduction, and I step up to the podium. I look out at the predominantly gray and white-topped crowd. My heart rate doubles, and a train engine chugs inside my ear canals. I glance at my notes. To my utter horror someone has replaced them with some kind of hieroglyphic rubbings. These aren't my words—I can't read this! I cannot make my brain understand what I'm reading.

I look up and meet the blank faces of the audience before me. There. There's Cora, all smiles and sunshine. She urges me on with a minute nod. I clear my throat. My knees threaten to fail me. *What the hell?* I can't get a grip on my nerves! I have no character to hide inside of. It's just me out here in front of the church people. The men have on suits. The ladies have on pantyhose. Here I am, some young kid, braless, about to ask them for several thousand dollars. *Hey gang, let's put on a show!* I think I might throw up.

The rest of the presentation is somewhat of a blur to me. After stammering and fidgeting for a moment, I go into survival mode, and some other entity takes over my mouth. I become Tony Robbins and lead them all across burning coals. I remember weeping when I spoke of the great work of Habitat—and damn if toward the end I didn't add an extra syllable to the name of Jesus-ah. Too bad I wasn't asking for a hundred thousand dollars—I might have landed it.

A week later: "Good news, Kathy!" Pastor Terry's voice is full of champagne bubbles and delight. "It's a go! The board has agreed to underwrite the production."

I'm not sure at first whether I'm ecstatic or scared shitless. Taking on a show is no small enterprise, especially as a producer/director. But we had money! That was a huge head start. As I allowed my mind's eye to call up images of opening night, I knew that this thing had the potential to rock. Of course it did, Jesus was all over it. He called me to do it, and He would see to it that all would go well. He had my back.

☙

Our church was quite conservative and traditional in terms of its worship services. The worship committee's idea of a contemporary service was to have an occasional up-beat Pat Boon song that someone would sing for a special occasion or to pull Cindy in for one of her rockin' solos. Except for the wall of sound generated by the gargantuan organ, the atmosphere was predictably quiet and reverent. Piano hymns, the melodious strains of the choir, an occasional string quartet were the usual fare.

Oh, at Christmas and other holy days though, they would get a little wild and bring in the hand-bell choir. That was a sight.

A long table would stretch across the front of the altar, draped in red velvet, upon which stood numerous large-handled bells, like a row of gleaming brass soldiers. Behind them stood two-dozen or so ladies in red satiny robes, each wearing a dainty pair of white gloves, like so many Minnie

Mouses. Bells and ringers alike would range in size from pint to jug, standing erect, like the human counterpart to the line of bells, waiting for the director. At the maestro's signal, the ladies moved forward as one, each taking hold of her bells, one in each hand. Without a sound (How the heck did they do that?) they would bring their instruments to their breasts and hold them at the ready. The whole preparation was so ceremonial and synchronized. They'd obviously put a lot of time into their timing. You'd find yourself anticipating a rapturous concert the likes of which one might encounter only in Heaven itself. What followed though, was more like:

The whole room is hushed. The director raises his baton. The music begins.

Jing . . .

. . . gle bells . . .

Jing . . .

. . . gle . . .

. . . bells Jing . . .

. . . gle . . .

. . . all . . . the . . .

. . . way . . .

The piece begins haltingly, at first—and then, haltingly it continues. The delay between notes is almost maddening. I mean, holy crap, you want to stand up and shout, "OH-WHAT-FUN-IT-IS-TO-RIDE-IN-A-ONE-HORSE-OPEN-SLEIGH-HEY!!" just to get the damn thing moving.

It wasn't their fault though. Unfortunately, in order to get any sound out of them, each lady had to give her bells a violent shake and then bring them back up to her boobs to quiet them. It was incongruous to see these docile and dignified church-lady bell ringers jerking their arms so hard in order to get their instruments to sing, that they nearly got whiplash. No wonder none of the men played, there would surely have been a few toupees flying.

Their faces would beam proudly all the while, with the exception of an occasional grimace of pain from a wrong note. They always ended with a magnificently stuttering flourish. Each song was met with thunderous applause. If this was all it took to bring down the house, it would be fun to see what the response to *Godspell* would be. Who knew, maybe it would inspire a little more life in the service. I'd heard that some of the more modern, charismatic churches had full-on rock bands that played on Sunday. I was fairly sure the sweet sound of rock-and-roll had not yet raised the roof off this place. I was a little scared and a little thrilled that I would be the one to bring it. Okay, so it wasn't going to be for a regular service, and it wasn't exactly like, you know, Ozzie, but it would be close enough for this crowd. The rebel in me was secretly hoping to ruffle a few feathers. I loved the idea of glorifying the Lord with cool music and clown makeup.

Meanwhile, as second-year exam plays came speeding around the corner, my Academy experience was nearing the home stretch. Those days were so incredibly intense and all consuming that I didn't notice them rushing by like so many summer fields. Except for the hope of being selected to participate in the third-year production company, it was likely that I would not see many of my chums again.

Third-year at the Academy was also by invitation only and was designed to create a type of repertory company experience for those who attended. Company members could invite agents and industry people to come to the shows, a great opportunity to show off what you were made of. Only a handful of graduates were selected to participate in Production Company; it was considered an honor to be chosen. Whether or not you accepted, you nonetheless kinda hoped you would be thought worthy. I mostly put it out of my head and tried to focus on digging into exam plays.

Although I took my conversion seriously and kept as involved at church as time would permit, I found that in order to stay sane I subconsciously compartmentalized my sacred and my secular lives. As my two worlds paralleled, artist-Kathy continued her passionate pursuit of her craft in all its bawdy glory, while church-Kathy watched her language and volunteered to help with the cleanup after the potluck or to pull a shift serving soup to the homeless. It was doable in the context of this particular congregation. Never in my wildest dreams, however, did I imagine how the construction of my compartmental walls would eventually be put to the pressure test.

☙

I'm fucking late for my graduation class picture taking. Shit. I can't believe it, after all the sweat, all the commitment, all the pain, and all the tuition; they can't hold the damn photo session for five minutes? All of my classmates there—immortalizing the memory of two of the most unforget-table years of our lives—together in that photo forever . . . without me. (I still have bitter feelings about that, even this far out.)

We gather in the main campus theater for our commencement. Guys in ties, girls in heels. My mom and mother-in-law have traveled down together to So-Cal for the event. They stand chatting in the foyer with Marie as the stage manager herds all of us grads into the auditorium for a final walk-through. The energy is high; this is a monumental day.

We finally settle into our seats and the stage manager opens the house up for the attending loved ones and friends to take their seats. Several of our teachers speak. A number of awards are given for outstanding actor/actress, most improved, most fantastic human, and the like. I don't receive any, although if they had one for most likely to become a Bible thumping, tongue speaking, Gospel preaching, servant of Jesus, I would have cleaned up on that one.

I'm pretty sure our special celebrity guest speaker is the person who did the voice-over for Charlie Brown's teacher. She steps up to the podium and congratulates us, inspiring us with her well-rehearsed speech:

"Bwah, bwah bwah bwah bwah, bwah bwah bwah bwah bwah. Bwah-bwah-bwah, bwah, bwah bwah-bwah-bwah."

And on it continues. It's such a heady moment—so full of anticipation, pride, inspiration, tears, and bittersweet emotion—that the address escapes me. Something, I'm sure, about you've never had it so easy, good luck in the real world.

Before I know it, my row is standing and filing toward the front of the auditorium. I turn to look for Patricia back in the W's, give her a fist pump; she smiles and waves. In turn, we each anticipate the calling of our name so that we can have our moment of glory, gliding across that stage to shake the hands of our soon to be industry peers and grasp the piece of paper that declares we have the stuff. I somehow manage to refrain from blubbering and falling into the arms of any of my teachers—on the contrary—I walk, goddess-like, statuesque and proud, to where my golden ticket awaits. I take hold of the leather-bound package and grasp the executive director's hand with confidence. And then, it is done. I slide back into the cracked, wine-colored Naugahyde of the ancient theatre seat and look down at my prize. I caress the smooth black leather and run my finger over the gold embossed emblem on the front. I gently lift the cover to peek at my name emblazoned on my hard earned diploma, but alas, it's empty.

Turns out they will be mailed to us in a few weeks. There would come a time in the not too distant future when I would look at that moment as a sign, a prophetic message from the Lord, telling me that my destiny lay along a different path. For this moment though, I turn my heart toward the great accomplishment of these two long years and the hope of another fat envelope in the mail.

A week later, I get my envelope. Well praise the Lord and pass the loan papers: it's fat.

❦

There is not much time to rest and revel in my invitation to third year Production Company. I was stoked, but I had a show to do: myriad details to be organized, people to be mobilized, sets and costumes to be stylized, not to mention squeezing casting in there if the dream of helping Habitat was ever to be realized.

The making of *Godspell* was an exhilarating challenge. I found that I had a pretty good knack for producing and directing, although doing both at the same time is the stuff of which high blood pressure and nervous breakdowns are made. Because I had a lovable bunch of theatre junkies helping (amateurs all, but faithful to the end) and the power of God behind me, I knew we couldn't fail. I'm not sure how in the world I convinced so many people to give of their time—I had no budget for salaries of any kind. Folks were just inspired, I guess. I even managed to talk a couple of my AADA friends into getting involved; Marie did the choreography and Patricia did costumes.

As far as casting went, I did question whether I should cast only Christians in the show. Assessing my talent pool—a handful of teenagers from youth group with lots of hormones and little to no theatre experience, a few dozen geriatric hand bell ringers, and the choir (most of whom are also the ringers)—I came up with two viable hopefuls: my husband and Cindy. That was that; time to take out an ad in the trades. Given that the show was being done in a church, I wondered if I would get much response from the secular world.

Well, apparently those dang actors will do just about anything if it gets them on stage or in front of the camera, so I had a fairly decent turn out. In addition to being talented actors, the folks who came on board also happened to be wonderful and interesting people. One gal was studying to be a pastor; another was a nurse who worked with end-stage AIDS patients. I felt that God had sent me the perfect group: full of talent, enthusiasm, good looks, kindness, and compassion; and not a prima donna in the bunch.

Did I cast Mike as Jesus? Hell no. A second go at playing the Lord? Are you nuts? He would have been impossible to live with! He would've had me washing his feet and other crazy stuff. "But imagine the money you could've saved on wine," you might say. Nope, not worth it. Besides, the guy I cast came with his own Afro.

By the time pre-production and casting were done, we had a tall order to fill with only four weeks of rehearsal (including tech) before the thing opened. We put in long nights. Everyone worked a day job, so needless to say by the time we hit hell week (that's the last week before opening, when you're sure you've made a terrible mistake), we were all dragging and frazzled. My mostly non-religious cast was more than happy to pray before rehearsals. Eager, in fact, at this point, as we had all forgotten the secret mystery of how—by some mystical unknown power—every show comes together in the end. Even if Pete never gets his lines right, the paint is still wet when the house opens, and the rubber chicken has gone missing, as is so beautifully stated in *Shakespeare in Love*:

PHILIP HENSLOWE (Geoffrey Rush): Mr. Fennyman, allow me to explain about the theatre business. The natural condition is one of insurmountable obstacles on the road to imminent disaster.

HUGH FENNYMAN (Tom Wilkinson): So what do we do?

PHILIP HENSLOWE: Nothing. Strangely enough, it all turns out well.

HUGH FENNYMAN: How?

PHILIP HENSLOWE: I don't know. It's a mystery.

Fellow thespians, you feel me.

And so it was, a mystery. Before you could say, "Places," it was opening night and I was calling, "Places!" (Did I mention that I was stage-managing as well?)

As the house lights dim, my heart rate starts that deep and expanding thud. Like the drummer driving the oarsmen on the slave ship in *Ben Hur*, thud, thud, thud, thud, steady and hard and progressively increasing in speed till I think it might exit my throat.

Then comes the sound of the ram's horn from the back of the house. Every time, I hold my breath. Will it be a triumphant blast, calling the faithful to come follow, or a sickening "phlaaaaaagh . . . rrrraaaa . . . phlaaaa . . . phh-hhhhht" like a laboring ewe with intense gastrointestinal distress? Tonight it sounds a pure and beautiful note. John the Baptist sings out clear and pristine, as he slowly makes his way through the crowd, "Pree . . . eee . . . eee . . . pare-ye-the-way-of-the-Lord . . ."

The show was a smashing success. Nearly every night, that sanctuary was packed like it was Easter and the crowd always roared when it was over. The show ran for about a month at numerous church locations across Southern California. We filled the house consistently (I mean, who doesn't love *Godspell*, right?) and after expenses, netted about five thousand dollars for Habitat for Humanity. It was long, grueling, nerve racking, and glorious.

GODSPELL - LOS ANGELES

LIFE AFTER PARADISE

As I hoped and suspected it would be, my production company year at AADA was pure heaven. To get to do one play after another with a group of exceptional actors in a real live theatre with a full production staff and nary an audition was absolutely sublime—and about as close to a professional theatre company as many of us would get for some time. Well, minus the Equity card and the paycheck. Every show was fantastic, and I was fortunate to have gotten the lead role in *Homesteaders,* a play that I loved.

My time in paradise came and went like a bite of dreamy Belgian chocolate: gone all too quickly, leaving only the lingering memory of its creamy sweetness and a longing for more. Leaving the Academy was like being orphaned. A few of my classmates stayed in Los Angeles to pursue their careers; but most went home to wherever they came from. I went from a tightly-knit, intensely intimate support group to nada—an adventurer reaching the end of the familiar cornfields and facing the deep dark of the woods, alone.

That was a little melodramatic, but in all honesty, it was a hard transition for me. The daily community of people working for a common goal was no more.

I did spend a bit of time with one classmate after finishing school; James and I did a short-lived gig together in a children's theatre company—a little taste to wet my whistle. My eagerness to get out there into the real world soon helped me refocus my energy on the search for an agent and the subsequent life of always working oneself out of a job.

Patricia was still around, but both of us were working long hours at our *real jobs*. I got lucky and landed a position as a sever at a hip, up and coming restaurant that was opening in Pasadena (a sister operation to the place where Patricia worked). I jumped at the chance to segue out of working in the lab, and my horrible fear of being found out. I kept the nature of my work a deep dark secret from my church family. Waitressing was a more appropriate, if not clichéd, day job for an actor anyway.

After the *Godspell* project, church life went back to its predictable weekly routine. I found myself growing increasingly restless; an old hunger was starting to gnaw at my gut. I couldn't put my finger on it, but it seemed like there must be something more to life with God than Sunday service and potlucks. There must be some way to take church to another level—to integrate my faith more fully into all areas of my life. Going through the motions on Sunday and then living life no differently than any heathen out there the rest of the week was starting to leave a weird taste in my mouth.

I don't think I recognized at the time that I was desperately lonely for my theatre tribe, for that special bond that we shared. But now, living in a relational vacuum, I turned my yearning toward my church experience, seeking to forge that same intense connection in the context of my spirituality. Although we had a few friends at church, most of the members were decades older than we were. The distance to church made mid-week drop-ins and spontaneous visits to the one or two folks we were close to pretty much impossible. I longed to find a family of believers from my own generation, who were as eager as I was to serve the Lord and explore the faith more deeply. My hunger for belonging and my desire for community were a constant dull ache. Meanwhile, I continued to read and study my Bible, pray, and see where God would lead me next.

ↈ

During my time at the Academy, Mike had been taking a few evening acting classes and diligently submitting for as many roles as he could while also working full time (this is the quintessential life of the actor). He did come close to landing a lead role as the bad guy in a major western film. He got called back twice, but in the end they told him he'd been too nice in his personal interview. Dumb asses. Actors can be nice and still play bad guys. That's what actors do: pretend to be other people. Or, they could just hire dangerous killers. But, whatever.

Back then, newbies in the professional acting industry had only one way to hear about auditions: through notices posted in either of two industry trade papers. This was mainly for theatre, much of it unpaid. Auditions for paid gigs in film and television came primarily through agents. And neither of us had one of those yet.

Getting an agent was, and still is, a career in itself. We had scrimped and saved so that we both could get our headshots done. Not only did we have to cover the cost of the photographer, but also having prints made, buying envelopes and the postage to mail them out to agencies (Email? What's that?). I still don't know how we managed to swing it on our income. We ate a lot of ramen and eggs. A couple hundred stamps and about sixty follow-up calls later, I finally landed interviews with both commercial and theatrical agents. For my theatrical interview, I manage to talk James (my children's theatre buddy) into being my scene partner.

The agent's office is in the heart of downtown Hollywood deep within an antediluvian building flanked by a dive bar and a vacant storefront. Its aging paint and smudgy windows warn, "I'd turn back if I were you," but I grab hold of my tail, my butterfly net, and my resolve, and in we go.

We venture up a narrow stairwell and down a gloomy hall until we find his placard. The outer door is open so we step inside. The Inner Sanctum (for this is what an agent's office is to the wannabe actor) is as dim and dark and cramped as the façade promised. There's no sign of life in the unattended front waiting area, which is the size of a breakfast nook. We stand there, hoping that someone will emerge from the one and only other door that stands slightly ajar before us. After a moment, the door swings open and out shuffles a rather rumpled elderly man (he is undoubtedly in his early fifties but to my twenty-something eyes, fifty is the new eighty), with a spotty shirt and disheveled greying hair.

"Come on in," he says, his voice flat.

James and I glance sideways at each other, considering our last chance for a quick dash outta there. But we proceed beyond The Door. This is Columbo's office. It's windowless and dank, with a hint of, what is that? Old spice? Bourbon? A massive walnut desk that predates the World Wars devours most of the room; two heavy leather chairs sit snug up to the edge of it. Floor to ceiling bookshelves line the walls and are crammed with the man's entire life—books, papers, files, bottles, knick-knacks, god-knows-whats, cobwebs, and dust. His desk is stacked with the same, plus headshots and resumes. Many of them.

He deftly squeezes around his desk and sits with a whooshy *frump* into his antiquated leather desk chair. James and I pull out our chairs trying our best to put as much space between the agent's desk and ourselves as possible. We gain about twelve inches of clearance.

He leans back and puts his feet up on the desk. For the first time I notice he is in his socks. Deep breath . . . or not so deep.

"So, wattaya got for me?" he says.

"We're going to do a scene from Hothouse," I say.

We'd done another scene from this play together at school. It's an edgy dark piece with lots of drunkenness and yelling.

We do our entire scene, which in actuality is very physical and intense, right in our two chairs with our knees touching. All things considered, it went well.

"That was good," the agent offers with his now typical languor.

He scratches his wanton hair then shuffles through the paper on his desk until he comes up with a blank piece of letterhead. "Have your resume printed on this. I'll be in touch." He stands, indicating that we're through.

"Ok, thanks," I say. I take his smudgy letterhead.

We make our way out into the crystalline light of day and welcome the enlivening fresh Los Angeles air into our lungs as we walk down Hollywood Boulevard to James' car.

"What just happened?" I ask my friend. We sit for a moment in the quiet of his tiny Toyota Tercel.

"I think you just got signed."

PLANTING SEEDS

Dear Ann Landers,

I'm a twenty-three year old woman. After gaining a good deal of theatre experience through my involvement in college, local, and regional theatre, I left my home and family and all that is familiar to me to pursue my dreams of becoming a professional actress. I have invested vast amounts of cash, sweat, tears, and yes, even a little blood to acquire professional training. I have secured both theatrical and commercial representation, am bursting with talent and confidence, and I'm poised to get out there and take Hollywood by the short hairs. What should I do now? Signed, ~Ticking Biological Clock

Dear Ticking Clock,
Have a baby. Signed, ~Ann

There are some choices that we make in life that appear to defy all sense of logic. In the case of our daughter, conception was a conscious choice, although I cannot say it was a logical one.

If Mike had gotten his way, we would have had a half-dozen kids starting on our honeymoon. I, however, was firm in my resolve to have a maximum of two children and not before five years of marriage. I didn't Google calendar that promise or set a timer, but somehow, the desire to start a family came hard and heavy about nine months before the five-year mark. I didn't do a bunch of deliberating or planning or plotting. I simply knew in my knower it was time.

We're standing close, encircled in one another's arms in our little 1940s kitchen with the turquoise Formica countertops. I look into his eyes and smile my *I want something* smile.

"I'm ready," I whisper. He leads me straight into the bedroom for a little unprotected nookie.

Warning: the following content may be considered by some disgusting and crass, and otherwise inappropriate for children under the age of 13. I agree, but it's fun and I gotta get this question off my chest.

So. What is the deal with people in the movies who have wild, crazy sex; then the chick hops out of bed and throws her clothes on or goes and makes pancakes or lays there and has a long leisurely conversation with her lover as if there isn't a whole lotta rapidly cooling stuff running down her legs? What is up with that?! Same with the guy – it's not like he isn't all sticky and icky either—what—he's going to jump back into his hundred-dollar silk boxers and his nine-hundred dollar Armani trousers without a little freshening up? Puleeeeeeaz! (And speaking of movie sex, don't even get me started on first-thing-upon-waking tonguing—even a kiss before brushing is poo-poo, caca, dog doo-doo.)

Okay, now back to the Conception Story. Given the determined nature of this particular coupling and knowing the anatomical and gravitational reality of how this works, it seemed a perfectly ingenious idea to me to, upon coitus completion, assume a yogic shoulder stand for at least a minute or two. Couldn't hurt to provide a little extra inertia to help the wee spermatozoa reach their destination. It's a wonder we didn't end up with sextuplets.

Six weeks later, the results were in: early morning pee-pee, plus two pink lines, equals: IT'S A GIRL!

৩

Upon signing, my commercial agent had me reshoot my photos (like I had a stack of hundred dollar bills to throw into the wind), which had to include what was known back then as a composite. The back of the main headshot would have a bunch of smaller photos of me in a variety of commercial settings: a cute gal in pigtails working on her bike with a wrench, a secretary looking perplexed due to PMS bloating, a soda jerkette at 31 Flavors, a sexy ski bum, and a tough bitch in a denim jacket. Being freshly knocked up didn't deter my determination to get my career rolling, so before the tummy started to show the bun, I had the shots done.

KATHY MARTENS

KATHY MARTENS

In all of my youthful optimism and phantasmagorical visions of the future, I figured it was plausible that I could immediately land some recurring role on a daytime drama, wherein I would play a young political intern who has an illicit affair with a senator and ends up in a predicament. As my condition begins to become apparent to all, I'm let go—with a handsome payoff—and return to Boston to study law by correspondence, have my baby, and plot my revenge.

While there, I fall in love with a handsome young Washington-bound congressman who has an affinity for smart, round-bellied women. He swallows the tragic tale of the hit and run bus death of the child's father and promises to help raise the illegitimate nipper as his own. What no one knows or suspects is that due to the dark and Luciferian activities of my long dead grandmother, I now carry the seed of Satan who is destined to rise in the world of politics . . . You see how this could go on for many seasons, right through my pregnancy, birth, and at least the first few years of my kid's life. Of course they would cast my kid to play my kid. Hell, it could go right up into his or her adulthood and my old age! We'd never have to audition again! And commercials? Who needs 'em?

Wait. Where was I? Oh yes, on the road to Tinseltown (or possibly the hatch). Anyway, I figured that I might get a few bites before I got too rotund, and if not, I'd lose the weight fast after childbirth and pick up my career where I left off.

Meanwhile, this bringing-a-new-life-into-this-world thing was in forward motion—no turning back. I was full of joy about it, but even so, found that I spent a few awake-in-the-dark nights, wondering how in the heck I was going to know how to do this parenting thing.

"Dear Lord, thank you so much for giving us this baby. I guess I'm pretty nervous about all of it. Well, I have changed my nephew's diapers, so I've got that covered. And I know I can nourish the little thing, although I'm sure you now see why I have always complained about the wee mammaries. I'm excited though, cuz I heard recently that some girls end up with a rather nice pair after childbirth so I'm kinda hoping this might be the case with me. If it's not too much to ask, could you possibly arrange for them to stick post-lactation? Is that too vain of me? Oh, also, as you know, income is a bit of a challenge. I know I can stretch breastfeeding out to six months in a pinch; by then one of us will surely have landed a paid acting gig or a promotion at the day job, but Lord, what I'm not sure about is, like, *raising* this new person. How are we supposed to know how to bring them up right? I need some support here. I need some New Mom community. Could you work on arranging that for me? Could you maybe help us find a church like that? One that's full of young families who love you and are radical and devoted to serving you. Is that possible Lord?"

BORN AGAIN
(PART II)

BORN AGAIN (PART II)

"It seems very pretty," she said when she had finished reading it, "but it's rather hard to understand!" (You see she didn't like to confess, even to herself, that she couldn't make it out at all.) "Somehow it seems to fill my head with ideas—only I don't exactly know what they are! However, somebody killed something: that's clear, at any rate."

~Alice on "Jabberwocky"

DOWN THE RABBIT HOLE

IN PREPARATION FOR THIS SECTION, I went out into the garage and sifted my way through a number of boxes to find my old journals. I took up journaling at some point early in my visit to Wonderland, as a means to cope, I suppose, with all of the Jubjub birds and Bandersnatches.

I knew when I began writing my saga that at some point I wanted to access the memories contained therein, observing them as they had been recorded by my own hand from the far off regions of that strange place. As the time neared to go box diving to locate them, I felt a gathering reluctance to look inside those worn and forlorn pages. I wondered if I would recognize myself. I wondered if it would hurt.

(March 12) *I am so thankful for the blood of Christ—that I am washed clean of my sins. Still, I will stand before the One who died for my sins, and I long to hear "Well done." I fear for having to give account for my careless words & deeds. I know I can't earn my salvation O Lord—I deserve to die. But because of your mercy I desire to please you. I desire to be a living sacrifice for you. I wish to bring you glory not shame . . .*

Yep. It's been a toughy, but I'm determined to look my manxome foe in the fiery eye, hoist my vorpal blade, and let it go snicker-snack, through and through, until the worm no longer haunts me.

CHURCH OF THE ROCK-N-ROLLERS

Every so often I step back and take a wider view of the path that led me to where I am. Whether it's Providence, destiny, synchronicity, happenstance, or plain crazy luck, I must admit that when I gaze left on my timeline and ponder the dots connected one to the next, it causes me to lean toward the idea of some kind of orchestration beyond pure coincidence. How's that for solid conviction?

The fact that Mike happened to choose one music store over any of the other multiple choices he had, and happened to strike up a random conversation with a supercool dude there, who then still more randomly mentioned he was a musician on the worship team at his church, which just happened to be one of those Rock & Roll churches, and would we like to come check it out; I mean, what are the odds? Weird, that at this particular moment in time, when I was praying to find a church that would lead us to a radical life with God, comes an invitation that would set us on a course straight down a rabbit hole and into a world that even Alice herself might wonder at—all because Mike broke a guitar string.

გ/ე

The Church of the Rock-n-Rollers met in the ritzy theatre auditorium of an upscale high school, in a well-to-do little bedroom community in the foothills of the San Bernardinos.

"Are we late?" I ask.

"I don't think so. I'm pretty sure Ron said nine o'clock," Mike says. "We're a bit early."

"A lotta people here already. Maybe they have Sunday School classes or something?" I say.

"Well, they meet in a school, so . . ." Mike says.

As we make our way toward the venue, music wafts from inside, and is carried off into the foothills on the morning breeze.

"Sounds like they've started," I say. We pick up the pace a bit.

As we reach the entrance, it's clear that church hasn't started, as there are people hanging around outside chatting, laughing, praying. Among them are people our own age. First good sign.

"Welcome!" the greeter calls as he makes a B-line for us, hand outstretched, beaming a hearty Sunday morning smile. I'm not a great judge of age, but he looks to be in his early thirties maybe. *Suit and tie though . . .*

"Hey . . ." Mike looks at the guy's name tag, "John. Mike Martens." They shake hands.

"Hi, John. Kathy Martens." I extend my hand and we shake.

"Well, praise the Lord, Mike and Kathy! We're glad you're joining us today! Your first time at ALCF?" he says.

Did we stumble into some kind of recovery group or something? "Uh, yeah," I say.

"Well, praise the Lord! Welcome! I hope you enjoy worshipping with us today. Head on in; the service will start right on time." He ushers us to the door.

We make our way through the lobby and into the auditorium. The venue is crisp and clean, like it was built last week. There are already a few dozen folks scattered throughout the rows of theatre-style seats, some sitting meditatively, others standing, hands raised in the air, eyes closed; and they're singing. They sing to the tune that the band is playing, but it's like everyone is improvising on the melody line. Many of them are singing with strings of odd sounding syllables rather than recognizable words. It's a new and strange thing to see and hear, but the effect it creates is somewhat ethereal and calming. Like the sound you might hear as you pass through the Pearlies.

The band, and I mean a band—like, a rock band—stretches across the entire breadth of the stage. They aren't down in the orchestra pit or off to the side like the organ player; they're the headliner. And right up there in the lead, guitar in hand, head back, eyes closed, singing his heart out, is the Supercool Dude from the music store: Mike's new friend Ron. Tall and thin, he looks a little like one of the Beatles; black slacks, white collared shirt, skinny black tie. His feathered black hair is still a little stuck in the late 70s, but the goatee bumps the look toward hip.

Our guide, John, smiles and gently steers us to a couple of seats, thankfully, near the outside of a row. I'm impressed that they allow newcomers the option for a quick getaway. He hands each of us a small folded program.

We sit and observe as the band plays on.

A row or two in front of us in the center of the seats stands a willowy young woman who captivates me with her slow rhythmic swaying, her arms reaching upward and smoothly flowing back and forth in a lovely graceful dance as she sings, her face upturned. Her eyes are closed, and she smiles wide like someone enraptured by a suitor. It's a very intimate moment I'm witnessing. It feels a bit inappropriate to watch, but I cannot take my eyes from this holy encounter.

The song (or songs, as it were) that everyone is singing swells and then comes to a seamless close, leaving a quiet reverberation swirling in the air above us. The worshippers stand or sit still in rapt silence, clearly in no hurry to leave their blissful state. Without a signal from anyone, the little band of pre-show prayer people (Prayer Warriors as I later learn) stirs from their unified trance and comes alive, stretching and smiling and sharing some insider secret with nods, grins, and glances.

The band members go about their musician-ly business, adjusting their instruments and stands, shuffling their sheet music, while the congregants mingle and those from outside begin making their way in. Ron catches Mike's eye and greets us with a goofy, enthusiastic wave from the stage. He puts his guitar on its perch, then makes his way down the steps and up the raked aisle toward us.

"Hey! You guys made it! Awesome! Praise God!" he gushes.

Mike holds out his hand and Ron grips it, pulling him into a brisk hug.

"Hey, Brother! So glad you could come!" he says.

In my typical fashion, I reach for a big squeeze myself and am a little surprised at the deftness with which Ron pulls some kind of Christian Kung-Fu move and spins me around to his side for a rather awkward sideways, arm around my shoulder hug. I'm not exactly sure what to make of it, but whatever—it's nice to be recognized and made to feel so welcome.

"Hey, I'd like you guys to meet Reed. He's one of our pastors," Ron says. He waves to a well-dressed guy who is coming in the door. He's a small fellow. If he wasn't sporting the neatly trimmed mustache and dressed so smartly in the well-cut suit, I would guess he was twelve. He looks to me more like a (very) young business executive or a pharmaceutical rep than a pastor. Reed makes his way down the aisle, greeting people and shaking hands as he passes. Many people embrace him with big smiley hugs.

"Reed!" Ron is a pretty upbeat guy. He ends many of his sentences with exclamation points. "I'd like you to meet some new friends! This is Mike and Kathy Martens." I'm impressed that he remembers our last name.

Reed, like Ron, pulls Mike into an energetic hug. "Praise God, Brother!" Reed echoes Ron's earlier ejaculation. He turns to me, and as I step forward for my hug, he holds out his hand for me to shake.

"Nice to meet you, Sister. So glad you guys could join us today," he says. Despite his polished appearance, he seems earnest. I take his hand, squeeze it with my most confident woman grip, and give it a pump.

"I hope you enjoy the service. I think we're ready to start," he says, nodding toward the stage where the other musicians have reassembled. Several chairs have been added to the stage and are now occupied.

"Hang around for a minute after church," Ron says to Mike. He heads back up to his post. "We can talk more then."

We make our way back into our seats and sit with the rest of the full house. Reed has now taken his place with the other men seated onstage. I assume they are also pastors since Ron introduced Reed as *one of our*. There are four altogether. Wow. That seems like a lot of pastors. I've only ever heard of a church having one.

They must be really blessed to have so many pastors. Or else really rich, I muse.

All of the men sitting on stage are meticulously dressed, except for one. On the end of the Panel of Pastors is a tall and impressive man, but with slightly thinning disheveled hair which at some point, perhaps yesterday, had been combed over in an attempt to make up for the third of itself that's missing. A creamy yellow Izod shirt (I didn't think Izods could get wrinkled) and Navy Dockers that have long since lost their creases, replace suit and tie. He looks around smiling and bouncing his right heel up and down to some enthusiastic internal beat.

The house lights come down slowly, and Ron starts strumming his guitar. The other instruments join, like an orchestra tuning up.

A tall, equally well turned-out pastor steps forward with a handheld microphone. He has on a red power tie, so I figure this must be the head guy. He smiles broadly. "This is the day that the Lord has made!" he shouts.

I'm startled as the congregation erupts in whoops and shouts of glee.

The drummer counts off four, and the band slams into a rocking tune, all instruments blazing. Behind Ron, is a trio of ladies and another skinny-tied young man—Ron's own Christian brand of The Pips—all lined up in a row. They do the step-touch in unison and clap their hands over their heads. Everyone around us jumps to their feet, hands shooting into the air, and the place goes wild. Folks are rocking out with total abandon, dancing, clapping, doing the pogo. There's a large screen hanging from the ceiling with the song lyrics projected onto it, but mostly everyone knows the words already. I'm glad to have something else to look at now so I can stop gawking at the people. There are a few here and there who stand quietly and a few elderly who stay seated, but the overall feeling is PAAARTAAAY!

Mike and I, of course, are still seated—I, on my hands, heart pounding, little prickles popping out in my armpits. I feel a scary compulsion to join in the ruckus but am mortified at the thought of making a spectacle of myself. After all my longing and internal bragging about stirring up my own church, here I am in the thick of some mighty stirring, and I'm rooted in my chair, with my ass glued to my hands.

This goes on for three more songs. With a final power chord prolonged by rapid incessant strumming, symbol crashing, lead guitar riffing, and back-up singers wailing, Ron smoothly transitions the band into the same ethereal sustained progression we heard coming in. Now the entire congregation joins in the angelic-choir-scatting like we heard from the Prayer Warriors when we first arrived. Faces are turned Heavenward, hands reaching or held out with palms turned up.

The tune morphs into a lovely lilting melody, acoustic twelve-string leading the way. Rich harmonies from the bass, keyboards, electric guitars, and violin join, and we enter into the easy listening set. The songs that follow are nothing less than the most romantic love songs ever written for and about the King of Kings. These serenades are astonishingly tender and amorous, filled with images of lovers walking through fields of gold, children dancing before their adoring father, and lost sheep being washed clean in the blood of the lamb. Okay, I admit that last one is a little freaky and disconcerting, but I get the gist. These aren't your bookish hymns.

A woman draped in a shimmery cape-like shawl floats down the aisle and comes up onstage as the band continues to play a soft and soothing tune. She approaches the unkempt pastor. He leans down a bit so she can speak into his ear. He nods and rocks back and forth rhythmically as she speaks. He bunches up his brow and looks intently at the floor like someone receiving a top-secret message of utmost importance. He gives her another nod and hands her a mic.

She steps to center stage and closes her eyes. "Shaaaabala Nanda Sahhh-nahnahnah . . ." she breathes into the mic.

WTF?! I blink and swallow.

"Shaaaaabala Nanda Sahhh-nahnahnah! Coooobiala, naahla babababababa," she chants with great fervor.

Yep, heard her right, but as I said, WTF?!

"My breath is upon you. My sweet breath of refreshing. You, my sweet child, who have come, thirsting for more of me shall be filled as I breathe my breath of renewal into your soul." My ears perk and my heart rate jumps a notch.

"I will sing my song, and you will dance your dance, and together we shall bring down the gates of Hell. Through your devotion and obedience to my Word and your sacrifice of praise, the heavens will be shaken and the Earth shall receive the bounty of my Spirit—shaaaalalala." She sways from side to side; the rumpled pastor rocks behind her.

Around us, the congregants echo their agreement, "Yes." "Amen." "Praise You, Lord!"

I'm not sure what to make of this. I've heard of prophesying in church and seen some of the televangelists doing something similar, but this is different somehow. It seems . . . genuine? People around us weep. Some warble with gentle laughter. There is a palpable presence among us. It's weird—and a little cool.

The rumpled pastor comes forward and takes the mic. Prophecy Lady floats back to her seat.

What comes next is the stuff of Amos, Ezekiel, Jeremiah, and the like. I'm not sure what all he's talking about, but with the fiery passion and force of an Old Testament prophet this guy goes on and on. He speaks with great conviction, his voice strained and croaky, spittle spraying forth in a fine mist that sparkles in the stage lights, body rocking and bobbing like a buoy on rough seas.

Much of what I hear is foreign to me—but I do hear a good deal about a

Ring, a Dark Lord, and something about the end of the world. It's mesmerizing.

The people respond to his energetic zeal with wholehearted agreement and mounting urgency. His speech is punctuated by individuals in the crowd, "Preach!" "C'mon!" they say. Not one person fidgets in their seat, leafs through their program or checks their watch. They gaze at him with eager smiles, leaning forward, lapping up his words. Some, with eyes closed tightly, hold up their arms, palms pointed toward him, as if they are pulling in his message through their hands.

When Rumpled Pastor—let's just call him Leonard, Len for short. When Pastor Len finishes monologuing, I figure we had just heard the sermon for the day and would be headed out to lunch soon. But no, it appears we're just getting started because up jumps Pastor Power-Tie . . . let's call him Jim. Jim for short. Up jumps Pastor Jim.

"Praise the Lord. Praise God. Welcome everyone. Good morning. We're going to jump right into the meat of the Word here, but first let's take a few minutes to greet one another. The Scriptures say that they shall know we are disciples of Christ by our love for one another. Let's show one another we care. Find someone new or someone who you don't know and take a moment to get acquainted."

For Mike and I, that's, well, everyone in the entire room. Except for Ron and our new friend Pastor Reed. As eager as I am to make new church friends, this mix and mingle kind of thing makes me uncomfortable. But in my deep desire to find community, I shove my trepidation down deep, grab Mike by the arm, and head for the nearest safe looking couple.

"Hi, nice to meet you. We're Mike and Kathy Martens," I say. I offer my hand to the friendly-faced gal. She throws her arms wide and gives me a sweet hug. Mike is receiving the same from her hubby, a rather tall and round around all the edges fella with ruddy cheeks and thinning hair. He looks like an overgrown little boy.

"Oh, well Praise the Lord," she says in a deep, sultry voice, a hint of some kind of southern dialect curling at the edges. "I'm Joan, and this is my husband Clive."

We do a kind of do-si-do and switch our partners. Mike endeavors to give Joan a warm and friendly hug, while simultaneously I reach to put my arms around Clive. Like a couple of ninjas, Joan and Clive each pull the

Kung-Fu move from earlier on us with head-spinning swiftness and grace, and we each end up in an oddball sideways pseudo-hug.

This was what I eventually would come to call the "Don't Press Your Boobs Agin' My Chest" hug. (It's a negotiation I would never understand and would eventually have to master, albeit somewhat begrudgingly.)

Pastor Jim is now calling us back to our seats. It's time to dig into the Word and his message for the day. I hope he'll bring his sermon down a notch. Don't know if I can take much more wheels within wheels or ass's jawbones. This's a lot of new stuff to assimilate all at once.

The message is fairly short and sweet, speaking about the great love of God and how we can receive His glory in greater measure through things like repentance, prayer and fasting, and a deep hunger for more of Him. Pastor Jim speaks about the laying on of hands, the gift of tongues—*so THAT'S what that was*—and the early church in the Book of Acts and how the disciples devoted themselves to the apostles' teachings, breaking of bread, fellowship, and prayer. *He's talking about community*—this gets my attention. I sop it up eagerly, like dry bread dipped in chicken soup for the soul.

When he finishes, he gives a short invitation for anyone who has not yet received Jesus Christ as Lord and Savior, to do so. We all bow our heads and close our eyes so that anyone who wants to receive Jesus can anonymously slip up their hand without anyone looking at them, but then once they do, we all open our eyes while they stand and come forward as a public declaration of their salvation. Feels a little bait-n-switchy, but whatever; several folks make their way down to the front. Pastor Jim lifts his arms encouraging us all to stand, "Praise the Lord! Let's all Praise God for these courageous souls," he says. He starts to applaud; the audience joins him with whoops and whistles and joyful shouts. Pastor Jim has to raise his voice over the happy ruckus, "Praise God! The angels are rejoicing in Heaven today as you come forward to receive Christ as your Lord and Savior. Praise God. Praise You Jesus."

A number of people, including all of the pastors descend on those who've come forward. The crowd quiets down as the pastors and others huddle around the newly converted, speaking quietly with them. Some of them nod their heads, listening intently; others close their eyes. The pastors put their hands on the people's foreheads and pray for them, several begin to weep. The rest of the congregation waits patiently. Prays. Mike and I watch. After a little bit, the people are led out of the auditorium through a side door. I wonder: More prayer? Counseling? A class? What? (!) Pastor Jim gets back up on stage followed by the other pastors as Ron fires up his git-fiddle for one last song of celebration.

I realize that we're now two and a half hours in. I'm about done, and can only think about a burger and fries. I'm hoping that we're gonna wrap up and call it a day soon, though I am enjoying this strange and mystifying experience. Everyone jumps around, dancing like they're on pogo sticks, and it all finally ends with a flourish and a Praise the Lord Hallelujah, Amen!

The congregation begins to move about; Mike and I wait as Ron wades through all of the people talking, laughing, and sideways hugging. He comes up to us, smiling wide, like a Jack-o-lantern.

"Awesome, huh?! Did you love it?"

"Yyyyyeahhh, that was . . . something else," Mike says.

"My wife and I would love to have you guys for lunch today."

So that is the deal. Lure us in with your supercoolness, knock us silly with your raucous rock-n-roll worship music, blindside us with strange languages and otherworldly messages, starve us for two and a half hours, then entice us into your home with the promise of food so that you can HAVE US FOR LUNCH?!! Who do you think you're dealing with here, a couple of gullible Pollyannas who would just walk into any ol' trap?

"Sure! Sounds great!" we say.

We make our way out into the sunlight, half expecting it to be dark by now, and walk back to the car. My limbs feel oddly clumsy.

We sit in the warm silence of the car for a moment. We've been here before, a few years ago.

"That was bizarre," Mike half whispers.

"I kinda liked it," I say.

"Yeah. Huh. Good music," Mike says after another moment.

I look at the church bulletin. At the top is printed, "How God spoke to me today." Below that are lines for taking notes about what God had to say. Ron has scrawled his address there.

Mike slides the car into Go, and we head off to find out if we're lunch.

THE NEW FRIENDS & FAMILY PLAN

As we pull up and park, it dawns on me that we have yet to meet Ron's wife. How in the heck did that happen? Did she even know we were coming? How odd to be about to go knock on a complete stranger's door and say, "Hi, we're here for lunch." Or possibly in this case "Hi, we're lunch." I marvel at my own sense of adventure.

A young boy answers the door.

"Hello, I'm Billy, you're having lunch with us," he says. He holds his face straight like the grown up version of himself but with a whisper of a sheepish smile at the corners of his mouth.

His mom calls from somewhere inside, "Billy, please invite Mike and Kathy in." He steps back and opens the door wider for us.

We enter to the aroma of something much more than sandwiches. It smells warm and thick and comforting.

"Hi, I'm Luanne." A smallish gal emerges from the kitchen, not quite June Cleaver (she wears pedal pushers and Birkenstocks) but donning June's apron anyway. She carries a dishtowel.

"I'm sorry I didn't get to meet you guys at church. I had to get Libby home for her nap."

"Libby's the baby. I don't have to take a nap anymore. I'm too old. I just have a quiet time," Billy assures us. "But sometimes I fall asleep." He's awfully cute, as far as little kids go.

"Thanks for the invite," Mike says.

"Well, sorry, it's so last minute. Good thing I made lots!" Luanne says. She has a large, pleasant smile. Her front teeth overlap at slight angles, like a hand of cards fanned out.

The décor is an early eighties Kid motif, mostly toys, books, stuffed animals, and such. Here lives a clearly busy family. I begin to be aware of a faint aroma I can't identify hiding under the lunch smell . . . is that ammonia? A large woven basket holds a pile of cloth diapers and crinkly plastic pants. Wait, you have to wash those yourself? I feel a little prickle of unease; I was intending to use disposables. Other laundry is folded and stacked on a large avocado-colored chenille recliner. The furnishings all look chunky and weighty. The couch upholstery has seen some spills and the laminate on the coffee table has had its wood-like finish worn to a lighter shade where people have propped their feet.

The long heavy dining table—oak maybe—has already been laid out. I wonder at how Luanne, like my sweet Cora, managed to spend all morning at church, then somehow be translated home, prepare an entire meal for guests with a fully set table, seemingly as easy as breathing. This must be the hallmark of a truly godly woman. Or else they have elves. I wonder what this means for me; I have no elves.

Ron comes walking in the front door and is nearly bowled over. "Daaaaaad!"

"Heeeey! How's my squirt?" Ron drops his armload of guitars and bags and scoops the little tyke up into a hefty bear hug. Butterflies take flight in my tummy realizing this is a scenario that will soon be played out in our own home. Weird. Exciting. I know Mike is gonna be that kind of dad. Our offspring will have a chance of surviving.

"Billy, wash up for dinner," Luanne calls from the kitchen.

He immediately complies. Unusual.

"So, glad you guys could come today!" Ron says. He heads directly for the table and takes his place at the head. Luanne comes in with a large casserole in her puffy oven-mitted hands. With her apron off, she looks less like June and more like, well like me. Unlike me, she wears a bra. She wears no makeup. She has a natural blush to her snowy cheeks; her almost black, shoulder-length curls are very shiny. Somehow I already like her and am eager to tell her our news and perhaps gain a newfound advisor. She clearly has the mom thing down.

"Thanks for your hospitality. This is quite a spread," Mike says. We both eyeball the large bowl of peas and carrots, stealing a secret *Oh God!* glance at each other. Peas are gaggers for both Mike and I. If anything, they're to be swallowed whole—like a handful of vitamin pills—with a big swig of milk. We both have our share of pea stories. Being out of our parents' homes and all grown up, we're somewhat out of practice at pea swallowing. This will be a delicate operation indeed.

"Let's bless the food," Ron says. He takes hold of Luanne's hand. We join hands around the table and close our eyes.

"Mmmm, Father. Thank you for this day, for your Word, and for a great time of worship this morning. We stand in awe of your mighty power," Ron says. His speech feels a little elevated, but there is something genuinely intimate in his intonation, like he's in some kind of inner circle with Jesus.

"We thank you for our new friends, Mike and Kathy," Ron says.

"Yes Lord. Yes, Father. Praise you Jesus," Luanne echoes, her voice breathy, passionate.

"We ask that your hand of blessing would rest on them and keep them."

"Yeeeeessss." Luanne's voice is soft and has an almost moaning quality as she punctuates Ron's prayer with her agreement and praise. If I were sitting in another room listening and didn't speak English, I would swear they were making love.

"Thank you for this food we're about to receive. May it nourish our bodies. Bless the hands that prepared it, in Jesus' precious name. Amen."

"Amen," we all echo.

Luanne passes the casserole to Mike, and we start to dish up. We scoop and pass and chat. Mike and I perform some clever sleight of hand, managing to somehow miss the peas altogether. Luckily there's also salad, so there's some green on the plate, which makes the lack of peas less noticeable.

Luanne, whose overall demeanor seems rather soft-spoken, surprises me with her boisterous laughter and lively conversation starters. Ron is equally engaging, although he frequently talks with his mouth full, smacking loudly as he chews and speaks.

Presently, a wee girl appears next to Luanne, hair tousled, cheeks flushed from a good sleep, beaming proudly and holding a roll of toilet paper. *Ah, here must be the storied Sleeping Libby.* She tugs on her mommy's sleeve, turns around and bends over so the whole table is greeted warmly by her bare bum. "Wipe me?" she squeaks.

Luanne jumps up, apologizing, and steers the little imp toward the hall bathroom.

"So Mike, come take a look at my little studio out back," Ron says.

"Can I come?" Billy asks.

"Sure squirt," Ron says.

"You mind?" Mike asks me.

"Nah, I'll hang out here, wait for Luanne, " I say.

I wander around the living room, look at a painting of a huge lion. It's painted on black velvet. A tiny lamb is nestled by the lion's side, eyes closed, a serene smile on its muzzle. I wonder if I should start clearing the table but then Luanne comes back, shy little girl in tow. She expertly tucks Libby into her highchair, dishes some noodle casserole into a small neon pink plastic bowl, and sets it in front of Libby who watches me with big brown eyes. Luanne motions for me to join her on the couch.

I say, "So, I haven't told you. We just found out that I'm pregnant."

"Praise God!" she says. "Oh, Kathy, that's wonderful! Children are a blessing from God, the fruit of the womb a reward!"

I want to giggle because, well, Fruit of the Womb.

"Yeah. We're so excited. I'm freaking out a little. Mike comes from a family of five, but I was practically an only child, so babies are kinda new for me."

"Oh-ho-ho-ho Kathy," Luanne says. Her laugh is tender. "You're going to be a great mom. God has given you everything you need. You'll see."

"Thanks," I say.

"I'm happy to help. If you have any questions or concerns, I'm here for you."

She hugs me, and I drink in her joy and attention.

"And, we have so many amazing women of God at our church who're full of wisdom. If you guys decide to join, you'll meet tons of young moms and be surrounded by lots of supportive older woman who can disciple you in being a mother."

"You guys really have a cool church," I say. "Everyone seems so nice."

"Well, we're blessed. God's Word is our teacher. It shows us how to live. And we have an incredible group of leaders and elders."

She reaches for her fat, well-worn Bible that sits open on the coffee table. The pages are a patchwork of pink, yellow, and blue highlighted passages. There are notes and exclamations scribbled in the margins and between the paragraphs, many sentences underlined. I envy this deep study. She reads a scripture from Titus 2 to me.

"Then they can train the younger women to love their husbands and children, to be self-controlled and pure, to be busy at home, to be kind, and to be subject to their husbands, so that no one will malign the word of God."

I feel like a sojourner in a foreign land, being taken under the wing of a genuinely loving native.

Such a strange and new language they speak here, such unconventional customs. But to my desperately lonely spirit, this all felt like community, nurture, safety, and love. And for some inexplicable reason, I felt I could trust this completely. I remember a feeling of falling while this was happening. Like I was going over an edge. I believe that it was at this particular moment, for some reason I can't fully explain, I abandoned reason and bought in hook, line, and sinker.

SEND IN THE CLOWNS

Now it is God who makes both us and you stand firm in Christ. He anointed us, set his seal of ownership on us, and put his Spirit in our hearts as a deposit, guaranteeing what is to come.

~ 2 Corinthians 1:21

It was sad to say goodbye to Pastor Terry and our sleepy little church in the Valley, but we quickly made the switch and started attending Abundant Living Christian Fellowship (ALCF for short) regularly. It was good to find a church community full of young families and so much closer to home. It was exciting to meet a group of believers in Christ who lived their faith with such authenticity, conviction, and enthusiasm. The services continued to be full of surprises.

The sermon this particular Sunday is about the laying on of hands, the receiving of the Holy Spirit, and speaking in tongues. As with all of the other messages given at church, it is spoken with great fervor and authority.

"When you received Jesus Christ as your Lord and Savior and were baptized in water, you had your ticket to Heaven. But if you really want to be able to serve God powerfully and withstand the fiery arrows of Satan so you can live a holy life, you need to be baptized in the Holy Spirit. Being filled with the Holy Spirit is evidenced by speaking in tongues."

Everything is laid out and backed up by plenty of Bible verses, so it all makes perfect sense. I want this. I want so badly to be full of God's Spirit. The speaking in tongues thing is interesting to be sure, but I'm terrified of looking foolish or being out of control of myself, so it is with utter dread that I rise up from my seat and make my way down front, heart pounding, palms sweating, when the invitation comes for the laying on of hands.

There's a good-sized group gathering at the front of the auditorium, so at least I won't be singled out. I hope. We're divided into smaller groups; the pastors and elders spread out among us. I feel somehow honored that Pastor

Jim—turns out he is the senior pastor—chooses to come and pray for my group. The worship band is back up on stage strumming soothingly and *singing in the Spirit*.

"Okay, guys, let's just begin to worship and focus our attention on the Father—shalalala kundaliabababa . . ." Jim's last few syllables melt into and join the ethereal chorus that issues from the singers onstage.

I close my eyes and tune into the gentle guitar and the waves of harmonious voices that ebb and flow in the air. I feel an upward drift inside my body as I let my mind float on the pretty sounds. I allow my imagination to paint a picture of the throne room of God in all its splendor. I stand at the foot of a magnificent white marble staircase that reaches high into the sky, its top overtaken by the brilliance of the King of Kings.

"Praise you, Father—shandala keeelia shabalalala," Jim prays, his voice full of earnest reverence. "Thank you for these your children who desire to be touched by you and to receive your precious Holy Spirit—lalalalala cooodialababa."

A chorus of strange words begins to increase from the congregation and the group around me. Pastor Jim moves among us, gently laying his hand atop each person's head.

"In the name of Jesus, receive the Holy Spirit," he says. His voice is soft, with gentle authority. Some people weep. Some begin to utter the otherworldly language. "That's it. Just let the words come. This is your new prayer language. It is freely given by the Holy Spirit."

For those of us not yet flowing with the tongues of angels, Jim exhorts further. "Just open your mouth and begin to speak. Let it bubble up from the depths of your love for God. Don't try to censor it, just start moving your mouth and using your voice. Trust the Holy Spirit."

A few more join in. My desire to be in-filled with the power of the Spirit is so great; I want desperately for my life to fully please God. But my self-consciousness is excruciating. Pastor Jim is in front of me now. I'm squirming inside my skin, but just can't—he lays his hand upon my head. I begin to weep and . . . wait, what is this? I can feel it—yes, yes I definitely can feel something coming . . .

Twas brillig, and the slithy toves did gyre and gimble in the wabe; all mimsy were the borogoves, and the mome raths outgrabe . . . No wait, that can't be it; surely I'm not going to manifest the spirit of Lewis Carroll as my sign. I squeeze my eyes tighter and continue to silently praise the Lord with all my heart, which is thundering in my chest. Pastor Jim lingers with me for a few more moments and then moves on through the crowd. My heart sinks in a mixture of downright relief and sharp discouragement. I can't do it. I can't speak in tongues. I feel a hot wave of shame wash over me. I'm sure I could feel Jim's disappointment as he passed me by. I weep some more, but this time not for the joy of the Lord, but rather, for my deep dismay with myself. I'm ashamed that I'm too full of my own dignity and pride to allow the Holy Spirit to move in me—a feeling that I will grow very familiar with over the course of the next few decades or so.

༒

We'd been attending ALCF for about a month when we met Harry and Mary. One might think them a comedy a duo, but they were just a married couple, and he was obviously a magician.

They approach us during the dreaded Mix and Mingle.

"We're new!" he says. He wears a big black eye patch and is pulling a long yellow silk scarf from his trouser pocket. He pulls and pulls and the thing just keeps coming. It goes from yellow, to pink, to orange, to blue.

"Did you know that the love of God goes on forever?" he says as he pulls. "Kinda like my wife after coffee." She rolls her eyes, gives him a swift elbow. She smiles. He chuckles. They seem to have an understanding.

He whips the last of the scarf out of his pocket, waves it with a flourish, and proceeds to stuff it into the fist of his other hand, pushing dramatically with his finger, tucking it out of sight as he talks.

"God's Word is magical, like my scarf here. If you hide it away in your heart . . ." He pokes the last bit of it into his fist, making sure it's good and packed. Using his thumb and greatly exaggerated effort, he gives it a final tamping. With a quick and nimble move, he fans his fingers outward to reveal his empty hands.

"See that? God's Word, which has been tucked away in your heart, can now grow and yield a bunch'a goodness!" With a big sweep of his arms, he reaches over and pulls a colorful bouquet of silky flowers from my ear. I'm pretty sure it came from up his sleeve, because I didn't feel a thing. The guy is pretty smooth, I have to give him that.

"I'm Harry; this is my wife, Mary, and this is the day that the Lord has made!" He has an infectious grin and energy to match.

"We just celebrated our tenth anniversary. Wanna know the secret to our success? It's cuz of our belief that marriage is grand . . . and well, divorce is twenty grand, so that's pretty much out of the question!" He cringes and takes a quick step to the side, just missing Mary's left hook to his shoulder. "I'm not paranoid! Which of my enemies told you that?" he says, laughing with glee. It's hard not to just stand there grinning stupidly at his inane quips, he's so sincerely goofy.

He doesn't wear a big orange wig or a red rubber nose, but the guy is clearly a clown. The one eye he uses to look at us fairly sparkles with joy. This is one of those happy for no reason kinda guys—and why not? What enthusiastic, magical clown pirate who serves God by doing tricks and telling jokes wouldn't be happy? I have a feeling we'll become fast friends.

We found out later that he *was* a clown, literally (and professionally). His stage name? Happy.

THERE'S NO PLACE LIKE HOMEGROUP

They devoted themselves to the apostles' teaching and to the fellowship, to the breaking of bread and to prayer . . . All the believers were together and had everything in common. Selling their possessions and goods, they gave to anyone as he had need . . . They broke bread in their homes and ate together with glad and sincere hearts, praising God and enjoying the favor of all the people. And the Lord added to their number daily those who were being saved. ~Acts 2:42ff

Homegroup was like mini-church that happened—yep—you got it, in people's homes. Bi-weekly, either on Sunday or some other weeknight, a number of the church Elders (usually couples) hosted these meetings.

In case it's not obvious to someone outside the fold, an Elder does not necessarily connote someone who is older, although sometimes this may be the case. Also, there is a distinction between *Elder* and *elder*, the former being a term of office or ranking while the latter is more about years as a believer. Although, as you will note in a few subsequent anecdotes in this story, *elder* (*Elder* too, for that matter) does not necessarily mean *mature*, in either possession of wisdom and understanding or in years on the planet. Additionally, *Elder* could mean one has served for many years, but not necessarily, as one could become an Elder while having been a believer less time than an elder. As well, an Elder could be all three: holding the specific church title, having been a believer for many years, and is old.

Clear as mud?

ANYWAY. Ron and Luanne were Elders (though not old) and also homegroup leaders. We'd visited their mid-week homegroup meeting a couple times. The atmosphere was akin to a family gathering: home-cooked potluck, warm hugs and fellowship (visiting), a time of worship and teaching (ok, so that might not be so much like a family gathering, but maybe), then more fellowship and usually dessert (!)

Making a commitment to a specific homegroup, as opposed to attending casually, was strongly encouraged.

"We would love it if you guys would join our homegroup," Luanne says.

"Mike, I was thinking it would be cool if you brought your guitar and played with me for the worship time," Ron says.

"Love to, " Mike says.

"We've got a couple other guys that play, we can jam a little." Jam always sounds good to Mike. "Maybe you could share some of your songs too!"

"Once a month we do a potluck," Luanne says, sweetening the deal. "Oh, and also, the ladies take turns bringing dessert, so maybe you could bring this amazing Mississippi Mud Pie you keep bragging about," she adds with her wide-toothed grin.

Ron and Luanne's homegroup consisted of about five or six couples, a handful of single people, and a slew of kids. I thought it seemed like a great opportunity to open up and share our lives with each other.

Harry and Mary also joined Ron and Luanne's homegroup. I was happy about that. Harry and Mary were, as I said, a little different. They were as nice a couple as you could want to know, but they were a bit atypical to the other ALCF couples. First off, they'd been married for quite a while but still had no kids. Mary was the main breadwinner, as Harry was disabled and hadn't been able to work—except for his clowning—for a number of years.

One evening at homegroup, after worship and bible study, Ron, Mike, and another guy lingered in the living room jamming on their git-fiddles.

My failure to manifest the gift of tongues had me perplexed, especially since Pastor Jim's teaching of the Scriptures made it clear that this was a sign that accompanied being filled with the Holy Spirit. My worries about this dilemma had me in rapt contemplation when Harry and Mary swept past and pulled me into their orbit.

"Why the long face, sunshine?" Harry says.

Mary slips her arm into the crook of mine, and we make our way to the backyard where the little ones scamper about with gleeful squeals and titters. I touch my tummy, which finally looks like a baby is living inside (as opposed to perhaps just a little gas). Four more months. So weird that before long, I'll be adding my own little squealer to this mix.

I quietly confide my troubles to our swashbuckling friend and his first mate. They somehow make me feel like my secret will be safe with them.

"I don't know. I feel like I'm somehow blocking the Spirit. Maybe I'm just too prideful or something."

Harry looks around to be sure he's keeping my issue confidential. "Hey, really. No big deal, Kathy. If you're worried about it, just make something up. After a while, it'll just kinda become your prayer language. Jesus doesn't really care too much about it. He just likes to hang out with you. I mean it all sounds the same to me: homina, homina shoulda boughta honda, but I boughta mitzubishi . . ."

When he laughs, his good eye gets all watery. He grins at me. I'm betting his bad eye twinkles too, safely hidden beneath its piratey disguise.

Mary giggles. I feel reassured. The sounds of a hot guitar jam float out of the back door and into the balmy evening.

"Now if you'll excuse me, I'm gonna go blow some harp," Happy says. He pulls a harmonica out of his sleeve.

"Wow, what the heck else you got hidden up there?" I say.

He hunches his shoulders up high around his ears like a cartoon burglar and tiptoes up the back porch steps and into the house to join the musicians.

"He'll never tell," Mary says. "Could be anything. A trombone, a side of beef, you never know with this guy."

Yep, homegroup was one of my favorite modes of doctrinal reinforcement. Committing, however, carried the understanding that the relationship between the homegroup leaders and the members became one of teacher and disciple. Although it was not necessarily spelled out that way in the brochure, the expectation was that you were submitting your life as an open book, a rough draft to be edited and adjusted by your leaders to help you perfect your story so that it was pleasing to God, a blessing to the Body of Christ (the church), and a testimony to the world.

I know, I know, you're thinking, *Did they serve Kool-Aid with dessert?* But honestly, it was a comforting atmosphere, full of love, support, prayer and yes, occasionally Kool-Aid. I made it my secret mission to be a star pupil and make my teachers proud.

TROUBLE WITH TRIBBLES

Luanne and I sit on the porch late one Sunday afternoon, swapping stories of salvation and shelling peas for dinner. You know how I feel about the buggers, but it sure is fun popping them out of their little cocoons. I'm glad salad is also on the menu.

The cement porch, once painted the color of brick, is now patchy and dull, the paint wearing away on the steps to reveal that before red it was Pepto Bismol pink. The eves are shedding their dirty skin as well. In L.A. if you don't sweep, wipe, power-wash, or paint things on a weekly basis—or pay someone else to—the sooty dust from the vast freeways settles itself on every surface. It's why so many of the rentals have twenty-five layers of paint slopped on top of one another. Each layer is whatever color was on sale when it came time for a fresh coat.

I'm telling Luanne about the sleepy little church where I had gotten saved and my funny story of the stunned congregation, the river of tears, and fountain of snot; how my friend Cindy was such an inspiration to me with her intimate love of Jesus and her unique, un-churchy ways.

"Cindy was a huge factor in my coming to know the Lord," I tell her.

Fond memories of laughter shared and tears cried emerge in the misty seeing-stone of my mind. I haven't talked to Cindy in a while—we'd had a few struggles during Godspell (the stress of a show can do that to relationships) and had drifted a bit, but I miss my curious Jew for Jesus and kindred sister of the big hair.

The last I heard, Cindy had found she was getting more nourishment from her TV church, so she was hanging out there more often than regular church. "Very tempting—going to Sunday service in your jammies," I say.

"So your friend Cindy isn't submitted anywhere?" Luanne asks me.

"Come again?"

"Well, it sounds like she isn't really submitted to proper church covering." Sometimes my new family speaks in a language that takes me a little time to fully process through my translator.

"Oh, well, um, yeah I guess she isn't really going anywhere in particular right now?" I'm wondering where this might be going. "I mean, she does still meet with pastor Terry for counseling sometimes, but . . ."

We sit quietly for a moment, zipping the long green strings, then running our fingers along the length of the smooth pods, popping the little vermillion jewels out into the pot: *ping, ping, ping.*

I attempt to bridge the rhythm of the peas, "Yeah, it was cool for a while, but neither of us felt like we were really getting fed, so Mike and I started coming here, and most Sundays she just hangs out in bed and watches TBN." I laugh. Cindy's such a cool rebel.

"Hmmmm yeah. That's dangerous," Luanne says. She brushes a stray hair out of her face with the back of her hand. *Ping, ping, ping.*

"What do you mean?" I ask. I'm ever the student, albeit feeling a little uneasy with this lesson.

"Well, she needs to find a church covering; she should be submitted under the authority of an anointed Man of God and be surrounded by fellow believers who can speak into her life." Her tone is urgent and grave.

I can feel the involuntary bunching of my brow—the beginning of the deep groove—I endeavor to relax my forehead and the space between my eyes.

"We're living in times of great sifting, Kathy, and God is separating the wheat from the chaff. It's so important that all of his children are under the covering and protection of Godly leaders."

I puzzle over this for a moment. Heavy sigh. Can it be that there's a difference in God's eyes between the level of authority of different pastors and church leaders? Are some more favored or acceptable than others? I mean, besides the ones that are touching young boys in ways they ought not, I'm thinking that it's more a matter of style and preference, not so much one being more God's man than another.

Luanne continues, "If you aren't under the covering of an anointed leader, you're open game for the Enemy."

"Meat's goin' on the Bar-B," Ron hollers from the side yard. I'm relieved to have an out from talking about these scary notions of believers who think they're safe, but who are actually in some serious doo-doo. I feel afraid for them and for me. Kinda like rabbits in a trap—they, trapped in the grip of Satan—and me, just . . . trapped? Where else can I ever turn if this gig doesn't work out?

☙

One Sunday afternoon, we're sitting together in Ron and Luanne's living room, Harry and Mary on one couch, Mike and I on the other. We've been invited to this New Member's class to learn a bit more about the history and structure of ALCF. Ron is seated on one of two heavy oak dining room chairs they've brought in for the meeting. They're simple, unadorned, sturdy. The old, dry wood complains with high-pitched squeals, snappy pops, and ominous cracks when Ron shifts his weight. He's holding Libby on his lap. The back of her head is a tangle of fuzz shooting out in every direction from a nest-like nucleus, a clear sign of a good nap.

Billy has enclosed himself inside a fortress-like wall of Lego bricks and is now building some kind of elaborate plane for his army men. The left wing keeps falling off—he's got the turbine situated too far out—but this doesn't seem to thwart his imagination; he continues to mumble the cockpit dialogue and patiently reattaches it each time.

Luanne brings in a tray with six tall glasses, two plastic Tupperware cups—blue and pink—and a gallon jug of milk. Red cap. Whole milk. I much prefer two-percent. I'm thinking milk is a bit of an odd choice until Mary pulls the lid off of the big tin she's holding in her lap. Homemade chocolate chip cookies. What other hope does one hold out when there's a big tin and a gallon of milk?

"So you just packed up your whole life and followed Pastor Jim out here," Harry says. He resituates his eye patch, rubbing under the black elastic band where it has left a long red indentation along his cheek. Turns out it was diabetes that took his eye. Twenty-three surgeries to-date. This is one tough clown.

Luanne says, "Us, Pastor Len, Pastor Reed and their families, and a handful of others." She sets the tray on the coffee table and sits in the other dining room chair next to Ron.

Billy hops over the wall of his citadel and plops down next to the coffee table and the milk. He looks at Luanne. She nods, and he carefully lifts up the big plastic jug and pours some milk into one of the two plastic cups—the blue one, of course. His pour starts a little stuttered, but quickly smooths, and he stops as the milk reaches the very top of the rim and arcs just above it. It seems impossible that it doesn't flow over. He looks at Luanne, his eyes wide, and gives her a nervous smile. She smiles back, eyebrows raised and gives him a quick nod of encouragement. Sometimes her eyes literally sparkle. He leans over and gently sucks the milk down with a loud slurp, just enough so he can gingerly pick up the cup for a bigger swig.

"Yep, just like the pioneers," Ron says. "We loaded up the covered wagons, and we all trekked across the prairie to Sunny Cali-forn-ai-yay!" He is now wearing Billy's little red felt cowboy hat, and Libby is trying to push the small red bead up the braided chin string to tighten it for him.

"Rah-ha-ha-han," Luanne laughs, accentuating Ron's name on the exhales.

"What's so funny wom'n?" he continues in his cornball dialect, "We staked our claim for Jesus, right-cheer, by golly!" he says, slapping his knee. Libby is pinning a shiny toy sheriff's badge to his shirt.

"Otherwise known as what we call a church plant," Luanne clarifies for us.

"Yup, boy-howdy, by golly! Yeeeee haaaaw!" Ron is on a roll. He bounces Libby on his knee like a bronco. Her laughter is loose and throaty like shallow water over smooth stones. It makes me giggle. She hops down and joins Billy on the floor. He pours some milk in the pink cup for her.

Luanne takes over pouring milk into the rest of the glasses. "We'd been praying for two years about Ron's calling as a worship leader when Pastor Jim and our Apostle, Tom Lorrack, approached him to join the team. It was an obvious answer to prayer."

She offers a glass of milk to Harry. He declines but reaches for a cookie. Mary smiles and slaps his hand, then offers the tin to Billy. Harry makes a pouty face, sticking out his lower lip like a big bass and winking his one eye at Billy.

Mary whispers, "Billy, would you pass these around to everyone?" He nods, taking the tin. He offers the first one to Harry.

"My kinda kid," says Harry, laughing. He looks at Mary. She shoots a cold glare at him. "What? " he says. "One isn't gonna kill me."

"Apostle?" Mike says. He takes two cookies from Billy.

"Tom Lorrack, yeah. Our Apostle," Ron says.

"Apostle? You mean like the Apostle Paul?" Harry says.

"Well, yeah, kinda," Ron says.

"So how do you know someone is really an Apostle? I mean, can I be one?" Mike says, smiling.

"Miii-hii-hiiike. You're so funny." Luanne says. She sends the kids outside with their cookies.

"I've heard that you're definitely an Apostle if you can drink Draino *and* if you can survive being bitten in the asp." Harry says. He bobs his eyebrows up and down.

Belly laugh from Mike. Tee-hee from me. Golf laugh from Ron. Luanne crumples her brow and smiles with one side of her mouth.

"Bitten *by* an asp," Mary says. "And here I thought you were a grown up," she adds, then elbows Harry.

"Ow!" Harry says. I think Mary could take Harry in a wrestling match.

Harry rubs his upper arm and says, "Hey, you're only young once. But you can be immature forever."

"Anyway," Luanne says, shaking her head, "today, Ron and I thought we would give you some of the background of ALCF and Disciples of Destiny."

Ron says, "In answer to your questions about apostolic leadership, the Bible clearly lays out the intended structure of the church in Ephesians chapter four."

He leans over and grabs his big black soft-covered Bible from the coffee table. He lets it part in the middle, and it does a floppy backbend before he lays it open across his lap. He gives a quick lick to his middle finger, and gracefully pinches the delicate paper of the Bible page, swishing to the left. It makes a crinkling sound like tissue paper. He leafs through two or three pages, looking for something.

We wait quietly for him to find the passage he's looking for. Swish, swish, swish. Ron has a cookie crumb stuck at the top of his goatee. I want so much for Luanne to reach over and brush it off for him, but she doesn't. He stops flipping the pages, goes back one, and runs his index finger part way down the page. The whole of the open book, similar to Luanne's Bible, looks like a Rubik's Cube, blocks of blue, pink, and yellow highlighter, all fitted together; some things additionally underlined in black ink. There are notes scrawled in the margins. He stops on a paragraph nestled in a large sea of yellow. It is also underlined. He continues.

"Christ himself gave the apostles, the prophets, the evangelists, the pastors and teachers to equip his people for works of service, so that the body of Christ may be built up until we all reach unity in the faith and in the knowledge of the Son of God and become mature, attaining to the whole measure of the fullness of Christ." Luanne reaches her hand out. Ron looks at her, she nods toward his lap, he hands her the Bible. She dabs her tongue with her middle finger and starts the same leafing process.

Ron says, "The mainstream church has strayed pretty far from the biblical model, but God put the offices of Apostle, Prophet, Evangelist, Pastor and Teacher into place to equip the saints so that the church could grow. This is how His Kingdom will be established on the earth, and the return of His son will be ushered in." He pauses and runs his hand over his chin, finally wiping off the crumb.

"We've been seeing him restore these offices over the years; we've seen Pastors, Evangelists, Teachers functioning in their specific gifts, and now we're beginning to see the offices of Prophet and Apostle restored too. Apostles to captain the ship, as it were, and Prophets to steer it with a fresh Word from the Lord." Ron smiles, looks at all of us, nods. He adds, "Pastor Jim also has a strong apostolic anointing."

Luanne says, "But he's actually operating in the office of Evangelist right now."

"And Pastor Len, obviously, functions in the office of Prophet," Ron says.

"Reed is definitely a Teacher," Luanne says.

Now I'm beginning to understand why so many pastors at ALCF. So many jobs to do.

Luanne reads, "'God's Word is the same yesterday, today, and forever,' Hebrew's thirteen, eight." She continues to read to herself, skimming the words with her finger.

"Yeah, God's Word is living and active, given to us to instruct us how to live. And how to do church. I'm pretty sure He never intended for His Church to be divided like she is now. If we were using the original manual to build the Church, we wouldn't have all the divisions and denominations we see today."

Harry breathes out a suppressed giggle. Mary gives him a sidelong glance.

"Sorry. Can't help it," he says.

"Joke," says Mary, "Ten-to-one."

Ron cocks his head a little and smiles at Harry.

Harry says, "I hear ALCF welcomes all denominations. Tens, twenties, fifties . . ." He laughs. Mike laughs.

Luanne shakes her head. "Ha-ha-ha-rry."

Ron continues, "The Bride of Christ is meant to be *one*. Spotless and beautiful. United in the Lord and equipped by the five-fold ministry. The ultimate goal being, of course, the fulfillment of Jesus' great commission: to go and make disciples of all nations. And in answer to your question, Mike, about how do you know if someone's an apostle? Well, we can know by the fruit they bear. Tom Lorrack is a mightily anointed man of God."

Sometimes the church lingo makes my head swim a little, but I'm starting to get it. It's kind of like watching Shakespeare. After a bit, you start to tune in.

Luanne says, "Tom has shown himself as an exemplary husband and father. He walks in great integrity, power, and biblical authority. Other apostolic leaders have confirmed his anointing, and he has powerfully led many to the Lord."

"He's been in ministry since back in the seventies," Ron continues. "He and his ministry partner, Chuck Mulroney, started with a little Bible study in Tom's living room. Folks came to hear them teach about God's plan for advancing the gospel. Pretty soon hundreds of people were showing up and they realized that God was leading them to take the Bible study to the next level and establish it as a church. Their numbers grew into the thousands. That's how Disciples of Destiny was born. They knew God's plan was for them to keep growing and to multiply and spread the Church across the nation and the world. See, the key is the building of the local church."

Mike says, "So, Tom is the Apostle over Disciples of Destiny, and Chuck Malarky is . . . "

"Mulroney. He's the Pastor over the main church, but they've split it up and spread it out into many local churches with their own Pastors," Ron says.

"But Tom oversees the whole shebang," Mike says.

"Disciples of Destiny is a kind of overseer, with Tom functioning as a part of an apostolic team of Pastors. See, by sending out teams and planting more churches, they're advancing God's Kingdom."

How do they keep all of this straight? I had no idea what a saga laid behind a simple question. A whole new world, and I have a cookie headache.

"Disciples of Destiny. Sounds like a boy band," Mike says and laughs. Harry and Mary laugh. Ron laughs. Luanne gets up to open the small windows in the adjoining dining room. I feel a little anxious, like maybe all the jokes are wearing on her.

"And Abundant Living Fellowship," I say. I watch Luanne open windows. "You guys helped start the church here?" My blood sugar is now around my ankles. I drink the rest of my milk. It's warm.

Ron says, "About ten years ago, Pastor Jim had a dream that God was going to send him to California and was going to do a mighty work of revival through him here. Others kept confirming Jim's dream . . ."

Libby comes screaming in from the back door with Billy laughing and roaring in pursuit.

"Ahhhhhh!"

"Rrrrrraaaaawrrrr!"

"Hey, hey, hey!" Luanne swoops in and corrals them with the finesse of a calf roper. "Shhhhhhh . . ." She kneels down and gathers them with her arms open wide. Billy whispers something in her ear, then looks back at the tin on the coffee table. Luanne shakes her head and says something softly. I know it's a *no* by the little drop in their shoulders, but it's only for a moment, and then they take off again for the back door, happy and cheerful as can be. I'm mystified. I would have tried harder.

Ron is still talking only now he's sitting up really straight and leaning forward in his chair.

". . . so awesome how God showed him this sign again and again. He even spoke to him through Pat Robertson. Get this, Jim is watching *The Seven Hundred Club* super late one night—I mean what are the odds, Jim up at midnight watching TV—and Pat gives a word that some young pastor is thinking about starting a church in LA! Awesome! What are the odds?" He laughs and runs his hands over his shiny black hair, smoothing back pieces that have fallen into his face. "So anyway, he takes it to Tom Lorrack and the rest of the leadership. They pray and fast and it's decided that a team'll be sent out with Jim and Len to plant the church here. That's where we came in—and how ALCF was born!"

Luanne says, "Our vision is an example of the Church living in true community, like in the Book of Acts. Now, we just keep replicating the model, planting more churches and expanding the Kingdom."

"That's quite a story," Mike says. "Makes me think of tribbles."

"Tribbles?" Luanne says.

"Yeah, churches . . . multiplying . . . like trib—never mind."

Harry raises his index finger, "Star Trek. Season Two, Episode Fifteen. Got it," he says, smiling.

Mike opens his eyes wide.

"Wow," I say.

Ron stands, stretches, and reaches for his guitar, which is on a stand next to the bookshelf. A stack of children's books is there on the floor, a set of small smudgy footprints mark the wall next to them.

On cue, Mike pulls his guitar from its case.

"Tom will be visiting from back east next month," says Ron. He strums a few chords. "You'll see what we mean when you hear him preach. He's an amazing speaker!"

"He's also written a number of books," Luanne says. She gathers glasses on her tray.

"Hm," Mike says. He strums his guitar.

Mike doesn't seem super enthralled. But then, he isn't impressed mcuh by position. He picks up on Ron's progression. They sound nice together.

The atmosphere in the room shifts to one of utter ease; a late afternoon post-sugar sleepiness has descended. Soothing guitar sounds, the close of a meeting, the start of fellowship.

Luanne adds, "Remind me, Kathy, I'll loan you Tom Lorrack's book on parenting. You'll love it. It's very helpful for young moms and dads."

"Sounds awesome," I say.

I was intrigued by how this big ship operated. I imagined what it must have been like back in biblical times, when the knowledge of Jesus was still fresh and new and the early believers were all united like a big loving family.

This was the sequel in modern times—the story of the True Church. Of course, in my mind it was very movie-like, only this one didn't star Robert Powell, and the people didn't wear robes. But it was like, *Finally, the real deal.* And for Mike: *Hey, guitars!*

THE DREAM LIVES ON

And this gospel of the kingdom will be preached in all the world as a witness to all the nations, and then the end will come.

~Matthew 24:14

We sit around the table together at Ron and Luanne's often. We finish up a big pot of Luanne's famous Mac-n-Cheese Supreme; a hearty super-version of macaroni and cheese studded with frozen peas (I swallow them whole), carrots, and corn, all smothered in rich, creamy Velveeta deliciousness. Even though Velveeta is classified as a pasteurized, processed cheese-food-product, and not really cheese at all, there's still something comforting about all that starchy, velvety heaven that warms the heart and strengthens the soul.

"So, you guys have done a lot of theatre. I've been thinking about the arts a lot lately," Ron says. He pushes back from the table.

"A lot of local and college theatre," Mike says. He stands and starts gathering plates. "And we both studied professionally."

"It would be so cool to see your guys's talent put to use for the Kingdom," Ron says.

"Pastor Jim has a real heart to see the arts used to bring in the lost," Luanne says. She mops up Libby's gooey face and hands with an old wet washcloth. The wee girl has a way of slathering every nook and cranny with whatever she's eating. I make a mental note for my baby preparedness list: *Lots of washcloths.*

"Have I told you about Toymaker's Dream?" Ron asks. "Oh my gosh, I haven't!" Ron's face lights up like the sunrise. "Oh my gosh!" he says again. "We have got to show you Toymaker!"

The way Ron gushes when he's excited makes me laugh. He's kind of a walking incongruity. At first glance he seems the epitome of the cool musician, someone you'd see playing in a dark, smoky jazz club; but the lanky, loose-jointed way he carries himself and his puppy-like enthusiasm reminds me of an awkward teenager.

"TOYMAKER! TOYMAKER!" Libby chants with utter glee, banging on her highchair tray.

"Are we gonna watch Toymaker?" Billy darts back into the dining room, his little cargo shorts still unzipped from his trip to the potty.

"Billy, zipper," Luanne reminds gently. She smiles at him. Billy smiles and rolls his eyes toward the ceiling. He turns around to finish the job.

"Not tonight," Luanne says. "Only forty minutes to bedtime. You guys can go play outside for a bit, then time for bath and jammies."

"Awwwwww!" the two whine in unison.

"No grumbling," Ron says. "Better head out, times'a wastin', and you now have a five-second head start before THE TICKLE MONSTER COMES OUT TO PLAY! Rrrrrrrrraaaaaaawwrrrr!" Ron howls with a goofy growly laugh, chasing the squealing kids out toward the kitchen back door.

"Maybe you guys could plan to come back Friday night and we can watch the video together," Luanne says. She starts wiping the table with the Libby washcloth. It's just kind of smearing the cheesy drops dotting the table. I'm hoping she's just getting the big chunks to start and plans to rinse and repeat.

"I do not know dees Toymaker's Dream you speak of," I say, breaking into a random Russian accent for no reason whatsoever. This happens to me sometimes. Dialect training. Oi.

"Oh my gosh," Ron wheezes, as he returns from his chase. "You guys are going to love Toymaker's Dream. It's a huge deal . . . multi-media . . . theatrical . . . extrava . . . ganza . . ." He stops, puts his hands on his knees, and sucks some air. "They tour all over the world. I'm surprised you haven't heard of them!"

"Cain't say as I have," I say, this time in Texan. Carb high. Must be.

"It's produced by Impact Productions. Out of Tulsa." Ron plops onto the couch. Mike joins him.

"Oh, my gosh," Ron says. "I would love it if we could do something like that here. They're so anointed. Such an awesome way to bring the Gospel message to the lost."

Luanne steps into the kitchen and rinses the rag. "I wonder if you guys could do something like that here. Like a Christian theatre company," she calls over the running water. She comes back for another wipe-down. I take in a deep breath and let it out.

"I hate to say it, but I haven't ever seen any Christian productions that I was very impressed with. Even ministries that have tons of money behind them. A lot of it is so . . . hokey and well, Christian, you know what I mean? I can't see how they can possibly be effective."

Luanne looks at me.

"What I mean to say is, most unbelievers aren't really interested in Christian entertainment. I know I wasn't. Before. They're kinda too savvy for that. Some of the production values are just too . . ."

Ron says, "These guys are different. We have a video of one of their performances—"

"Come Friday," Luanne says. "We'll have a movie and popcorn night. The kids'll be so excited."

I'm a bit nervous about the invitation. I'm not meaning to be condescending or elitist, it's just that people cavorting around on the stage in tunics and fake beards is something that I'm terrified of being associated with. I'm hoping that come Friday, we won't end up in that awkward silence where you're supposed to say, "That was great!" but instead you want to crawl under the sofa cushion.

"Cool!" Mike says.

"Popcorn!" I say.

On Friday, we arrive at six for movie night. The kids, all bathed and snuggled into their faded and pilled footie jammies, greet us with their usual whole-hearted hugs and giggles. The soft plastic bottoms of their p.j. feet make swishy noises as they scramble around the wood floor.

"Yay! Mike and Kathy are here for movie night!" Billie cheers.

"Toymaker! Toymaker! Kitty Cat!" Libby chants.

"Kitty cat?" Mike says.

"Yeah!" Libby squeaks. "I like the kitty cats!"

Oh dear.

"I like the motorcycle cat!" Billy says.

Oh dear, oh dear.

We relax on the couches in front of the TV. Luanne brings in a huge tub of popcorn and the kids scramble over to fill their colorful little plastic bowls. Ron slips the video out of its crumpled cardboard case and says, "You guys ready?" The kids cheer as the VCR slowly sucks the big black cassette tape into its rectangular mouth. Ron plops back down on the well-worn sofa. Billy climbs up and sits with us; Libby curls up between mom and dad.

The music begins. A little wobbly at first as the tape gets settled and going. I take a deep breath and try to keep a positive attitude.

The next hour and a half takes me utterly by surprise. Although the production values of the video itself aren't spectacular, it is plain to see that the live show is something special and impressive indeed—like a cross between *Godspell*, *The Nutcracker*, and a *Kiss* concert.

The story, a thinly veiled allegory of the Gospel, is told through a spectacle of jazz, ballet, acrobatics, mime, and martial arts. God is the "Toymaker" whose creations (toys) live in "Dreamland." The "Dream Hater" (a kind of Satan/Gene Simmons look-alike) schemes to trick the toys into rebelling against the Toymaker. The cunning devil introduces the innocent toys to a gang of very 'cool cats' (the characters were literally cats—like from the Broadway show Cats) led by a big burly motorcycle-riding feline, who shows the toys how to really have fun. The toy's fraternizations and indulgences (or sin) create a barrier that then separates them from their beloved Toymaker. Of course, the Toymaker has a son, the metaphorical Jesus, who is sent to redeem the lost and broken toys by creating a doorway through the barrier with his own body, freeing them from the clutches of the evil Dream Hater.

"Wow. I'm surprised," Mike says as the credits roll.

Luanne puts her finger to her lips. Libby has passed out on her mom's lap. Billy pops up off the couch; bits of popcorn scatter from his lap onto the throw rug like confetti after a wedding. Ron scoops up the snoozing princess and sneaks her into bed. Luanne follows behind, gently steering Billy in the same direction.

Mike and I remain.

I just sit, blinking for a minute, gears grinding.

"That was kind of amazing," I say. *Christians can be full of surprises.*

Ron returns grinning. "Soooo? Huh? Huh? Yeah?"

"Oh—my—gosh," I say.

"I TOLD—" Ron starts to yell and then whispers, laughing, "I told you!"

"I'm mightily impressed, my friend," I say humbly. I'm also quite relieved.

"That was an awesome level of dance talent," Mike says. "And they obviously have a sizeable budget . . ."

"About a quarter-million bucks in their equipment alone," Ron says. "Pretty powerful stuff, huh?"

"Yeah, wow. I had no idea. Now that is a show I could be excited to be a part of," I say. The gales of a brainstorm are beginning to kick up in my noggin.

"The Dream's been performed for more than a million people. Forty states and eight countries." Ron says.

How have I never heard of this?

"Including Moscow and Leningrad. 75,000 Soviet citizens packed something like 18 performances in Russia."

Luanne has rejoined us. She says, "The cast and crew aren't even paid; they raise their own support. Like missionaries. When they're touring, they stay in the homes of the people of whatever church is hosting them in their city."

"The production company also has ongoing supporters who donate to them on a regular basis through their home church in Tulsa. They're touching many lives for Christ. So powerful," Ron says.

"Very professional," I say.

"Hey, sweetie, the kids are ready for prayer time," Luanne says softly to Ron.

He grabs his guitar, "You guys wanna join us?"

We gather in the kid's room. Billy and Libby are already swaddled, still, and drifting off. Ron strums tenderly and prays for the Father's protection over his children. As the two cherubs dream of lambs and lions, my mind wanders to the land of new possibilities.

Suddenly, my hope for a way to utilize my talents and training in theatre is being kindled to a blaze. The whole concept ignites my imagination and fills my heart with such deep longing that I think I might burst. This is exactly the kind of thing I've been yearning to be a part of. But how to take a baby on the road? This was our quandary. I figured I would just have to see what the Lord had up his sleeve. For the time being, I would, once again, tuck yet another little jewel into my heart and wait upon the Lord's timing.

KATHY GETS TONGUED

She lies alone on the bed in the heat of summer. Sweat shimmers on her chest, forming a slim rivulet that trails between her swelling breasts. Her breath comes slowly, rhythmically. She can feel his nearness. She silently waits for him to enter her. She hears him softly whisper.

"Say it. Say the words I want to hear."

Her heart becomes a cudgel against her heaving ribcage. She feels the urge rising up from her loins. The words rising up and filling her completely until she can no longer contain them.

"Ooooh shandala keelia shabalalala . . . crap, no that's not it. Lalalalala cooodialababa—arrrrgh!" Nooo, that just sounds like Pastor Jim's prayer language!

"Ooooria coria shandala coria cooorabaa yabba-dabba-doo . . ." *That's a little better. That sounds pretty good . . .*

Even though I am utterly alone in my bedroom as I experiment with these bizarre sounds, I am mortified with self-consciousness and embarrassment. I push on nonetheless, trusting God that I will find my prayer language.

And find it I would, come hell or high water. Caaaria shodala curia sobria . . . Shooda-botta-honda-but-ai-botta-mitzubishi . . .

LIFE IN THE SECOND CHAPTER OF ACTS

As the baby's due date approached, our concern for how we were going to make ends meet on a single income grew rotund right along with my belly. Soon I would have to stop waitressing; our faith in the Lord's provision was going to be put to the test.

Ron and Luanne and family have come to our little abode for lunch after church. We're sitting under the back carport of our 1950s bungalow, looking out over the sprawling yard full of blooming purple iris, creamy gardenias, and huge old avocado and walnut trees. It's a lovely early summer afternoon. The camellias are in full bloom around the walls of our little rented cottage; Mike has trimmed the wide bushes up high so they look more like camellia trees dressed in fine crimson ruffles. It gives the place a manicured look. I like the way it makes me feel—a little taste of the swankier neighborhoods around the corner. Neat. Tidy. Like some things in life can be controlled. I'm not sure how this hobbit-sized house ended up alone on such a huge lot. I feel rich when I look at the kidney shaped lawn. We got lucky snagging this place.

One of the mammoth avocado trees grows in a slow arc downward and has kindly, over the last thirty years, lowered one of its burly arms to about a foot above the ground. It looks like a gentleman at the Giant's Ball bowing gracefully to his waltzing partner, saying, "My Lady . . ." Billy and Libby are pretending to be tightrope walkers on the long branch that runs parallel to the earth. They hold their arms out straight to the side tottering and wind milling their way back and forth. A dangerous affair to be sure, given that their *rope* is a mere sixteen inches in diameter.

We've brought out the chairs from the old chrome and yellow Formica kitchen dining set. It came with the place and adds a vintage flair—along with the wallpaper of hand-drawn herbs labeled with their Latin names; Petroselinum crispum, Salvia, Rosmarinus officinalis, Thymus vulgaris.

It's hard for me to get comfortable when I have to sit up straight. I caress the tight sphere that has replaced my lap.

"Do you think you'll give your notice at work soon?" Luanne asks.

"Last night I knocked the salt and pepper shakers off one of my tables with my belly," I say.

Everyone laughs. Billy and Libby have started a game of hide-and-seek.

"I don't know. Mike is pulling as many hours as he can get at the country club right now. I'll probably wait until like maybe two weeks before our due date," I say.

The subject of finances makes me feel anxious. I'm trying hard to keep it light, but the truth is, I just don't know what the heck we're going to do once the baby comes. Even with both of us working we're living pretty much to the penny every month as it is. I hold this bit back out of embarrassment but somehow hope it comes out anyway. Mike always says that when something is bothering me, I pretty much wear my heart on my face.

Luanne says, "Ron and I've been talking about your situation. With the baby coming soon and all, and since you won't be able to work, we were thinking, well, that things might get a little tight for you guys."

Ron finishes Luanne's intro, "Our single will be moving out next month, and we'll have two bedrooms free upstairs. We need to rent them out and were wondering if you'd be interested in moving in up there."

(A *single* is a term used at our church for someone who is not married. It's used, interestingly, almost like a title or a station designation. Or a condition.)

They go on to propose an affordable amount that will cover rent and utilities and suggest that we could take our meals together as well, sharing food costs. It would be true community living.

"You'd be all settled in just in time for the baby," Luanne says.

I'm very attracted to the idea of having a built-in support system for this new form of existence called motherhood.

"That's an interesting proposition," Mike says. He holds his chin and with his index finger strokes the little divot above his upper lip. He looks up at the trellised carport ceiling. He's quiet.

"Sounds like it could be from the Lord," I say.

In all honesty, I've already been thinking about it. Luanne told me a few weeks ago that their single was moving out and that their upstairs bedrooms were going to be open and I had been germinating a silly idea . . .

"We'll talk and pray about it," Mike says.

We lay in bed later that night, further considering the notion of starting to build our little family while sharing someone else's home. I lay propped up on every spare pillow we own. I look at my ripe tummy melon as it pulls my oversized t-shirt nighty tight around my middle. It looks like I've shoplifted a basketball.

"I dunno, Kath. I kinda like our privacy," Mike says.

"Yeah, I know. Me too. Might be a little tight with all of us and a new baby."

"No more screaming during sex," he says.

He rubs my belly like I'm a Buddha. Clockwise, because it's good for digestion. My belly button pokes up through the thin pink jersey. So weird.

"Welcome to parenthood, anyway," I say.

"What, no more sex?" he says, aghast.

"Well, yes sex; but quiet sex," I say.

"Good luck with that," he teases, grabbing the supremely loaded tickle spot just above my right knee.

"Aaaaaaaa! Stop!" I scream.

"See?" he says.

"That was hardly sex," I say, crossing my legs, "you're gonna make me pee."

"I guess I would miss this little place," he says. He rolls onto his back, propping his head with his hands.

"Yeah, I really like our sweet little Gramma house too," I say.

Mike sits up. "Me too, but I don't know how long we'll be able to afford this place once you quit the Croc."

"Yes, eating could also become an issue." I sit up too, Indian style, now holding my big ball in my lap like a large fortune-telling monkey; I just need a satin turban. "Ya know, I wonder . . ." I say.

"Uh-oh," Mike says.

"Well, who knows what the Lord's got in mind for us. If we end up on the road with some kind of touring theatre company or even in Africa building homes . . ."

Mike rolls his eyes, "I thought we retired that," he says.

I think about the letter to Millard Fuller still quietly tucked in the desk drawer.

"Did we? Well, we don't know what He's gonna call us to do; this might be good practice for living in community. Like training for living on the road with a production company, or—"

"Whoa, Nelly," Mike says, like he's slowing a horse. "Maybe we should just get through having a baby first. I gotta focus on one thing at a time here. Like how are we gonna pay the bills."

"I know. Just thinking . . ."

"That's dangerous," he says.

"Okay. So just from a practical standpoint—we'll have the whole upstairs to ourselves, and our own bathroom; and we cut our living expenses in half. That makes all the sense in the world," I reason. "Plus, we get to live in community," I add.

"Well, community aside, it seems like it could be a good situation for us," Mike says. "Financially."

The proposition seemed to answer several concerns, as well as one great big longing that I (alone, I'd wager) was carrying—the desire for community. I was now nursing an intriguing idea. True Believers living together, loving one another, and giving up their lives for the brotherhood of the Saints. It had such a Biblical ring to it. Well, this would certainly put that to the test.

And so after another few days of praying (I would have also fasted, but I had never fasted before, and besides, I was eating for two) it was decided. We packed up our meager household and moved in with our friends Ron and Luanne.

❦

We grew close with Ron and Luanne during the time we spent sharing a household with them. When I think back about it now, it seems like we lived with them for a lifetime, although it was only a year. Because we experienced one of our most life-changing events so intimately with them (the birth of our firstborn), and because we chose to basically live as if we were one big family, our lives during that time became deeply woven together. We shared most of our meals, chores, grocery shopping, all of the holidays, and plenty of colds and flus.

Luanne and I quickly fell into a comfortable rhythm of switching off cooking meals and cleaning up the kitchen. She ran her household in a scheduled and efficient way, and I learned some valuable homemaking skills from her. I remember my first introduction to such organized living.

"Once a month, I sit down and plan the meals for the whole month. Ron gives me a monthly cash allowance for groceries, so planning out the meals helps me stretch my budget. See? Here's the menu."

Hanging on the fridge under a little dough-art Lion Laying With Lamb magnet is the current month's calendar, each day's dinner menu all neatly laid out square by square. Monday: Mac-n-cheese Supreme with green salad. Tuesday: Chef Salad, French bread. Wednesday: Spaghetti with Meatballs, green salad, garlic bread . . . We will apparently be eating very well. And regularly.

"Billy, the timer went off fifteen minutes ago, it's time for your phonics lesson," Luanne calls to Billy, who is busy in his room erecting a massive Lego space station.

Libby is sitting at the little table in the back kitchen nook where Luanne has set up a classroomy-looking homeschool area. She seems happy in her miniature chair—the old metal and blond wood kind, like in kindergarten—assembling a wooden puzzle—the old chunky kind with only seven or eight pieces.

"Mom! I'm almost done with the landing bay," Billy calls. His voice ratchets up a half step, "Can I have ten more minutes?"

Homeschool starts promptly at nine a.m. Luanne is super meticulous about setting the small, round, eggshell-hued kitchen timer for ten minutes before a scheduled activity—like homeschool or chores—to help the kids wrap up their playtime and transition into the next required task.

"Billy, you need to obey Mommy right away," Luanne says.

"Mom!" Billy says.

"Bil-ly." She draws the syllables of his name out and down just a little, which makes it sound more like: "You're disappointing me."

"Just ten more minutes, please!" he calls. I begin to feel nervous.

"Billy, please come here, and please bring the rod with you."

Uh-oh.

After a few moments, Billy emerges from the hallway, shoulders slumped, head down, wooden spoon in hand.

"Billy, what do we do when the timer goes off?" she asks.

"We clean up our toys and come in for school," he says.

"Should Mommy have to call you to come in?"

"No."

"Did you come in when I called you or did you argue with Mommy?"

"Argued."

"Mommy shouldn't have to keep asking you to obey, Billy, so now I'm going to have to give the rod," she says. She closes her eyes and takes a breath; there is a subtle drop in her shoulders.

Billy hands the spoon to her, "Yes, Mommy," he replies. His voice trembles. He sniffs and glances at me briefly, a dart of the eyes.

Luanne leads Billy back into the bedroom; I just stand in the middle of the kitchen feeling awkward and a little like I'm the one about to be swatted.

I have a clear view across the hallway; a tiny lamp on the dresser casts the otherwise kid-friendly room in close shadows. From outside, the bright morning sunlight frames the opaque pull-shade that remains drawn as an early intervention to the scorching summer rays that will hit that side of the house around two o'clock.

I can hear Luanne speaking softly to her son. I can hear his quiet murmurs in response. I move a little closer to the hallway and make it my life's purpose to analyze the bulletin board that hangs on the kitchen wall just next to the hall door. Homeschool calendar, chore chart with multicolored foil stars, Bible verse chart with little cross stickers, an adorable crayon drawing of Jesus sitting with little children gathered around his feet—signed by Billy—another crayon drawing that resembles a pile of green and yellow pick-up-sticks—signed by "Liddy." Die-cut alphabet letters in all the primary colors create a scholastic border across the top of the wide corkboard.

Some odd, if not morbid, curiosity keeps me here to observe Luanne's parenting techniques—the secret ritual that produces such sweet and amazingly well-behaved children.

"Billy, it's so important for you to have a heart of humility and obedience toward Mommy and Daddy," she says softly. "What does the Bible tell us about obeying your parents?"

"Children, obey your parents in the Lord, so that you will have a long life and things will go well with you."

Wow. This kid knows his Bible.

"Did you obey Mommy when the timer went off?"

"No."

"No. I had to call you several times. What does the Bible say about disciplining our children?"

Wow. I wonder if he can get this one too.

"Foolishness is bound in the heart of a child; but the rod of correction shall drive it far from him."

Amazing.

She starts to help him pull down his little elastic-at-the-back-of-the-waistband jeans. I'm compelled to turn away, give him privacy.

"Turn around please," she instructs him, her voice soft and calm.

I want to leave the house. Go upstairs. Or outside. But I stay to bear witness to this strange new ritual. I rub my basketball tummy and look out the window over the sink. The dish drainer is piled high with freshly washed breakfast dishes. My mind is reeling.

WHACK! Comes the sharp slap of the wooden spoon against soft bottom flesh—it makes me jump—then a loud cry, followed by weeping from a small boyish voice. I look over at Libby. She continues with her puzzle, unconcerned. I rub my belly.

WHACK again. And then two more, each punctuated by Billy's cries.

"Shhhhhh," Luanne sooths. Billy's yowling is quickly assuaged. Apparently it's over. My heart is beating fast.

"Let's pray," Luanne says softly. Billy sniffles and coughs. "Jesus . . ." She pauses.

"Jesus," Billy echoes, coughs again.

"Please forgive me for disobeying Mommy."

"Please forgive me for disobeying Mommy," he repeats, a small shudder in his voice.

"And?" Luanne prompts softly.

"And please help me to obey right away with a good attitude, so things will go well with me," he says on his own.

"What do you need to tell Mommy?" she asks.

"I'm sorry for disobeying you," he says.

"And . . ." she says.

"And thank you for disciplining me so I can learn how to obey God too," he says.

Then it's quiet. I hazard a glance. Billy is wrapped in a gentle hug followed by a kiss on his forehead. As she releases him and he turns to leave, I quickly make myself busy studying the menu on the fridge.

Billy sniffles as he quietly walks past and into the homeschool area without looking at me. He retrieves his little blue phonics book from the plaid contact paper-covered work bin on the shelf (Libby's is papered with bright daisies and tiny green hearts). He pulls out his little chair, sits, and opens his book.

"Wanna build a fort in our room?" Libby asks.

"Sure. After homeschool," Billy says. He sniffs.

"Okay!" Libby cheers.

Order is restored and all is well.

This extreme close-up of the inner workings of my new universe brought a fresh feeling of free-falling. The way Luanne administered Billy's discipline was systematic, so quiet and calm, so orderly and constrained. It felt right and wrong at the same time. Or did just the witnessing of it feel wrong? What did I know? The whole parenting piece was uncharted territory for me. I had so little exposure. Yes, I had witnessed various techniques, but only in a sort of once-removed kind of way—I had only ever been the auntie. None of my friends even had kids yet.

So far, Mike and I had not explored the notion of what disciplining our children might look like. We knew that it was our job to nurture, protect, and provide for them, but as far as how we were supposed to manage behavior once they were past the laying in our lap making goo-goo eyes at us stage, we were kinda clueless.

This day brought my new path into sharp relief. I knew that committing to our new church family carried a certain expectation of complicity in the accompanying ideologies around family life. Was I ready to dive in? Soon, this corpulent little ball of personality was going to come rolling into the world and require our wisdom, and guidance, and . . . discipline. Would we be up to the task?

✂

Ron and Luanne were the exact same people in their private lives that they projected to the world publicly. We saw each other at our best and at our worst, but I must say that I can't recall a single argument between the two of them, and they rarely raised their voices at their children (apparently the rod was sufficient for inspiring obedience). For the most part, we got along well. We had many pleasant times together, around the dinner table, watching movies, playing with the kids (Mike was always amazing with kids), joking, laughing, and playing music together. All in all it was everything one might hope for in a communal experience . . . for those who hope for that kind of thing.

"Pass the mashed potatoes please," Mike says. The happy ambient dinner music of tinkling flatware on plates and random conversation is sweet in the air.

"So, I've got a new song for the worship team this week," Ron says. His partially masticated meatloaf reveals itself as he chews, and smacks, and speaks. He passes the taters. "I'll play it for you after supper. It rocks. It's like an older Keith Green tune, but I've put a new spin on it."

"Love to hear it," Mike says.

"Can I be excused?" Billy says.

"Clear your plate, please," Luanne says.

"Yes, mom." He slides down out of his little blue Naugahyde booster seat.

"Me too!" Libby calls from her potato-painted highchair.

"Down you go!" Ron grunts as he liberates Libby from her holding device.

The group moves into amiable action as everyone clears the table, and the two men move to the living room to pull out the git-fiddles. I love seeing Mike flourishing in his music. He's writing more and more, and I bet it won't be long before he'll take his rightful place on the stage.

The kids scamper out the back door for the final half-hour of playtime before their baths.

It's a rather warm and balmy late-June evening, and I'm feeling happily satiated after a lovely shared meal. I find relief from the sticky heat in my typical comfy summer duds. My bulbous tummy tests the limits of my stretch-shorts, dwarfing my pint-sized ladies who are free in the breeziness of my baby-doll tank top. The atmosphere of love and community is waxing pleasant when Luanne sidles up to me as I churn up the warm soapy dishwater I've prepared for my turn on wash duty.

"So, I just wanted to encourage you, Kathy; I know you wouldn't want to cause any of your brothers to stumble," she whispers. Her voice is full of tender concern; she gently strokes my back as we face the steamy sink.

What? My heartbeat quickens, but I'm not sure why.

"I thought I should mention to you that maybe you might want to think about wearing a bra. I can see your nipples, and like I said, I know you would probably want to be modest in considering your brothers in the Lord." She keeps her voice low, seasoned with tender but firm resolve.

I have no response to this. I feel my face flush and my heart constrict, as I glance down and for the first time ever become aware that my nipples (perky as they are) do present themselves somewhat proudly to the world.

I mean, I guess I've always been vaguely aware that yes, indeed, I do have nipples, and yes, they do sometimes poke out from the fabric of my shirts, but the girls are so petite; it never occurred to me that they were imposing on anyone. I now suddenly feel what I imagine is a little kinship with Eve after that cursed apple had opened her eyes and she noticed her nakedness for the first time.

"Yeah, okay," I say slowly. I feel suddenly detached from my body. I sort of float up the stairs in stunned slow motion to go strap the twins into submission as images of all of my braless wardrobe choices worn in front of pastors and other church family members dance before my eyes. How many other people have noticed my nipples? How many others have now categorized me as immature and lacking in discernment? Hot shame bursts inside my chest, creeps up my neck to my cheeks and squeezes tears out of my eyes.

I had always felt comfortable and unselfconscious in my braless bliss. It never occurred to me that it might be a stumbling block for my male breth-ren. Besides, it wasn't like I needed the structural support of a brazier (this was way before bras that came with boobs already in them), so what was the point? It was like a dagger to my heart. My integrity was in question and my freedom diminished. Was this the way of the Lord? Must be.

Later that night Mike and I sit upstairs in bed, shoulder to shoulder reading our Bibles. I close mine. The sting of my earlier conversation with Luanne is still buzzing around in my chest; I've read the same verse a half-dozen times and I still can't remember what I just read.

"Do you think I'm a person of integrity?" I ask.

"You're the most honest person I know. To a fault sometimes," Mike says. "Why?"

"I mean, do you think I dress provocatively?"

"Yes. You wear the sexiest maternity clothes I've ever seen," he says.

"Stop. Luanne said that I was being a stumbling block to my brothers because I don't wear a bra and my nipples show." The tears start again.

"Luanne is just uptight. God gave girls nipples—which I'm kinda thank-ful for; He just happened to give you exceptional ones. But, I kinda think He's got more important things on his mind than whether or not you wear a bra. I wouldn't worry about it."

"So you think I should wear a bra then?"

"You care way too much about what people think of you, Kath. You should do whatever makes you happy," he says.

I roll onto my side and hug the fatter of my two pillows. The last of the lights illuminating the windows of the big, white house is extinguished. Mike spoons around me in the dark, kisses my neck.

All is quiet.

"Night, Dad," comes the young boy's voice from somewhere inside the snugly tucked-in abode.

"Night, Billy," answers the comforting voice of the dad.

"Night, Libby," warbles the loving mamma.

"Night, Mamma," comes the little squeak.

"Night, sweet wife," my handsome prince whispers into my ear as he caresses my rotund belly and fondles my tender breasts, "I love you so."

I DON'T KNOW NUTHIN' 'BOUT BIRTHIN' NO BABIES!

For you created my inmost being; you knit me together in my mother's womb. I praise you because I am fearfully and wonderfully made . . .
-Psalm 139:13-14

The kitchen window is a black square in lemon pudding. Five old jelly jars holding plant cuttings stand in a line on the sill, white and cloudy, layered in calcified water rings, roots spiraling in mossy green liquid, ready for soil three months ago. A spoon rest in the shape of a child's hand offers a fistful of treasure: a small bolt, a cat's eye marble, a penny, a washer, a safety pin.

"Oh, Heavenly Father, thank you so much for your faithfulness," Luanne prays softly over my big, round belly. "Thank you that your hand has always been upon Kathy and is even now upon her as we prepare for the arrival of her little one."

It's two-thirty a.m., and we've all been asleep long enough that a little gargle with Listerine would have been in order. But, my water has broken, my contractions are two minutes apart, and I love Luanne anyway for her prayers of comfort and protection.

"Thank you for this new life, for a speedy and safe delivery, and for your peace that passes understanding that is now residing in Mike and Kathy's hearts." She gives me a hug and smiles her huge smile at me.

Mike hustles down the stairs in rapid-fire steps and bursts into the kitchen where Luanne and I are praying. He looks like he's off on holiday.

"Okay, I've got your bag and your purse. Anything else?"

His slightly skewed mullet is pressed to one side like a Gumby-doo. He wears the somewhat apprehensive, but mostly silly grin of an adolescent on his first date. Luckily, he has managed to change out of his jammie bottoms and into his pink and silver snakeskin-print sweats—I'm not convinced it's an improvement, but it's the 80s and pink is in. I'm pretty sure he's as excited at the prospect of driving as fast as he wants without fear of a ticket ("She's in officer, labor!"), as he is about our new baby coming to town for real.

"Do you have the Phil Keaggy tapes?" I ask, breathing into the next contraction. Music is a must in the labor room and *Wind and the Wheat* is an all time favorite album.

Luanne makes gentle circles on my back with the palm of her hand. "Our room will be all ready for you when you come home," she says. "Ron and I are gonna camp out in the kid's room for a few days so you don't have to climb the stairs."

How incredibly sweet and generous our friends are. I feel comforted by the fact that we will be going through the process with the support and encouragement of wise and loving people who genuinely care about us.

"Yep, Phil Keaggy—check! Okay, let's do this!" My gallant hubby bundles me into the car and we make our way down the darkened highway to the little Catholic hospital in the foothills.

"How ya doin', my sweet wife and mother of my adorable child?" Mike asks without looking over at me.

Eyes on the road . . . good man. Especially since he is doing eighty.

"I'm fine," I answer. But all time is slowing around me; the dark highway seems to stretch out longer as I watch it through the windshield. "How do you know he/she will be adorable?" I ask.

"Because *we* made her/him," he declares. Big smile.

Breeeeathe iiiiinnnn . . . and ouuuuut . . .

"How ya doin?" he asks again.

I continue to breathe. Even in the face of this utterly foreign happening (you know the one where you push something roughly four times the size of your vagina through it), I feel strangely calm.

"Good. Fine. A little nervous."

"Well, remember what your mom said: 'Just like poopin,'" he says.

My mother always spoke of my birth as being one of the most wonderful experiences of her life. Not just that she got wonderful me out of it, but the actual birthing experience itself. She said that it wasn't painful to her, but rather, it was strenuous, exhilarating, and totally satisfying; "Like a nice big BM."

Even though this is something completely new and unlike anything I have ever done—unless perhaps it is, as mom claimed, just like a nice big BM—we're prepared; we've taken our birthing class and have had all of our questions answered. My mom's stories of her absolute peace and joy in my accouchement, along with my newfound faith in the goodness of God, brings a great sense of confidence that my first delivery will be no less marvelous.

The love of my life was by my side through the whole six-hour process, praying with me, soothing me, feeding me little smooth, round ice chips as I labored. He faithfully coached me through all of my breathing exercises and didn't hold against me the fact that I tried to bite off his finger during the *Blow out the Candle* technique we employed to get me through transition. I will forever remember the amazing melodious echoes of Phil Keaggy's *March of the Clouds* and *Wind and the Wheat*—two of the most sublime pieces of music to ever grace the universe—softly bringing me peace and comfort, while serenading and coaxing our little girl out of her watery haven and into the light of a new day.

♋

I would like to say that an angel from On High descended and announced that our daughter shall be a girl and she shall be called Emily Katherine, but that just ain't how it happened. She was thus named because, well, because that's the name she picked, by golly. And she picked it years before we got pregnant or even met God for that matter.

"Mr. Toad's Wild Ride, Dumbo, or Teacups first? What is your pleasure, my Lady?" My handsome prince held out his hand.

"The Teacups make me barf," I answered.

"Mr. Toad it is," he said, kissing my hand and leading me through Fantasyland.

Soon we stood, tangled up in each other's arms, awaiting our wild ride. I followed Mike's rapt gaze to the young lady in front of us.

"Should I be jealous?" I asked.

"You know you're the only one for me."

"I know that someday, some little girl will steal your heart," I said.

"Yes, but she will steal yours too," he said. Kiss.

Just ahead of us in line, a little princess slept sweetly in her daddy's arms; chin resting on his shoulder, bouncy curls unfurling in the hot Disney sun. She was crowned with her official Minnie Mouse ears upon which her name was whimsically scrolled: *Emily.*

"Emily," Mike whispered.

"Will she be called Emily?" I asked.

"What do you think?" Mike asked back.

"So let it be written," I decreed.

"So let it be done," Mike seconded.

And so it was.

We came to find out later, when we were getting ready for the real deal, that the name Emily translates from its various derivations as *industrious, diligent one* or sometimes *rival,* and that the personality profile of this name kinda goes like this:

"People with this name tend to initiate events, to be leaders rather than followers, with powerful personalities. They tend to be focused on specific goals, experience a wealth of creative new ideas, and have the ability to implement these ideas with efficiency and determination. They tend to be courageous and sometimes aggressive. As unique, creative individuals, they tend to resent authority, and are sometimes stubborn, proud, and impatient."

Our first clue as to the aptness of her naming came to us before we even left the hospital; you could hear her caterwauling above all the other newborns in the nursery. Yep, our little lastochka came out singing like a diva—of course, Mike being the papa and all—and she never stopped. A force of nature that one turned out to be.

❦

It was surreal to now have a real live human being there, outside my body, utterly dependent on us for everything. When she was inside, no sweat, just eat right and put down the crack pipe. But this, this was no gerbil, no goldfish that you could feed every few days and change their bowl of water once a week. This was going to be pretty much 24/7 for a long time (at least a week, right?) and then pretty darn regular for the next eighteen years.

The bizarre and cool part of it was, with the gestation and birthing process, so too was born this incredible love that was so deep, so intense, so captivating that we would have given up our lives to protect and nurture it. Where did this come from? I didn't feel anything remotely the same for any other little babies I had held in my arms.

When I was a teenager, you couldn't pay me enough to babysit. I didn't hate kids, but the idea of spending multiple hours with them made me squirm. I wondered how in the heck young moms could stand just hanging out with a baby day in and day out; how they didn't go mad from the boredom. I still sometimes wonder that I ever tuned into my reproductive instincts at all.

But this, this was so different than I anticipated. I found myself surprised by how long I could just sit and look at my baby.

Her wee noggin fully wigged in thick, shiny brown curls; her elfin mouth, like a little archer's bow, pink and juicy; her teensy round nose, like a smooth button mushroom. Her long, slender fingers especially fascinate me: perfectly formed grown-up fingers but they can only just wrap around the whole of my thumb. Her nails are round-cornered squares, like ten of the smallest Chiclets on earth.

I sit on the old scratchy sofa, her little body nestled just right into the meeting of my two thighs. This is perfect for baby gazing. I run my fingers over the soft rolls and creases of her chubby arms and legs, her little tummy; watch her delicate ribs expand and drop as she breathes and sleeps. Something is compelling me to memorize every bit. Now that I can see and touch and smell the promise that has been rolling around in my belly for so many months, I just want to lap it up and take it back in again. Luanne told me that these days would be short, that Em would grow quickly, and it wouldn't be long before all of these miraculous details were just memories. Until now, these words didn't have a lot of meaning for me. Sitting here, looking at her, I understand, and I want to hang on to the details.

I didn't account for the way motherhood would make me feel. This feeling was immense and full. It was like the kind of ache you get in your whole body when you miss someone you have lost. When I lost my mom a few years ago, the emptiness that was there after she left made my awareness of my love for her bigger. It squeezed on my insides and made me feel gravity more intensely, running down my limbs, down into the ground. Looking back, I remember this newly birthed love for my daughter felt kind of like that, only in reverse. It was sweet. And expanding. And warm. A low humming that ran upward, permeating every layer of muscle, connective tissue, and skin.

My new church family often spoke of the love of God and the Father's heart for his children. Was this what those things were like? Was this how much I was loved by God? It was in a few of these quiet moments, watching my slumbering child, when I felt God was showing me something of Himself. If I could still my thoughts enough—like the stillness in my slumbering daughter's face, her utter trust—I sometimes touched the heart of my faith. If I could be still enough.

As for boredom . . . ha! Between nursing and burping and urping, and wiping and diaping and de-rashing, and bathing and soothing and more pooping and wiping, and more nursing and napping (she and me), there was little room for boredom.

"This is your new life," Luanne told me. "It's designed to teach you about God's constant love, patience, and nurturing affection."

This made sense to me. I knew that with His grace I could do this; I could be a good mom.

Right up until the colic hit. Um, this was new. This was not so fun.

At about three weeks old, the Divine Miss Em developed an extreme case of colic that subsequently lasted for the next three hundred years (okay, three months).

3 p.m. nursing. Baby is happy. Mommy is happy.

Twenty minutes later. Baby starts to fuss. Mommy gears up for five hours in purgatory.

"How long?" Mike asks as he walks in the door from a long hard day of sales calls. He has to raise his voice to be heard over the ruckus.

"Two hours," I respond.

"Nice hairdo," Mike says. He sweeps the screaming cherub from my arms, the faint aroma of aged cheese following in her wake.

"You're lucky I have any left," I shoot back.

"Did you burp her?"

I roll my eyes.

"Bicycle?"

"Tried that."

"How about the taco fold?"

"One Lilliputian toot." We high five.

"I love you," he says, doing the tummy-knee bounce. He's a ninja at that one.

"Only three hours to go 'til her battery should wear out," I breathe and flop back on the sofa.

"Praise the Lord and pass the ear plugs!" he grins.

As long as I've known him I've marveled at how absolutely at ease Mike is around children. He's like the Pied Piper, they flock to him and dance to his tunes. He can jack them up and then just as easily calm them into unconsciousness. Maybe this comes from growing up with four siblings and then practicing on a gaggle of nieces and nephews. Maybe he was just born with an awesome daddy gene. All I know: This guy's good; glad he's mine.

After dinner (Mike and I take turns eating, otherwise one or the other of us would eventually starve) the wee banshee is momentarily quelled while nursing. She sobs and snorts and takes shuddering breaths as we prepare to switch boobs. I sit her up and apply gentle but firm back-pats, attempting to coax a teensy belch.

Emily: "Ruuuuuuup!"

Mike and Kathy (and Luanne and Ron and Libby and Billy): "YAAAAAY EM! YIPEE! WOO HOO!

Emily: "WAAAAAAAAAAAAAAAAA!"

Mike announces, "Time to employ operation Princess Pillow." The secret weapon.

He places the howling nipper upon her satiny body pillow and . . .

"Three, two, one, blast-off!" he yells. Like Aladdin on his carpet, Em soars through the air, from the living room to the dining room, through the kitchen and back to the living room. Up the stairs and down again, through the dining room and back to the couch. Baby is laughing. Baby is happy. Mike makes a safe and expert landing onto my waiting lap.

A message from the dashing captain, "Ladies and gentlemen, we would like to thank you for choosing to fly Princess Air with us today. We trust you've had an enjoyable flight. Please visit again soon."

"Oh, have no fear. She will fly again. Very soon," I say.

A five-minute respite and then: baby snuffles and sputters and revs her engines for the instant replay. Again and again for the next two hours.

Finally, just shy of mommy throwing her precious bundle out the window, the petite princess magically and mercifully falls asleep.

Daddy lays the snoozing baby gently in her crib. "We made it," he whispers, ever so softly. Then prays, "Father, thank you for this sweet girl. We love her so much."

He hovers his hand over her back—not willing to risk a touch that might reawaken the little thing. "Please, Lord, have mercy on our sweet girl—"

"And on us," I add.

"Have mercy and heal this colic, Lord. We ask in Jesus' name."

And we both say, "Amen."

We watch as she sleeps so peacefully.

"Sweet angel," I whisper.

"We're gonna make it through this." Mike smiles and kisses me on the forehead.

"Okay, we can keep her," I whisper.

Finally, our cries for mercy (mercy on our sweet baby for her pain and on we, the collateral, for ours) must have been heard. God took pity on us all, and come day ninety-one of this nerve-wracking trimester, as quickly as it came, Miss Em's colic abruptly stopped. And we all breathed a great sigh of relief, and a very grateful hallelujah.

Later, I would tell people that this trying time turned out to be a blessing in disguise.

And we know that in all things God works for the good of those who love him, who have been called according to his purpose. ~Romans 8:28

I would say they were Em's early days of training, a vocal boot camp, as it where. For only God could have known that these seemingly endless daily doses of ear-splitting wailing would build a set of pipes in her that would result in a singing voice so splendiferous, so wondrously capable of producing sublimely pristine sounds, notes so rapturous and pure as to bring tears to the eyes and cause one to catch and hold one's breath for the sheer beauty. And I'm not being biased. I'm not. Nor am I exaggerating. A truly divine gift.

A LITTLE ON CHURCH FAMILY STRUCTURE

ALCF as a whole was a fairly eclectic mix of people and cultures, but throughout the Disciples of Destiny church movement there was a clear template for what the godly Christian family looked like. The folks in positions of leadership (from those at the helm of DOD, down to those on church staff, and those appointed as Elders) modeled this with great aplomb. For the hopelessly left-brain-dominant types like myself it was convenient and comforting that you could fit the archetype into a nice, neat bullet list:

- husband is the head
- wife is the helpmate
- minimum of three children, but the more the merrier
- husband is the sole bread-winner
- wife is the homemaker
- children are taught to be obedient
- children are homeschooled or at least Christian schooled

Simple to understand as far as structure goes. In terms of how this organism operates, the following scriptures are a good summation:

Wives submit to your husbands as to the Lord. For the husband is the head of the wife as Christ is the head of the church . . . Now as the church submits to Christ, so also wives should submit to their husbands in everything. . . . Husbands, love your wives, just as Christ loved the church . . . each one of you also must love his wife as he loves himself, and the wife must respect her husband. Children, obey your parents in the Lord, for this is right . . . that it may go well with you and that you may enjoy long life on the earth. -Ephesians 5:22ff

Now I have to admit, I was down with the *husbands love your wives* thing and the *children obey your parents* thing. I could even do the *wives respect your husband* thing, but the other thing, well, Annie Oakley sang about it courtesy of Rogers & Hammerstein:

"I agree to love and honor, love and honor yes, but not obey!"

I couldn't see at the time that trying to reconcile some of the church's ideologies (especially related to the roles of women) would set me on a collision course for the Cliffs of Insanity (as you will see). The Lexicon could be subtle and confusing and the language used to teach these doctrines was pretty and intermingled with great nuggets of wisdom. The people were nice and seemed to know so much about the Bible. It was all very compelling and I was drawn like a moth to a flame. Despite the fact that my wings were starting to singe and bound to eventually catch fire, the cognitive dissonance by which I found myself living my life was simply interpreted by my conscious mind as the Mysterious Ways of God. To appease my intellect, I filed those harder to swallow pieces safely away in the Chat With Jesus Upon Kingdom Come file, and did my best to conform and transform into a woman of God.

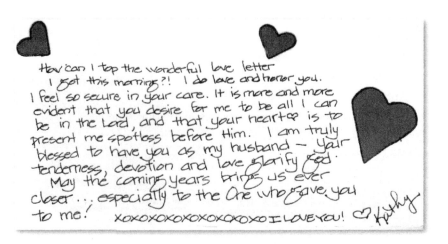

❧

Behold, children are a heritage from the Lord, the fruit of the womb a reward. Like arrows in the hand of a warrior are the children of one's youth. Blessed is the man who fills his quiver with them! He shall not be put to shame when he speaks with his enemies in the gate.

~ Psalm 127:3-5

Funny, how God took us from the Church of the Over the Hill Gang, to the Church of the Open Womb. We did ask for it, in a manner of speaking, but honestly, I exaggerate not when I say that a gaggle was standard for the mom's of ALCF. To be fair, most of them seemed suited for such sizeable menageries, although some did appear frazzled and exhausted. Of course, not a one ever breathed even a hint of any dreams or ambitions (seriously, for the female type, these were dirty words) outside of motherhood.

"Kathy, how are you doing sweetie?"

One of the pastor's wives stopped by to bring a meal and a little gift for us. She brightens the room as she enters, her noisy covey effusing through the door behind her.

"Look at your sweet Emily!" she coos.

She adeptly scoops my girl out of my arms with expert mommy finesse. "Awwww, I bet you're so happy!" Two elongated dimples form parentheses around her glorious smile.

"I'm tired and grumpy," I say. I look around at her brood jubilantly hugging and giggling with Luanne's two.

"Awwww. Drink it in while you still only have one!" She winks and smiles. She gently bounces Emily, putting her instantly to sleep with her magical powers.

"I can hardly imagine more . . ." I say; a faint flutter of panic tickles my tummy.

Pastor's Wife has a most gracious demeanor; she is soft spoken and emanates a sweetness akin to the melty fig wrapped in the bready goodness of the Newton. She fixes her dark, doe-like eyes on mine, smiles, is quiet for a moment. Then just a hint of shininess glosses them over.

"I understand. I wouldn't trade my precious ones for anything, but there are times . . . " She pauses and swallows.

"Well, we've chosen to let the Lord decide when we get pregnant," she says. Tears are welling now. "I've gotten to almost dread being intimate with my husband for fear of, well . . ." She drops her gaze to her slightly distended abdomen. She has three little muffins already and number four in the oven.

I try to relax my face with empathy so as not to betray my shock. Firstly, this is a woman who seems the incarnation of motherhood. Second, this is a pastor's wife. That she would confess her doubtful feelings this way is a little unnerving. I already know that they made a conscious choice to abstain from using birth control, but that she would share her misgivings with a newbie like me takes me completely by surprise. I find myself suddenly moved with compassion and very much in love with her. For a heartbeat, I imagine a younger, less tired, more carefree version of this lovely lady; one who enjoyed sex, and quite possibly might have deftly performed an occasional little lap dance for hubby during their early pre-parturition romps in the hay.

Then as suddenly as she has expressed her innermost self to me, she vanishes behind her veil of modesty. "But children are a blessing from the Lord; the fruit of the womb a reward. Blessed is the man who fills his quiver with them," she says with a sunny smile. She hands my snoozing cherub back to me and wipes away the moisture from her cheek.

I have no response to this. I feel like I should just erase her admission because she never meant to say it; this information was not really meant for me.

Later, I pondered why she would confess something so personal to me. There are some who would say (likely in a sermon or a motivational speech) that she was merely hooking into my negativity and allowed herself a momentary lapse in her complete trust in the faithfulness of God. I ultimately surmised that my honesty in the moment gave her permission to be honest back; and somehow, by some crazy ephemeral enchantment, God gave me a glimpse of the authentic person inside the persona so I could love her for real.

As much as I would have liked to become this gal's pal, it was never to be. We always maintained a friendly relationship, but it was ever one of teacher and disciple, mentor and mentee, pastor and flock. It was just too impossible for someone in such a prominent position of leadership to be completely open and transparent about her weaknesses and doubts. The leadership, for whatever reason, was expected to be a model of strength, a strong tower, above reproach, and stable in all their ways. What an incredible burden to bear. I would have cracked under the weight of it, which may be why I was spared from ever reaching that summit.

EXTREE EXTREE! GET YOUR GOOD NEWS HERE!

The sharing of the Gospel was one of the most important mandates given to believers. To be faithful in witnessing about the need for salvation, Christ's sacrifice on the cross, and the infilling of the Holy Spirit was un-equivocally stressed as a non-optional act of obedience and proof of love for Jesus. If you were uncomfortable or afraid of doing this, it was shameful. If you didn't do it, it was considered tantamount to forsaking the Lord:

> *If anyone is ashamed of me and my message in these adulterous and sinful days, the Son of Man will be ashamed of that person when he returns in the glory of his Father with the holy angels.* ~Mark 8:38

Whether you were laying out the plan of salvation or telling someone your own personal testimony of how you were saved and how the Lord was changing your life, the goal was to be a constant witness to the world for Christ and his power to save.

In an attempt to be faithful witnesses, many of our kind went to great lengths to find ways of working the Lord into every conversation with anyone we came in contact with. Co-workers, the lady in the grocery checkout line, the dentist, the pizza delivery guy, the Jehovah's Witnesses or Mormon missionaries at the door, the neighbor kid who was over for popsicles: all of these encounters were "divine appointments" in which to share the Good News.

And if someone you spoke with was already a Christian, if they weren't a Radical-Spirit-Filled-Christian, then their salvation was questionable and they were considered to be lukewarm. And God hates the lukewarm Christian.

> *But since you are like lukewarm water, neither hot nor cold, I will spit you out of my mouth!* ~Revelation 3:16

We charismatics counted—even if only subconsciously—our *mainstream* Christian friends and family as marginal Christians which, according to our interpretation of Scripture, was a dangerous thing to be.

If this wasn't out and out preached, it was most certainly implied both from the pulpit and among the flock. If friends and family were not

Christian at all, then it was your absolute duty to witness to them, else their blood be on your head.

Needless to say, this was a lot of pressure. The last thing I wanted to do was deny the Lord by not sharing my faith with people.

This very pressure nearly cost my friendship with my old theatre buddy Marie back before Emily was born. I hadn't premeditated an evangelistic outreach when I made that phone call; I just wanted to thank her for the gift she brought to my baby shower. I was given two showers, one by the church ladies and one by the crew at the restaurant where I worked. Marie also worked at the cafe for a while, so she'd been invited too. We weren't in touch often. She'd been busy working with friends to build a small repertory company in Hollywood; I'd been busy with my new church friends and preparing for motherhood. I missed seeing her. I didn't want us to lose touch, and if the Lord came up, well . . . the thought made me instantly nervous.

"Hey Marie. Just wanted to call and say hi; see how you're doing," I said. I suddenly felt all jittery and started to sweat. *What the heck?*

"Hey, Kathy!"

She's happy to hear from me. My chest loosened, but that could have been because my heart was karate chopping it from the inside like a hyperactive masseuse. Now my hands were tingling, a slight ringing in the ears. *Holy Spirit?* I wondered.

"I wanted to be sure you had our new number," I said. "We moved out of our little place in San Gabriel. We're in Alhambra now."

"Oh, I didn't know you moved. You're due soon aren't you," she said.

"Not soon enough. Two more weeks. It's so hot."

"I bet!" she said.

"I've finally got some boobs to sweat under." I shot a glance toward the kitchen. Luanne was in the kids' room for jammie time. Marie laughed. I missed her laugh. I wasn't sure why, but for some reason, my mind was scrambling, trying to find a way to work God into the conversation. I tried to relax, just focus on keeping it light, keeping it casual, but there was a little push underneath that felt urgent.

"So are you still at the cafe?" she asked.

"I worked my last shift about a week ago. Thanks by the way, for the cute diaper bag. I hope it's a girl," I said. We both laughed.

"Yeah, I wasn't sure I should get pink since you guys don't know the sex—you don't know do you? But I couldn't resist," she said. We laughed again. "I guess you could still use it for a boy," she said.

"We don't know the sex," I said.

"Or a dance bag for you," she added.

"Yeah, don't know if I'll be doin' much dancing anytime soon," I said.

"So, in other news, we've moved in with a family from church."

Marie was quiet.

"It's such a blessing, since I won't be working anymore. God is so good. It's going to be way cheaper, and they're really nice and have two really sweet kids. I'm sure I'll glean a lot about being a mom from Luanne."

Another pause. "You guys are really getting into the church thing," Marie said.

"We like it. They're a pretty cool bunch of people. And they really love God. I'd love to have you come some time."

She remained quiet.

"And we love the worship. The music. It's so different from our old church."

"Yeah, I'm not really into the church thing. I've kinda got my own thing with God," she said, finally.

I took a breath. *Here's the in.*

"I worry about you, Marie. I love you, but the Bible says that Jesus is the only way to God. I don't want you to go to hell. I want you to know God."

No response.

"We're all sinners in need of forgiveness—I include myself in that—but you've got to humble yourself and let Jesus into your heart. Only his blood can cover you, it's only by his blood that we can be in the presence of a Holy God."

"I . . . Kathy, I—"

My mouth just kept going. "I used to think that I knew God. It wasn't 'til I surrendered my whole life to him that I really understood. I'd been living a lie. We've all been blinded by our sin nature." The words felt weird and new in my mouth. There was a slight feeling of disassociation as I let them flow out of me. I wasn't sure I recognized my own voice. At the same time, I felt a kind of headiness, a confidence that emboldened me.

"I have to go Kathy. I can't talk to you right now."

"Wait. Marie. I—I'm sorry. Wait." I was choking on my desperation.

"I just don't know what to say to you. You've changed. You sound like someone else. All this esoteric language—do you even care what I think? What I believe? I can't . . . I've gotta go."

"I, Marie—" She hung up.

Marie and I shared so much history. It was because of Marie that I found out about the Academy and pursued my professional training as an actress. But I found myself weighing her against my new worldview and it worried me. She had a definite date with fame and glory, but according to my new Christian paradigm, she was also utterly lost.

I instantly regretted that conversation; yet, it seemed so inevitable. I cried about it for days. I cried for the condition of her soul, for her blindness, for her rejection of the Gospel. Her rejection of me. But I just didn't know what to do about it. I knew that this was part of the deal—sharing the Gospel with the risk of rejection—so I had no choice but to just let the space between us grow.

◌

I'm seated across from my commercial agent Joan. Heart pounding in chest. Sweat.

The purpose for my visit is three-fold: reconnect with her and with the commercial industry, lay out my new Christian boundaries, share the Gospel if possible.

"So, now that Emily is a little older, I have more time and think I'm ready to start having you send me out, but the thing is, well, I'm a Christian now, and uh, well . . ."

Blank stare.

"Well, I just wanted to be sure that you understand that there are certain things that I just can't go out on . . ."

Slow nod from my agent. Blink, blink.

"Well, and well, there are certain kinds of things I just couldn't do, I mean, I'm not willing to compromise my faith."

"I'm a Christian . . ." Joan draws her words out slowly, like, *soooooo what the hell are you inferring?*

"What kind of things were you thinking I would be sending you out on?" she asks. One of her eyebrows seems higher than the other.

"Well, I don't know, you know, stuff that might compromise my Christianity."
Like, I don't know, ads for Hustler or Budweiser or heroin or something!

I'm sinking fast. I'm a freak.

"Ok. So you want to be sent out for commercials, but you don't want to compromise your religion." Her eyebrow definitely seems even higher now.

"Mmm hmm. Like maybe just family type stuff."

She sighs. "I might be able to find something for your daughter; I get a lot of breakdowns for moms with babies. Maybe we can see how that goes."

"That would be great," I say. I happen to have a couple of photos of Emily and also Mike's headshot with me.

"Oh yes. Very nice. I can probably send you guys out as a family."

I think she sent us out twice after that. Gerber and Pampers or something. We got a call back on one of them, but after that, well, the calls dried up. A fortune in headshots, postage, and dogged persistence to finally get a good commercial agent, and like a handful of crumbs, I tossed it to the wind with one conversation.

I didn't continue to pursue her either; I could feel my grip on my dreams faltering, in the context of the secular industry at any rate. I questioned whether God approved of this passion I was still clinging to. Was this an idol? Perhaps he was closing doors. If so, I was going to have to trust that he had better plans for me.

⁕

It took a few years and several similar attempts at sharing the Gospel with my family (my sister and my dad, both of whom exercised great patience with my zeal) for me to start to see that I needed to take a step back and re-evaluate my tactics. I remember eventually adopting the secret opinion that all new believers should be locked in a closet until they calmed down. For Marie and me though, that revelation may have come a phone call too late. It certainly came too late for my potential career.

But, my heart ached for the world to be converted and for everyone to know and love Jesus. I had a genuine desire for people to not be eternally separated from God and for them to have *the peace that passes understanding*. Funny, this peace was a thing that was supposed to be a huge boon in the life of a believer, but something that I found nearly impossible to enter into.

Even though I felt compelled by the constant barrage of warnings that my loved ones and the world were all going to perish into eternal depression and teeth gnashing, I inwardly loathed having to tell people this. Every time I crossed paths with a stranger, I would feel the pressure start to mount to find a way to bring up Jesus. If it did come up, I would instantly start to sweat, my heart would pound, and I would shake all over. Of course, not wanting to admit that this was extreme anxiety, I attributed it to the power of the Holy Spirit, which only made me feel a stronger compulsion to convince whoever I was talking to (and frankly, myself) of their need for Jesus.

I think this is why I wanted so desperately to deliver God's message through story. That, after all, was how Jesus did it. If I could use my creative gifts in the arts to bring the Gospel, it would perhaps somehow relieve me of some of the guilt over my feelings of absolute dread of having to pitch the Good News one-on-one.

PARENTING 101

Children, obey your parents in the Lord, for this is right. ~Ephesians 6:1

The raising of godly children was serious business at ALCF. It was number two only to world domination on the Stuff to Do Before Jesus Comes Back list put out by leadership. Very practical, in a corporate sense; if the conversion numbers are down, at least you're ensuring church growth from the inside. Takes a bit longer, but hey, whatever works. And besides, what parent doesn't want godly children?

It was easy to be amazed and delighted by the orderly, well-mannered behavior of the Church Elder's progeny. But what about the Terrible Twos? How were we to cope with the dreaded grocery store tantrums, the smashing the other kid over the head with the Tonka truck moments? What if she succeeds in launching herself out of my arms and right on to her brainpan, breaking her fragile little infant neck? What about the nightmarish teenage insurrection years? Huh? HUH?! What about those?

Ah, children—such interesting and complex little beings—no two alike. It's unfortunate and rather unfair that they don't come with an operating manual.

I'm sure that even at this young almost-toddler age The Divine Miss Em was thinking in complete sentences, but she refrained from speaking them, keeping her superpowers hidden so as to not attract the media. And so, like all nine-month old infants, she took to displaying (with vigor, I might add) her disdain for being told *no* by stiffening up and flinging her body backwards like a dolphin doing a backflip. I had seen this plenty in other children but must confess that it was a bit disconcerting to almost drop my kid because she unexpectedly tries to launch herself out of my arms. Wow—a show of will. Whatever shall we do with this?

"Well, it's not too early to nip that willfulness in the bud." Luanne's gentle nudging can always be counted on.

"Spanking? So soon?" I'm nervous; it's all about to begin.

"Well, no, I wouldn't call it spanking. Just a swat on the fatty part of her thigh to let her know that this behavior is not acceptable to you, or to the Lord."

"Oh." Sigh. I think about when I first witnessed Billy getting the rod. My heart breaks.

"We started at nine months with both kids. As long as you approach it with calmness and love. Oh, yeah! I was going to give you Tom Lorrack's book on parenting." She scans the living room bookshelf, thumbing past *My Utmost for His Highest, The Pilgrim's Progress, Mere Christianity, The Cost of Discipleship, Hind's Feet on High Places.*

"The Scriptures are very clear about how we should be raising up our children. Tom lays it all out in such an easy to understand way. I know I've still got a copy here somewhere . . ."

She lands on a diminutive volume, "Ah! Here we go. This'll really help. It's a great little guide for godly discipline techniques." She hands me my new parenting bible.

"All the pastors and elders in the DOD churches follow this model. Our kids are such a strong testimony to the world. It's so important for them to be raised to be humble, teachable, and obedient."

"But, nine months?" I say.

"Hey, instructing our children to obey us right away and without question could save their life. What if Em were running out into the street when a car was coming? Wouldn't you want her to stop immediately if you called for her to stop?" She has a point.

"It's never too early to teach them not to pitch themselves out of your arms," she says with a wink. "Don't worry. You'll get the hang of it. You can thank me when she's a teenager and still a delight to be around!" She smiles broadly.

I smile weakly. "Thanks."

I stand there, holding the definitive manual on child disciplining in one hand and my sweet baby girl in the other. Being the gargantuan force of will that she was upon her arrival on the planet, our tenacious firstborn would soon have her first run-in with the rod . . . before she even mastered the art of walking.

⌘

"They're dreadfully fond of beheading people here; the great wonder is, that there's anyone left alive!"

~Alice, Alice's Adventures in Wonderland

This has been the hardest section of this book for me to write. So here's the short (paraphrased) version of the Discipline Manual:

THE WHY:

The world is very screwed up. This is mainly due to the degradation of the traditional Christian family. Men have abdicated their proper place as the leaders and breadwinners of the household and women have forsaken their responsibility in their home by seeking careers.

Parents are deceived in thinking that the delicate psyches, self-esteem, and personalities of their children need to be nurtured rather than their sin nature being driven far from them through proper disciplining.

Foolishness is bound in the heart of a child; but the rod of correction shall drive it far from him. ~Proverbs 22:15

Kids are born innately selfish and prone to evil. If not disciplined in the way prescribed by the Bible (spanking), they will most certainly forsake God, end up in a life of misery, and bring you shame. Also, if you do not keep God's word in this department, you are not only disobedient yourself, but you hate your children, are the cruelest of parents, and responsible for ruining their lives.

Whoever spares the rod hates their children, but the one who loves their children is careful to discipline them. ~Proverbs 13:24

Whoever causes one of these little ones who believes in me to sin, it would be better for him to have a great millstone fastened around his neck and to be drowned in the depths of the sea. ~Matthew 18:6

Conversely, if you discipline your children for their folly, they will be a joy and you will ensure their salvation and that their lives will be awesome.

Correct thy son, and he shall give thee rest; yea, he shall give delight unto thy soul. ~Proverbs 29:17

Because all Scripture is from God, we can rely on and trust the many specific directives held therein regarding the way in which we should discipline our children (even if most of the proverbs cited were written by a guy who in the later years of his life turned away from God, hmmm).

Train up a child in the way he should go: and when he is old, he shall not depart from it. ~Proverbs 22:6

THE HOW:

The rod should be given when a child has displayed either willful disobedience or wrong attitudes. It should always be administered in an atmosphere of loving calmness.

This can commence as early as nine months old.

In regard to obedience: Children should obey willingly (without grumbling or questioning), completely (pick up *all* of the toys, not just *most*), and immediately (I won't say it twice). If any of these are violated, the rod (*loving correction*) will be administered.

In regard to wrong attitudes: These include, sulking, fussing, arching the back defiantly, pouting, complaining, holding the breath, waking up grumpy, walking around with a sour look. All of these are evidence of bad attitudes and should be corrected with the rod.

The rod is to be given after a clear, calm explanation as to why they are being punished. You should use a neutral object not your hand. (We had a bamboo spatula beautifully engraved with Emily's name, Proverbs 22:6, and flowers.) The swats should be hard enough to be painful, but not break the skin.

The spanking should be received willingly and without struggle. If they are repentant, tell them that Jesus forgives them and you forgive them, ask them to say they are sorry, and restore them with a hug and a kiss. Now you can send them on their way, happy and well adjusted. If they are not repentant, the rod should be applied until you feel they are truly sorry. You will learn to hear the difference in their crying. Once their will, not their spirit, has been broken it is important to restore them by forgiving and displaying affection.

This is, of course, a truncated version of the teaching, but this was what we embraced and basically what we subjected our children to for the first several years of their lives.

So that you don't hate me, I must tell you right now that we eventually abandoned this way of disciplining—I'll elaborate later—but in their early years, every fuss, challenge, test of the boundaries, or roll of the eyes was met with a spanking—all in the name of training them to love and obey God. Oh yes, we achieved compliance, but at what cost? I'm sure I could write a whole other book on this alone.

This is an area of deep, deep regret and shame, and something I do not think I will ever be able to find complete resolve for. Knowing that we required our highly emotional and sensitive children to basically stuff all show of emotion, preference, and will, is probably one of the most egregious results of our full buy-in to the ways of Wonderland.

BIG SHOES, BIG . . . VISION

Pastor Jim was a man of huge vision; he knew that he had a big destiny as a leader of men and an apostle to nations. It had been foretold in his dreams and visions and corroborated by strangers who had also had dreams and visions. This was beginning to be further confirmed as our robust band of radical servants of Christ was steadily growing, and our little high school auditorium was busting at the seams. Pastor set his sights on a much bigger building, a gargantuan multi-use building on the campus of a prestigious seminary. So much room for growth.

We soon called it home and began to enjoy the excitement and novelty of numerous "famous" guest speakers and people of note from within the charismatic movement frequenting our new voluminous worship space. In addition to our own Apostle and Prophet, we had other well known Apostles, Prophets, Evangelists and Teachers from far and wide come to deliver their compelling messages (along with their latest books and tapes which were available for sale in the back of the room).

Big vision. I have always been of that ilk myself, so naturally the thing that tripped my trigger about our new church home was, now we had a place that could also serve very well as a performance venue . . . as in theatre . . . as in concerts . . . as in *Toymaker's Dream*.

The auditorium is vast, like an overgrown gymnasium; the area could hold two full-size basketball courts, and in fact it does—contain a basketball court. The space is divided in two by a gigantic black theatre curtain. On one side of the curtain are the main stage and the seating, and behind the curtain, is the court. The open ceiling is a maze of metal trusses, ductwork, and industrial lighting. The walls are banked at the top with large windows, all covered by blackout curtains. No outside light gets in here. A single truss spanning the front of the stage is modestly outfitted with a dozen lighting instruments—not enough for the productions I have in mind, but certainly enough to set the mood for a worship service.

I stand in the middle of all this theatre potential with visions of high drama playing out in my head—dancers leaping and turning; raw, edgy scenes with characters weeping and yearning—

"Hey, Kathy." My friends Lynn and Nate interrupt the reverie. They stand quietly with me for a moment, following my gaze around the room. There are a number of couples in church that are enthusiastic supporters of Impact Productions and big fans of *Toymaker's Dream*. Lynn and Nate would be at the top of that list, probably even before Ron and Luanne.

"This space would be awesome for Toymaker," Lynn says.

"Oh my gosh, yes," I say. *Oh my gosh. Did I just say, oh my gosh?* I shake my head. "I was just thinking that!"

"Nate and I have been talking about it. Wouldn't it be amazing if ALCF would host a performance?" she says.

"Think we could produce it here?" I say.

"Oh yeah." Lynn has long hair that reaches down past her butt. It's always clean and shiny. She doesn't wear makeup. She looks comfy in her cargo pants, Birkenstocks, and flowy sleeveless tunic. A kind of utilitarian hippy. I can tell she was a dancer at some point by the way she pulls up from her center. Ms. Evelyn hollers in my head, *"Pull up! Straight line from your butt to your crown, and on up to the ceiling! Drop your shoulders! Squeeze that tush—no bouncing basket balls in my class."* I involuntarily lift and then drop my shoulders.

Nate is grinning. He's a man of few words, but when he grins I get the feeling he has good ideas and a clear plan brewing. He's a physicist at a nearby jet propulsion lab. He parts his bowl-cut hair neatly in the middle; it flares outward slightly all around the edge. If you flipped it over, it could be something my mother might have served nuts in.

Over the next weeks, we pull together a production team led by Nate, who brings the idea before Pastor Jim. Knowing that he is big into evangelism we feel pretty optimistic that we'll get the green light. And indeed, Jim and the rest of the pastors jump on board. We secure a date during the company's West Coast tour and work hard to get the word out to area churches. We push to get as many tickets distributed as possible; nothing better than a packed house, especially when souls are on the line.

Arrangements are made for housing the cast and crew—a mighty tall order to place a company of thirty-plus people—but, not impossible with a congregation of four-hundred-plus members. One of the dancers, Karina, will be staying with our household. I can't wait to meet her, to make a connection with someone who is living my dream: a trained professional, serving the Lord and performing at the same time. All of the preparation makes me feel like I'm five with adrenalin and bubbles in my tummy.

Finally, arrival day comes and the company descends upon the auditorium with their two semi-trucks and multiple tour busses. Baby in tow, I wander about, watching the adept crew as they move with practiced purpose. I begin to feel that old familiar achy tug in my gut. I drink them in as they assemble and erect their massive twenty-foot high lighting truss towers and perform the alchemy that turns piles of metal whatsits, doodads, and thingamajigs, into a mammoth forty by forty-foot custom stage. It looks like a child-giant's erector set. They roll out the dance floor surface; it winks at me with its inky dull sheen, ready to absorb flying leaps, tour jetés, and back-flips.

Myriad chrome-cornered road cases, like so many treasure chests, are rolled in and emptied of their precious cargo: ellipsoidals, par cans, Fresnels, and other magical instruments for which I know no names. Miles of cable coil neatly at regimented intervals, an army of black snakes awaiting the flutes of their handlers. It's a circus—a mechanical bazaar, systematic chaos, the crazy mayhem that is theatre tech—executed with skill, swift precision, and occasional outbursts of song and laughter. With the exception of nary a cuss word being uttered, it feels delightfully familiar to me, something like home.

I close my eyes and the camera pans down and down, through the floor, down to the bowels of the theatre. I sit before the mirror. Six more just like it span the wall to my right and left. My face is lit by a dozen light bulbs of odd sizes, naked and bright around the chrome frame of the glass. I flutter my eyelids to dry the tacky lash glue; two fringy black butterfly wings wave back at me. Behind me, reflected in the dim light of the cramped dressing room, is my old friend Marie, one foot stretched high above her head in a wide standing split. She slowly bends her supporting leg, as the opposite arm and leg reach for the sky. Like a Barbie doll with her leg rotated completely beyond the natural confines of her hip joint, Marie manages to make it look effortless and beautiful. Oh, to be so flexible. The twelve of us are all singing and warming up together in this impossibly tight space, knowing that in the auditorium above us the audience is already milling about and finding their seats. The air is thick here in our dark and magical little transformation space; hot with breath, sweat, nerves, and bliss. "Five minutes," calls the stage manager. We go silent for a moment. Heartbeats quicken, stomachs tighten; we take a collective breath deep into our diaphragms and let the nerves out so the energy can flow. "Break a leg," we all say, like a blessing.

ᥱᏒᦆ

"We are the music-makers. And we are the dreamers of dreams."
~Arthur O'Shaughnessy via Willy Wonka

I stand in the kitchen, telling Mike about the stage set-up. Luanne is preparing mac-n-cheese and a tossed salad. She has chopped the lettuce, which makes me wince. In my head, my mom's voice: *Always, always, tear lettuce. The knife browns the edges.* But even tearing must be done ever so gently, so as not to bruise the tender leaves. Salad was my job growing up, and my mom taught me well. Luanne scrapes in a pile of diced tomatoes, along with all the juice. *Oi.*

Mike is keeping Em gleefully entertained by holding her like she's sitting in a chair, her back against his belly so she can see what's going on in the kitchen. Every minute or so, without warning, he pretends to drop her by quickly lowering her bottom toward the floor. This is met every time with a string of bubbling giggles from Em and a slight intake of breath from Luanne.

"It was so awesome!" I say. My stomach hurts a little from the excitement and the longing. "These guys know what they're doing—there must have been a hundred instruments on those trusses—and the stage—holy mmmmmoley—lasers—flash pots—huge scrim—these guys know what they're doing—it was Heaven!"

"Kaa-ha-haaa-thy." Luanne adds syllables to my name, floating each one on a titter. "You're so funny."

Mike can't find a place to stand without being in Luanne's way. It looks like they're doing some kind of stilted square dance. She turns to get to the fridge, and there he is again. She finally just stands and looks at him.

"Dinner will be ready in twenty minutes," Luanne says. She isn't smiling. Then she smiles.

"Let's go upstairs and play Em," Mike says. "Kath, wanna play?"

We go upstairs and sit on Em's floor. She plays with her white stuffed kitten that my old friend Marie brought over for her a few weeks earlier.

I was kind of surprised to hear from Marie. We'd seen each other but a few times since we graduated from the Academy. Our last interaction nearly a year prior had been the phone conversation that had ended badly when I told her she needed to "get right with Jesus."

Lucky for me, she hadn't given up on me completely. She showed up ten months later, peace offering in hand, to meet our new baby.

We sat on the floor with Emily and the new toy kitty Marie brought for her.

"You guys made a pretty baby," Marie said.

"I'm sorry if I blew you out of the water the last time we talked," I said.

"Yeah, that was weird," she said.

"I know."

"I was really mad at you," she said. "I felt all you wanted to do was proselytize me. Like you didn't care about my feelings or me, you just wanted me to get converted or something."

"I know. I'm sorry."

We groped around trying to find our friendship again.

Em held her new practice pet by the tail and banged its head on the hardwood floor. She flung it at the bookshelf, then squealed and took off after it with her newly mastered one-leg-straight stumpy crawl. It was amazing how much ground she could gain with this unique style of locomotion. It was a normal hands-and-knees crawl but with one leg stuck straight out to the side like Long John Silver. She levered herself forward with her foot, like it was a paddle. She stopped face-to-face with the bookshelf and the very interesting row of VHS tapes neatly lined up there. She sat back on her bottom and looked at them. Then she looked back at me.

"Em," I said.

She kept her eyes on me and reached out her pudgy arm toward the tapes.

"Em," I said again. "Those are no-no."

With one smooth movement, she rolled onto her hands and knees and with great dexterity pulled on the tops of the tapes, capsizing several of them onto the floor. She looked back at me again.

"Mommy said those are no-no, Em." I scooped her up and gave her a stinging swat on the fatty outside of her thigh. She burst into a wailing cry.

I could feel Marie's eyes on me. I looked at her. Her brow was bunched into a fleshy little knot in the middle, like a little pink mushroom had bloomed there.

"Sorry. Just need to deal with this." Then turning back to Em, "You need to obey mommy," I said. I felt so grown up, like a real parent.

I sat on the floor by the pile of tapes and propped Em on my lap. I picked up one of the tapes and showed it to her. "This is no-no!" I put the tape back on the shelf. "These are no-no!" Em hollered and wailed some more.

I put the rest of the tapes back and stood with my caterwauling girl. I held her against my chest, bounced her gently and soothed, "Shhhhh, it's okay. It's important for you to obey mommy, Em. Those tapes are no-no." In a few minutes, her upset settled to some shuddery snuffles. I picked up the snowy kitten and gave it to her.

"This is Emily's kitten. This is okay."

She hugged her kitten against her chest. She looked at Marie and was wracked with a single big quivering breath. Marie looked at me. Her eyes looked hard and shiny; her brow was still rumpled.

"Sorry about that. We're working on Em obeying right away."

"But why do you keep the tapes right there where she can get into them?" she asked.

"We don't believe in baby proofing. We feel like it's important to take the time to train her to know what's okay for her to touch and what isn't."

"But that seems like . . . I don't know." She took a deep breath, ran her hands over her head, pushing her hair back and then letting it drop. Her loose, dark blond curls bounced and settled. "Like an awful big temptation to just leave stuff in her reach."

"I know, but better for her to learn to obey immediately. What if she were running into the street, or putting her finger in the electrical socket or something?"

"I guess," she said.

We were quiet for a few moments. I watched Em's eyes as they began to droop and her head gave a few little nods. I rocked her gently. It had become a natural rhythm for us. Her body grew heavier and her chin dropped again, eyes closing. She jerked her head up quickly, blinking, then shuddered once more and finally laid her head against my chest.

"I'm gonna go lay her down," I whispered. "Be right back."

When I got back downstairs, Luanne had returned from dropping the kids at a birthday party. She was putting apples in the fridge and talking to Marie.

"Oh, hey, hi Luanne," I said. "Sorry, I guess you've met my good friend Marie."

"Marie was telling me that you guys grew up doing theatre together."

"We both graduated from the American Academy," I said.

Marie leaned against the doorframe with her arms folded, parentheses around her ample cleavage. She crossed one leg over the other. She had a way of leaning into her hip and pressing her shoulder down toward it that Bob Fosse would've loved. Her purse was slung over her low shoulder.

"Are you going already?" I asked.

"Are you pursuing a career in the movies?" Luanne asked at the same time.

"I'm doing theatre right now. I'm part of a rep company in Hollywood."

"I just don't know how anyone can stand it there. Hollywood, all the perversity and homosexuality," Luanne said. She shook her head and pressed her lips together into a straight line as she pulled a can of pork and beans from the cupboard.

Uh-oh. A turn I so did not want to take.

Marie's head tilted to the side ever so slightly and her eyes narrowed.

"I guess there are a lot of gays involved in the theatre," Luanne said. "Does that bother you?" She squeezed the handles of an old hand operated can-opener. The black rubber grip had peeled partway off of one of the handles so it was mostly bare, slightly rusted metal. The can of beans let out a quick gasp as the little round blade bit into the edge of its lid. Luanne cranked on the T-knob with some effort. She had strong hands.

Marie's silence made me feel like I was sinking. I couldn't find any words at that moment, no lifeline to grab hold of.

"A lot of my—our," Marie turned and looked at me, "very good friends are gay." She sighed, laughed, rolled her eyes upward, and shook her head. "I—"

"The Bible is very clear about homosexuality," Luanne said. She looked up at Marie and smiled. "God rejects it. He calls it an abomination." She had cut up a pile of Hebrew National All Beef Kosher Franks into bite-sized medallions; she scraped the little rolling meat coins into the pot of beans.

Faces of some of our mutual friends flashed in my head—Tony, Matt, James, Geoffrey (who played one of the Leads in Sugar; he was no longer with us). I quickly added, "But God hates the sin, not the sinner." I wanted to be clear that I didn't believe God hated gay people, but I knew this was not helping. Marie's eyes were bright with tears; her plump lips drawn thin.

"I can't believe . . . I can't . . ." She shook her head. "I find your assumption that I would agree with such a backwards homophobic attitude so offensive."

"Well, I'm sorry if it offends you, that wasn't my intention. But that is what the Scriptures say." Luanne was firm, unruffled, but she didn't sound unkind.

My heart was bashing against my chest walls, splitting itself in half between my two worlds; watching my friend slip away.

"Marie, I'm sorry. I'm—"

"I have to go. You know this is wrong. We have friends . . ." Red blotches were blooming on her chest, spreading out like fingers reaching for her throat. She wiped her cheek hard with the heel of her hand and turned for the door.

I followed after her, desperate. It was like part of myself was leaving, and my feet were rooted deeply in warm, wet sand, held fast by the suction.

She turned and looked at me when she reached the porch. "I don't know who you are anymore, Kathy. I'm sorry." She got in her little midnight blue Nissan Sentra. I could see her through the smudgy passenger window; she looked like a starlet behind a soft lens. She wiped her cheeks again, and drove away.

This day was a disaster. I loved Marie. So much history. But I couldn't make her understand this new worldview. It was utterly foreign and repellent to her. I didn't know if this could be overcome; I was committed to my new life in Christ, and that meant sacrifice.

"It's so hard at first," Luanne said when I came back inside. "I lost one of my best friends when I got saved."

She gave me a hug. I wiped my cheeks.

"'If anyone comes to me and does not hate father and mother, wife and children, brothers and sisters—yes, even their own life—such a person cannot be my disciple.' Luke 14:26," she said. "Friends and family don't always understand the ways of the Lord. It can be hard to stand firm in the truth, but He will always give you grace."

Em is gnawing on the little pink bow attached to the kitten's ear. She has worked at it with her two new front teeth until the edges have a little twisty fringe, like a string of fuchsia meringue peaks.

"I guess I am alone in my Toymaker mania," I say to Mike.

"We should probably cut this off before she goes and swallows it," Mike says, gingerly loosing the small toy from Em's grip. She squeaks with annoyance.

"Luanne doesn't get it," I say. "She just doesn't get the awesomeness of it all."

"Nope, she doesn't." He cuts the little bow off with his pocketknife. Em hollers and holds her hands out for her kitten.

"Here you go punkie." Mike hands it back to her. She frowns and lets out an exasperated whine. She hugs the kitty, and sinks those two sharp front teeth into the kitty's head—where the bow used to be. I think of Marie.

"It's like, I don't know. Being around theatre again. It makes me all giddy and sweaty," I say. A slight warmth that feels a little like sadness spreads across my chest.

"Like really good sex," Mike whispers. He bobs his eyebrows up and down.

I laugh and then tease, voice low, "Yeah, I can feel it buzzing all the way to my hair follicles." I smile and glance toward our open door. The kitchen is just at the bottom of the stairs. I can hear Luanne running water in the sink, clanking pots. We don't often talk dirty anymore, but once in a while it's hard to resist.

Em erupts with a frustrated yowl. She now has a tuft of white kitty fuzz stuck to her tongue. She paws at her tongue, poking it in and out like she is testing a bite of something hot. Mike adeptly plucks the bit of fluff off just as it emerges on an out-poke. I marvel at his precision.

He says, "I think I'm getting on Luanne's nerves."

"I know. I'm sorry," I say.

"I got another lecture about missing trash day, " he says.

I screw up my mouth. "I heard."

"What am I, twelve?" he says.

"No, you're three and a half," I say.

"Okay, six. But I don't see how forgetting the trash relates to my integrity. I didn't want to be late for a meeting with a potential client."

I lean over and kiss him. Em is caught in the middle. She hollers again.

"I think you are an amazing man of God," I say. "Thank you for busting your butt for our family."

He sighs and looks around the room. "This house seems smaller than it did when we first looked at it."

"Is it bad that I get so worked up over Toymaker?" I say.

"It's who you are, Kath. You don't need to feel bad about it. Not everybody gets it. It's part of what I love about you."

"I guess not everybody gets *us*," I say.

⌘

Theatre. The preparation, the collaboration, the performance—all of it—this was the stuff that made me know why I was breathing air. When I was in it, it was all I could see. I missed it like an amputated limb.

One afternoon Luanne, Lynn, and I are hanging out with our Toymaker guests, Karina and her friend Anna. Anna, who plays the part of a China Doll, is staying with Lynn and Nate. She's a tiny girl of Korean descent, a spunky and densely muscled gymnast and dancer. Karina, one of the Kitty Cats, is tall and statuesque, a Scandinavian warrior princess. Karina pushes Em in her stroller, and Anna walks beside me. Luanne pulls up the rear with Libby stopping to pick every dandelion and stray weed she comes upon. Billy is at a friend's house for a play date.

Dancers have a distinct way of ambulating, feet turned out, torso pulled up tall, shoulders pressed down, chest lifted. They stroll with a languid, feline roll in their hips and feet. Even walking down Main Street, they promenade like they're on stage. Just moving along the sidewalk with these two ballerinas elicits a visceral response from my dance muscles. *Pull up! Shoulders down!* Ms. Evelyn makes her appearance once again. I am nursing my typical feelings of desperation. The more I get to know our adopted thespians, the more my urge to throw myself around their ankles and beg "Please! Please tell me you guys can't live without me." And then they would say something like, "Kathy, we can see that the Lord made you to be on tour with us; please, please, pack your kid and your stuff and we'll hide you in the baggage compartment," because I know they must get me, they really must.

"So, I have like a million questions. Like, how did you get involved? And how in the world do you manage to support yourself on the road? And how often do you get to be home? And are there plans for other shows and expansion? How often does the company audition new members, and do they take married-with-children types?"

"Ka-ha-ha-thy," Luanne says.

Karina and Anna laugh.

"Where would you like us to start?" Anna says. She smiles.

"Uh," I say.

Karina looks back at me, all smiley and conspiracy-eyed. "Is someone wanting to run away and join the circus?" she says. She has a slight gap between her front teeth. It makes her look rather faerie-like, despite the fact that she stands about five-foot-eight. Her silky dishwater blond bob waves at me in the breeze like a shiny flag saying, *Come, come away with us.*

"Busted," I say. The two girls laugh.

"Libby, hold Mommy's hand while we cross the street," Luanne says.

"I imagine road life isn't exactly for families," I say. I hold Libby's other hand as we cross the street. She pulls down on our arms, trying to get Luanne and I to swing her.

I say, "One, two . . ."

"Three!" Luanne and I say together. We lift Libby up and swing her onto the curb. She dashes ahead to pick another dandelion from the crack of the sidewalk. Luanne paces on to keep up with her little one.

Karina says, "As a matter of fact, the guy who plays the Dream Hater is married to one of the Toys and they tour with their little boy. He's playing baby Jesus."

Anna adds, "It's been tough on them though. I don't think they'll continue beyond this season. Remember last winter, Karina, little Evan barfing all over the bus?" She laughs.

"Uuuugh. Gross. Spaghetti. Yeah, poor little guy. Traveling with the flu. No fun for any of us," Karina says.

My heart sinks. I know in my knower that we have chosen our road, and it doesn't involve raising our kid on a bus. The tears come. Then, like I sometimes do, I share too much of my intimate desires and yearning with people who don't even know me, and I find myself trapped in an awkward silence.

Anna slips her arm into the crook of my elbow. She looks up at me. "You know, Kathy, the Lord knows the desires of your heart. He put them there. The trick is to trust that and not try to push things into happening before their time. It's important to do what the Lord has put right in front of you to do; sometimes that means blooming where you're planted."

Pastor Jim's wife had used that same phrase at a woman's gathering I attended. My guts clenched then too. The primordial go-getter in me jumped up and down when these words were spoken, like a petulant kindergartner who doesn't want to come in from the monkey bars and sit at a desk.

I knew she was right though; it's just that I ached so badly for my craft that I found myself constantly trying to figure out every conceivable way that it might still be possible to be a Christian wife and mother *and* an actress.

I tried to find comfort in the knowledge that a group like Impact was producing such high quality, cutting-edge Christian entertainment; it gave me hope for the future. The fact that it was winning souls for the Kingdom made it all the more sweet. When I thought of it that way, my mind would relax and let go some, but only for a while.

Later that evening, Karina nibbled on her raw veggies, apples, and cheese. All the dancers were very disciplined when it came to their diet; none of them fancied being dropped on their noggin during a lift. One too many muffins could be a dangerous thing.

"Why don't you come tomorrow to dance class? You can warm up with us. It'll be fun," she says.

"Really?" I say. I have an urge to crawl inside myself and hide. I want this. I fear this. "I haven't been in class in like, over three years."

"You'll be fine. Alex won't mind, she's cool. You can just hang out in the back and do the warm up."

The next day I dig around in by bottom drawer. For some reason, I still have an old, moldering wad of tights and leg warmers stuffed in there. Like any minute I might need them for class.

I hold up an old pair of tights. Ballet-pink. They hang there like a deflated balloon. The elastic waste band crunches like a bunch of crackers under a rolling pin as I stretch it out; it doesn't snap back, they would now fit around Mike's waist. I wad them up and toss them in the trashcan. Deep sigh.

I opt for an old pair of sweats and faded Crocodile Café T-shirt. I doubt Alex will have any interest in seeing my body alignment, let alone me in her class. I look at myself in the mirror. I only gained twenty pounds with my pregnancy, and half of that came out with Emily. The rest was gone with a few months and a few hundred sit-ups. Now I'm looking at the same girl who once pushed her body to its limits in that sweaty dance room. Could she still manage a plié? Another deep sigh.

Luanne agreed to watch Em the next day for a few hours. I drive Karina down to the auditorium, jabbering all the way to ease my nerves.

"Two years on the road," I say.

"Yep," she says.

"Do you miss home?" I ask.

"Yep," she says.

"Boyfriend back home?"

"Mhm."

"Is it hard? Touring?"

"So hard."

"But you love it."

"Wouldn't trade this experience for anything," she says.

Class takes place behind the curtain and between the hoops on the shiny wood floor of the indoor basketball court. The company lines up in rows; Alex, the choreographer, stands at the head like a drill sergeant. She is lean and tall. Her dark hair, shorn close, pushes her height even more. Karina is toward the front of the group. I stay in the back—way in the back, on the fringe—a large buffer between the last row of dancers and myself. I don't want to draw attention if I can help it, and I certainly don't want anyone tripping over me.

Alex calls out a combination, "Let's start with pliés; demi, demi, demi, grande, three times; then cambré side, and side, and back for one, and soutenu to change. In first, second, fourth, and fifth. She demonstrates as she calls the steps—she's a young tree in a breeze.

She strides off to the side—like a stately Lipizzaner—stops at the boom box, bends at the waist, knees straight, like a toy soldier, and punches the play button. Even the most basic of things, like walking to the tape player, is executed like a piece of choreography. She takes her place again in front.

"Five, six, seven, eight, and one . . ."

On the *one* count, the class moves as a single unit. Well, except for the stiff giraffe in the back. I eke my way through the routine, grand pliés stopping a half a foot higher than the rest of the pliable bodies on front of me; my side and back bends are more like geriatric leans compared to the graceful arcs executed by my comrades. Once upon a time this was easy for me.

We move on to a combination that involves our feet and half a dozen steps, including, of course, jazz-turns. It's lively and quick. The terms are all familiar to me, but the movement has become a foreign language to my body. My mind scrambles to make the translation, but the signals from my brain stop halfway between my cranium and my poor confused feet, lodging firmly in my chest and transmuting there into supreme embarrassment. The harder I try, the greater my frustration and mortification. Somehow during the night, as I dreamt of coming here and keeping pace with the pros, some trickster transplanted the feet of a clumsy oaf onto the ends of my legs.

I stumble through the rest of the routine and part of the next, always three beats behind the group, before finally slinking to the far edges of the room and oozing to the floor to observe the remainder of class. I hold my face straight and proud, doing some innocuous floor stretches, feigning a little nursing of some old dance injury—*oh this ol' trick knee*—and trying not to cry. Karina catches my eye. She smiles and waves cheerfully. I blow her a kiss.

Watching those dancers, strong and in their prime, was like gasoline on the flame. Just being around the smell of sweaty leotards and piles of dance bags and cast off shoes stirred up the juices to the point of distraction. But the atrophying of my skills was more distressing than anything. The farther away from school and class I got, the more the reality of losing all I had worked so hard to gain loomed heavily. This dance class brought my fears into painfully sharp focus.

~

The Toymaker troupe had a second, smaller production that they some-times used to entice the local high school youth into coming out to see the main attraction. The theme of the show encouraged kids to resist bowing to peer pressure, to go against the flow, and to be true to themselves. It was only about twenty minutes long, completely secular, and highly professional, which made it an easy sell to administrators. It was purposefully crafted to put teenagers at ease about coming to see a performance sponsored by a church. Nate made arrangements for them to do the show as part of an assembly at the local high school.

Mike and I sit in the bleachers surrounded by a crowd of noisy, rowdy teenagers. I feel anxious because they're big and unwieldy; so much unbridled juvenility could hurt a person. Mike just grins and talks easily with the kids. Assemblages of large, hormonal ganglions make me want to go home and hide.

This group is generating its own weather system from all the bump-ing together of sweaty bodies, pubescent urges, and plumes of pheromones. Being all jammed together in this warm, sultry gym brings out their gamey aroma. I never realized when I was in high school that we smelled so weird. Just a minute ago I was one of these strange creatures; now at twenty-six, I feel positively middle aged.

The kid next to me keeps hitting my leg with his foot, which he has crossed over one knee and jiggles nervously. Part of his sock pokes out where the thinning sole of his tattered Converse high top has split open. He has small, angry constellations blooming on his cheeks and forehead. He drums his fingers on his thighs and darts glances around the room like he's looking for someone. He looks at me, smiles, then quickly closes his lips. Braces.

I smile back. I remember how awkward being a teenager could feel.

On the main floor of the gym, there are of a number of tall, graffiti covered, reversible flats standing at different angles to provide coverage for the entrances and exits of the dancers. This is the only set for the show.

The gym lights snap off. The hullabaloo around us is shocked into silence. The sonorous buzzing of a sustained synthesizer chord rumbles through the overhead sound system. It echoes around us and up to the cavernous rafters. The sound of car horns, city traffic, and jackhammers underscores the dark, ominous music.

A strobe flicks on, slicing the gloom with stuttering bursts of syncopated light. Walking toward us in a slow motion lockstep is a New York City crowd. In unison they move, like a Wall Street gang headed for the Exchange by way of deep water. They're dressed in identical, slightly bigger-than-life business suits; double breasted, exaggerated shoulders, sleek lines; all in varying shades of gray. The guys wear fedoras and carry briefcases, the gals have their hair slicked back and braided severely to their skulls. All faces are hidden behind blank white masks. They move as a tightly huddled mass, like so many automatons, in perfect precision.

The music shifts into a driving electronic dance tune and the house lights come up. The crowd breaks formation and there is a momentary scrambling of suited bodies as they reform and become a human escalator—business people getting on and off one-by-one, disappearing down into the subway tunnel, then rising up out of it again. They look like they're descending into, and rising out of the floor as they pass behind a *wall* of humans. They do this with their bodies alone, without the use of any set pieces.

My breath catches in my chest. Supremely cool, as I hoped it would be.

The music and movement continue to paint a world of compliance, order, and efficiency—a well-oiled machine—powered by robotic, automated life forms. Through the course of the story, one-by-one, the cogs in the machine grow tired of the grind. The music begins to shift to a more fluid, uplifting rock style, and in turn, the dancers begin to shed their cookie-cutter suits with a single yank to reveal multi-colored patchwork costumes, no two alike. Masks fly to uncover real faces bedecked with unique and vibrant tattoos. The rest of the show unfolds with an unrelenting onslaught of smokin' hot choreography and impressive gymnastic stunting. Buck the crowd. Be unique. Celebrate! is the message.

When it's over, the music is replaced with thunder from the bleachers. The kids applaud, stomp their feet, holler, and whistle their approval. We take out our flyers for the upcoming performances of Toymaker. Oh, they'll be there, yes they will.

❡

On opening night for Toymaker, after wishing our adopted dancer *merde* (means shit/good luck—don't ask, long explanation), I leave my offering (a big veggie platter) at the altar (the dressing room table). Being backstage brings a flood of familiar images: I'm fifteen again for a moment, playing Robin in Godspell, leaving a shoe as an offering to the Lord. I'm Frenchy, smacking my gum and rolling my eyes. I'm—

"Five minutes," the stage manager calls. She points me toward the door.

I make my way out into the main auditorium as the seats are filling up. I'm barely involved in this part of the production, yet I feel such a sense of ownership in the show and kinship with my new actor/dancer friends, that I find myself beaming with pride as I take my seat next to Mike. Full house, oh yeah; can't stop jiggling my foot.

The spacious stage is bare but surrounded on all sides by the towering light trusses, which are studded with a gazillion lighting instruments. The length of the back of the stage is filled with a huge scrim, behind which numerous slide projectors have been assembled that will shoot images from several angles onto the great wall of white. The audience can't see this, but I know they are there, being an "insider" with a backstage pass and all. I'm also privy to knowledge about flash pots, fog machines rigged into the stage, and the laser set up in the back of the room.

As the house lights dim to black, my heart rate increases its rhythm to double-time and I can only manage shallow breaths from the top of my chest. Mike reaches over in the dark and finds my hand, giving it a little "I know you're freaking out" squeeze of reassurance. From the void comes a deep, resonant voice, "In the beginning, lived the Toymaker, and his son." Then: rock and roll. Giant imagery splashes across the scrim. The Greatest Story Ever Told unfolds before us in flashing, driving, Technicolor glory.

The next hour and a half is everything I dreamed it would be. Lights, music, explosions of fire, flashing lasers, dancers skillfully leaping and flipping through the air, all masterfully woven together to bring life to this strange yet captivating tale.

With the final blackout, the audience is on their feet, hooting and hollering their delight. After the curtain call, the Toymaker's Son, who interestingly does look like Jesus: Caucasian, bearded, handsome, dressed in lederhosen (you get it; he's a toymaker, you know, kinda like Geppetto . . .) ANYHOO, the guy playing Jesus comes out and gives a brief, very hip and compelling gospel message, and an alter call inviting the unsaved to get saved and the unserious to get serious.

What a triumph. I was ecstatic. The show was amazing and souls were being saved; this was a signpost for me. I felt that this perfect storm—excellence and efficacy—validated my certitude that the arts were a powerful vehicle for the delivery of the Good News, which in turn, gave me hope that there was indeed a place for me in this world.

Among the crowd that came forward I did recognize a number of folks whom I thought were already saved. Hm. Well, the message was about giving your life to Jesus, and you just can't do that too many times. Born again, again, I guess.

When it came time for the company to pack up all their magic and hit the road again, I hugged my friends tearfully and ferociously.

Karina held my hands and looked in my eyes. "I would give anything to have what you have, Kathy—amazing husband, beautiful daughter—you are truly blessed. Don't miss out on it." She smiled, turned and stepped up into her rootless home. Anna waved from one of the windows.

The diesel engines belched black as they roared to life. I stood and watched with tight throat and achy eyes as the buses pulled out of the parking lot. I felt like a piece of my heart was tearing itself from my chest and wrapping itself around the bumper like some love crazed Elvis fan. Being an official bra wearer at that point, I could have easily ripped mine off and flung it at the convoy as they drove away from the church and out of my life.

As it turned out, the spellbinding presence of *Toymaker's Dream* did linger in our world for some time after their departure. In fact, they revisited the area again a few more times over the next several years, and we housed another couple of cast members. It was like a sweet itch that was so satisfying when scratched but maddeningly impossible to quell completely.

✆

We sit on the bed together. Me with my legs crossed, Indian-style; Mike with his long legs crossed, straight out to the end of our old lumpy mattress. It isn't cooling off even though the window is wide open. No breeze. You can smell the attic on hot nights, like warm mothballs and forgotten things stowed for another time. It's still light, but Em is conked out in her crib, maybe for the night, maybe not.

"I wrote a letter," I say.

"Another one? You like to write letters," Mike says. He reaches over and touches the large mole perched on the side of my left heel. It looks like a plump, fleshy raisin. He likes to press on it like it's a doorbell. It holds the shape of his fingertip for a second before puffing outward again. I was mortified of this blemish when I was in grade school but have grown to accept it, mostly. I've thought about naming it, but never got around to it. Its color is starting to fade around the edges.

"To the president of Impact Productions," I say.

Mike gives me a kind of one-sided smile. He drops his chin to his chest like he suddenly fell asleep.

"About the possibility of us paying a visit to Tulsa," I say.

"Kath," he says.

"I know, I know. I just can't help wondering if the Lord might have some connection for us there. I don't know. I can't stop thinking about how awesome it would be to do something like that here. We could go and learn something from them," I say. That tight, frantic feeling is squeezing my chest again.

"You know I'm not going to tell you what to do," he says. "This is your thing, Kath. I got my plate full. But I'll support you in whatever it is you need to do." He smiles at me. My heart goes all juicy.

One afternoon a few weeks later, I get a call from Nate.

"So, Lynn and I were praying about it, and we feel like the Lord wants us to help get you to Tulsa to meet with the Impact team."

"Oh! Wait. That would cost . . ."

"We know. We've already priced out the flight and hotel, and we feel like we need to support you in your dreams. Your calling," he says.

Their offer makes me feel humbled and a little dizzy and out of control.

"I've already spoken to the company director, and he's open to you coming, although he said it's an extremely busy time for them, and he's not sure how much one-on-one time he has to give. You might just have to kind of hang out in the background and see what you can learn."

My heart drops a little. I try to imagine what I would do there. It's not as if the production company is some kind of factory that I can walk around, you know, tour the Chocolate Room; see how the Oompa Loompas make Exploding Candy for Your Enemies and Fizzy Lifting Drinks; take a boat ride to the Clotted Cream Room . . . I suddenly feel foolish about the whole thing. We aren't ready for this level of production, or any level, for that matter. Inadequacy rolls up my back and curls over my head like a wave of shame.

"I don't know, Nate. It's an awful lot of money; we have a long way to go to put anything even remotely like Impact together here. I'm stunned by your offer; I just don't know. I'll talk to Mike."

What was this lapse in confidence? This was not like me. Just a few years ago, I would have jumped all over an offer like this. What was I afraid of?

We prayed about it, and Mike's conclusion was, "Go for it!"

But I still felt weighed down with trepidation. Worries and fears spun around me like rabid bats. *You have a kid to think of. Your place is at home, tending to your family. Who do you even think you are? Are you stepping out of your place? Would Pastor Jim and the leadership bless this?*

Anna's words kept banging around inside my skull, *bloom where you're planted.* In the end, I convinced myself that the trip was premature; this just wasn't God's timing.

Young ambitious dreamers, full of gigantic cinemascopic notions of ministry set against dioramas of tidy Christian family living. Two jigsaw pieces trying to fit into diametrically opposed puzzles.

I did, for a number of years, continue to secretly nurse my fantasy of us running away to join Impact—a life of adventure, creative excellence, and theatre a' la road. Unfortunately (or fortunately, who knows), we opted to stay firmly planted in Wonderland, coloring inside the lines with the prescribed palette.

Impact productions went on to play with the big boys, becoming a professional faith-based film and television boutique. They subsequently produced feature film projects with Hollywood mogul the Weinstein Company. I wonder what would have happened if I had taken Nate up on his offer.

BROTHER'S KEEPERS

"Tis so," said the Duchess, "and the moral of that is- 'Oh, 'tis love, 'tis love, that makes the world go round!'"
"Somebody said," Alice whispered, "that it's done by everybody minding their own business!"
"Ah, well! It means much the same thing," said the Duchess.
                                        ~ Alice's Adventures in Wonderland

Luanne, Deacon's Wife, and I sit on decomposing lawn chairs in the backyard one pleasant early summer noontime. The baby monitor crackles intermittently from the bathroom window, my lifeline to my little sleeping beauty upstairs. The tinkling laughter of the older kids fills the air.

In the bullseye of a lonely green circle, a single sprinkler shoots rainbows of water in lazy curling arcs. The kids squeak as they crisscross through the cool spray that keeps the tiny oasis alive in a sea of brown—our already burnt southern California weed-lawn. Water is expensive, and this mini emerald isle is the only vacation spot we can afford.

The eldest of our creative li'l adventurers club has set up a second pleasure destination: a Slip'N Slide that Luanne picked up at a yard sale for fifty cents. It doesn't really work right, so it's Libby's job to keep pouring little sand pails of water on the length of the sunflower-hued plastic. Each squealing mud and grass-coated urchin in turn scampers through the falling rainbows and then flings themself belly first onto the long, wet alley like shining slippery tuna being hoisted onto the deck of a fishing boat. They skid along and then come to a sudden tumbling stop in the sludgy puddle at the end of the yellow slick road. How they can bear the little round sand burrs that stud the lawn like so many tiny piranha-balls is a mystery to me, tender foot that I am.

"We've decided that it's time for me to think about going back to work," I say.

I try to sound confident in my resolve. I know the Church's stance on moms working outside the home, but we are not making ends meet. I'm grateful for the affordable housing for sure, but the picture of our little collective growing old together, sitting in our rockers on the front porch with our corncob pipes and knitting just isn't the movie of Mike's and my future that I like to play in my head. My Utopian idea of a communal lifestyle is fairly quickly losing its luster. If I can pick up some hours somewhere, perhaps it will hasten our ability to afford our own place again.

"Oh," Deacon's Wife says. "Is Mike in agreement with that?" Small diamonds of sweat stand out along the deep wrinkle of her brow, which has formed a wide letter v across her forehead.

"Oh yes!" I blurt-laugh. "He pretty much asked me too," I say. My regret is immediate. "Well, not so much that, but we talked it over, and we just really would like to be putting some money away, and his income is just barely covering our expenses right now . . ."

Silence. Nodding heads. Kids yipping and yapping.

"Well, what about Emily? She is your priority right now." Deacon's Wife's voice is soft and firm. Kind and cutting. "Mary-Joy," she calls to her eldest, "be a servant; let your little sister have a turn with the hula-hoop." The lanky girl deflates and limply acquiesces, turning the hoop over to her sobbing younger sibling. "Mind your attitude now, Mary-Joy," her mommy cautions. "It's more blessed to give than receive, honey, and God loves a cheerful giver!"

Mary-Joy hands the big fuchsia ring to her sister. Her little face is rather like stone, but knowing what will befall her if she doesn't adjust her attitude, all interest in the hula-hoop is abandoned with a sigh and a quick smile.

Mike emerges from the back kitchen door. "Hey, my sweet!" He plants a big kiss on me. Good golly but that man can trip my trigger. I bet the other ladies have to suppress a little tickle themselves. He has stopped in for some quick lunch on his way to another sales appointment.

"Kathy was just telling us that you want her to go back to work," Deacon's Wife says.

I say, "Well, I was just saying that we discussed it and agreed that it would be very helpful." It sounds like a hasty cover and I instantly feel like some kind of traitor for having shed any negative light on my handsome prince.

"Oh, yeah, well . . . yeah," Mike says. He smiles and cocks his head to the side just a little, then turns to go get the plate I left in the fridge for him. He's not one to feel the need to explain himself to anyone.

Deacon's Wife says, "Gerry and I have made it a priority for me to be able to stay home and take care of the kids. We think it's important that we let him be the head and me be the helpmate." I honestly don't think she hears her condescension, but this stops Mike in his tracks.

He turns around. "Yeah. Well, I would love to stay home and take care of the kids. If we could, I think Kathy and I would happily trade places. I'm a great Mr. Mom." He smiles. He can be so charming and disarming in the way he executes his smack downs.

"Oh." Deacon's Wife looks down at her hands, fidgets with her cuticles. Luanne is silent on the subject, although I know where she stands.

"See ya in a bit, Kath," Mike says as he disappears into the kitchen.

Luanne finally makes a contribution. "Kathy is going to go back to the

Crocodile Cafe. They offered her a position tending to the indoor landscaping." I'm touched that she is somehow kind of defending our decision—in a non-committal sort of way.

"Yeah! It'll be like having my own business. I get to make my own hours, so it's super flexible, and I can bring Em with me!" I'm strangely too enthusiastic—trying to win Deacon's Wife to my side in the matter.

"Oh. We've eaten there before. Gerry and I both sensed such a strong spirit of homosexuality in that restaurant. Do you really want to subject yourself to that?"

I'm beginning to steam a little, but I have no response to this. The manager, Mitch, is a bit on the effeminate side, yes, although I don't know for sure if he's gay and frankly don't care; I love him. He's soft spoken and kind, has impeccable style, long slender fingers with immaculately manicured nails, and is one of the nicest people I can think of at the moment. I have a sudden deep urge to run. Run away from this upsetting dialogue.

I can't explain myself, I'm afraid, sir, said Alice, because I'm not myself you see.

As if on cue, Em warbles into her baby microphone. "Oops, there's my girl," I say. I make my exit from this maddening conversation, confusion and guilt topped with a dollop of utter indignation follow me into the house and up the stairs.

❧

We did friendships differently at our church. They were not the same animal as what Mike and I had known back in our BC days. You know—*friends*—like how most heathen folk do it; comrades, chums that live their work-a-day lives, call occasionally, get together on Friday or Saturday night to play Nintendo and have a cold one, or go bowling and have two or six cold ones. In our new world, friends didn't just *hang* and, you know, live and let live. Relationships kind of carried a super-objective that was the driving force behind all interaction.

Usually, within the encouraged framework of church friendships, there were distinctive roles and a somewhat elusive sense of hierarchy. The expectation was that the duty of the *older* Christian (meaning years served) was to bring up the *younger* Christian (meaning newly converted) in the ways of the Lord. And 'the ways of the Lord' were often interpreted to the nth degree, right down to whether or not you wore a bra, took out the trash at the appointed time, had an occasional Bartles and Jaymes, or put your kids in public school. I don't even need to touch on R-rated movies, necklines below the collarbone, shorts above the knee, or secular rock-n-roll. If you wanna talk about premarital petting, porn (even the soft kind), or masturbation: here we tread in the realm of the Evil One. The list of areas for potential correction was as vast as the small print in a Viagra ad.

The sense that someone was your peer, at least among us common folk, was rare. Within the structure of a group of friends, if everyone was basically on the same level in terms of *spiritual maturity* there was still often an undercurrent of *teaching*, a kind of *brother's keeper* mentality that flowed as an unspoken rule.

This was puzzling to me, especially in light of the scripture James 3:1 which says, "Not many of you should presume to be teachers, my brothers, because you know that we who teach will be judged more strictly."

This modus operandi was often subtle and tacit. Much of my observation of it was made subconsciously with my resistance checked at the door of brotherly love and holy obedience. The rules came in many packages and were upheld in a variety of ways. Some were understood by way of comments made, like Mike's level of spiritual maturity being measured by whether or not he was on time to meetings or got the trash to the curb on Thursday mornings. Some were just a clearly stated ordinance, like unmarried young couples (I mean college age) being required to only spend time together within a group setting or with a chaperone. Sometimes rules were enforced by admonition which took a much more drastic form and was just in your face, like pressure to stand before the congregation and confess that you were a regular jerker-off-er hooked on Hustler or a repentant homosexual in need of deliverance.

Most of this steady diet of *loving correction* was so prettily wrapped in yummy pastel lick-able paper with cotton-candy tissue and rainbow licorice curling ribbon that it went down so easy. All that lovin', however, led to a slow rot in our bones . . . one that went on undetected for many moons.

A WORD ABOUT THE PROPHETIC

"The time has come," the walrus said, "to talk of many things: Of shoes and ships —and sealing wax—of cabbages and kings—And why the sea is boiling hot—And whether pigs have wings."
~The Walrus, Through the Looking-Glass

Gifts of the Spirit are special abilities provided by the Holy Spirit to in-filled Christians for the purpose of strengthening and serving the body of Christ. A short list of spiritual gifts includes wisdom, knowledge, faith (yes, even the ability to believe is a gift), healing, miracles, prophecy, discerning of spirits, speaking in tongues, and interpretation of tongues.

The Gifts of the Spirit were a big deal in our church. The gift of prophecy however, held a lot of weight. The purpose of the New Testament gift of prophecy, like all of the gifts of the Spirit, was to edify and build up the Church through encouragement, consolation, and correction. It was a gift that we were encouraged to pursue eagerly—both on the giving and the receiving end.

While any one of God's children was potentially a transceiver through which the Holy Spirit could speak, there were those who carried a special calling or *mantle* of the prophetic. These *Anointed Ones* were held in high esteem and looked to with great respect and often more than just a little awe. The sheep were always eager to receive a *fresh word from the Lord.*

At ALCF we were lucky. We had our very own prophet in Pastor Len. Pastor Len was a man on fire—a modern day Elijah—bursting with his passionate message for the faithful to prepare the way of the Lord.

"I believe the Earth is headed for a great stand-off. The line will be drawn in the sand between Elijah and Jezebel, and they will stand toe-to-toe. And not just here, but all over the planet!"

The sheer force of his message was riveting. I always loved to hear him preach. Everyone did. He preached with great fervor, conviction, and authority, his voice gradually rising to a fevered shout as he proclaimed the holy myster-ies of God. He would plant his feet wide and rock forward and back, bobbing his head in a kind of groovy funky-chicken. His movement and words would become a rhythmic dance that seemed to hypnotize both speaker and hearer.

"The warriors will be the prophets of God standing against the prophets of Baal and there will be no middle ground! There will be a generation, the forerunners for the coming of Jesus, who are known not by their niceness but by the intensity of their passion." His words were strung together and poured out like a gushing stream with little time given to swallowing, so he would baptize those sitting in the front row with the light mist of his saliva. It was as though he was chewing and savoring the words, and they made his mouth water.

"Jesus is going to make war on everything that stands against love. His eyes will be like blazing fire and on his head will be many crowns. He will be dressed in a robe dipped in blood and his name will be the Word of God. The armies of Heaven will follow Him, riding on white horses and dressed in fine linen, white and clean. Coming out of His mouth will be a sharp sword with which to strike down the nations. The Kingdom of Heaven suffers violence and the violent take it by force!"

His messages often sounded like they were coming straight from the War Room of God. Other times, he painted beautiful word pictures worthy of the walls of some vast cathedral in Rome. Usually focusing almost exclusively on the Old Testament, Pastor Len taught and read from the Scriptures as if he knew every jot and tittle. As if God Himself had composed every line as a love letter to him personally. And yet, he also peppered his sermons with a humor and familiarity that was extremely endearing and disarming, leading us all to great depths of open heartedness and receptivity. He was forever proclaiming that a great move of God was about to break loose on the earth. Casting his magic spell, he never failed to fill us with a longing to see God's Spirit poured out in some mighty way.

Every once in a while, without warning, Len would grab Ron's guitar and lead us all in a rousing song of worship and celebration. He wasn't much of a musician, but he always managed to bang out some lusty tune and would muster just as much enthusiasm in the house as Elvis could in a room full of bra-swinging devotees. He would sing with all the gusto of a Hobbit hoisting a pint on a tavern table, pounding poor Ron's fiddle 'til nigh on every string broke. He wailed about abandoning all dignity and dancing neck-ed like David did before the Lord of Hosts. The whole house would break out in wild abandon; stomping, and twirling, and cutting a jig like a raucous horde of partiers, clapping, hollering, and sweating ourselves into a crazy, joyous, foaming frenzy. Though no one ever disrobed, oh what unbridled merriment! What utter madness. What zaniness. More fun'n' a bunch'a pirates set loose in a whorehouse.

It's no wonder that he eventually became famous. To this day, Pastor Len is gathering masses of restless young outcasts and misfits around his fiery message, building an army of prayer warriors to usher in the next great revival.

THE VERNACULAR OF THE SACRED

In order to always be clear that we were "*in* the world but not *of* it," well-meaning church folk would often adopt Old Testament language to refer to certain things. There was a strange aversion to calling things what they were for fear of appearing worldly.

For example, in order to steer clear of the worship band being thought of as a . . . well, a band, Ron dubbed the worship team The Minstrels.

"Hey Mike, if it's something you think you'd be interested in, I'd love to have you join the Minstrels."

"The what?"

"Minstrels."

"But I'm a dude."

"Yeah, no. I mean sing on the worship team."

"Oh, okay. But I'm not wearing tights."

Perhaps in Ron's mind, if it sounded Shakespearian, God would be down with it. He sometimes referred to his guitar as his *harp;* and the ladies in the band, like Miriam of old, played with their *timbrels.*

This was a lingo that was hard to embrace without giggling. I always saw tights and poet shirts. Mike just blushed crimson and rolled his eyes.

Church life came with its own vernacular that became so prevalent for us that we didn't even recognize we were speaking it. Looking back, it's no wonder our unbelieving friends and family often appeared so puzzled. Just for shoots and goggles, here follow some linguistic substitutions and their interpretations:

"I heard that you've been wrestling with your thought life, and I just want to encourage you in the Lord to guard your heart and make yourself accountable to someone in leadership."

Translation: "Stop ogling Sally's boobs or I'll have to tell the pastor."

"You've really been on my heart lately, so I know it must be a God-thing that I ran into you."

Translation: "Wow. What a coincidence."

"I think the Lord may want me to bring a word to her about the secular music she's been listening to because it's ruining her witness; I'd hate to see the Enemy get a foothold."

Translation: "Ugh. Kenny G."

"One question, Kathy: How's your heart?"

Translation: "Got any juicy sins you'd like to confess?"

"I wonder if she's backsliding; I haven't seen much fruit lately."

Translation: "All she does is play tennis. Whore."

"Randy complains that we haven't been having enough intimate fellowship."

Translation: "Randy is too . . . well, randy."

"I know that you are still young in the Lord yet, bless your heart, so you haven't really considered that wearing those tight jeans could be a stumbling block to your brothers."

Translation: "My husband keeps peeking at your ass, and it's pissing me off."

"I'm so blessed that you brought that word of correction. He was on a slippery slope."

Translation: "Nice smack down!"

"He and I have been really struggling with some times of intense fellowship."

Translation: "I just hate the bastard and really want a divorce."

"After church we're getting together for a time of breaking bread and fellowship. Would you like to join us?"

Translation: "Let's do lunch."

"I'd like to ask you to covenant with me in this commitment to forty days of prayer and fasting."

Translation: "You're fat."

"I wish he would stop watering down the Word. I'm done with milk; it's about time he finally brought some meat to his message."

Translation: "Ummm . . ." Sorry. Just can't do it. You figure that one out.

As you can see, I'm fluent; well, some of these may be a little off; I'm a tad rusty. Besides, it took me a long time to shake this way of speaking, and I don't want to backslide. I'm finally reorienting myself to the language of my heathen roots—Praise the Lord, Amen and Amen.

ROCK'N ROLL HOOCHIE KOO

Sing to him a new song; play skillfully, and shout for joy. ~Psalm 33:3

Playing skillfully was a biblical mandate, so they were choosy about the musicians who were invited to be on the team. Of course, it didn't take Ron long to see Mike's ability as a musician—that was abundantly clear right out of the gate. At some point, I guess it was decided that, although he was a fairly new believer (spiritual maturity was also an important factor), he was *teachable* enough to be a good addition to the team. My guess is Ron knew a good deal when he saw one; he wasn't gonna let that set of pipes slip past.

Ron's position as a worship leader was strictly volunteer, so a day job was required. He, like Mike, had not taken the traditional path: degree, career in banking or corporate management, then retirement. As far as vocation went, Ron was pretty much piecing it together. Quite the entrepreneur, he always had his eyes open for new and exciting endeavors. Over the years, he managed to convince Mike to buy into a handful of multi-level marketing opportunities.

"Try this."

"What is it?" Mike asks.

"K-M."

"Looks like tobacco spit," Mike says.

"No. Really. It's really good for you. Come on, try it."

Ron squeezes the clear dispenser bottle over the little white plastic cup. The bottle has no label, it looks like a small whisky flask—the kind you see guys pull out of the inside pocket of their sport coat when they think no one is looking, only it's not silver, it's plastic. The brownish sludgy liquid rises in the cup, pushing its way to the thin line that says *2TBS*. Mike downs the whole thing. He coughs violently.

"This has got to be tobacco spit!"

"You'll make fifty percent of markup," Ron says.

I think Mike sold . . . um, like six bottles of that stuff. To us mostly. It tasted so bad. Like fermented dirt or maybe steeped rain gutter debris . . . or tobacco spit.

Then there were the 3D cameras:

"I think these are going to take off like wildfire," Ron says.

"They really take 3D pictures?" Mike asks. He turns the boxy camera over in his hands. It's chunky and unsophisticated like a kid's Playskool toy, only black.

"Yeah, look at these."

"Wow." Mike holds up one of the photos, tilts his head a little and squints. "Look at that." He rotates the picture back and forth. "Kinda reminds me of the 3D pictures they used to put on the back of cereal boxes. It makes me a little dizzy."

Ron says, "But they're so life-like, don't you think?"

"Well . . ."

"Fifty bucks for every one you sell!"

I think Mike sold three of those. But not to us—we couldn't afford one.

Oh yes, and the little plastic I.D. wallets:

"Identa-Kid."

"Identa-what?" Mike asks.

"So you have something to give the police if your kid gets snatched."

Mike picks up the little red plastic booklet from the breakfast table. A smear of milk from Libby's Cheerios glistens on the cover. Mike wipes it off with his thumb. He rubs his thumb on his jeans.

"Why not just give 'em a recent photo?" Mike asks.

"This has a recent photo right in it. And all their pertinent info—you know, fingerprints and stuff. Look at this nice vinyl cover!"

"Why would the police need my kid's fingerprints?" Mike asks.

I don't think Mike sold any of those.

And on it went:

"Okay. This circle is you. And these circles are your friends and family. That's called your downline . . ."

So you get the picture.

For all of his wacky endeavors, what I think Ron was in actuality was a closet rock star. He lit up the most when he was talking music. All the evidence was there, four or five different guitars, little studio hidden away in the old barn in the backyard, most of his spare time spent with his instrument strapped on. I knew the signs; I was married to one.

"No, I mean it. We should form a rock band!"

Ron is strumming his twelve-string. Mike is thumbing through a stack of rumpled sheet music looking for a song.

"You, me, Tom, Jon, Todd. And Harry on harp." Ron plays a short riff on his guitar.

Mike is quiet. He crosses his arms and holds his chin with one hand, his right index finger pressed against his lips. He squints at the ceiling like there's fine print there.

Ron says, "Almost every one of us writes, so we've got lots of awesome material."

"True," Mike says.

"Between all our demos, we could put an album together pretty easily," Ron says. "Besides, I already have our first gig lined up. Well, Tom does."

"What?" Mike says. He smiles and shakes his head.

"Calvary Chapel is hosting a free concert next month. Evangelistic outreach."

Mike laughs. He's now strumming too. "Okie dokie," he says.

"Pastor Wright ministers to this huge biker congregation, and they have this awesome outreach ministry. Anyway, Derek Dansfeld is headlining this concert. Tom set us up to open for him."

"Derek Dansfeld? You mean the Blues legend? That Derek Dansfeld? How'd Tom swing that?" Mike says.

"You know Tom . . ." They both laugh.

"So, Kathy, will you sing backups?" Ron asks me.

Well, let me check my daytimer. Holy cow! Are you kidding?

Of all the schemes, here was one that didn't make me want to cry. First of all, it didn't involve selling any weird junk, and second of all: Me! Onstage! Singing!

Cutting our debut album and opening for a bona-fide rock star, and we hadn't even had our first practice! Is this how it happened in the Christian rock world? Here was the creative outlet I was looking for. I was all in.

We gather for our first rehearsal in the living room of the drummer, Tom. He also sports a cool-cat goatee, but he somehow wears it more honestly than Ron does. Like maybe he was born with it. He's a gifted drummer and the second Born Again Jew I ever met. He sells organic stuff like tofu and toasted kelp and puffed rice. He had a reputation as one of the slickest salesmen on the planet, which, I'm sure, is how we got this gig.

I don't know how we find room for our bodies with the sheer amount of equipment that is assembled here. We squeeze ourselves here and there in the crevices between stacks of old banged up Peavey amps, their black pleather skins peeling at all the corners; a gaggle of microphone stands, music stands, and guitar stands; Tom's full drum kit; and one huge road-weary Fender Rhodes, topped with four or five racks of other spaceshippy-looking keyboards, all strategically tied together in a snake's nest of cables and cords. It's chaos, but it feels so . . . rock-n-roll.

"Test, test, one, two . . ."

Ron's mic squeals with ear-splitting feedback. Tom's teenage son turns a few knobs and adjusts a sliding button on the mixing board.

"Yeah, so I'd like to introduce my new song tonight. It's called *Throw Me a Rope*. Kathy, I'd like you to sing lead vocals on this one, if you're interested. You up for it?"

"Ummmmm . . ." The bottom of my stomach shakes hands with my left ventricle. "Of course." I clear my throat. That familiar tingle pops out in my armpits.

I know the song. Ron has already played it for Mike and me a number of times and had me goof around with the melody a little, but we haven't practiced yet. I like the song; it has a hard driving rhythm and melody, like something Pat Benatar would do, except it's about Jesus. I secretly started practicing after Ron casually mentioned that he thought I might have the voice for it. I knew that, given the chance, I could totally rock it.

Now my chance has arrived.

Ron starts the pounding opening guitar riffs, kinda like the beginning of Heartbreaker. Mike joins him on acoustic, and Tom jumps in with his double-kick bass drum, which replaces my heartbeat inside my chest cavity.

With a skillful chromatic squeal, our buddy Harry (Happy the Clown) slides into the mix with his wailing harmonica. Now by some magic, Jon and Todd have figured out the chord progression and together are rounding out the big, fat refrain with keys and bass. The sound is crashing against the dingy walls of the cramped living room and then reverberating through our skin, pushing into our bones.

I'm a little dizzy, my throat feels like there's a potato lodged in it. The metallic smell of the mic hits my nose as I step in close. I shut my eyes and I'm standing on stage at the Hollywood Bowl; the lights consume my vision. I rip into the opening lyrics, giving it all to ten thousand screaming fans. No more potato. Just electricity and sound and raw vocal energy. It's all part of my rock-n-roll fantasy.

So here we were, headed for Contemporary Christian Music glory—in my head anyway—and I was gonna be the next Joan Jett—well, the Christian version, anyway.

"So, I've come up with our name," Ron says. His smile is so big.

I'm thinking: The Warriors or Guardian or Sword.

"Homegroup!" he says.

Homegroup. Sounds like The Waltons. Please, no.

"Homegroup," I say. It makes me squirm a little inside when I say it, like saying, "I'll take a shot of milk . . . in a sippy cup," in bar full of construction workers named Mac.

I think I can feel the whole room blushing but, well, he is the leader and all.

⌘

The night of Homegroup's big gig comes cold and wet. Ron, Harry, Mike, and I pile into Ron's old van, its rear end sagging toward the pavement with age and the weight of all the gear. The rest of the band follows in Tom's car. Our little caravan makes its way down the long road to Calvary.

"I cannot believe I'm gonna blow the harp on the same stage as Derek Dansfeld," Harry says. His grin is wide and unstoppable like a six-year-old boy with a pile of presents. "He's like the god of harmonica."

Did he really just say that? A god?

"I mean, the dude can blow like, I don't know, like Dylan, or Young. If I didn't know better, I'd bow at his feet."

Ron laughs a little. Nervous laugh.

Wow. Wow. Careful there, Happy. I wonder if he's just being funny. Isn't this dangerously close to idol worship? But there's something about Harry's jubilance that I recognize as my own. I still have my idols, people whose art does something powerful to my heart. And now, some of them are Christians: Phil Keaggy, Matthew Ward . . .

"He's in like, the Blues Hall of Fame," Harry says, then sings one of Danfield's bluesy refrains: "People are you lis'nin' . . . there's a wind that's blowin'. . ."

Ron says, "Yeah, and now he's preaching the Good News with his music, and his testimony."

Harry continues to sing, "Don't fear that sound, now . . . it's gonna put you right . . ." He blows a little of the tune on his harmonica.

Ron says, "Wait'll you hear Pastor Wright preach tonight. Total evangelistic anointing. He really knows how to reach the biker culture. I've seen him minster to some pretty gnarly dudes."

This, of course, makes me sure that we have taken the wrong moniker.

We pull up in front of an old warehouse. It's dark by now, and the rain is pelting the windshield. The shadowy parking lot is already filling up with cars and motorcycles. On the long side of the building, a single fluorescent tube lights the words *Jesus is Lord*. The rain softens and amplifies the glow, spreads it out into the night, the lone beacon of hope to the neighborhood.

At the entrance, a solitary shop light hangs from a curved pipe illuminating two windows, caged in wrought iron, above a set of industrial double doors. The sputtering bulb adds a backbeat to the raindrop rhythm on the van roof. My stomach does a little flip-flop.

The rain soaks the equipment and us as we hustle to get it all into the building. Not churchy on the inside either; it's doggone cold and cavernous and well, warehousy. Green, blue, and salmon hued metal chairs give the only color in the room, each one with its own set of bumps and bruises and slightly skewed posture. Everything else is grayscale. The seats make crooked rows in front of a plywood stage. It reminds me of a black box theatre, only hollow and less cozy. I'm curious to see how Jesus will bring his warmth here. Still, I love the idea of a church that doesn't feel churchy.

Already a crowd of maybe a hundred folks are here—men and women— some seated quietly, some talk and laugh, some are praying. Many wear leather in some form or another: vests, chaps, hats, and of course, boots. Lots of boots.

The stage area is filled with the main act's equipment. It looks like a real rock show is gonna happen here. Derek's band members are busy onstage, tuning and warming up like the orchestra before a symphony but with electric guitars and a Hammond.

Where are we supposed to set up? Did they forget we were coming?

"There's Derek. I'll go scope it out," Tom says. He heads off across the room.

There *is* Derek. Shaggy long hair, fringed leather jacket, shredded jeans, chunky rings on every finger. An emblem of rock and roll, a portrait of the blues. It suddenly comes home to me that these guys are the real deal. I suddenly feel completely out of place.

"I guess we just set up our stuff wherever we can squeeze it in," Tom says after his conference with the star. "If we're quick, we can get in a little sound check. They said I should just use his drummer's kit."

I feel like we're an afterthought.

The boys all jump into action to set up what they can. I scoot into the bathroom before our sound check to dry off with paper towels, try to salvage my two-hour hair and makeup job, and to pee (which doesn't matter because it's inevitable that the moment it's time to step on stage, I will have to pee again).

Then, I make an awful discovery.

My period has decided it's a good day for an unannounced visit, and of course, I have none of the tools of the trade with me. They don't happen to have one of those amazing magical tampon machines in their ladies' room, so I carefully craft a makeshift maxi-pad out of twenty-five layers of toilet paper and wrap it neatly into a paper towel. This is tricky—it has to last for our whole set—but we girls can be very industrious. I have horrific visions of my improvised Kotex working its way up the back of my undies and out of the top of my pants. Fortunately, we're only doing four songs. Unfortunately, I'm wearing white pants. Tight ones. (Hey, it's a rock show— don't judge me.)

I sidle up to Mike at the back of the platform. The sound check is already underway. "Look at my butt," I whisper.

He leans in closer. "What?" he yells.

"My butt! My butt! Can you see the stain?"

"What's wrong with your butt?" he says too loudly, and laughing.

I pull his head to my mouth with more aggression than I mean and seethe into his ear, "My period! I just started my period, and I don't have any tampons!" I feel tears starting to clump up at the base of my throat. "Can you see the stain?"

Mike takes a half step behind me as nonchalantly as he can in the overcrowded space. He surveys the butt.

"No sign of leakage," he reports with a whisper.

"How about a bulge? Is my butt bulgy?" My relief won't be complete until I know my derriere is clean and smooth.

Mike peeks again. He wraps his arms around me from behind and pulls me in close. Leaning over my shoulder he murmurs with a bit of a dirty grin, "Very nice."

I give him a little elbow in the gut. "Stop! Smooth or lumpy?" Desperation has taken over. All spirituality has long since flown out the barred windows.

"Ow! You're fine!" he laughs. "*Very* fine."

"Stop! You're relentless!" I giggle. The tightness in my chest loosens a bit, and I take a deep breath.

We take our places onstage to no great thunder of applause—more like a golf match than a rock show. The house is full to capacity and the audience looks a little confused. They blink up at us. A guy in the front row leans over and says something into the ear of the woman next to him. She shakes her head and shrugs her shoulders.

I'm in a dream; none of it feels quite real. Except for the mattress in my pants. Tom counts off four and Ron drives into the opening riffs of my song as he says, "Evening, everybody. We're Homegroup."

I involuntarily shrug and roll my eyes in apology, and then to compensate: I rock that song for all it's worth. The short set goes just fine, despite my anxiety. We play well and I have my moment in the spotlight—in my gleaming white pants with the hidden blot. And all those big burly bikers . . . well, they smile and listen politely, then clap politely.

We finish and Ron introduces Derek and his band. They take the stage, and the energy in the room shifts, pushing the mercury right over the top. The crowd erupts with wild applause, whistling, shouting, praising. Derek starts off, of course, shredding that harp as they launch into the first tune of their set with the energy of a freight train.

I look over at Harry. He fits in well here with his black eye patch. The stage lights cast a gold halo behind his short fuzzy hair. Tears run down his face. He often gets teary over stuff. I love that about our happy little clown. And, I get it, I really do. I watch the band with awe and realize I am an ant among mastodons, T-Rexes, great whites; masters of rock and roll, who have come to bring the Good News.

They end with the tune Harry played on the way: *People Are You Listening.* A smooth, sexy classic blues tune that primes the heart and touches the soul. The set finishes on a sweet note. Derek praises God, thanks the crowd, and the pastor steps onstage.

"The Derek Dansfield Band!" pastor says.

The crowd hails the king. The band points toward Heaven and heads offstage.

Pastor Wright smiles and waits as the caterwauling settles. He's in his forties, small of stature with a large mustache that is bested, astonishingly, only by his nose. His baby blue button down shirt is belted neatly into his khaki slacks. Penny loafers. He is a bonsai among cacti. How did he ever come to shepherd this barnacled flock? He seems gentle and unassuming— so quiet compared to the reverberations that have heretofore filled the room.

"Praise God," he says softly. "Father, you are glorious."

Many in the congregation echo his praise. "Amen." "Praise you, Father." "Hallelujah." The gentleness of the voices juxtaposes the hard exteriors—an uncanny shift after the the last forty-five minutes of pure adrenalin.

"Thank you for blessing us with the amazing talent of brother Derek. Thank you for gathering us together here tonight in the name of Jesus."

After speaking for a few minutes, he steps off the platform to floor level. He's carrying a cordless microphone. He approaches two very large men in the front row.

"Hey, Rudy."

"Pastor," says Rudy.

Rudy towers over the pastor. He's wearing a black leather vest that is decorated with a collage of cryptic patches sewn on the front of it. I don't know what any of them mean. I doubt any of them are for merit, but some of them are shaped like crosses. Pastor turns to Rudy's sidekick. I'm thinking his name might be Goliath (it's like these bikers have a special hugeness gene).

"You came here tonight with your friend? You came with Rudy?" Pastor uses his mic with the finesse of a skillful news reporter.

"Yeah. Rudy's been buggin' me to check out his church."

"What did you think about the concert?"

"Pretty cool, man."

"So you don't usually go to church?"

Giant Tattoo Man laughs; it is boulders rolling through deep gravel.

The audience laughs too. It feels friendly, warm.

"What made you decide to come here tonight?"

"I don't know, man. Free concert, I guess."

More laughter ripples through the crowd.

"Have you been thinking about coming to church?"

"I don't know, man, maybe. Rudy talks about it a lot."

"What's your name?"

"Buzzard."

Of course.

"Buzzard?"

Buzzard laughs again, the sound of ten thousand cigarettes.

"Well, Buzzard. Can I ask you a question?"

"Sure, man."

"Do you consider yourself to be a good person?"

Buzzard stands like a mountain, shrugs, looks up toward the ceiling.

"Yeah, well, I guess I'm good . . . and I'm bad," he says.

"Can I ask you a few more questions about that?" Pastor Wright says.

"Why not."

"K. So you know the Ten Commandments?"

"Yeah, sure, I know 'em." Buzzard looks over at his buddy and gives him a flick of his chin, laughs. "Uh, let's see . . . thou shall not steal, thou shall not lie, thou shall not . . . thou shall not uh, commit, uh . . ."

"So you know some of them," says Pastor.

Buzzard nods, shifts his bulk from foot to foot slightly, looks at the floor.

"That's okay," Pastor says, "just an experiment. Can we take a look at the Ten Commandments to get an idea of how good you are? After all, that is the standard by which God measures goodness. Can we do that?"

"Uh, sure."

"Okay," says Pastor. "So, have you ever lied?"

"Yeah."

"Well, you said it yourself, the Ten Commandments say thou shall not lie. So if you tell a lie, what does that make you?"

Buzzard folds arms like hams over his corpulent middle. He could flatten the wee man in front of him with one blow. "A human being," he says.

The air tightens a little around us. Nervous chuckles from the audience.

"Of course, but if someone tells lies, what do you call them? If I lied to you, what would you call me?" Pastor persists.

"A liar," Buzzard says.

"A liar, yeah. You ever stolen anything?" Pastor asks.

"Hey, man, like I said, I can be good and I—"

"No it's okay, it's okay. I appreciate your honesty here. Have you? Have you ever stolen anything?"

"Yeah." Buzzard levels his gaze at the pastor.

"So if you've stolen, what does that make you?"

This is nerve wracking. I feel a little shaky; my body is vibrating all over. I can see where this is going. Can't tell if Buzzard is gonna get mad though. He's a very big man.

"A thief," Buzzard answers. He drops his arms and hooks his thumbs in his front pockets.

"A thief. The Ten Commandments also say, 'Thou shall not commit adultery.' And Jesus said in Matthew five, verses twenty-seven and twenty-eight, 'You have heard it was said, *You shall not commit adultery. But I tell you that anyone who looks at a woman lustfully has already committed adultery with her in his heart.*' Have you ever looked at a woman lustfully?"

Buzzard smiles and looks up at the ceiling again.

"Well, yeah, like I said, I'm a human being."

Laughter.

"Of course you have, of course you are," Pastor says.

"Have you?" Buzzard asks.

The crowd laughs.

"Of course I have," Pastor says. "But let me ask you, if the seventh Commandment says 'thou shall not commit adultery,' and you've lusted after a woman—which Jesus says is the same as committing adultery in your heart—that makes you an adulterer, doesn't it?"

"Well . . ."

"So according to God's perfect law, 'cause that's what the Commandments are, God's Law, you are a lying, thieving, adulterer. Wouldn't you say that's true, according to God's perfect law?" the pastor asks.

I am in awe at how gently Pastor Wright delivers this terrible news. He seems so kind; his voice is so mild, but with a mysterious authority and confidence that I find mesmerizing. He is standing next to danger itself, yet he wields God's Word with no sign of fear and an absolutely captivating precision.

"So Buzzard, we've only covered three of the ten and you've broken all of those so far—oh, and I'm as guilty as you, by the way—but if you were to stand before God on the Day of Judgment and have to answer to His perfect law, would you be innocent or guilty?"

"Uh, guilty, I guess," Buzzard says.

He stands still, a tree deeply rooted.

"Buzzard let me ask you this: Where do you think God would send you—Heaven or Hell, if He found you guilty?"

"I don't know. Hell, I guess."

"Well, He'd have to if He was a just judge. And I'm sure you don't want to go to Hell. But the Bible says that all liars will have their place in the Lake of Fire, and no adulterers or thieves can enter the Kingdom of Heaven."

Buzzard looks at his friend. Rudy tilts his head, blinks slowly, nods.

"Buzzard let me ask you this. Do you think God is good and just? Do you think that God is a good judge?"

"Yeah, of course. I think God is forgiving. Maybe I would ask Him for forgiveness."

"But is He a good judge? The Bible says He is. Good and just. Let me ask you this; have you ever gone to court?"

"Yeah."

"So if you were standing in front of a good judge, and he pronounced you guilty of crimes that you actually committed, and you said, 'Please, Your Honor, please forgive me of these crimes.' If he were a good judge, would he just say, hey, no problem, Buzzard, you've committed these crimes, all the evidence is there, but I'm just going to let you go? Would he be a good judge?"

"No."

"No. He has to pass sentence and see to it that you face the punishment for your crimes. So say he fines you half a million dollars. And what if, say, some guy you don't even know walks into the courtroom and hands the judge a check for five hundred thousand dollars and says, 'Judge, I sold everything I have so I can pay Buzzard's fine,' and he pays your fine and you go free. How would that make you feel?"

Buzzard looks at the ceiling, then at Pastor.

"Grateful."

"Yeah! Well, that's what God did! Two thousand years ago, God came to earth in the form of a man, Jesus Christ, to die on the cross to take the punishment for our sins. It's like, we broke the law, and Jesus paid our fine. He died for you. And for me."

Buzzard nods. His cheek muscles are rippling like he's clenching his teeth.

"And the Bible says that if you will repent, turn from your sins, once and for all, and trust in Jesus, put your faith in him . . . give Him your whole heart, He'll forgive you. He will give you what you don't deserve: eternal life, a new heart, a clean heart, a new life."

Buzzard is nodding slowly and shifting his weight back and forth.

Pastor continues, "But you've got to give God your whole life, man. He wants it all. He wants you to turn away from all the bad stuff you've been doing and put all your faith in him. Trust in Jesus for the forgiveness of your sins and give God your whole life."

"I've done some pretty bad sh—stuff," Buzzard says.

"Jesus paid the penalty for that. All of it. All you have to do is trust and believe and turn from your sin," Pastor says.

Rudy puts his hand on his buddy's shoulder. Buzzard wipes his eyes with his meaty thumb and forefinger.

"Buzzard, I care about you. I care about what happens to you. I don't want you to go to Hell," Pastor says.

Rudy and Buzzard are nodding.

"I don't want to go to Hell either," Buzzard says. "I need to get my life right," he says.

"We can take care of that right now, Buzzard," the pastor says. "Would you like to pray with me?"

"Yes."

I weep to see this hardened man melt before the Lord. I feel connected to him somehow. I remember my own moment of surrender. I feel my own desperation for truth, my own longing to be okay with God.

In the end, many come forward to receive Christ. Pastor's ministry team gathers the seekers into intimate huddles around the room. The atmosphere is hushed and solemn; arms are draped over shoulders, heads are down, prayers go up. Here and there, earnest conversations are taking place with eyes meeting eyes. It's clear to me now that there is something much bigger at work in this place than my rock and roll fantasy, my period, my moment in the spotlight. This was about getting hearts ready. Ready to meet the Lord. There's a headiness to it all that makes me feel a little giddy. It makes my stomach quiver and my breath shallow. I want with all my heart for this to be my calling. I want to be able to lead others to salvation in this powerful way.

After the service I approach Pastor Wright. "Pastor, thank you for being such an amazing example of how to share the Gospel. I was blown away."

"Praise God, sister. He's given us everything we need right here in His Word." He strokes the cover of his Bible. The black leather volume, worn and soft, folds over his fingers as he holds it up. "God's perfect law will never let you down. It's a constant reminder of how utterly sinful we are and how utterly forgiven we are in Christ. It's a powerful tool for the saving of souls."

"You make it seem so easy, sharing the Gospel. I get so nervous, I can't think of what to say."

"It takes practice. But trust the Holy Spirit. It's the Spirit's job to convict men of their sin. Know the Word and your own testimony, trust the Spirit, and you'll see the power of God move."

This experience set me on fire. I felt I had tasted something that was so real, raw and powerful—the cold steel church, the driving edgy music, the crowd of rough characters all gathered there, hungry. And then, to witness these people—most of whom had been dealt some pretty tough cards in their lives—surrender to the message they were hearing, soften and break apart like sand castles in the tide. Watching Pastor Wright and Derek in action, how powerful they were with the message of the Gospel, was like trying to catch my breath. It made me ache for air. I wanted this to be the kind of ministry God had in mind for Mike and I. It was exhilarating, and the truth was, as spiritual as all of it may have been, it was also dog-gone fun.

But my enthusiasm was dogged by another persistent worry.

"Use your talents to glorify God, but be careful not to cross the line into *performing* and claiming any of that glory for yourself."

This was a message we heard again and again. It seemed to be leadership's go-to warning for the artist.

My own mind echoed it back to me for weeks (and subsequently years) after that concert. I became consumed with feelings of guilt over the rush I got from the performance.

> (October 20) *I'm afraid my heart was prideful, Lord . . . that my burden wasn't for the people so much as it was for my "performance." Please deliver me from this pride, O God. Purify my heart . . .*

I wondered at how Pastor and Derek found a way to wrangle their egos and freely utilize their gifts to serve God without actually performing. Or were they? Performing? What a puzzle this was for me. They each were seemingly sincere guys and they were also good showmen, each in his own way. Was it possible to be both? I ruthlessly questioned my own motivations, the thrill I got from being on stage, singing for the audience, praying for people. I craved the power and grace with which these men were able to minister. How did they manage to keep themselves pure in their hearts through it all?

Performing had been part of the core of my being for my entire life, and now I was forever wrestling with how to make it something else. Something holy. Something pleasing to God. I was taking this church concept of performance being a bad thing deep into my bones. A perspective that was becoming like a virus in my cells. I could not figure out what the definition was supposed to be for the artist who also ministers. It was a delicate dance, a mixed message mambo that muddled my brain and crisscrossed my neural connectors into a tangle that took years to sort out.

Well, I needn't have worried about it so much. When I say *moment* in the spotlight, I mean it. Homegroup did a total of like, three gigs. And then petered out. The beginning of a long pattern of petering for many of my artistic church endeavors. Also, apparently no one else noticed that I had performance issues, because not long after our whirlwind tour, I was invited to join the worship team and shake my timbrels alongside my hubby and the other minstrels. Maybe I had an in because I was sleeping with one of the guys in the band. At least in the worship environment, it would be much easier to just focus on the Lord and not so much on the audience, wouldn't it?

A ROOM WITH A VIEW

We apartment-sat for some friends while they were away on a short-term trip to India. I think they asked because they knew we could use some space to get away from the stress of communal living and spread out for a few weeks, just the three of us. They were thoughtful that way.

It was during this time that a couple from our homegroup approached us with an opportunity. Jan and Barry were house parents in a home for the developmentally disabled.

"We think you and Kathy would be a fantastic addition to our home," Barry says.

"What Barry means," Jan clarifies with a giggle, "is that y'all would make great house parents."

"Oh, yeah," Barry laughs, "I mean as house parents. We have an opening for a second team at Vista Manor and we thought you guys would be perfect."

"Oh . . ." I'm trying to wrap my mind around the concept.

I've seen the place once before, a huge two-story house (seven bedrooms, six bathrooms, sprawling manicured gardens, kid-safe fenced backyard—a mansion to us), in an upscale neighborhood in Altadena.

"We've been doing it for a year now and have been able to sock away a pretty nice little nest egg. We're hoping to have enough for a down payment on a house in a couple more years. It's a really sweet arrangement," Jan says.

Barry continues the pitch, "Lots of perks: no rent, all utilities and meals provided, and a salary to boot. You'd have your own suite and private bath, and only have to be on duty every other week. We've only got six adult clients, all out of the house from just after breakfast until just before dinner-time. They're all very independent. It's pretty easy; we've really enjoyed it."

Sweet. A tempting deal indeed.

Mike and I deliberated about it for a few days.

"So waddaya think, Kath," Mike says, bouncing the divine Miss Em on his knee.

"About The Home?" I say. "We definitely should be in one."

"Well, it couldn't be any harder than the one we're living in now," he says.

I scrunch up my lips and use my scolding Shirley Temple voice, "That's mean," I say.

"Well, you know what I mean. I mean, no offense to Ron and Luanne, but I'm kinda starting to feel like we have our *own* house parents," he says. "I like them and all, but I sometimes feel like Luanne thinks she's my mother; it's getting on my nerves."

Sigh. "I know. I do love them, I do, but . . . Maybe this could be our clean getaway."

"And a chance to actually get ahead financially," he says. "I mean, if we're gonna live with a bunch of people, it seems way smarter to get paid for it."

And what an opportunity for ministry! Here was a missionary calling right on our own soil. No bugs, no dirt floors, no thronging crowds of the abject poor in my face reminding me of the desperation of this world. Just shiny hardwood floors, Spanish tile, live-in housekeeping staff, and six lost souls who needed compassion and the love of Jesus.

Okie dokie, where do we sign?

Now we were faced with the task of breaking the news of our decision to Ron and Luanne. I brought it up during a seemingly innocuous phone conversation.

"Oh, hey, Luanne! How are ya? We'll be coming back home day after tomorrow when our friends get back from India. Any mail come for us? By the way, we'll be moving out next month. How are the kids doing?"

Luanne was gracious. Of course they both were. They were our friends. Even though it sometimes did feel like they were our parents.

❧

Vista Manor stands tall and gleaming, red tile capping white stucco, stark and clean against the clear blue sky. The rugged Altadena foothills tower behind, so close and crisp now viewed beyond the smoggy curtain of the valley. We park in the semi-circular driveway, perched high above the doublewide street. I sit for a moment before getting out of the car, pretending this is my house. I have never set foot in anything so grand, and now I will be calling this place home.

I'm not sure what made us think that moving from one communal setting to another would be anywhere near helpful in relieving our need for space. Yes, the house is infinitely bigger, and yes, it's quite lovely, but now, instead of sharing life with another family of four, we will be cohabitating with ten people, six of whom are total strangers. Nay, not simply living with, but responsible for "parenting" a whole new set of very large children. I'm only barely juggling one. Now six. Out of the frying pan, into the fire, as they say.

It's not too late. You can still run away. It's downhill to Pasadena. Oh come on silly, Jan and Barry have been doing this job for a year now and haven't lost their minds. Yes, but, Jan is a nurse, she's used to "patients." Yes, but they had no prior experience working in this particular type of situation either, and they've somehow figured out how to do it.

We get out of the car. I check my feet to make sure they're actually touching the ground. I try to pretend I'm not terrified. Jan greets us in the driveway as Mike pulls our sweaty little girl from her car seat.

"Hi, guys! Hello, Miss Em," Jan says as she scoops Emily out of Mike's arms and hoists her onto her hip like a bag of groceries. "You ready to see your new home?"

Jan and Barry's little boy, a year older than Em, is hanging onto Jan's shirttail. He looks up, wide-eyed, at his new live-in playmate. We stroll up the incline to the cement veranda. Jan says, "You guys are going to do great! Don't worry, it's all pretty simple, really." My face feels all pasty and weird. "Let's go in and we'll introduce you to the clients."

Jan leads us through the massive mahogany front door and into the expansive living room. The hand-plastered walls are a pristine white; all ornamentation is heavy dark wood and black wrought iron. Standing under the arched entryway, I feel like a Spanish noble arriving at her hunting villa in the highlands of Madrid. Shining hardwood floors stretch away through a sort of parlor into the formal dining area, creating a long continuous corridor perfect for sliding in your socks.

Six sets of curious eyes peer at us from around the sprawling dining room table; they look like they are gathered for a board meeting. Some meet our gaze directly; others dart back and forth nervously, only daring to lock on for a nanosecond.

"Everybody, we would like you to meet your new house parents." The air fills with the howling chorus of heavy wooden chair legs dragging across wood flooring, as the whole group pushes back their massive throne-like seats. They stand at the table as if the president has entered the cabinet.

"These are our good friends, Mike and Kathy, and their daughter Emily." Barry's friendly voice booms boisterously and then dances around on the vaulted ceiling. His ear-to-ear grin seems to leap off his face and land squarely onto the faces of a few of the clients who in turn smile broadly, as if taking Barry's joyful zeal as a sign of safety. One funny fellow catches my glance and, rolling his eyes bashfully, shrugs his shoulders and looks away with a rosy blush of embarrassment, kinda like Dopey getting his forehead kiss from Snow White.

One man, tall and slender and very serious indeed, slowly slips up his hand like a student in class.

"Jimmy," Jan urges cheerfully, "did you have something you wanted to say to Mike and Kathy?"

Jimmy, whose eyes are magnified to several times their natural size behind slightly skewed glasses, nods solemnly.

"Hey Jimmy! How ya doin'?" Mike steps forward casually, hand outstretched.

Jimmy throws back his shoulders, puffs out his chest, clears his throat, and engages Mike's handshake. "Me and my wife, see," he says with a Cagney-esque intensity, "we been here for five years." He pushes his glasses back up and then puts his fists on his hips, like Peter Pan.

A small pixie-haired woman stands next to Jimmy. Her somewhat portly shape is an absolute juxtaposition to Jimmy's stick-like physique. She seems intently focused on the terra cotta tile under her feet, but she manages a whispered, "I'm Bridgette."

Bridgette's eyes flick up to meet ours, but only for a moment.

A rather burly young woman croaks her rapid-fire inquiries at us in a husky voice. "You guys gonna move into Jess and Anita's room? You guys gonna take their place? Why'd you guys wanna take Jess and Anita's place? Is that your kid? Tonight's not my night on dishes, I'm on floors." She wears a mischievous grin that I find slightly disconcerting; it bears a resemblance to a look that I might have, in another life, categorized as *shit eating*.

"Candace," Jan says. She speaks firmly, yet kindly. "Let's not overwhelm the Martens with so many questions at once. Yes, they are going to be our new house parents, just like Jess and Anita. We're going to all work together, like a big happy family." Spoken like a true house mom.

"Is that your last name? Martens? Mike and Kathy. Martens. I like that. New house parents. Just like Jess and Anita." Candace processes her thoughts out loud like a semi-automatic rifle.

"Yes. New house parents. That's what Jan said. She told us already yesterday, Candace," the blushing flirt shoots across the table. The bashful fellow apparently also has a sarcastic side.

"Shut it, Walter," Candace fires back at Bashful, her face twisting into an angry grimace. I feel suddenly nervous, like we could be on the verge of some kind of incident at the Home . . . already, in the first five minutes of our arrival.

Barry laughs his infectious laugh. The boom of his voice slices through the clients' tension with some kind of jovial authority. "Okay, okay, you two. Remember, we all agreed that we wanted to make our new friends feel welcome." His sunny face, made larger by his receding hairline, seems to warm the room. "Walter, would you like to introduce the rest of our group?"

"No," Walter says, rolling his eyes; he goes rosy again with a smile and a demure shrug of his shoulders.

A rumpled young man—I guess about eighteen, but small for his age—steps forward to shake our hands.

"I'm Tom, and this is Anmarie." He motions with his head to a blocky woman standing just behind him at the end of the table. She lifts her chin to look at us through smudgy glasses but does not smile. "She's not my wife. And she's not my girlfriend either."

Tom wears his baseball cap backward like a rapper. He has a silver hoop in one ear and a Walkman stuffed in the waistband of his baggy jeans, the headphones draped around his neck like a skinny torc. He also wears a feisty grin, a rebel *I got this shit handled* kind of grin. He pulls a cigarette out of the pocket of his hoodie and pops it between his lips with smooth James Dean-like finesse.

"Tom, no smoking in the house!" You would think it was Jan's firm command, but this reminder comes with surprising force from the diminutive little Bridgette.

"Yes, me and my wife, see, we won't have any smoking in this house," says Jimmy.

"Fine," Tom says. He slips the cigarette behind his ear. He points to each person in turn around the table. "K. So, you met Anmarie, Jimmy and Bridgette." Jimmy nods like a CIA agent; Bridgette looks at the floor. "And Candace, who is full of questions." She sticks her tongue out at Tom. "Which just leaves Walter who doesn't want to do the introductions."

"Who made you the boss?" Walter says. He presses his lips together, narrows his eyes at Tom, and shifts his head to the left, like a middle-school girl giving a smack-down.

"Well, you obviously didn't have the cojones, Walter," Tom says.

"Okay, okay, guys," Barry chimes in again. He seems to be the calmer-downer. "Mike and Kathy, we're super glad to have you as part of our household. I'm sure we'll have lots of fun together." He wiggles his eyebrows up and down quickly. But not in a creepy way—more like in a *no really, it's gonna be fun, please stay* kinda way.

Fun. Of this, I am forming my doubts. Interesting, however, I am sure of.

"Okie dokie guys. Chore time," Jan calls. "Jimmy and Bridgette, Walter, your night for dishes. Tom and Candace on floors. Anmarie, trash. Let's do it!"

The whole crew jumps into action like, well, like a herd of reluctant first graders. Jimmy is clearly in charge. "C'mon, Bridgette," he directs his wife. "I rinse, you load." He speaks to her with the affection of a drill sergeant.

Candace turns back as she heads for the kitchen, "Bye, Emily! Bye! See ya later," she says, her voice now way up high, like a little girl.

Barry turns to us and adds some icing to the deal, "Well, you won't have to do dinner dishes but a few times a month for the next two years!" He smiles, mouth open, nodding vigorously.

☙

It's our day on duty and I'm making the rounds for client bedroom check. We do a daily sweep to inspect for cleanliness and contraband. By now, I'm an old pro.

From inside Candace and Anmarie's shared room, an unfamiliar male voice softly croons.

"You're so pretty."

What the? I stop outside the door to listen.

The clients have all left for the day. I didn't see Candace leave . . . Did she have some dude in there with her? Was she secretly doing the dirty with some guy—sneaking him in through the balcony window? I imagine it for a split second: Candace, a hefty woman-child in her crash helmet, seductively unstrapping and tossing it aside in a steamy striptease. (She wears the helmet from time to time because she occasionally blacks out, one time hitting her head on the pavement, but she mostly dons it as a fashion statement or a cry for attention.) Her slack-jawed lover reclines on one elbow atop her single bed, partially draped in her Pink Power Ranger bedspread—

Interrupting my lurid, if not disturbing soap opera fantasy, the soft male voice echoes the sweet words again from behind the door, "You're so pretty." A screechy voice cuts in, "Penny wants a cracker. Rrrrrah!!" Penny is Candace's parakeet. I open the door. Candace left her cassette player running with a Parakeet language learning tape repeating her favorite new phrase, "You're so pretty." So far Penny seems to only be into crackers.

Candace keeps her side of the room with amazing meticulousness. She likes pretty things and keeps her myriad little girlie knick-knacks arranged in seemingly specific, yet completely unrelated groupings. Ballerina jewelry box, stuffed kitten with lifelike fur, Elvis button, matching hand mirror and brush; lamp with feathered trim, empty Madonna Pez dispenser, tiny sequined coin purse, Pink Power Ranger Big Gulp cup. To look at her frou-frou taste in keepsakes, you'd think she was a petite little blond princess with bouncy curls and petticoats. She mostly dresses in khaki Dockers and plain Izod T-shirts, kinda like a boy. She wears her hair in a stick-straight bob, bangs chopped across the brow, (which has never seen a pair of twee-zers), no make-up, although she keeps a collection among her whatnots. She likes to carry a small handbag on a long strap slung across her chest in the touristy style, a feminine touch to her warehouse stockperson ensemble.

Most of the time, Candace speaks in her machine gun rapid-fire gruff-ness, with occasional lapses into an affected little girl voice. When she wants something from you, out comes the charming young lady and up goes the timbre of her voice. Except for that one time, when I tried to share Jesus and offered to pray for her, and her upper lip curled into a snarl and she actually growled at me. Like a mean dog.

Anmarie's half of the room is the Oscar to Candice's Felix. Her side is always just barely passable; her faded, threadbare, grayish spread haphaz-ardly tossed over her pillow; lumps and bumps betraying the jammies and clothes and whatever else from the day before obviously hidden beneath. In terms of inspection, for Anmarie, contraband includes candy. She's diabetic and hopelessly addicted to sweets. She buys herself tons of sugar free good-ies, but we sometimes find a Snickers or a Three Musketeers tucked away in her nightstand and have to confiscate it, which invariably leads to days of pouting and snarling from Anmarie.

Oh heck, let's face it; Anmarie is just a grump. All the time. She lumbers around the house like a very big ten-year-old, grumbling and cussing under her breath. She has terrible personal hygiene and mumbles colorful epithets when sent back upstairs to brush her teeth. She hates being made to walk all the way back up there because anything that resembles exercise is absolute torture for her. Anmarie is a lot of work, and she loathes being told what to do.

One day she was sitting by herself at the dining room table playing solitaire. Everyone else was in the TV room. Anmarie rarely hung out with the other clients. I grabbed another deck of cards out of the buffet drawer and sat down.

"Hey Anmarie, can I join you?"

"There's no law against it, I guess," she said.

"How many games have you won?" I asked.

She stopped in the middle of putting down a card, looked at me perturbed, then went back to her game.

"How come you never wanna hang out with us on movie night? Hey, next week we're gonna watch Jesus of Nazareth. Have you seen it?" I asked.

"I'm not watching any Jesus movie," she said.

"It's a great movie," I said. "We'll make a bunch of popcorn and Jan is gonna get some sugar-free Fudgcicles for you." Anmarie picked up a column of cards, moved it onto another column, and turned the next card face up.

"Five of clubs. Jesus Christ," she said.

"Anmarie, language please. You know the house rules."

"Sorry, slipped out."

"The Lord can help you with that, Anmarie," I said.

"Don't be coming at me with any goddam fucking preaching. I don't need any of that shit," she said.

I was becoming pretty well convinced that Anmarie didn't like me much. Can't blame her. I wouldn't like someone who kept taking away my sweets and getting in my business either.

One morning, however, out of the blue, while I was poking her finger for her blood sugar test, she looked up at me and said, "Kathy, I like you and Mike. You're alright." Then she smiled her big, stinky, grimy-toothed smile at me.

"Awww. That's nice Anmarie. I like you too. Now, please go brush your teeth."

INTO THE DEEP

This is your last chance. After this, there is no turning back. You take the blue pill—the story ends, you wake up in your bed and believe whatever you want to believe. You take the red pill—you stay in Wonderland and I show you how deep the rabbit-hole goes.

~Morpheus

During some worship services, it was common for folks in the congregation to demonstrate great displays of emotion: weeping, crying, calling out to God in all sincerity and utter abandon. This was usually the case on the occasions when Pastor Len was at the helm. He would often lead the group into long sessions of prayer and repentance that were akin to a visit to the Wailing Wall.

But this abandon part, it somehow eluded me. My heart ached for God, but I continued to feel constricted and self-conscious. My inhibition became a source of deep shame and distress for me. Was there something wrong with me? Why couldn't I work up the tears? With all my heart I desired to, but like my early struggle with tongues, I could never fully enter in.

I remember the night the tide finally took a turn.

Len would sometimes pop into our Worship Team practice as a kind of guest worship leader. What he lacked in musicianship he more than made up for in zeal. He would bang on his old beach guitar and the team would back him up.

This night he has joined us because he has a new worship song that he wrote and wants to share with the team. Len has a small entourage of prayer warriors that often do tag-team prayer and prophesy with him in services and such. A couple of these intercessor ladies—Beth and Jolene—have joined us tonight.

We start, as usual, with Ron and Mike strumming a soft melody on their guitars. There's a heightened sense of anticipation among the group, an almost palpable electricity in the air. This always happens when Len is here.

"Father," Len says, softly. His body rocks back and forth, bobbing like a buoy on a gentle sea. "Abba," he says, which means papa. He draws the name out on a long ragged whisper. Len's voice has become shredded from years of fervent preaching.

The two ladies begin a soft harmonious song with words that only God and the Angels understand. The other musicians sing too, a soft undecipherable chorus. The sounds swirl together, rising and falling, ebbing and flowing like the tide.

Len's voice continues breathless and low, "Holy Spirit. We call upon you to come. Inhabit our praises. Let our songs of love be a pleasing incense, rising to the throne room of God. Praise you, Lord, blessed be your name."

"Yes, Lord," we echo back, all the voices together, drawn out, a little slurry, a little drowsy.

I realize I'm distracted by Len's presence with us. I squeeze my eyes shut tightly, trying to focus my mind, point my love toward the sky.

Len starts to play his little beat up vinyl-stringed guitar. The others are quiet.

"Your love . . ." he sings.

"Your love . . ." echoes Beth.

"Awakens my heart . . ."

"Awakens my heart . . ." Beth and Jolene echo.

"That I might love . . . you more . . ."

They echo him again.

"Your love . . . changes . . . me," they all sing in unison.

Four simple lines sung again and again. Each time sweeter, more heartfelt.

My heart feels like it's being drawn from my chest—pulled by some great magnet. As I breathe out, I try to picture my love floating there on top of the breath and wafting upward and outward. My torso is buzzing, my body expanding. I raise my arms like a little girl to her daddy, her Abba: *Hold me.*

I join the song because it's coming up from my toes. I begin to weep.

A soft voice speaks into my right ear, "I'm pricking your heart to relieve the pressure." It's one of the intercessors, Beth, I believe.

"The things I've placed in your heart—your desire to serve Me, your love for the lost sheep, your commitment of your life to expand My Kingdom—these are as foreign objects there, and they're inflaming and irritating the *old man*. Thus, the need to prick your heart and relieve the pressure that builds up."

The dam breaks, I fall to my knees and up from my inmost being gushes forth sorrow upon sorrow. I wail and cry like a baby there on the floor as Beth gently caresses my back and prays softly in tongues.

(August 17) *Last night at minstrels I was touched by the Lord as never before. My heart finally broke before Him—I was able to weep and mourn over my hardness and sin which has hurt Him—yet this is only the beginning—He's taking me even deeper into the things of His Kingdom. Lord, You are tremendous! Your faithfulness abounds.*

. . . he said nothing about healing or completely ridding me of the old heart. I have a desire like never before to be totally purified within – for Him to seek out and expose every dark area. He must want me to be strong, and therefore must allow me to persevere through pain and suffering as He banishes my old sin nature. All of this must come through worship, prayer, and fasting.

I know. But I'll remind you again: Red Pill.

೧

Following in the footsteps of pastor Len (I must admit that he was an odd hero of mine—I was so drawn to his intense passion), I felt a persistent compulsion to try to fast and pray for days on end. Not that the idea of going without food appealed to me in the least, but I wanted so much to be part of what I was being told would unleash the next great revival (and also to try to quell my dark and sinful tendencies).

Len had successfully completed a number of forty-day fasts, like some kind of Christian Gandhi. I could usually fast through lunch anyway, but the PBJ called with such ferocity, I would ultimately succumb. This, of course, was always followed by utter disappointment in myself for giving in to my carnal nature so easily. I think the longest I ever succeeded in fasting all food was three days. I would like to say that it opened the heavens for me, but in actuality, it was pure torture. I couldn't even call anyone and say, "Hey, three days . . . yep, three days . . ." because Jesus said you're supposed to wash the *I'm starving* look off your face and comb your hair and keep your fasting a secret so God will reward you.

I was also desperately trying to find my place in the sun. I felt such a deep longing to be using my gifts to serve the Lord and save the world. Everything was urgent and revival was just around the corner. I met with Pastor Len to get some counsel on what to do with all this evangelistic and artistic angst.

"You've got such a heart for the lost, sister—that's fantastic!" Len says.

When Len smiles, his mouth spreads wide across his face; his slight underbite causes both upper and lower teeth to show. A little bit like a bull-dog, but nicer. This, along with his dancing eyes, makes his smile huge and infectious—a very disarming trait.

I sit there on the pleather couch in his office, soggy tissues crumpled up in my lap. "I get so frustrated. I want so much to do something that's radical, and relevant, and effective for communicating the Gospel. I know the Lord must have provided my professional training for a purpose. I look around and see so many deceived and lost. I want to use my gifts and my training to bring them in."

Len doesn't look directly at me as I talk. He rocks gently, brow fur-rowed, eyes set intently on the floor between us.

"I know I'm called as a wife and mother first, but I just get so full of some kind of, ugh! I don't know. There has to be a balance in here somewhere."

"Kathy, I've never much believed in balance," he says. "I'm afraid I have more of the lion in me than the lamb." He smiles that warm doggy smile at me, chuckles. Despite his kind temperament, Len effuses intensity. His outer layer of approachability just barely cloaks the dervish that whirls be-neath. "Like me, the Lord has given you a passion that'll always burn in your bones. He'll help you find an outlet for it. Just keep fasting and pray-ing. He'll show you your calling."

"But it all feels so urgent."

"Well, the days grow darker. Revival is coming, and He's rousing his fiery ones. He'll assemble his army in all its splendor. You're a warrior-artist."

This guy knows how to whip up the crowd—even a crowd of one. I suddenly feel like I'm the Grasshopper, here with my wise Kung-Fu Master. I look around for the glowing brazier, so I can lift it with my forearms.

"Take heart, Kathy. As you seek the Lord, He'll make a way for your gifts."

"I believe He will, Len. It's just so hard to be patient." I decide to lay my cards on the table: my truest desires. "Maybe somewhere down the line He might make a way for me to head up some kind of a production company or something." I'm clueless how this can ever come to fruition—from what I've seen so far, there are few actors in our midst. Seems I'm forever fully equipped and sorely under-staffed.

Len cocks his head, squints to the left.

"I think a street evangelism team would be powerful—like, skits. For outreaches to the college."

Inward eye-roll. I can't help it. I'm thinking *The Royal Shakespeare Company*; he's thinking *Our Gang*—but I say, "Yeah. I'll have to give that some prayer."

"Give my wife a call. After four kids, I'm sure she can give you some words of wisdom about balance. She's a master at balancing motherhood and ministry. And keep fasting and praying, sister—you'll find your answers there."

So, I walked away with no concrete solutions, but at least Len seemed to understand my intense longing, and his encouragement was a strange kind of comfort to me. There was a real softie side to the fiery prophet, and I felt a private little sense of pride that he saw something of a kindred spirit in my own passionate soul.

JARS OF CLAY

Claude and Lilly were new to our church. They had recently moved cross-country to be a part of ALCF. They were cut from wholesome, earthy, mid-western stock, but they were not bumpkins by a wide stretch. Claude was a longhaired musician type, handsome and ruddy. Lilly was of faerie blood, eyes full of mischief and a head full of long bouncy black curls. They were several years younger than we were and had no children.

We invited them over for dinner. It was always an interesting endeavor entertaining guests at the Manor. I was impressed with how in-stride they took our rather colorful housemates. Lilly was full of compassion and kindness toward the clients. Claude was very laid back and easily engaged them in conversation. It was our week off, so after supper, we retired to our little apartment suite; Mike and Claude broke out the guitars.

Lilly joined me as I plopped Em into the tub for her bath. We sat and chatted as the girl splashed and played, capturing mounds of bubbles in her colorful measuring cups that floated about on the water.

"I've seen you dancing at church a few times," I say to Lilly.

"Worship was great today," she says. "Really felt like the Spirit was hanging out with us. It was fun."

"I love watching you dance," I say. "So expressive. Really lovely."

"Aw," she says.

Em slaps the bathwater with her open hands, splashing Lilly and I and sending a wad of bubbles into her own face. She squeals like a banshee.

I chuckle. "See?" I say. She fusses as I wipe her face with a clean wash-cloth. "There. All better?"

Em exhales an exasperated "Huh!" and then lets loose a diatribe of gibberish as if to say, "Mother, I fail to see the humor in the stinging of my delicate princess eyes, I would appreciate a little empathy here."

"Oh-ho-ho, you're fine," I say.

"I like watching you with your daughter," Lilly says. "Seems like being a mom comes very naturally to you."

I laugh and shake my head.

She adds, "Claude and I don't feel the Lord has called us to have children."

"No kids? You sure?" *Definitely not natives of this neck of the woods.*

"I don't think so. I feel like I've had a definite word from the Lord on it. We know God's going to use Claude's music. We feel like we've got a strong calling to ministry, and we just don't know where the Lord's gonna take us."

"Kinda young still. You might change your mind."

"Maybe. How about you guys. Lynn and Nate told us you guys are called to minister through the arts."

I pull my wriggling fish out of the water and swath her in her baby towel. I put the little corner hoodie of the towel on her head and let it hang down her back like a superhero cape. It used to completely cover her with about six inches to spare. Now it just reaches the floor. "Go see daddy," I say.

Em squeals and takes off running out of the bathroom, her bare feet slapping on the hardwood floor, adding rhythm to her squawks. From the living room Mike hollers, to Em's giggling glee, "Woo-hoo! Naked girl! Naked girl!"

I continue chatting with Lilly as I drain the tub, mop up water, stack toys. "Mike's and my training and experience is in theatre, music, acting, dance. Mike's also an amazing songwriter. I know we're called to use our gifts, we just haven't figured out what the Lord wants to do with us. Well, I mean besides the worship team. I've been kicking around ideas for some kind of theatre or production company. Have you heard of Toymaker's Dream? Impact Productions?"

"They're amazing."

"I would so love to do something like that. So powerful for bringing in the lost."

She nods. "The Church should be leading the way in the arts. So much of what we do is just embarrassing," she says.

Yup. I look at Lilly and smile.

Em comes running back in, letting her stomping feet push out a string of syllables "Mah-ha-ha-ha-ha-ha-ha!" with every step. I snatch her up with a big swoop and muzzle a big raspberry onto her tummy. She screams and laughs that deep unhindered laughter that's so matchless in little kids. It'll be short lived tonight, for now begins the comb-out of the tangles. From here on out, conversation will be impossible.

"We need to talk more later," I say.

"Absolutely," says Lilly. "You're a good mom," she adds.

Happiness rises up in my chest.

Claude and Lilly soon became our bosom friends and partners in dreaming. We shared a passion for communicating the Gospel in a way that wasn't preachy or churchy. We wanted to live our lives as authentic, radical representatives of the King of Kings, winning souls by whatever means necessary (as the Apostle Paul said)—especially if it involved the arts and particularly music.

DO A LITTLE DANCE . . .

Let them praise His name with dancing and make music to Him with timbrel and harp. ~Psalm 149:3

Worship dance. This was another funny thing practiced in the charismatic church. But we're not talking Alvin Ailey here. This was the Pentecostal version of the bell choir, only dressed in pseudo biblical attire, with high-necked shimmery frocks, tinsel bedecked tambourines, veils, sashes, hair wreaths, and the like. The style of dance involved cavorting around doing grapevines and folk dances from Fiddler on the Roof and waving streamers and flags. This was not my gig.

Thankfully, there wasn't a whole lot of it going on at ALCF at the time, although people did dance around in the aisles. This consisted almost exclusively of the pogo (bouncing straight up and down) or the Jr. High bop (you know: step-touch-right, step-touch-left).

Some churches, however, had full on teams of worship dancers. My friend Cindy and I saw this phenomenon on one of her TV praise shows on a couple of occasions. It made me feel embarrassed just to watch.

"Looks like a school of Esther Williamses out of water," I told her.

"Like Little House on the Prairie—The Musical," she said.

We stopped just short of pointing and laughing. I tried not to judge, but it made me shudder. I'm pretty sure I told God that while I was open to the idea of using dance as a means of worship, I would rather go live as a missionary among the bugs in a third-world country than participate in the likes of the Pentecostal Follies. I'm pretty sure he high-fived me on that one.

Lilly's dancing was something altogether different. She would find an open space, kick off her shoes, and twirl about barefoot in classic faerie fashion. She had no training, but she moved with a natural grace that was full of beautiful expression and lyrical style. She just flowed, like a watery nymph. Her movement wasn't wild, but it was uninhibited and childlike (and dare I say, a little sexy).

A rather buxom sprite, Lilly let the cleavage lead in all its glory as she swirled and skipped around before the King. It wasn't that she was flaunting; her ample girls just couldn't help the way they glorified their maker (although I think she would've been mortified to know that it was noticed— she was delightfully unselfconscious). I'm sure the leaders would have preferred she wear the standard issue high-necked frock, but I loved her flowery, breezy, feminine dresses.

Watching her move always added something sweet to my worship experience. I longed to be that free in my expression toward God. Her intimacy with him somehow brought me closer too. I could see why God called for dancers.

However, this was also a dangerous notion. Women moving. Their bodies. In reckless abandon. Very sexy. Yes, this was dangerous ground indeed.

Of course, I wouldn't have admitted out loud that women dancing was a sexy thing. In truth though, I'm sure it's why dance took on such a bizarre form in church. There's something intrinsically alluring about women moving in time to music. It's just the stuff of which we're made, I'm afraid.

In order for this to happen in church, however, it had to lose all manner of sensuality to not be considered worldly, immodest, or inappropriate; hence the loathsome smocks and limited movement. Definitely not sexy. Wouldn't want the brothers to stumble, don'tcha know.

I did finally give it a go myself. Not in a regular service though—I wasn't that brave. Yet.

(June 5) *Last night in minstrels practice God had me step out in faith and dance . . .*

Yes, yes I did. It was conservative: some arm movements here, a little chasse-lunge-turn there. Nothing radical. No major leaping and certainly no double jazz turns, but I was most definitely dancing. I entertained the idea of trying it again on a Sunday morning, but I just couldn't find the courage to let it all hang out. Perhaps I was waiting for some kind of permission. Instead, I just tucked it all back in like a shy little turtle and tried to forget about it. I don't know what held me back. It was Lilly who finally coaxed me out of my shell.

∽

"Kath," Lilly says. She pushes a chunk of unfettered curls back from her face, "I really think we should dance together. See what the Lord does."

This wasn't the first time she'd proposed the idea, but of course I would always instantly clench when she brought it up. *What if she thinks I'm too worldly? Or worse, that I'm a total goof?*

I was so hopelessly perfectionistic and obsessed with what people thought of me. She was so free and obviously pure in her movement before the Lord. She also had a little wild gypsy blood in her.

Many weekends we would drive out to Claude and Lilly's place and hang out together. They were living as caretakers on a huge rolling estate in the foothills of Topanga Canyon. We would gather in their tiny cottage, praying and worshipping and weaving fantastical visions of rock and roll ministry backed up by the Streets of Solid Gold Dancers.

"C'mon, it'll be fun!" Lilly says. She's relentless.

She leads me out onto the vast tennis courts, which are overlooked by meandering paths and lush rose-gardens. She sets down her little scuffed boom box and pops in a cassette tape. The air is soon filled with the intoxicating strains of Phil Keaggy's sublime guitar.

Lilly's full cheeks bunch up high as she smiles at me. Her grin always comes all the way up from her toes. Even her dimples have dimples. Adorable. Giggle inspiring.

"C'mon, Kath." She starts mini-skipping in a little circle around herself. She brings her arms up and begins the most intricate and deliberate hand movements. Like they've been given choreography of their own

"Are you . . . signing?" I ask.

She smiles. Her hands move to the lyrics of the song.

"You are!"

She nods a groovy side-to-side nod and winks.

Lilly had worked with the deaf and was fluent in sign language. It never occurred to me that it could be put to dance. It's quite lovely.

"C'mon!" she whispers loudly, and twirls off across the tennis court like a badminton birdie floating on the breeze.

My heart is pounding, I want to be absorbed into the smooth surface of the court, but nevertheless I compel myself to my feet and force out a couple of stiff plies, like some old woman with bowel problems. *Oh brother.*

Finally I throw off my mortification. I close my eyes and let the beauty of the music move me, swaying side to side like a rigid and bashful tree. *Come on, goofball, you're a trained dancer for goodness sake!* My limbs feel awkward and sluggish, like someone has transplanted one of Vista Manor's client's arms onto my body.

Then larger movement takes over and invites the rest of my body into the dance. Lunge and reach, arms outstretched, head down, bowing before the King. Scoop down and then open to the sky like a blossoming lily. I do what I can in my acute self-consciousness and the two square feet of tennis court that I'm willing to explore.

Lilly is flying around the place, flitting inside and outside of the boundary lines like Salome.

She skips over to where I am, takes hold of my hands, leans back and skips us around in a circle. Soon we're spinning and spinning, leaning back in opposing directions, faster and faster. We're two five-year-olds on the merry-go-round, her wild black curls bouncing and blowing in the centrifugal force. She throws back her head and laughs. I'm grinning like an idiot.

We let go our hands and continue to leap and twirl and lunge and sway around one another, until we collapse on the red clay, sweating and panting and laughing.

It was ridiculous. It was glorious. And fun. And possibly sexy.

(June 5) *Danced with Lilly for the first time. Felt so free. My fleshly mind was confounded as we jumped and swirled around the tennis court. But God created us to express ourselves with this kind of freedom, didn't He?*

LIFE IN THE HOME

Jimmy nervously taps his stubby pencil point on the little black scribble, as if his insistent tapping will somehow make us understand what it is he's drawn.

It's game night at Vista Manor and Pictionary is on the menu. Boys against girls.

"Uh . . . it's a dot!" Mike calls out. I shoot a sideways glance at him.

Jimmy shakes his head vigorously. Jaw clamped tight, neck muscles straining. He pushes his thick glasses back up on his nose.

"A uh, a uh . . . a tiny ball of thread!" Claude hollers. He reaches his hands up and feigns pulling out the hair of his spikey mullet. "Aaaaaaahhhh!" he bellows.

Jimmy is one of the more uptight clients at Vista Manor; he keeps tapping on the spot with his pencil point, leaving little crumbs of lead and additional dots on his artwork. He's laboring with all his might to not give verbal cues. He's a strict follower of rules.

How can we possibly divine from a little black splotch and his fretful repeated pointing what the heck that is? Time for intervention. I can't bear having Jimmy go into some kind of fit over a game of Pictionary.

"Okay, Jimmy, time's up. What is it?"

"It's a bee. A bee. A bee! A bumble bee!" He blurts. *Can't you see that, you morons?* He glares at us through his crooked glasses, eyes bugging, head cocked.

"Ohhhh! Of course . . . why didn't we see that?" is our chorus.

Jimmy's wife Bridgette mumbles in her low monotone, "It looks like a bunch of dots." Jimmy casts a stern look at his wife but holds his tongue. The hint of a smirk twists the corner of her mouth. I'm beginning to believe there is more to her than meets the eye.

It's my team's turn. Lilly and I are wicked good together at this game—a formidable duo. Claude and Mike always accuse us of cheating because we can literally guess each other's drawings with the first scratch of pencil to paper.

This go-round is stumping me though. Lilly has drawn what looks like a butt with something coming out of it.

"Poop or pee? Poop or pee?" I say low, trying not to move my lips.

"No helping!" Jimmy hollers. He taps his pencil on the table even though he isn't the one drawing. Beads of sweat stand out in a row along his hairline.

Mike starts giggling. Claude soon follows. So does Bridgette.

Lilly taps on the somewhat obscene cartoon. Funny how we somehow all believe the rapid pointing helps.

"Poop or pee?" I breathe through my teeth, desperation setting in. We are way over par by now.

The last grains of sand slide to the bottom of the timer as Lilly and I dissolve into puddles of laughter across the table. Jimmy's having a conniption, wordlessly huffing and sputtering and tapping as Bridgette giggles coyly. Mike and Claude are falling out of their chairs, crying and peeing their pants.

So much for this round. Game night is always interesting at Vista Manor, and Pictionary with developmentally challenged adults (and I mean all of us) is always a kick. I highly recommend it.

But what was Lilly's drawing, you ask? I think it was either poop . . . or pee. I don't remember.

❧

Tom and Walter were roommates. They were an unlikely pair. Walter was one of our more meticulous residents, in his mid-forties, soft-spoken, shy. His side of the room was always spit-spot, and he kept his clothes impeccably clean and pressed. Tom was eighteen and I had my doubts as to why he was a client in this home. He was in his tattoo, earring, cigarettes, and banging chicks phase; perhaps this was his parents' way of handling it. He may have had a slight delay, but all in all, he seemed like a pretty normal kid to me.

Of late, Tom and Walter were having some altercations. Walter had developed a tendency to snoop around in Tom's stuff (there was likely some porn stashed in there somewhere) and this was pissing Tom off. When confronted, Walter would blush, stiffen his neck, and deny it with the most annoying smug smile on his face, which would send Tom through the roof.

"But I walked in while you were rifling through my drawer!" Tom says. He jerks his backwards ball cap off and then quickly slides it back on again, smoothing his hair back in the process. A tiny gold cross dangles from his ear.

"Walter, we've talked about this so many times. Do you think Jesus likes it when you invade Tom's privacy and take his stuff?" I can't help speaking to Walter as if he's a child.

Still smiling and blushing, Walter rolls his eyes, shrugs. "No."

"What are we going to do about this, Walter?" Mike asks.

"I don't know." Walter's face drops, and he seems suddenly genuinely sad about the situation.

"Your attitude has been kind of stinky lately too," I say.

"Yes. I've had a bad attitude lately," Walter says.

"Well, Jesus could help you with that, Walter," I say.

Tom chimes in, "Yeah, man, you need to pray to Jesus."

"Would you like to pray about it Walter?" I ask.

"Yes, I would like to pray." He smiles at Tom. Tom rolls his eyes.

We all bow our heads and pray for Jesus to help Walter change his attitude and to help him turn from his sin and know Jesus better.

"That was cool," Tom says afterward.

"I'm sorry I got into your things," Walter says.

"S'okay, man. Just don't do it anymore."

"I won't, Tom. Friends?" Walter puts out his hand.

"Yeah, okay," Tom says and gives Walter's hand a pump.

As gentle as he was, Walter could be a pill at times, refusing to do his chores and making snide comments to the other clients. He had a subtle Jekyll & Hyde thing going on that was a little unnerving, and of course we had our suspicions as to who the Hyde part was being influenced by (here's a clue: t'weren't no angel).

We'd been talking to Walter about Jesus for a while, and he often seemed repentant when we did, so we decided to strike while the iron was hot and invited him to a time of prayer and worship to see what the Lord might want to do.

❧

Claude, Lilly, Mike, and I are gathered in the small living room of our apartment at Vista Manor. I think the truth is, we're all sporting a possibly misguided curiosity about what might truly be behind Walter's predilection toward mischief. Would we encounter a little demonic activity? Could be interesting . . .

The lights are low. Mike and Claude gently strum their guitars. We sing together of God's amazing grace and the sweet blood of Jesus.

Walter sits, back straight, feet neatly lined up, hands resting just so on his lap, short-sleeved button-down smartly pressed. He holds a placid smile and seems cautiously relaxed.

Lilly and I sit on the polished hardwood floor, its blond surface gleaming where the dimmed wall sconce casts a warm glow. Em is asleep in the walk-in closet, which doubles as her nursery. We had to get creative with space in our Manor suite. She sleeps well in her little cubby—our somewhat moderate wardrobe hanging along the walls forms a nice sound barrier.

The tranquil music swirls around in the air as we wait there for the Holy Spirit to lead us in our prayer time.

"Praise you, Father." "Bless Your holy name." "We invite Your presence to fill this place." Our praises echo off of one another. A soft chorus.

"Father, we're so thankful that You have touched Walter's heart to be here with us tonight. We ask for Your blessing to be upon him, Lord," I begin.

"Yes, Lord. Yes, Jesus." Lilly's voice is angelic, like a little girl.

Claude says, "Father we ask that You'd loose your Holy Angels into this place. Surround us, God. Push back the darkness and let Your Glorious Light shine." As he speaks, the intensity of the chords he's playing grows, the cadence quickens, the beat becomes more insistent, warlike.

"Yes, Father," Mike says. "We take authority over any spirit of darkness that may be hanging out in this place . . ."

"Yes, Lord! Yes . . ." Lilly and I both say.

I open my eyes to check on Walter. He sits like a statue, blinking, smiling, eyes darting.

The mounting urgency of the guitars seems to speed my heartbeat and pull the warm air in close. Lilly is now up and swaying in a tightly contained dance within the small floor space she occupies. Walter watches politely.

I stand and rest my hand on Walter's shoulder. He tenses slightly, shrugs, rolls his eyes, and purses his lips.

"Yes, Lord, we command any foul spirit that has attached itself to Walter, any spirit of contention or rebellion that is harassing him, we command you to GO! In Jesus' mighty name! Shabababa coolia cooriaba sholiariaba . . ." Blood is pumping hard through my chest. My hands are buzzing. The others also pray in tongues, voices rising into the air, declaring war in the heavenly realms.

Walter's smile has faded, and he seems fidgety. He sighs deeply. A strong sense of anticipation pulses in the air—any moment something could happen, some manifestation of the demonic.

"Lord, we know you love Walter. You gave Your only son, Whose blood was spilled to cleanse him of his sin. You gave this freely to Walter because of Your love. Please, Lord, deliver him from The Oppressor. Help him to walk with You. To trust in You and turn away from the evil that seeks to lead him astray."

Lilly is sweeping the air, her arms circling in graceful arcs around were Walter sits, like she's pulling curtains of protection around him. He drums his hands gently on the tops of his thighs, patting nervously.

"Okay," he says. "Thanks guys. I've gotta get back now. It's probably time for Wheel of Fortune. Thank you for your prayers to Jesus." He smiles and casts his eyes toward the floor.

"Okay, Walter," I say. "Do you want to pray? Do you have anything you want to say to Jesus?"

"No, thank you. I think Jesus is going to help me to be nicer to Tom now. Thanks, guys. I'm gonna go now."

So off to the TV room goes Walter.

And so went our little ministry time, like a scene out of The Diviners, only Walter didn't drown in a river while we prayed. What a good sport he was, smiling and sitting patiently as we ranted (which I'm certain at the time we took as a sure sign of some demonic influence). We probably should have been arrested. I can only say we're lucky Walter didn't turn us in. This interaction was totally inappropriate and unprofessional, given that we were there as hired house parents, not counselors or even clergy for that matter.

(September 16) *We had a great time of worship last night with Claude and Lilly. Prayed over Walter. Everyone was ordering spirits around. Really sensing a need to be more wise and discerning in this area. I felt a lot of striving going on. I feel we were in danger of doing more harm than good. Need more insight from God and to be careful not to operate in the flesh during warfare. Too dangerous.*

The idea that Walter might be afflicted by some kind of unclean spirit felt very real and scary to me. Our duty as believers filled with the Holy Ghost however, was to take authority over such spirits. Though it was weirdly easy to get caught up in the zeal of the moment, I sometimes felt like perhaps things might get out of control. Images from *The Exorcist* would dance in the back of my mind: what if we unleashed some kind of evil thing that did some harm to Walter? What if we caused some kind of irreparable emotional scarring? As heady as it all could be, I was feeling that perhaps we should be leaving this kind of stuff in the hands of the big boys.

I'll say it again: red pill.

SIGNS AND WONDERS

The idea of demon possession and the Devil totally freaked me out. I think this fear was part of what drove me into the protective arms of the Lord in the first place. Funny though, before I became a believer I only had to avoid the movies about children who could spin their heads completely around and projectile vomit pea soup at will (I find demon-possessed children to be particularly creepy and awful).

In church, we found devils crouching behind every bush, lurking in every stray thought, and waiting eagerly at your back door to pounce on your every unguarded moment. Every *victory in the Lord* was expected to be followed by some kind of attack of retaliation from the Enemy. We were living in a war zone. The Evil One and his minions—and these critters were not cute little yellow guys wearing goggles—sought every opportunity to take you down.

Every human behavior that was considered to be negative had its designated demon, and it became a regular practice to look for and point out the afflicting spirits of others.

"She had a spirit of lust all over her."

"He is clearly struggling with a spirit of pornography."

"He needs to be delivered from a spirit of homosexuality."

"I can't be around her; I sense such a divisive spirit."

"We really should pray for Cheryl, her obsession with tennis has turned into such a spirit of idolatry."

When it came to evil spirits, it became easy to get a little carried away and cross over into some pretty wild and wooly ministry. If someone sought prayer for some malady that was determined to be the work of a demon attaching itself to, or worse, inhabiting them, the atmosphere would often become angry and a bit out of control. I've been in meetings where gentle and loving prayer gave way to yelling and commanding and bullying, and though it was being directed at these *spirits*, it almost felt as if the person being prayed for was the actual problem. Depending on what was going on with the person, they might even respond with violent twitching or shaking or retching, as if to confirm or accommodate what was being spoken around them.

If someone responded in some outward way, it would often create an even more elevated response from those praying, much like the increasing frenzy at a WWF match or a rugby game, with the equivalent of victory roars and fist pumping. At first, I thought it was rather cool to wield the power to cast out demons. There was something intoxicating about feeling like you were some kind of devil ninja, but soon it just felt upsetting and ugly. I eventually started avoiding this stuff like the plague, but I worried about it nonetheless. I never did see anyone levitate, turn their head around backward, or vomit pea soup, but Candace *did* growl at me. I don't blame her though; we could be downright annoying. I don't know. It could just get pretty weird sometimes.

I hold just about anything as being possible. The wide world and the vast universe abound with so many mysteries and marvels. I'm fascinated by the idea that the nature of our existence is only just starting to unfold for us. We're discovering new things all the time about matter and energy, consciousness and the mind, imagination and creativity. I've always had a vivid imagination and felt pretty sure that just about anything we humans can imagine we can eventually create.

Signs and Wonders—supernatural occurrences—are part of the very fabric of the charismatic Christian experience. It was a central dogma that the proof of God's favor was the manifestation of his Holy Spirit through the demonstration of the supernatural. Perhaps this was part of the allure for me. I wanted to *experience* God, in all His amazing, magical power.

Pastor Jim and many of our distinguished guests preached heavily on the importance of miracles, particularly in the area of physical healing. This was how God revealed his character of goodness and displayed his power.

Miracles were a sign that we were pleasing to the Holy Spirit. They were also deemed necessary for the preaching of the Gospel to unbelievers. What could be more convincing than having your missing left pinky toe grow back, or having that huge goiter drop off your neck, to convince you to give your life to Christ?

Amazing stories often came forth from the pulpit. We regularly heard tales of modern day miracles of biblical proportions: the dead being raised, the blind receiving their sight, the lame being made to walk, the demon possessed being delivered to freedom. But these miracles always took place at this or that conference or at so-and-so's church or in some remote village in Mexico. We talked about it so much, but frankly, the actual occurrence of such amazingness was something we just talked about and longed for, but I personally never saw.

The belief that miracles should be a common occurrence for the Spirit-filled believer was an area of deep frustration and grinding tension for me. I desired this with all my heart. I did see people (myself included) claim to have been healed of a headache or a sore knee, but I always had a little voice in the back of my head explaining it away. I tend to believe in the mind's amazing ability to heal the body, so in the absence of any astounding incidents of eyeballs growing back or people sitting up in their coffins, I was never sure if the more minor healings that some claimed were just occurring naturally.

I wrestled mightily with the shame of my secret seeds of doubt. This constant struggle was aided and abetted by my inner accuser who told me that I had something wrong with me. I was walking around with two strikes: I couldn't seem to manifest this proof of my position in God's Kingdom and I entertained sinful contemplations that maybe, just maybe, the stories being told were slightly, well, let's just say embellished.

The deeper down the rabbit hole we went, the curiouser and curiouser it got.

DRAMA QUEEN

I was a born leader (my Kindergarten teacher said so), and as you know by now, theatre was in my mitochondria. It was such a natural thing for me to dream of being the leader of a theatre ministry. When I spent time contemplating it, my soul came home again, and I felt expanded and more connected to God. And since ALCF was where we were planted, I was determined to bloom.

The collaborative work of bringing the Toymaker production to church drew me into the orbit of a few other theatre-minded people, like Miriam. A talented actress and musician, she and I seemed destined to eventually team up. She had trained professionally in the performing arts, had zero tolerance for schlock, and had the same weird OCD-like affinity for detail as I did. I was immediately drawn to her quick wit and confident intelligence. At the time, she was married, but I never really got to know her husband. Unbeknownst to most at the time, her marriage was undergoing some massive challenges—a saga in itself—but she managed to walk through it with grit and courage and without broadcasting her private hell to those around her.

Miriam and I started brainstorming the concept of utilizing drama as a means to bring a contemporary creative punch to church services. We decided to get organized and see if we could make it happen. We gathered a handful of thespian types to kick around some ideas. What came out of these sessions was the concept of creating a series of short dramatic scenes based on the theme of the pastor's message that could be used as sermon illustrations, complementing and bringing them to life.

The first order of business, however, was to get buy-in and permission from the leadership. Despite my utter confidence in my knowledge, training, and experience, the idea of pitching Pastor Jim filled me with dread. I don't know what it was that intimidated me so much about the idea of a formal audience with the head pastor; he was just a guy after all. I finally summoned my inner cojones, and Miriam and I took the vision to the big Kahuna.

"Well, we don't really refer to them as skits, we're thinking more along the lines of professional-level dramatic sketches," I clarify for him.

Pastor Jim nods and smiles. He shuffles papers on his desk. Checks his watch. Miriam says, "We want to keep this at a high level of excellence. We think just because this is being done in church doesn't mean it has to be amateur. We really want to raise the bar."

"Yeah *skit* is kind of a four-letter word for us." I laugh, but my joke and my regret of it just kind of hangs there in the air for a moment. I try to suck it back into my mouth. "Christians should be leading the way in the arts. We shouldn't settle for cute or unpolished just because it's church."

Jim is looking at me and also just past me. I'm not sure he's really here in the room with us.

"So, if leadership agrees, we'd get your sermon topics as far in advance as possible, write the scripts, cast, rehearse, and then be ready in time to go up one Sunday a month," Miriam explains.

"I think your idea is interesting. You would need to submit the scripts in advance for me to approve the content," Jim says. "And you'd need to be submitted under the authority and oversight of one of the pastoral team— I'm thinking probably Pastor Chris.

The youth pastor. Is he thinking this is a youth thing?

Okie dokie. No problem. We can work with this. At least he didn't say no entirely.

So our little dream was beginning to sprout some stumpy wings. Our group started meeting weekly while we waited for Jim's sermon list; we figured we could start getting some of the potential cast warmed up. I was all into it. I had us do dance warm-ups and stretches and some acting exercises. I was a twenty-something version of my beloved Cora: "Arm circles everyone!" We batted around a number of ideas and did some improv games.

I'm not sure if it was because people were too busy, or whether I just didn't like any of the ideas that came to the table, or if maybe I was just too much of a control freak, but once we had a topic list in hand, I ultimately ended up writing the first few sketches myself.

I gave my scripts to a guy in the congregation who was a professional screenwriter and also a professor of writing at a couple of the local colleges. He sold a number of film and television scripts and was a super intelligent, all around normal guy. I asked him to take a look at my stuff and give me his professional opinion; I desperately wanted to be reassured that I wasn't writing rubbish that I was going to regret putting up on the stage. He wasn't involved with our group in any way (he steered way clear of any fraternization with amateurs—I got that), but he looked it over and told me that he thought my writing was good.

"I'd put my name on this," he said.

You know how sometimes someone gives you a word of encouragement that sorta stays with you like, forever? For some reason, it has always stuck with me and when I contemplated finally writing this story, it popped back into my world like permission to pass go. For this gift, I'm very grateful.

❧

Father's Day. Our first sketch is going up this morning. The stage lights dim and three men each take their place at stage-right, left, and center. I'm seated in an aisle seat, near the back of the room, nerves ablaze as if I'm the one up there about to do this scene.

Mike I know has got this, no problem. The other two guys, being complete newbies, well, we'll see. Three fathers, three interwoven monologues.

Light up on Father One (Mike): Sits at a table, backwards baseball cap; he folds and unfolds a dollar bill as he speaks. "I tell you my boy is gonna do great things. Goin' places, ya know?" He's playing it with a Brooklyn dialect. Maybe a tad cliché, but I'm okay with it.

Light up on Father Two (Martin): An older gentleman, he stands holding a letter. "Three years. Three. Not one call from my girl. And now out of nowhere she blames me. For everything."

Light up on Father Three (Barry): Down on one knee. "You're doing great sweetheart. You're a real trooper, hun. Breathe now, in . . . and out."

I realize I've been holding my breath, and let it out. The three fathers go on, intermingling their stories of pride, hope, regret. The audience is riveted; so far, not one line is dropped; my actors are nailing their scenes. My heart is so full.

Each monologue ends with a little twist: proud father rolls up his dollar bill and takes a hit of cocaine from the table, regretful father tears up the letter and remains blind to his daughter's pain, hopeful father celebrates the birth of his first child: "Doctor!" he says, "It's a baby!"

Lights out. Applause. Yeah.

GIRLS, GIRLS, GIRLS

"You're not the same as you were before," he said. You were much more . . . muchier . . . you've lost your muchness."
~ Mad Hatter, Alice's Adventures in Wonderland

My buddy Miriam was an anomaly at ALCF. She was a woman who loved Jesus passionately (still does) and knew her way around the Bible like a New York Cabbie knows the Big Apple. She was also not afraid to apply her intellect and speak her mind boldly—to men and women alike.

When a friend of Miriam's, who was on staff at the church, was fired from her position, Miriam showed her metal. The *official* reason was never announced, but it boiled down to the pastors feeling that her leadership position put her in an unscriptural place of authority over men.

Miriam was vehemently opposed to this, decrying it as a cold act of patriarchal legalism and was quite vocal about her feelings. Her absolute disagreement with the leadership on this issue alarmed me on one level and intrigued me on another. Were we allowed to disagree? Wasn't that dissention? Rebellion? I had been taught that submission to church authority was a good and godly thing, and fully trusted that our pastors understood and acted upon the Scriptures in a righteous way. Could she have a more accurate understanding than they did of what the scriptures had to say about the issue? She presented them (and me) with very compelling arguments as to why it was not a scripturally sound decision, including a twenty-some-odd page thesis that had vast biblical references to back up her point of view. At that time, though, I defended our venerable pastors, even in the face of abundant evidence that they may in fact have been misinterpreting and misusing Scripture. I loved my church family. To question our leaders was to risk the unraveling of the underpinnings of my new community, a group of folks I was now emotionally invested in. To refute our leaders' wisdom and understanding of Scripture could open up a whole other can of worms: what else could they be wrong about?

Years later, Miriam told me (we remain friends to this day, and I love her dearly) that my response to her warnings broke her heart because up to that point, she thought I was different. She said that she knew when she met me that I was not like the typical sheep, that I didn't fit the mold. She said she mourned that I, for some crazy reason, was buying into the club mentality.

So here was one of the main areas of conflict I was rubbing up against:—women in leadership was against the rules. I didn't understand this mindset and though I tried to swallow it, I was finding it increasingly hard to stomach. But there it was, right there, in the Bible: women were not to have authority over men. And according to the Apostle Paul, women were basically just saved through childbearing—*What the fuh?* Yep, it says it right in 1 Timothy:

> *But women will be saved through childbearing—if they continue in*
> *faith, love and holiness with propriety.* ~1 Timothy 2:15

I never fully got that verse. I do know that pushing a baby out of that tiny opening makes all us mothers badasses and must surely count for something.

In the beginning, it didn't occur to me that being a woman would pose any problem for me or for my dreams. My first directly personal experience with this issue came with our second Sunday Sketch when I decided to up our production values with a piece that was a bit more technically complex. Miriam played the starring role, and she took her work seriously. I was proud of what we put together and felt that this one would be particularly effective.

I started voicing my expectation that we should be given equal access to the stage and lights for tech the week prior to the performance, and light and sound checks the day of. I was told that this was not going to be happening; there just wasn't anyone authorized to run the light and sound-boards during the week for rehearsals, and our request was in direct conflict with the worship band's time before the service. This raised my dander just a skosh. Call me rebellious, but since some of the scenes involved crazy things like lighting and sound cues, film clips, and set pieces (albeit simple ones), I thought it'd be a given that a little tech rehearsal in the performance space wasn't an unrealistic thing to expect. Okay, so I admit that when I'm in full on director mode, I can get a little intense. Never disrespectful or mean, mind you, but perhaps a little, er, well . . . manly? For the craft! For the work! It was for the Lord!

The morning of, we get about fifteen minutes to set everything up but no rehearsal on the stage and no sound check. We've run this sketch a hundred times. A story in three scenes about a young lady who gets busted at the airport for possession of marijuana, ends up in jail, and has to turn to her father for help. Miriam inhabits her character with an earthy realness; I feel utter confidence in her performance, but I don't know; I'm worried about the tech. Josiah is running the light and sound board, but he's never looked at our cue sheet and we've never tested our secret weapon lighting special in this space. Or any of our music cues, film cues, or ANY GOL DARN CUES! (A "special" is theatre speak for lighting that has been designed to create a special effect of some kind.)

Scene One: At the airport. Miriam stands in line as airport security searches the bags of the person in front of her. She carries a backpack slung over her shoulder. She waits her turn, calmly, no big deal man. Subtext: *I'm totally freaking out because, crap, I forgot to ditch the weed before I got to the airport.* Miriam knows her craft. No fidgeting, no shifting around, no "acting" or "showing" us that she's nervous. The guard, played surprisingly well by Len's prayer warrior intercessor Beth, finds the weed. With convincing force, she spins Miriam around, gruffly pats her down, and cuffs her (she mimes this as well as can be expected; we couldn't get any real cuffs). Lights to black. Lights! I said (!) . . . Finally, blackout.

Cue music: The Rolling Stones "Sympathy for the Devil." Cue music. Cue . . . Gaaaagh! Miriam transitions to the next scene in total silence. I close my eyes, sigh.

Lights up. The special works, praise the Lord. Miriam stands center stage in harsh light with slightly skewed vertical shadows running across her body like jail bars. Yesssss. Brief monologue about her family, her fears, her need for forgiveness. Miriam freezes: Cue blackout. Blackout! Miriam stays frozen in the light. Ahrrrrgh! I dive from my seat three rows back to the front of the stage where our special sits on the floor and yank the &%$@!! plug. Blackout.

Final scene. The phone call. The moment of truth with her father. Lights up on Miriam who picks up the receiver from the telephone sitting on a table stage left. She takes a deep breath, dials the number (we're talking old school rotary phone here; the story was set in the 70s). She closes her eyes and waits for her father to pick up. I look to the giant screen hanging upstage of her, where the prerecorded video of her father is supposed to appear to hold the other end of the conversation. Cue video. Nothing . . . Cue—her father appears; I unclench my jaw. But the video flips a couple times as it tracks and he freezes there holding the phone with a goofy look on his face. My heart sinks. This wasn't supposed to be a still life. Miriam is left to improvise the whole of the two-sided conversation on her own. I hold my head in my hands and try not to cry. When she finishes, Miriam turns and exits in full light because Josiah has no idea when to go to blackout.

Pastor Jim comes onstage, clapping, cuing the audience that they should also clap. He then goes on to recap the entire story, beginning to end. As if the people hadn't just watched it. I just stood there blinking. I couldn't feel my feet. Only my hot cheeks and my pounding heart. It felt like a train wreck, despite the fact that Miriam had still somehow managed to deliver a deeply emotional performance.

After church folks politely congratulated us and said they liked the skit. Miriam later told me that she had walked off stage, fuming all the way out to her car. She sat inside, sobbing and raging at pastor Jim. She started to drive away, but changed her mind and came back. She didn't want me to face my mortification alone.

That sketch had so much potential if we'd just been allowed to do a few run-throughs to work out the technical kinks. I just couldn't wrap my mind around why there wasn't more support. Then I thought of Miriam's friend whom leadership had fired. Now I was finally getting the concept that having a woman heading up something the size and scope of which I had in mind, might not ever happen. The truth was, a woman heading up anything of any size or scope that placed her in a leadership role *over* men was verboten.

Along about that time, a famous traveling Evangelist / Giver of Prophetic Words moved to the area and became a new member of the church pastoral staff. Let's call him Frank. And gifted? Frank had been in the ministry for years and had already travelled the world, attracting quite a following with his uncanny abilities as a speaker and evangelist.

He was super good at this because, well: 1) he was a mighty fine looker; and B) he was an entertainer. A fetching singer, storyteller, writer, musician, actor, and evangelist, all wrapped up in one dashing package.

And he had a huge vision. Like me.

For a number of years he had been developing a concept for a huge multi-media-effects-studded-rock-n-roll theatrical extravaganza. It was written to appeal to the secular world while delivering a strong Gospel message and was to star none other than, well, him. He also lined up some other ex-heathen who was a semi-famous actor to co-star, but I can't recall who that was.

Frank and his family were an attractive bunch. I mean that in all sincerity. He, his wife, and kids were about as beautiful as they come. Not only that, but also well-spoken, intelligent, kind, and well dressed; they were natural leaders and all around nice folk.

One impressive trick that Frank had down cold was giving *words of knowledge*. A word of knowledge was when a believer would receive some kind of insider info from God about you or for you, meant to give you guidance or instruction, or possibly just to wow you into the Kingdom. It was a kind of Christian fortune telling sometimes referred to as *reading your mail* (I alternately loved and hated the idea of having my mail read; ya just never knew what someone might find in your fine print or under your plain brown wrapper).

Being of the same theatrical mindset, I had secret hopes for some kind of artistic partnership with the likes of Frank. I never spoke of this, of course, but the fact that he had so much going for him in terms of the respect of the pastors, his many years of ministry, and now he was part of our church leadership. Hmmm, seemed like some kind of sign from God to me; perhaps my dreams were closer than I thought.

ℛ

Our relationship with Claude and Lilly was growing steadily. We spent more and more time together, imagining our futures in shared ministry, envisioning multitudes coming to Jesus through music and our genuine love and compassion for the downtrodden.

It wasn't long before Mike and Claude started playing more music together, and they soon teamed up with another guy, and then another, and well, you know what that kind of thing leads to: a band was born.

We were also now attending the same homegroup as Claude and Lilly; this one was located much closer to Vista Manor. Frank and his family started attending our homegroup meetings as well.

Being in the same homegroup as Frank came with the perk of having some pretty exclusive access to receiving personal words of knowledge and wisdom from him.

One evening, trying to play it cool, I corner him in the kitchen during the snack and mingle time. His hair is perfect, like Richard Gere, only jet-black.

I share a little about the vision I have for ministry and the arts (okay, it may have been more like babbling and gushing); he listens kindly, smiling and nodding enthusiastically.

He puts his hand on my shoulder, "Kath," he says, "you're full of intense passion, and that's awesome, but . . ."

He called me Kath.

He picks up a book of matches from the counter. "You see these matches? Hold out your hand."

I narrow my eyes and smile a little sideways smile at him.

He laughs, flashing a perfect row of immaculately white teeth. "Hold out your hand."

I hold out my hand; he drops the matches lightly into my palm and says, "Don't close your fingers."

We just look at it there for a moment. He says, "I love what you're doing with the Sunday morning sketches. You're on to something there. But don't grasp. When God gives you something, you've got to hold it loosely. Let *Him* steer the ship."

Soon after, we had a little get-together at Claude and Lilly's pad to fellowship (lingo lesson: fellowship is a verb) and break bread with Frank and his family. Our band of ministry hopefuls decided that it would be cool to test the waters with Frank and get his feedback on our collective endeavors and ideas. We hoped that maybe he would have some words of insight for us.

We had a lovely lunch, and afterward their two kids jumped up and offered to take care of all the dishes. We were all very impressed. Teenagers. Offering to do dishes. How unusual.

We sat on the floor around the coffee table and laid out our dreams about the band and music and arts in ministry. He was supportive, although he did caution us against jumping ahead of God. Something about still having some maturing to do. After some prayer time, he had a few words for us. For me:

(February12) "You *are a worrier and tend to allow anxiety to rule. At these times you need to rest in Jesus. Turn your anxious energy toward intercession* [prayer]. *You are the motivating force behind your husband, but you need to rest in his leadership. Your tendency to worry leads to nagging. It's okay to encourage and motivate, but be careful not to nag. Mike is a special gift to you from the Lord—he brings you balance.* [Well, Amen to that, brother, that he does.]

Who me? Worrier? So, fine. He pretty much nailed me on that one, but nag? Really?

For Mike:

"I see *integrity and a solid foundation. I see a mantle of leadership upon you, but be aware; there is also a tendency to take your eyes off the Lord and put them on yourself when success comes in the areas of your gifting.*"

In other words: Yes you rock. Don't get cocky.

He also said he got a word that his evangelism extraordinaire show would do extensive international touring in the year to come. He'd been doing some fairly aggressive promotion of the whole hullapalooza complete with slide presentations, songs, and scene excerpts. The pastors were pretty excited about it.

There seemed to be all kinds of divine artistic energy swirling around us: the drama ministry, the band, Frank and his whole gig. As long as we kept our hearts right and trusted God for the details, I was convinced that something big was just around the corner. But this was also a mindset that was intensely propagated in the Church. Whether it was the next big Revival or your own personal advancement, the urge to strain forward could be very strong, like the urge to push out that baby.

೧೨

My heart is pounding in my chest and I'm feeling a bit barfy as Miriam and I sit in her car for a last review of our meeting strategy. My gaze is stuck on the windshield, at the wreckage of a moth that has met its unfortunate demise: death by wiper blade.

"You hold his arms down and I'll stuff the script in his mouth," Miriam says. She smiles at me, takes a last drag off her Virginia Slim, and blows sideways out the window. There's still two-thirds of it left, but she carefully snubs it out, putting the remnant back in the pack. Nobody at ALCF smokes—except Miriam. When she smokes I feel like we're a couple of teenagers in the school bathroom: all rebellious and sneaky, a secret little thrill.

She gives herself a quick squirt across the chest and hair with her Impulse body spray and pops a Breathsaver into her mouth. Mysterious Musk fills the car. Her taboo ritual and recalcitrant humor somehow calm me. I check myself in the visor mirror. Pale.

"I'm dreading this," I say. I check my shirt for signs of sweat.

"Look, Kathy, this was totally underhanded and unfair. Something has to be said." She has a way of bringing me back into my skin, reminding me of my worth. "Leadership can't just walk on people—no regard for people's time, money, effort; not to mention their feelings."

Pastor Chris informed us the day before that we needed to revamp our sketch for the upcoming Sunday service. This was our third sketch—a sketch we'd spent three weeks preparing—and we're supposed to just dump it and come up with something else because pastor Jim decided not to use the sermon topic he'd sent us. Though this wasn't the first time we'd been blind-sided by leadership, we were still stunned. And pissed.

"I don't know why this makes me so nervous," I say. I try to unsmudge the smudgy mascara under my bottom lashes.

"Because you keep forgetting that these guys are just guys, and you keep caring what they think about you," she says.

We'd fumed and ranted and prepared our argument. But now that it's coming down to it, I'm losing my grip on my aplomb. Miriam, however, has both barrels loaded.

And it's a good thing she does, because once we sit face-to-face with our leader, I freeze like a little girl in the headlights.

Miriam wields her reproof like finely honed Elvish steel.

"So we're just wondering if you would explain to us why you felt it was okay to just pull this sketch at the last possible moment."

"Explain?" Jim seems genuinely surprised and a little confused. He smiles widely at us.

"We're wondering if you considered at all the impact your decision might have on the people involved." Miriam looks at me like, *feel free to jump in any time here Kath.*

My lungs expand involuntarily, and I'm suddenly thinking that I might possibly be levitating or just in a weird dream. *Get a grip, woman!*

"We know you must have a good reason," I finally manage.

"I don't feel that I need to explain myself to you, but I will say that I felt the Lord was leading me in a different direction, and I had to be obedient to that," he says.

"I have to ask you, Jim," Miriam says. She sounds like a corporate exec at a big board meeting: so cool, such confidence. Jim squares his shoulders. She continues, "When we agreed to enter into this partnership, what was it you imagined we would be doing? Were you thinking that we would just be throwing together some cute little skits for you?"

Jim's eyebrows fly up. My armpits start to tingle. I can't speak. My job is to joke and charm, not calmly and intelligently point out the errors of authority, so I'm no help whatsoever.

"I wonder if it occurs to you how many hours go into the preparation for these sketches." She's taking a binder out of her briefcase. "I thought it might help you to see, for example . . ." She pops open the binder rings, *snap*, pulls out a legal sized spreadsheet that's been folded at the end to fit neatly into the volume. "This particular sketch has about twenty hours of writing time invested, another twenty hours of rehearsal with eight cast and crew members, all volunteer, of course; not to mention expenses for printing of scripts and transportation to and from rehearsals, all paid for by said volunteers." She pauses for a moment. I hold my breath.

"Look, Miriam," Jim says. He's smiling, again. His eyes are bright like steely marbles. "I understand that you're upset, and I appreciate that you two have been so committed to doing these skits. You've been faithful, and the Word says, 'Be faithful in little and He will make you faithful in much . . .'"

Oh my. He's quoting scripture at her . . . about our skits. Oh my. I think I hear a shotgun being cocked, *chuck-chuck!*

"Forgive me, Jim," Miriam says. Her voice is calm, her cheeks a little flushed, which makes her freckles stand out. "But I must say that you obviously don't appreciate our commitment. Nor do you respect our training, our expertise, nor our time or resources. You have not been supportive in providing anything in this endeavor, least of all space to rehearse or time in the sanctuary for technical considerations. And now to completely brush off the many hours of people's time and hard work to bring something of excellence to the Sunday morning service—I guess I should just turn that scripture right back around to you, Jim."

"Whoa, whoa, there Miriam. I'm going to have to ask you to calm down."

She actually is quite calm. I'm trying to wrap my mind around how she can so boldly confront someone in such a position of authority without losing her composure. I'm in awe of my brave friend.

Jim says, "As I said, I appreciate that you and your team have worked hard to put these ski—sketches together. But when I say that I'm being lead in a different direction, then I'm sorry, but I just don't need to explain that to you. This is the decision I've made, and you're just going to have to learn to be flexible."

"Then I guess we're through here," Miriam says, closing her binder with another sharp snap.

I can't stand up and gather my purse and sweater fast enough.

"Thanks for your time," I mumble. And we're out of there.

And so, our regularly scheduled "show" just got . . . well, canceled, before it even got started.

CH- CH- CH- CHANGES

After a year at Vista Manor, it was becoming all too clear to me that I wasn't cut out for social work and wasn't going to survive it for another year without needing to be put in a home myself. Our initial plan was to stay for two years, long enough to pay off our debt and have a little nest egg. I was trying to love the clients in the name of Jesus, but it seemed like I was just becoming more and more impatient and downright cranky with them. I dreaded our weeks on duty. We decided that we wouldn't be signing up for round two.

We started looking and soon found a sweet little Cleaver house that I fell in love with, but was a bit out of our price range and a ways from church. Of course, we prayed and I agonized over whether we should *step out in faith*.

Mike was able to work out a deal with the landlord—a little yard work barter and some kind of payment plan for the deposit. We had the gift of resourcefulness, and that often had a way of paying off.

Ah yes, another gift came about this time as well. In the midst of all the hubbub and upheaval, a lovely surprise indeed, the other most favorite thing that ever happened in my life (there are three all together): our second little sprout was planted. Bambino numero dos.

☙

Mike and Claude and the boys were turning out to have a pretty nice sound together. They officially dubbed the band "Surrender."

They were asked to be the official *Outreach Band* for the evangelism team trip to our sister-church located in: Manila (!) They would do a couple concerts on the college campus and then lead worship for the evening and Sunday services.

"The Philippines?" I'd been thinking more along the lines of a US tour, maybe the Hollywood Bowl. I'm trying not to panic.

"Wow. Cool. How long will you be gone?"

"Ten days."

Pout.

"It's a great opportunity for us. Pastor Jim is pretty excited about the band."

"Of course he is. You're guys."

They *were* very hip and cool—Mike in his pink snakeskin pants (yes he still had them), Claude in his grungy jeans and white T-shirts, the right mix of mullets and feathered and clean cut—they had the look and the sound goin' on. They were the boys for the job.

So off to the distant exotic land of crazy jeepney drivers and maligamgam eggs my hubby flew. For ten days—the longest we'd ever been apart in our seven years of marriage—he was an official, church sanctioned, on-fire, gospel-preaching rock-star.

(July 17) *Surrender and the rest of the team went to Manila for 10 days. Been through lots of ups and downs since I last wrote. Retaliation from the Enemy for the work done in the Philippines.* [Translation: My emotional struggles are an attack by Satan in response to Mike's evangelistic endeavors in the Philippines.] *Many lives changed—many snatched from the realm of darkness and added to the church. Mike was visibly touched. He got such a rush out of the intense Gospel sharing. God is undoubtedly moving in and with the band.*

This was the gig I was sure would launch the rock-n-roll ministry we all hoped for. From our humble beginnings, dreaming in Claude and Lilly's tiny living room, to the far off shores of Manila; we were on our way to Christian fame and glory: singing, dancing, and saving souls.

SURRENDER

YEP, THAT HAIR. THOSE GLASSES.

✌

"I don't know what you mean by your way," said the Queen: *"all the ways about here belong to me."*

~The Red Queen, Through the Looking-Glass

After Mike's return from the Philippines, everything seemed to begin shifting and changing for us. It seemed like God was getting tired of our current jigsaw and was crumbling the pieces into a pile and reconfiguring the picture into some new puzzle.

At some point the pastors got it into their collective head that it would be a great idea for them to take into their own hands the redistribution of human potential throughout the homegroup system. Rearrange the chess pieces, as it were. In other words, they wanted to be the ones to decide who got to hang out with whom. So they unplugged families from one homegroup and reinserted them into another.

And so my sweet Lilly and her Claude were assigned to another homegroup where they could establish new relationships and where their gifts could be shared with another part of the church body. Gotta spread around those guitar players.

Perhaps the leaders were just bored. Perhaps they worried that the tribbles would get ideas and start planning their revolt. Who knows? All I knew was that they were yanking Lilly and Claude out of our life and sending them off to build community with other folks. I saw this as leadership meddling with people's relationships and it pissed me off and messed me up.

I finally found what I thought I was looking for—friends that I felt I had a covenant with, that I had a future with, that felt close as family. Now my leaders were telling me to let them go, to find someone else to bond with (apparently, *covenant relationships* were something allowed only for those at the top). I was utterly confused and honestly becoming disturbed by this seeming manipulation of people's lives. It was starting to feel to me less and less like a family and more and more like some kind of big corporation or institution. Did I say anything?

Of course not.

We remained close with Claude and Lilly, but as I feared, they began investing more and more time in their new friendships and other ministry opportunities. *Surrender* lost steam as the individual band members turned their attention toward other things like solo projects, marriage, careers, and growing up.

Also, during this whole time of rearranging, another pastor was added to the church leadership line-up—yes, another, because six wasn't enough—and he loved to sing. He was a favorite sent to us by the DOD leaders. In short order, through some delicate slight of hand, Ron was driving the worship team from the back seat and the new guy was now front and center. This move left a lot of people scratching their heads, not the least of whom was Ron. There was no announcement or vote. Just a switcheroo I guess they hoped no one would notice. This kind of behavior at the top, however, was beginning to chip away at my confidence in the absolute impeccability of our leaders. It wasn't anything I was articulating yet; on the contrary, it was executed so subtly and justified so skillfully that I just couldn't bring my reaction to it to the surface of my consciousness. Especially since I had so thoroughly immersed myself into the belief that our pastors carried some kind of God ordained anointing that elevated them above all reproach or questioning. But it was there, swimming around so deep that it was like glimpsing darting shadows in the murky depths of a swampy pond. Despite my acquiescence, I started to harbor dissension against the way this ship was being run. It was about this time that I secretly re-dubbed Disciples of Destiny: The Mother Ship.

NEBUCHADNEZZAR TOUCHDOWN

What you know you can't explain, but you feel it. You don't know what it is, but it's there, like a splinter in your mind, driving you mad.

~Morpheus

As life in Church was beginning to dry up and curl around the edges, a new couple entered our world and although they didn't wear awesome cape-like leather jackets and supercool frameless magical-stay-on-your-nose shades, they were instrumental in the beginnings of our awakening from Wonderland.

Matt and Cheryl were atypical of the kind of folk that inhabited our church world. In fact, they were complete foreigners. But the brief year or so they sojourned among us was one for which I am ever so grateful.

Matt and Cheryl blew into ALCF like a fresh breeze on a smoggy summer day. I still don't understand what drew them there in the first place. Perhaps God sent them—armed and dangerous—as a rescue team for our family.

As I've said before, the doctrines and teachings that underlie the doctrines and teachings of our leadership were very tricky and hard to get square in the center of one's sights right away. As many years as Matt and Cheryl had walked with God before coming to ALCF, even they didn't spot the rot right away.

Matt and Cheryl did well for themselves, and they weren't ashamed of enjoying the fruit of Matt's labors. They lived in an upscale neighborhood, shopped at Costco, and belonged to the country club. Cheryl was an ace tennis player and could work that funny little skirt like nobody's business. Matt obviously enjoyed Cheryl's sexiness and didn't attempt to hide his hots for her. They were a little bit older than us and had three kids, one of whom was a teenager. They'd been married for like a million years but were still very outwardly affectionate if not out-and-out horny.

Mike and Matt hit it off right away, since Matt was a drummer extraordinaire. He had played with one of the first Christian Rock bands back in the 60s when hippies were really hippies and some of them were Jesus freaks. I knew we were gonna get along well when I saw Matt's photo on one of their albums (they cut three) from back in the day, when he had amazing giant hair, like mine, only ginger colored.

Their youngest micro-unit (this was Matt's loving term for *kid*) was Em's age and they were instant best buddies.

Matt and Cheryl both had hearts of gold and treated us like family from the get-go. And salt of the earth? Boy were they salty—kindred salt. And straightforward . . .

Cheryl, another church lady, and I stand outside together after women's Bible study group. Sunshine, birds chirping, children scampering and squawking after their release from the kid wrangler.

"I've been so irritable," Church Lady is saying. "Maybe it's hormones? I don't know; he comes home from work and then disappears into his den. I can't even remember the last time we had a date night."

"And sex?" Cheryl says.

"Excuse me?"

"Sex. Regular orgasms are very helpful," Cheryl says. "They cheer me right up." She laughs—a big wide-open laugh—and grabs my arm like she needs me to keep her from falling down.

"I . . . b—I . . . uh, well . . ." Church Lady says. A red glow is rolling up her neck and into her cheeks. She laughs nervously.

"Jeeeez, you're a married woman! What, have you never gotten laid? You've got four kids for God's sake," Cheryl says, of course, in the most amiable, if somewhat pitying way.

I just giggle and fall in love a little more. Hairline cracks were beginning to appear in the walls of Wonderland and a glorious light was spilling through.

ON THE WINGS OF ANGELS . . . AND JULIOS

Now that we were once again living in our own space and expecting our second little bundle, we began to feel the pinch. A friend of ours was looking for a place to live. I was loath to enter into another shared household situation, but he was as sweet a guy as could be, absolutely adored Emily, and we had a spare bedroom with its own bath. It was a no-brainer.

Angel and Mike were friends from way back before our tumble down the rabbit hole. They both had worked as temps at Bank of America. Angel was having some emotional struggles, and Mike invited him to church (this was back at our old church) and introduced him to pastor Terry. Angel was a gay Puertorriqueño with shiny black hair that he meticulously quaffed into a tight afro-mullet. He thought Mike was a hottie. Mike just liked Angel as a friend. At work, they would hang out at lunch together and talk about the Bible and life and stuff. Angel and pastor Terry hit it off well, and at some point, Angel gave his life to Jesus and with Terry's gentle prompting, decided to try to abstain from his homosexual "lifestyle."

When we joined ALCF, we kind of lost touch with Angel for a while, but he eventually reemerged, and before long, he was attending ALCF regularly. Like any good Christian ex-gay, he jumped into church life and took heterosexuality for a spin. He hung out with the singles group, got involved in street ministry and with my drama group (he was a salsa and ballroom dancer extraordinaire; we knew that somehow God would find a way to use that). Angel was head-over-heels for Em and soon we pretty much adopted him into our little family.

For a while, people at ALCF didn't realize that the gentle boy from Puerto Rico was of *that persuasion*. But on the heels of a sermon about confessing your persistent sins before the assembly, Angel made up his mind that he wanted to make a public declaration, renouncing his homosexuality. Mike tried to talk him out of it. He warned him that he would not be understood nor embraced and that he was only opening himself up to heartache and judgment. Angel was determined to do the *right thing*, so he confided his story to the pastors and made arrangements to give his confession.

The church had recently installed brand new gigantic screens on both sides of the auditorium that allowed for broadcasting the face of whomever was speaking all the way to the houses on the next block over. So when Angel's time came, Mike and I watched with heavy hearts as he, with his giant face splashed across two billboard-size screens, bared his soul with tears and genuine repentance. Afterwards, there were some encouraging words, prayers, and hugs for Angel, but he was never treated the same again after that day. It was subtle, as always, but we knew it and so did he, although he didn't speak of it for a long time.

Angel had a brother, Julio. Angel had been sharing his new found salvation with his brother and finally succeeded in getting him to come to church too. Julio was also gay, but he was deeply unhappy and in search of true connection and a sense of acceptance and love. Well, he found the right place. The loving folks of our church embraced him with open arms and no judgment. Well kinda.

Eventually, Julio too came to know Jesus and forswore his attraction to the stronger sex. This was a hard thing indeed, but with careful discipleship and guidance he came to see that God wanted him to have a wife and be normal like everyone else. This made everyone feel much more comfortable.

Mike and I grew very close with Angel and Julio. Soon after Angel moved in with us, Julio took our third bedroom and we were indeed a happy little ex-gay Puerto Rican-American family. Em loved them and took to calling them both Uncle. They were amazing with her and except for the fact that they both left their aftershave on everything they touched, including the community block of cheddar cheese (which drove me batty), we got along quite amiably. Angel taught me to make Arroz con Pollo, and I taught him to make homemade mac-n-cheese supreme.

"You are a good cooker!" he used to tell me.

We lived together for about seven months. As the time neared for our bun to come out of the oven, Mike and I decided, once again, that we needed to spread out into our own space. We also wanted to live closer to church, as we were currently about thirty minutes away, in an adjacent city. Angel and Julio decided to get their own place together.

Shortly after that, Julio fell in love. With a lady. A lovely church lady. She was a single mom and highly prized by the leadership. She and Julio were spending quite a bit of time together and of course, he was amazing with her kids as well. This did not escape the notice of the pastors, and the situation was alarming them.

Pastor Len called Julio into his office and in no uncertain terms told him that he was absolutely forbidden from having any further contact with Single Mom Church Lady until he could prove that he did not carry the AIDS virus, which, unfortunately, he could not do—because Julio was HIV positive.

When Mike found out about this outrageous act of bullying, he confronted Pastor Len. Len told him that this lady was under his covering and that it was his responsibility to protect her. This was the decision of the leadership, and if Julio was truly saved and committed, he would abide by that decision, or else help himself to the door—which, of course, he did.

Julio and Angel both were deeply wounded by this blatant homophobic behavior, but for some strange reason Angel stayed. For a while. Julio moved out of their apartment and in with friends. Non-church friends.

Now one might think that this behavior alone was cause for Mike and I to head for . . . well, just about anywhere else, but we were stuck fast. At that time, I in no way accepted or embraced Angel and Julio's sexual orientation on a doctrinal level. I held to the love the sinner but not the sin mentality. However, it was a topic that I had never entered into discussion about with either of them. My brain had been thoroughly washed with the notion that being homosexual was a lifestyle choice, one that was utterly disdained by God. I disagreed with the way their situation was handled; nevertheless, I did nothing. Said nothing.

Prior to slipping and falling down the deep hole, many of my friends in the theatre and dance world were gay. I never gave it a second thought; they were who they were. I didn't fully understand it; I just accepted it. Once

I began learning about what the Bible and the Church had to say about it, I went along with the program—didn't want to be accused of swallowing a camel. I never crossed over into full-blown homophobia, I just kind of steered clear of the subject if at all possible.

Somehow Angel and Julio had both been convinced of the church's absolute stance on the sinfulness of homosexuality. They tried to commit themselves to being something else, someone else's idea of what was right. In retrospect, I know that this is rarely possible. Not without terrible emotional and psychological consequences. This in and of itself should give one pause to reconsider the *lifestyle choice* paradigm. Is it a *choice*? At any rate, somebody else did the dirty work and messed with these boys' hearts and psyches. I suppose I'm guilty by association for the damage done. The only thing I can say is that I loved those two brothers, and I wish like hell I could take it all back.

SHOW ME THE MONEY

"I think I should understand that better," Alice said very politely, "if I had it written down: but I can't quite follow it as you say it."
~Alice, Alice's Adventures in Wonderland

There were so many doctrines and beliefs put forth in church that I accepted without question, even though they were diametrically opposed to everything I knew to be true. There were some teachings that we were expected to swallow, however, that from the get-go turned sideways and lodged firmly in my craw. The subject of giving was one of those. Even though outwardly we nodded yes and Amen'd and dutifully gave our tithes and offerings, I always secretly bristled when this topic was addressed from the pulpit. Let's face it; it was hard to be poor and giving your widow's mites to the guys in the suits with the nice homes and cars.

We were a house of highly compelled and enthusiastic givers. Tithing (giving ten percent of your gross income) was considered an act of faithfulness and obedience that ranked in importance right up there with, say, breathing. Special offerings for special speakers, building fund, pastor appreciation day, supporting The Mother Ship . . . these were equally stressed, right up there with say, using your inhaler.

The following statements (well, half of them) are taken from an actual teaching on giving:

"Everything you have belongs to God; you are His steward."

"But I'm broke and in debt."

"You're first indebted to God. You must not rob God to pay others. Tithe and be blessed. Don't tithe and be cursed. It's up to you."

"But I thought we were no longer under The Law."

"Jesus requires more than The Law. This is God's test. Will you pass?"

"But do we tithe on the gross or the net?"

"The gross, of course. And don't forget profits on investment, cash birthday and Christmas gifts, money given to you, the hundred bucks you made on the yard sale, and the penny you picked up and put in your shoe last week."

"Okay. I guess my kids can figure out how to pay for college."

"Oh yes, and your kids, don't forget about them."

"Wait. What? You mean I gotta give my kids?"

"Oh yes. It all belongs to Him. Well, your firstborn son anyway. In Exodus God tells us, 'You shall set apart to the Lord all that first opens the womb. All the firstborn of your animals that are males shall be the Lord's. Every firstborn of a donkey you shall redeem with a lamb, or if you will not redeem it you shall break its neck. Every firstborn of man among your sons you shall redeem.'"

"Holy Crap—sorry, I mean wow! Break my kid's neck? Wait. What the hell does this have to do with money now?"

"It's a lordship issue."

"Oh, well, since you put it that way."

∽

There were always plenty of opportunities for giving. Each year, there was a strong push for everyone in the congregation to make a pilgrimage to a far off land to take part in a regional conference hosted by DOD corporate headquarters (The Mother Ship). People from church plants across the country made the trek to hear from the DOD Fathers. It was a four-day soirée filled with lively worship services, dynamic teaching, and an extended time of fellowship. Many among the well-known higher-ups were to be there to enlighten us with their wisdom, bringing the Word with great authority and style. We were sure to come away filled with vision and mightily equipped to take hold of our destiny.

Although attendance was not "required" (because it wasn't free), the appeal to our deepest needs, desires, and fears was made with great marketing savvy. If there was any way to scrape together the resources to go, one did so. And heck, who didn't need a vacation? Bless their hearts; the organizers did do their best to make sure that there were lodging alternatives for those of us lower on the economic scale. Because the conference was held at a university, dorm rooms and cafeteria passes were available as a part of the hillbilly package—we were all over that.

Carpooling helped save on gas too; our new friends Matt and Cheryl offered to give us a lift. It was fun to have company, and the seven-hour drive through the desert with two families stuffed into a truck with a camper shell wasn't so bad either. Well, having a kid barf on you in the back of the truck wasn't so fun. (Glad it was Mike and not me; I rode up front, in the air-conditioned comfort of the extra-cab—I was pregnant. Don't judge me.) But it made it possible for us to go and be a part of this holy extravaganza.

As promised, our supreme leaders from DOD, Tom Lorrack and Chuck Mulroney, plus Pastor Jim and Len, and a number of other well known speakers gave their most compelling sermons about being true people of destiny, people called for such an hour as this, poised on the threshold of revival. The music and worship times were sweet and the atmosphere was highly charged with a sense of nebulous anticipation.

The whole shindig was to culminate in a huge celebration on the final day. What we didn't fully understand was that the main point of the final service was to lather us up for the big pitch. Yep, you got it. The whole shebang was a brightly colored packaging for a full on, unabashed, Give-Fest, all proceeds of which would directly benefit Disciples of Destiny.

Now, I figured that an offering would be taken—this is to be expected at any Christian gathering—but once again, I had to wrestle my rebellious streak into submission. My little money-grubbing demon just got so irked by this scenario: well-to-do ministers of the Gospel asking the lowly sheep for more. Nay, not asking. Not really.

And by this point, we were all tired, and I was more than a little grumpy. After four full days of non-stop services; lumpy mattresses cradled in sagging, squeaking metal jail cots; lukewarm cafeteria food; listening to our neighbor retching all night from said epicurean fare; dragging my big round belly, a toddler, her potty chair, and her thirty-pound bag of books (yes, we were in the middle of potty-training, and Em required a minimum of a dozen books to be read while making a poopie) from one end of the vast campus to the other for meetings, all in one-hundred-plus degree heat, it's a wonder they got one damn dime out of any of us. But they did. MANY dimes. Luckily, they had a monthly payment plan to break up that big fat sacrificial offering. But hey, it kept The Mother Ship afloat and headed toward her Destiny.

And the special guests of honor, well, it was a grueling travel, speaking, and teaching schedule and all, but they did ok. We made sure they were taken care of at the Hyatt so they could get their beauty rest. Oh, and the special-special offering helped offset their off-campus meals. And their flights. And their stipends. It was a tough row to hoe, but it's the price one must pay for a holy calling.

Now, I can't help but wonder how these guys got away with such a thinly veiled heist. I mean, we paid to attend the silly thing, and they were all on salary as it was. I'm just sayin'. But I wouldn't have dared to think it back then. No, I did the godlier thing; I kept it locked up in my inner-most psyche in case I might, years later, want to see what chronic fatigue or PTSD was like.

Wonderland was a land of mixed messages. This made it so hard to look this sort of thing square in the eye and call it what it was: manipulation and usury. Surely these men of integrity were operating out of the most noble of intentions, weren't they? And after all, we got something out of it. Didn't we?

MIRACLE BABY

Timothy: One who honors God. David: Beloved of God. Martens: Of superhero lineage.

A medical doctor and scholar crunched the numbers and came up with the odds of you or I actually having been born. His computations concluded that probability of you or I existing at all calculates to 1 in $10^{2,685,000}$ (yep, 10 followed by 2,685,000 zeroes). Before he was even born, our son illustrated this weird math: when his big sister tried to kill him.

I just said that for dramatic affect. We did almost lose him early on in the pregnancy though. One fine afternoon we were hanging out with Claude and Lilly. I was about four months pregnant and I was reclining on the living room floor, legs outstretched, propped up on my elbows. Em was scampering around the room jabbering her hilarious gibberish and pretending one of her fanciful pretends when, without warning, she came trotting up beside me, turned around, and plopped herself down, right on my tummy. She probably only weighed a scant twenty-five pounds, but she sat down with the force of a Monday Night Football fan dropping back in her Barkalounger after a missed touchdown pass. Besides having the wind knocked out of me, I didn't notice any other pain.

Two days later, I started to bleed. A lot. Coincidence? Maybe. But Em was truly a force of nature and not one to be trifled with; she may have been getting an early jump on letting this little interloper know who was boss.

Mike and Emily laid hands on my tummy, and we prayed for God's healing intervention to stop the cramping and bleeding. We stood firm on our vision of a blessed life for our son. That day, the bleeding stopped.

❦

A month and a half to go. Still no name.

"I guess we ought'ta decide. We can't just let the little feller be nameless," I say.

Mike sidles up beside me on the couch. "Feller? You know this?" He runs his big hand over my round belly like a fortuneteller with a crystal ball.

"I have a feeling. And I look like I've shoplifted a basketball." I hold my tummy with both hands—it pokes straight out, like I could just detach it and hand it to Mike to hold. "I've read boys like to ride high and up front. Girls tend to stretch out wide and low."

"Now that just sounds— "

"Hey! Baby in the room," I say. "We need to decide. Unless you want to wait 'til he's born and just call him Baby. Or Hey Kid."

"So if she's a she—I still like Laura Anne," Mike says.

"I like that too. That would make my mom happy."

"But I don't think Miss Em is gonna allow another girl, so if he's a he—"

"I'm sorry, honey, I really don't feel right about Mike Junior," I say. He makes a pouty face. "I'm sorry. I just feel weird about the junior thing.

You'd never know which one of you I was yelling at."

"You don't love me."

"Don't say that. He'll hear you." I cover the baby's ears—where I think they are. "Besides, there could only ever be one Mike Martens," I say.

"Fine. Next time we get a puppy, we're naming it Mike," he says.

"Why don't we pray about it," I say.

We pray together, nothing lengthy or grand, simply asking God to impress upon us the name of our son. We sit in the quiet for a while.

"I'm thinking Timothy," I say. "A young leader who's genuine in his faith, wise beyond his years, and not afraid to stand firm, even in the face of intimidation or hardship."

"I'm thinking David," Mike says. "A worshipper who isn't afraid to dance around in his Underoos." And so was chosen our son's name.

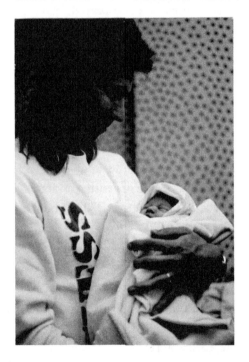

Six weeks later, in the wee hours of a fine spring morning, Timothy David Martens was born. The doctor set our wet and wriggling son atop my belly, arms and legs stretching and pedaling vigorously, unfolding fully for the first time. I raised my head and gazed at the biggest pair of feet I had ever seen on a newborn baby, ten perfect toes topping a promise of great height. Our jolly Jamaican nurse laughed a deep voluminous laugh as she scooped up our new joy declaring:

"Look at doze balls! Doze is de biggest balls I'evah seen on a new bahn child!"

Mike puffed out his chest. "Yes, well, he is a Martens boy!"

Tim and Em were pals from the day he breathed air and continue to share a precious closeness that is unique and rare. I'm so grateful that her evil plot to take him out was foiled. I can't imagine our lives without such a sweet, loving, and truehearted boy. I know Em would agree that she couldn't wish for a better brother and partner in childhood adventure.

৩

Our church had a cool ministry that organized meals to be brought to new mothers so they didn't have to cook for two weeks after the baby came. This was amazingly helpful for me since we were now living on our own. We would have to eat pancakes every night if it was left to Mike (he does, however, make delectable pancakes).

Cheryl sweetly brought a meal to us after Tim was born. She stayed and visited for a bit while our two little girls reveled in their reunion. After watching me change Tim's tiny diaper, they ran around the house with gleeful peals of laughter as they squealed "Eeeeeew! Poopie!" This went on and on, a never-ending source of cheerful amusement for them and for Cheryl and me.

Our friendship with Matt and Cheryl was blossoming and our two little girls were becoming fast friends. We frequently had dinner with them, usually at their house because it was huge and beautiful, and ours was, well it was small and homely (homey yes, but mostly homely). As I said, they had their financial poodoo together and we were still among the abject poor. Going to their house was like a mini vacation for me. It was a taste of how real grown ups lived. They had a massive backyard complete with a tree fort and a swing set and miles of lawn. Green lawn. Without weeds. It was a joy to watch our girls go bounding across it without going "Oooooo! Ow! Eeee! Oooo! Ow!" as they ran. Cheryl didn't hold a regular job. She mostly just raised her awesome kids, kept their gorgeous home, and played tennis.

She would invite me to bring the kids over, and we'd sip iced tea as we lounged on color coordinated deck furniture on the back patio, while Em and her bosom friend had adventures on the great green sea. Two sweet peas, they both loved pink and yellow flowery dresses and hair ribbons, and several years later both concurrently joined the ranks of the tomboys, ne'er to wear a dress again for many moons.

For me, Cheryl became a deep well of God's grace. That's Christianese for she was so free, so comfortable to just be who she was without the need to fit someone else's idea of how a godly woman should look or act. This gave me permission to just be myself as well (when I was around her at least). I loved this dangerous liaison with freedom. It was fascinating to me that these crazy ex-hippies could love God so passionately while in no way resembling the only example I had experienced so far of devout followers of Jesus. They continued to hold onto their individuality within a very compelling atmosphere of conformity.

"And Father, please help Cheryl to be the mom you've called her to be, grant her your sovereign grace that she might be able to sort out her priorities as a wife and mother, and be free from anything that may be binding her, like a Spirit of Tennis."

No joke. This (or something damn close) was prayed over Cheryl one Sunday when she asked for prayer for her son who was struggling with some emotional issues. Yikes. It's a wonder she didn't slap that church lady upside the head. I think I may have in my mind. Cheryl was a fiercely committed, adoring mother and Matt a loving and devout father, albeit their parenting practices in no way mirrored those of ALCF leadership.

SHOT TO THE HEART

One morning, Mike comes downstairs heading for the shower. He pops his head into the kitchen. His spikey mullet has been smashed flat and pushed to one side so it's now pointing due west. Tim's in his little baby seat perched on the kitchen table watching me make toast.

"I had the worst dream," Mike says. "It was so real. And messed up." He glances toward where Em is playing just outside the kitchen back door in our mini-backyard. If I threw a rock from where I stand, it would hit our neighbor's kitchen back door.

"I came home from work and the house was empty. I could hear the faint sound of Em crying. It was all muffled. I couldn't figure out where it was coming from, so I called out for her, but I couldn't find her anywhere."

"Where was I?"

"You weren't here. I finally came in here, in the kitchen, and right here," he walks over and points to the floor in front of the pantry cupboard, "there was a big stack of heavy books on the floor, and I could hear Em crying underneath it."

"Under the books?"

"Yeah. I mean, no. She was underneath the floorboards. I moved the books and I could see her through a knothole in the floor. She was buried under there, crying." He runs his hands through his hair; a large vein has popped out on his forehead.

"That's awful." I put down my butter knife and caress his shoulder.

"I don't know how she got there, " he says.

"What an awful dream. I wonder where that came from."

"I was lying in bed thinking about it after I woke up. I was so upset. I prayed about it."

"Did you get anything from the Lord?"

"Yeah. I think so. I want to talk to you about it."

I take Em her toast and some milk in her favorite pink sippy-cup. She sits at her Little Tikes picnic table for a morning tea party with her stufties. Mike and I sit at the kitchen table. He lays Tiny Tim in his lap, nestling him in the space where his thighs meet. He gazes at his boy.

"I think the dream was from God," he says.

"Really? I would think the opposite."

"No, I think it has to do with how we're disciplining her. I feel like God was saying that we're piling so many rules on top of her and being so strict with spanking that we're kind of . . . burying her. I think it was a metaphor for that." He looks at me. The blue of his eyes has gone almost purple.

"What do you mean? Like, that the Lord wants us to stop disciplining her?"

"No. Well, I don't know. I just think he's saying we expect too much from her. She gets punished for the littlest thing. I just think he's saying it's too much."

My heart sinks. Confusion nips at my mind: *What about all our training? What about leading a child in the way he should go? We're just following the rules as laid out and practiced by our Godly leaders; why would the Lord contradict them?*

So, then, it gets bizarre:

A week or so later, Cheryl stops by to see me. Mike's at work. She seems kind of upset as she comes in the house.

We're in the kitchen, and she stands there, in her little tennis skirt; her short muscular legs are sun kissed and freckled. Hands on her hips, she looks me square in the eyes and says, "You're killing your kid."

You remember I told you Cheryl's a straight shooter.

"I'm sorry to be so blunt, but we love you guys, and we love Emily, and you're killing her spirit with your heavy-handed spanking and disciplining. She's just a kid, and she can't even breathe without getting a damn spanking; you're suffocating her."

I have no response to this. The old feeling of hot shame rushes into my cheeks. But this shame is more akin to guilt. Guilt being produced by truth. I know she's right. Then I remember Mike's dream.

Words cannot convey how grateful I am to this day for Cheryl's gut level honesty. This was correction that was coming from someplace very different than what I had become accustomed to from church people. It was coming from a place of genuine concern for our daughter's wellbeing, one of just plain old love.

I would like to say that we immediately abandoned spanking from that moment on. But, how then do we discipline? What about what the Bible says? What about everything our leadership taught us concerning discipline? After much discussion, we opted to lighten up on the use of the rod, saving it only for flagrant disobedience. Looking back, I honestly can't think of any reason why we should have needed to ever spank either of our children again. They were amazingly well behaved kids. But alas, we (I, really) didn't completely forsake the use of the rod for many years yet.

In discussing this with Mike recently, he confessed that he had disdained using the rod so much, that after his dream, his swats (which were few and far between anyway) had the force of a fly landing, and usually his hand was between the blow and the flesh. Cheater.

SEEING THE LIGHT

When she thought it over afterwards it occurred to her that she ought to have wondered at this, but at the time it all seemed quite natural.
                    ~From Alice's Adventures in Wonderland

Not long after, Matt and Cheryl began to share their concerns with us about some other things they were observing in the leadership practices of DOD and ALCF.

Cheryl and I sit in the shade of a wide patio umbrella. Mike had worked at this country club briefly when I was attending the Academy, but I'd never actually sat by the pool as a guest. I roll Tim's stroller back and forth with my foot in an attempt to keep him asleep. His copious curls are all sweaty and stuck together, cheeks flushed. His little round Buddha belly spills over the edge of his diaper, rising and falling rhythmically. Our two wet girls are laid out next to the wading pool on the hot concrete like two beached mackerels.

Cheryl stirs her iced tea. Her upper lip and forehead glisten. She slides her Ray-Bans off and looks at me.

"Have you ever heard of the Shepherding Movement?" she says.

"No, what's that?"

"We brushed up against this nasty thing back in the 70s. In the church we were a part of back when Matt and I first got saved. The pastors were emotionally abusing and manipulating people; it was all about control and building their own ministry platforms. At first it was subtle, but it just got sicker and sicker. It was called the Shepherding Movement. Sometimes I get glimpses of that here. It's upsetting." She dabs her chin with the back of her hand.

"So you think ALCF is part of the same thing?"

"The Shepherding Movement? Well, no, I think the movement itself is pretty much dead, although the guys that had a hand in starting the damn thing are all still in ministry. I'm not saying Jim and Len and the DOD guys are trying to carry this stuff on in a formal sense, but there are a lot of similarities. Child abuse—I mean disciplining techniques—aside, Matt and I are getting very concerned about the emphasis on doctrines of submission and obedience to Church authority. It just . . . well, it stinks."

I feel nervous that we're steering dangerously close to gossip, or subversion, or worse—speaking against Church leadership.

"Go on," I say.

Cheryl is buttering herself generously with sunscreen. Her bikini, while fairly conservative—bandeau top, skirty bottom—makes no apologies for her shapely figure. I, on the other hand, have adopted Luanne's style of swimming attire: one-piece, well covered by an oversized men's T-shirt and Bermuda shorts (and the T stays on for swimming). In another life, I would have worn the stringiest of strings while basking. Now modesty (and self-consciousness) reigns.

Cheryl says, "I keep hearing so many inferences—actually, no—out and out teaching from the pulpit that there's some kind of standard that has to be met in order to really please God. It can be so subtle, hard to pin down, but this emphasis on gaining spiritual acceptance by speaking the right speak, wearing the right skirt length, listening to the right music, being the right gender, drinking the right Kool-Aid; it's legalism, plain and simple, and Jesus hates it."

I somehow know she's speaking true, but it makes my head swim. I say, "It's weird, because it seems like they're always saying that we're saved by grace, but . . ."

"There's always a *but*. Some other behavior or requirement tacked onto the end of grace. Like, you're saved, yeah, but true right standing with God depends on the other hoops you gotta jump through. Religious perfectionism. Hey Ashe, come here, honey, and let me put some more sunscreen on you sweetie," she calls to her little befreckled sunflower.

The girls scamper over to us, and we slather them up and then set them loose like a couple of piglets at the county fair. They squeal and laugh as they dash back to the kiddie pool."

"No running!" Cheryl calls.

"Maybe that's why I'm so darn tired all the time," I say.

"From chasing kids?"

"From trying to please everyone."

"You think?" she says.

"Hey, how's my sexy woman?" Matt glides up behind Cheryl and kisses her on the neck. "Mmmmm, I like's 'em salty," he says and smacks his lips.

"Hey!" Cheryl laughs. "Whatcha doin? Stop by for a swim on your way home?"

Matt grabs another deck chair from an adjacent table and pulls it over to ours. His otherwise smartly pressed dress shirt has a roadmap of sweaty creases across the back. His tie hangs at half-mast and his top few buttons have been loosed.

"Yep. Called home, Meg said you were here. Thought I'd see if I could catch you in your bikini. Looks like I got lucky." He grins and pumps his eyebrows. "Hey, Kath, how ya doin'? Didn't know you'd be here too."

"We were just talking about legalism," Cheryl says.

"Ooooo. I'd much rather talk about grace," Matt says. When he smiles, his eyes go all soft, like a great big St. Bernard puppy dog.

"Daaaaad!!" Ashe hollers and capers over, flinging her wet body into her papa's lap.

"Hey! You're wet!" Matt says. He gives her a hug anyway, and she's off again. "No running," he calls.

As Matt begins to paint a picture of God's grace and the kind of rest we were meant to experience in our relationship with Him (Matt can always be counted on for sermonettes about love), I remember a brief time when I first met Jesus, when it was more like just hanging out with someone who loved me just the way I was and just knowing him made me cool with God. How had I lost sight of this?

"You know," Matt says, "Jesus said, 'Come to me, you who are weary and burdened, and I'll give you rest.' But I bet you didn't know he also said, 'Except for a few odd-balls like Fred Astaire and Gregory Hines, tap dancing is just too damn much work. Don't do it.'"

Matt leans over and plants a big smooch on Cheryl's lips. He pulls back and they just smile at each other for a moment. "See you later," he says.

"Yes, you will," she says.

"Ok," he says and smiles.

Oh my gosh, get a room you two.

So Jesus was like this wooden fishing boat called "Rest in Me" that offered a free ride along with afternoon naps, fruity cocktails, and pupus. But I had taken passage on the ship "Do As I Do," that offered indentured servitude along with endless rowing, watery Kool-Aid, and poo poos. Somehow, I had missed the better boat.

Not long after these conversations, Matt and Cheryl brought some of their concerns surrounding this topic of legalism to the church leadership. Of course they would. Despite their mature, unassuming, and diplomatic approach, they were kindly invited to use the back door, which, of course, they did post haste.

As a parting gift, they gave Mike and I a copy of a helpful little book called *The Subtle Power of Spiritual Abuse*. It woke us up. It finally gave us a name for the stuff about church that was nagging at our knowers.

In this world that we inhabited, there *was* no other world. Well, there was *The World*, which was defined as anything and everything that was not submitted to Jesus Christ as God and Savior—that world we were *in* but not *of*. What I mean is that in Wonderland, everything about life was connected to the Church. No area went untouched or unexamined (except, of course, the church leadership). Every activity, every relationship, every decision, was undertaken with the filter of Church dogma firmly in place. Redirecting all of life through this small peephole was difficult to maintain—it was also directly responsible for any varicose veins I now have. The constant reinforcement of these concepts through the sermons, songs, Bible studies, special teachings, one-on-one discipleship relationships and other programs, along with the irreproachability of our leaders, kept everything knit together and the ship floating along nicely.

Our conversations with the superhero duo and the new understanding we were gaining finally brought into sharp focus the need to take flight from Wonderland.

BREAKFAST IN BED

(August 22) . . . I have been struggling and striving to measure up. I have been whipping myself, denying myself and stuffing my feelings for years so that I would be recognized as a person of excellent character.

Now that some of these things have been brought into the light, I'm left confused, bitter, and unsure of myself and my ability to discern correct "philosophy." I have fears that I'll only fall for someone else's wrong or off teaching.

. . . I feel so torn, realizing how much of myself I have invested in our church. How I have based all of my life decisions around ALCF. How I have let the teachings of the church dictate who I am . . .

. . . I am so ready to know Him without all the rules and regulations, expectations, and heavy yoke . . .

The decision was made. We were goin' home. Back North to . . . well, to no friends, but at least to family that loved us and of course, to whom we might minister (yikes, somebody put that girl back in the closet).

The more we contemplated and discussed the spiritual abuse we had not only been subject to but had also perpetrated on others (most especially our own children), the more urgent became the need to get out.

We found ourselves increasingly withdrawn from ALCF, not in terms of attendance, but certainly in terms of active participation and interaction with folks. I felt like I was floating around in a sort of emotionally detached fog, not wanting to think too deeply about saying goodbye to people who had essentially been family to us for the last five-plus years. The little book of freedom that Matt and Cheryl gave us blasted open our horizons. It also scared me. The idea that we would be making our own choices and living our own lives without seeking the approval or okay from some authority figure was a daunting to me. Would this be too much freedom? I'd been thoroughly convinced that to be out of Church was to be out of God's protection.

When we told Matt and Cheryl about our plans to leave, they were very supportive. Mike, always up for an adventure, was excited and ready. I was neurotic and anxious. Matt and Cheryl allayed my fears, telling me that God would hold me fast in the interim; He could see that our hearts were bent toward Him and that our hunger was for Truth. He would not lead us astray.

"Think of it as a nice season of Jesus bringing you breakfast in bed," Matt said through his frisky smile. "Time to rest."

I knew he was right. They had spent many years outside of Church, having breakfast in bed with Jesus, and they had done just fine. Now, they too were—yet again—seeking healthier pastures, and pastors.

Petrified as I was, I wholeheartedly trusted God's love for us.

(September 29) *I love you like never before. I trust your plans for our family. I trust your unfailing, unconditional, tender love. Heal us, Father. Show us your way.*

Still, it was a confusing and painful breakup. While we were eager to move on to this new season in God (prime example of the lingo there), we were mourning the leaving behind of many friends. I had alienated myself from every one of my pre-conversion relationships, and my ALCF family was all I had now. This was wrenching beyond belief for me. But I was so tired; I was more than willing to make the sacrifice.

As far as what our exit would look like, we had two choices: Be honest and speak openly about the issues that we were seeing and why we could no longer abide them, thereby opening ourselves up to misunderstanding, offense, rejection, and the now common invitation to the back door, or, mumble some cock-and-bull story about how Mike just couldn't find adequate work and that we wanted to be closer to family and blah, blah, blah. The truth was, this wasn't malarkey at all, Mike had been job-hunting for seven weeks, and though he was doing temp work, our prospects were sketchy at best. We were tired of being poor and constantly struggling to make ends meet.

Being the less confrontational route, we chose door number two.

We were so adept at not rocking the boat that the rest of our church friends readily accepted our story. Ron and Luanne threw us a big going away party complete with a video of each family wishing us well with individual goodbyes and words of encouragement and exhortation.

Many folks including Ron and Luanne, Angel, Matt and Cheryl, Claude and Lilly, Miriam, Jan and Berry, all helped us load up our little moving van. They gathered on the curb and waved farewell as Mike pointed the truck toward I-5 North, and our little family drove up and out of Wonderland.

THERE AND BACK AGAIN

I would so love to say, "And they lived happily ever after, loving Jesus and skipping in the fields with the little lambs. The End."

Unfortunately, rabbit holes sometimes have more than one opening.

We did indeed spend the next year in Northern California enjoying family and breakfast in bed, which, incidentally, had Prozac on the menu for me. All of the tap dancing I'd been doing had taken its toll.

In retrospect, it's obvious that I'd been courting depression for quite some time; I just didn't identify the nasty critter for what it was. In Wonderland, I'd been taught that psychotherapy was a secular-humanistic device used by the Devil to distract people from allowing God to heal one's mind. The renewal of the mind happened by the careful and constant intake of the Scriptures and by prayer and fasting. I did try, but often ended up just heaping the blame upon myself and spent years doing the self-hatred tango, reinforcing my belief that there was something intrinsically wrong with me—that I was irreparably flawed by nature.

Happily on meds, I was finally getting my head on straight again when, to the astonishment of our very patient, generous, and loving family, we did the strangest thing. Once again, we packed up our crap and headed back down south, leaving our kin shaking and scratching their heads.

You see, we still had pesky dreams bumping around in our noggins. The deep craving for professional careers in the arts continued to haunt both Mike and I, and this was part of the impetus to be back in Los Angeles again. We were convinced that LA was the only place this could really happen. Unfortunately we were also still locked into the struggle with finding a way to meld our Christianity with said careers. The vexatious belief that we were called to use our creative gifts in some kind of *ministry* stuck with us like a chronic case of eczema, refusing to be cleared, no matter how many topical creams we applied to it.

ON TEA PARTIES AND MADNESS

"Curiouser and curiouser." ~Alice

We came to find out that in the time that we'd been gone from Los Angeles, much had transpired in Wonderland. Soon after our departure, there'd been a huge upheaval and a bit of a coup within the ranks of Disciples Of Destiny. Tom Lorrack and his sidekick of many years had had a falling out and an ugly breakup ensued. The destruction rolled down the mountain like a deluge and Abundant Living Christian Fellowship was pummeled by all the churning debris. Apparently, we left none too soon. Nearly all of the folks we'd previously been close with had up and left for new and healthier pastures: Ron and Luanne had gone back east, Claude and Lilly had gone back to the farm in the Mid-West. Miriam was still around; but she was doing church alone in her apartment now—well, she and Jesus—free from all the hubbub.

Pastor Reed and a few of the elders had taken over what was left of the flock and had moved to a smaller building; Jim (the Apostle) and Len (the Prophet) and a handful of folks had taken to meeting in Jim's living room.

After a year away, it was strange to be back haunting the streets of our old stomping grounds. Especially when we would run into ex-church family around town.

"Hey! Mike and Kathy! How ya doin'? Long time no see! Where ya goin' to church?"

"Nowhere, actually."

Silence.

"Oh. Okay. Well, nice to see you."

People steered a wide path around us with this news.

On a very sad note, while we were away, after a hard battle back home in Puerto Rico, Julio succumbed to complications from the AIDS virus. And now Angel was also sick.

He was no longer going to church and was alone and full of anger—toward the church, toward God, and toward us. We visited him, but I was such a coward about everything that happened to him and Julio, that to my shame, I couldn't bear to spend much time with him. Mike, on the other hand, was persistent and would give him rides to the doctor for his medication and checkups. Other than that though, they didn't hang out much. Angel became increasingly reclusive and belligerent, and it got harder and harder for Mike to bring any comfort.

&

We spent a year trying on a number of the churches in the area that we heard were cool. Most of them were huge and we just kinda felt lost in the crowd. We had no idea where we would land.

We started hearing some interesting rumblings about strange and wondrous things that were unfolding back at the old ALCF auditorium. Jim and Len had paid a visit to a church up in Canada that had been experiencing some kind of crazy phenomenon for an extended period of time. They dubbed it *The Blessing* and everyone was talking about powerful visitations of the Holy Spirit. Well, those boys brought a little dose of it back with them. Upon their return, a similar raucous and wacky visitation started falling upon the little band of believers right there in Jim's living room. It wasn't long before so many people were showing up that they had to move their revival meetings to the old auditorium.

We heard stories that people were actually getting blitzed at church. Yep, I mean inebriated, trashed, stoned, fu'd up . . . in the Spirit, of course. Apparently, the Holy Ghost was hanging out and partying with this group, and He brought the *big* bong; it was wreaking all kinds of havoc. Folks were laughing uncontrollably, stumbling around like drunken sailors, barking like dogs and crowing like roosters. Children were seeing angels and the cloud of God's glory was hanging around the rafters.

I of course, had to check this out for myself. I figured there was a lot of exaggeration going on, but I just had to see. Mike wasn't interested in revisiting old ground, so he stayed home and played with the kids.

I had a strange and secret little aril of hope that something fantastical and fun would happen that night that would once and for all blow away every shred of doubt I ever had about God's superdeedooper magical powers.

But I wasn't prepared for the likes of this stuff.

I sneak into the back of the auditorium; I'm not interested in any reunions and want to have a clear shot at a quick get-away. The group has outgrown Jim's living room by a thousand-fold, but so far all seems fairly normal. I only see a few vaguely familiar faces.

Worship begins. A very young band is leading; I don't think there's anyone over twenty-five on the team. The music is fresh and rather sweet with an edgy alternative feel to it. I suddenly realize that I have deeply missed the music. I miss the feeling of being caught up in lively worship, singing songs of praise together with a bunch of young people (though at thirty-something, I'm probably considered elderly to most of this crowd). As we sing, my courage is bolstered by our shared love for Jesus. I begin to relax a bit, so I venture down to find a seat a little closer to the front. I feel a little inkling of hope. For about a minute.

Not long into the service, someone comes up to give a prophetic word . . . and then the fun begins. The lady giving the word starts to shake. I mean like, her head gets a serious case of what appears to be Parkinson's on steroids. I don't know how she manages to speak as her head shakes from side to side so violently I think it might come clean off.

This isn't completely unfamiliar to me; I've seen people shake and gyrate before, but this is so intense it makes me fear that soon I will see complete head rotation and pea soup fountains.

Soon, bursts of laughter erupt from various parts of the room. As it increases and spreads, I sorta feel like I'm in Uncle Albert's flat with Mary Poppins, Bert and the kids. Perhaps we all might float up to take our tea on the ceiling, which might have been fun, but then it just turns a corner somehow.

The entire row directly in front of me starts a little herky-jerky rave. Seemingly in unison, they're shaking and rocking and swaying their bodies around in wide circles in a kind of yogic dance. Then the moaning and wailing starts. Perhaps these are cries of holy ecstasy; they're something close to orgasmic, but rather spooky nonetheless.

Oh, and now, of course, there is retching. Somewhere off to my right. The green river will be flowing eminently; I just know it. When I venture a peek at the retchers, I see that they aren't in fact vomiting—which, by the way, I have a serious phobia of—rather, they're praying in tongues and prophesying. After they holler their declarations with great gusto, they double over as if they just took some massive gut punch, exhaling loud explosive grunts and groans. They then stay bent over and continue to groan and bob up and down, bowing like tweaking Japanese businessmen trying to outdo each other's greeting.

I make for the exit.

I wasn't much interested in whatever sermon might follow the three-ring circus. Though I hadn't yet been given the pleasure of witnessing the barking on all fours (I'd heard reports of such shenanigans), I had seen enough. The show had already gone a tad outside my weirded-out zone and I didn't think I could bear the second act. I tried to be open. I really did. But instead, I felt alarmed, unsafe, and pretty much all around freaked out.

I can't say I was surprised by what I'd witnessed. Jim had always had his sights on the big and mighty; after all, his destiny had been foretold. What did surprise me was the sheer numbers of people that were participating in this cacophony. This tomfoolery. This unhinged pandemonium.

Even more unsettling was that this thing was spreading. People were coming from far and wide to get in on this *blessing* (or at least to just stand and gawk) and then they were taking it back home with them. It was breaking out in churches around the globe to the tune of thousands more sheep clamoring for the clamor. It was like a whole new Pentecost, only this time, they were *barking* in tongues.

Jim and Len's services started being held seven days a week, and this went on for three years. The new church that formed out of this hullabaloo was dubbed *The Harvest*. Its gathering energy was creating a whirling vortex that started sucking up a number of other small local churches to create a new and more terrifying storm. And I thought the church *corporation* was scary. This new thing would go on to eventually reassert its efforts toward world domination long after the bleating and giggling subsided. More on that story later.

So what the heck was all this? Was it God? Was it mass hysteria? Who knows? Were these young folks just desperate for something new? Could it be that there were (and are) so many young, intelligent people aching for some kind of experience other than the grinding reality of everyday life? Were there so many disillusioned college students facing soul-sucking nine-to-five purgatory in a world headed for Hades, that a planet-wide movement was being spawned? You betcha. Many crusades are birthed that way.

I'll grant you, I'd always been up for a little wild abandon and it was hard for this rebel—who rather liked a little spice with my church service—to admit that this was more like taking the little shaker top off the Tabasco bottle and pouring the whole damn thing on the guacamole. It ruined the sweet, subtle flavors of the avocados, cilantro, and garlic, and turned it into something else completely. The other problem for me, besides the fact that it was downright disturbing and rather embarrassing, was that this behavior kinda flew in the face of scripture. The Book clearly taught that the worship service was to have some semblance of order and be easy to understand, so that the unbelievers who wandered into your midst would not think you were bonkers.

For God is not a God of confusion but of peace. ~1 Corinthians 14:33

Of course that particular passage also goes on to say that it's shameful for a woman to speak in church and that she should be quiet and save her brazen comments and maddening questions for her wise and learned husband, so I don't know. Hard to swallow the latter with the former, so can you trust any of it?

When I came home that night and shared my psychedelic visit to Wonderland Gone Wild, Mike's indifference was fanned into a bit of twisted fascination. He too had to go see for himself, which he did soon after.

"Yep," he concurred. "They have all gone mad."

Needless to say, our curiosity was quickly slaked and we set our faces firmly in any other direction but that one.

RECONNECTING WITH THE REAL

Meanwhile, Matt and Cheryl found a sweet little church in the next town over where the folks were fine and the pastor had a day job. That sounded just right; maybe we'd found a home.

We ended up hanging out there for several years. It was small and intimate, the people were, well, normal. Matt was drumming on the worship team, and of course, pretty soon Mike was playing as well. We quickly made some friends and always had a blast at Matt and Cheryl's homegroup. Yes they had those, but this was truly different. More like friends hanging out. We even had a few beers sometimes. Sacrilegious!

About six months in, Mike was asked to take over as worship leader. Turns out the current one got caught bangin' the Sunday School teacher, which may not have been as big a deal if he wasn't at the same time engaged to the pastor's daughter.

One fine Sunday, the guy got up in front of the congregation to announce that he would be stepping down as worship leader. He mumbled a bunch of stuff: something about sin, and a dark lord, and some goofy allegory about a jet airliner and warning lights blinking in the console.

"Do you know what he's talking about?" I whispered to Mike.

"I can't be sure, but I think he just confessed to something."

I didn't get it, but whatever; I wasn't crazy about the guy anyway, he seemed a smidge too slick.

After his *confession* he was escorted by the pastor and his shotgun, right out the damn door. (Finally, an appropriate use of the damn door, and not really about the shotgun part, but it sounded good.) The lucky horndawg. If it'd been our daughter, this story would'a ended here with me visiting Mike in prison for the next forty years. Okay, so at least this church wore its issues right out there on its sleeve.

I could cope with that. Real people. How refreshing.

  

Speaking of real people. Though my friend Miriam and I had known each other fairly well before our first exodus, it was during this second go-round that she became as close to me and my family as a person could be without *being* family. She, as you have likely guessed, was another one of the rescue posse that God sent during our stay in Wonderland. It took leaving and returning for me to figure that out. Though she herself had been an official resident thereof even longer than we, she somehow managed to retain her senses: her sense of self, her sense of worth in the eyes of God, and her sense of smell. She could smell rotten motives and doctrinal crapola from a hundred paces, and wasn't afraid to say when she was smellin' it.

She too had weathered some intense bullying from the ALCF leadership when she had finally come to the end of her marriage. Suffice it to say, the pastors had sided with the he of the couple. Patriarchal hierarchies are not kind nor sympathetic to wives stuck in cancerous marriages. They also have a zero tolerance policy for anyone who has the gall to speak up when they disagree with something that comes across the pulpit (you get double demerits if you're a girl and triple if you're a girl who can adeptly back up your arguments with your knowledge of the Scriptures). Miriam too, was acquainted with the ALCF back door policy. Boy, that thing got a lot of use. I think they eventually just installed a swingin' door, like at Miss Kitty's saloon.

A couple times a week, Miriam would amble by and we'd sip coffee and sit in the morning sun while the kids played in the trees out front (there was lava everywhere and it wasn't safe to tread upon the ground).

We would talk for hours about Jesus, and movies, and sick churches, and depression, and menstrual cycles. Those conversations were a precious comfort to me. She would give me much-needed breaks from the wee ones (she loved them like they were her own) and the shirt off her back if I asked.

I so envied Miriam's special relationship with Jesus. She, like Matt and Cheryl, seemed to really get the idea of unconditional love and grace at a level that almost completely evaded me. I understood it with my brain, but my heart only experienced it in fleeting snippets.

I remember Miriam sharing with me once during a particularly hard time she was going through, how Jesus had visited her while she was soaking in a bubble bath. He just showed up, sat on the edge of the toilet (lid down, of course), and had a nice chat about all kinds of stuff. He gave her advice; they shared recipes, the latest gossip, and then had a long talk about how huge his love for her was. Look, I'm telling you, she is super-intelligent and quite lucid; this is just the way she experiences her faith and her connection with Jesus.

I have a very small tribe of people in my life who love me with the same kind of unconditional love that Jesus had, and I have to say, Miriam is one of the chieftains. I think I would have to do something pretty underhanded and mean to be abandoned by her, and even then I have a hunch she would still leave the back door ajar, just in case.

During this time, I had the opportunity to take a short trip to the Midwest to spend a week with Lilly and Claude. Miriam graciously agreed to take care of the kids during the day while Mike was at work. Tim was about four years old; Em was around seven. Miriam always had the greatest stories to tell of her adventures with our progeny. My return home held one of the best.

"So, we had an interesting little outing to Thrifty's for ice cream on day three," she tells me.

I level my gaze at her. Smile. You never know what it's going to be.

She laughs.

"Well, Tim was having a rough day," she begins.

"Aw. I'm sorry. Did he give you a hard time?"

"Oh, he was fine, just a little testing of the boundaries thing. Anyway, it was so hot and I decided that we would all go get an ice cream after we picked Em up from school. So we get to Thrifty's and they take like, forever to decide on a flavor. We finally get our cones and on the way out, Em stops and is totally entranced by the toy machine . . . you know the one with the big claw hanging over the pile of toys inside the bubble, all the really cool ones are on top, but only ever delivers the crummy toys . . . fifty cents for some silly little thing."

"Yeah, did she bug you for a toy?"

"She asked me if she could borrow fifty cents so she could try to get the little brown monkey that was right on top. She really wanted it badly. She says, 'I know I can get that monkey—I have a dollar-fifty at home, I can pay you back.' She stood there studying it like she could somehow, by the power of thought, will that toy to come to her. I told her it probably wouldn't work, that those machines never deliver any of the ones that are on top, but she was so sure. I tell her, 'Fifty cents, Em; that's a third of your money—you sure you want to spend it on this? There's no guarantee you'll get the monkey.' She stares at it. 'Yes, I know I can get the monkey,' she says. 'Okay,' I tell her, 'but will you pay me back even if you don't get the monkey, no complaining, no whining?'"

"Uh-oh," I say. Miriam laughs.

"Yeah. So I gave her the quarters."

"And she didn't get the monkey. Did she freak?" I say.

"Um, oh my gosh. End of the world. She's shrieking, 'No! No! Aaaaaaaah!' And I'm looking around like, 'I'm not beating the kid! I'm not!' People are looking at us, and I'm like, 'Ok, let's just go eat our ice creams outside,' and I shuffle them out. We sit on the curb in the shade cause I don't want ice cream all over my car. Em's sobbing and snuffling and we're all licking our melting ice cream off our cones and hands; I'm trying to console her and she's starting to settle down. I wasn't really paying close attention to Tim. He's sitting there fiddling with his shorts, and all of a sudden Em lets out another blood-curdling scream, 'TIIIIIIMMMM! Stop it!!' and I look over. Well, I didn't notice when I put his shorts on him that morning that there was a little hole in the crotch. While I'd been trying to comfort Em, he'd worked the crotch of his shorts up to the front and managed to wiggle his little fingers inside that hole *and* inside the fly of his undies and had pulled his penis out through both. He's sitting there, ice cream in one hand, holding his penis by the very tip and stretching it out as far as it can possibly go . . . "

Miriam is cracking up; I'm mortified, and cracking up.

"Em is screaming bloody murder and Tim looks over at me—huge grin—and goes, 'See, look!' Em is like 'Tiiiiim! Stop iiiiiit!' and he says, 'Can I pee?' I'm like, 'Uh, that would be a NO. In fact, put that back in your pants please.' 'Why?' he says. 'Well, because we're in a public place and that's not really allowed. We're not allowed to pull our penises out in public.'"

"A few people giggle as they pass. Tim gets all deflated. I say, 'Can you put it back please.' With great effort and disappointment, he pokes it back into the hole, rearranges the package. I ask him, 'Do you think you can walk?'"

We both laugh.

"So we get into the car, Em is still upset because the universe has betrayed her and it's the end of the world. She's looking at her toy—which was not a monkey—and fuming and snuffling and getting worked up again. Tim says, 'It's okay. Em, I'll take the toy,' trying to cheer her up. She snaps at him. 'Shut up!' and she starts throwing herself around the back seat in an apoplectic fit – tears streaming again. 'Go ahead take it then!' she yells, and throws the toy at Tim's head! She keeps wailing, 'This wasn't supposed to happen! It wasn't supposed to happen this way! I thought I could make it happen and it didn't!'

"I pull the car over, before she hurts herself, and she gets the lecture. It's freaking hot out and we're sitting in the car, all sweaty, and I'm trying to comfort Em; Tim's just sitting there being a perfect angel. She calms down some and I tell her she still has to give me the 50 cents."

"Ohhhh. Bad timing?" I interject.

Miriam nods, "And the wailing starts again. Tim says, 'I'll give you my quarter.' 'No! No! I'll do it. I'll just do it,' she howls—utter despair. Finally we drive home."

"Oh. My gosh," I say.

"But wait, there's more," Miriam says. "So we're home. Tim is sitting on the couch next to Emily and they're watching cartoons. Now we're not in public, so he pulls that thing out again! Em has another fit. 'Tiiiiiim!!' I make him put it away, again. Em is inconsolable—all red-faced and sobbing, and Mike walks in from work.

"He says, 'Whoa, what happened in here?' Em goes off about what happened. She recounts the whole story from her perspective, 'He's being inappropriate!' she bawls. Mike listens attentively to her, trying not to laugh. Then, he gets all serious. Tim is so over it; he's playing in the living room. 'Tim I, need you to come here,' Mike says. He's like, so serious, now *I'm* scared. Tim climbs up in his lap. 'We've talked about your peeper, son. Did you take your peeper out in public at Thrifty's?' 'Yeah!' 'I've told you your peeper cannot be out in public. Do you remember that? It's against the rules. Do you know what happens to people who do things like that?' 'What?' 'They go to jail.' Eyes like saucers. 'Do you want to go to jail?' 'No.' Tim's lips start to quiver. Em's in the corner with her arms crossed, hip cocked, like: *'Mm hmm, that's what's gonna happen to you!'*"

This wasn't the first—or the last—penis incident, all hilariously innocent, of course. For little boys, there is apparently no lack of curiosity or comfort to be found in that little member, and our inquisitive young lad was no exception to that rule.

Some weeks later, we lay in the dark, Mike on the top bunk with Em, and me on the bottom bunk with wee tiny Tim. Nightly, when we put the kids to bed, we would sing a worship song or two, pray with them, and then just snuggle for a spell as they (and Mike) fell asleep.

On this particular evening Tim has something on his mind. In the sweetest little boy voice on the planet, he says, "Mom, I wanna ask Jesus to come into my heart."

Warm joy spreads across my chest. This is a sovereign moment. From before their birth, we have prayed for our kids, that they would be healthy and happy, would choose to know and serve the Lord, and would meet and marry their soul mates. Now, here he is, without any overt instigation from us, asking to be saved.

Our family prays together there in the soft glow of the nightlight, for Jesus to come and make his home in our little boy's heart.

Healthy and happy: Check. Saved: Check. Soul mate: a little soon yet, but we feel pretty sure God will deliver the goods on that one too.

I lay there, listening to my boy's breathing, slow and even as he drifts off into the land of dreams. I wonder what prompted this sudden desire in a four-year-old.

At the time, I took it as God's amazing faithfulness in drawing Tim into his arms. Looking back, I sometimes wonder, miracle? Or fear of jail . . .

***

During our SoCal sequel, Mike and I did manage to complete one pretty cool project. It was one that we had started before we departed Wonderland, so I must back up a bit.

A few years prior to leaving ALCF, we had both read and fell in love with a beautiful book. It was an allegory of the gospel written in the most eloquent pairing of prose and verse. Mike was of course immediately filled with music inspired by the writer's masterful symphony of words. He composed a theme song based on the book, and was soon developing the concept of creating a stage musical based on this exquisite retelling of the story of redemption. The more we discussed it, the stronger we felt that this was something God was calling us to. I wrote a letter to the publisher, asking for permission to adapt the work, which they granted.

When the time came for us to pull up stakes and vamoose to the Land of the Far North, *The Project* was safely wrapped in bubble wrap with all of the rest of our dreams, mismatched dishes, and Precious Moments figurines, packed in a U-Haul box, and filed away for later. Perhaps we would look at it again when we were settled safely on the other side of the Looking Glass and able to get on with our lives.

Once back in Los Angeles, we knew that it was time to pick the ball back up and see if we couldn't score a touchdown. We were part of a caring and encouraging church—albeit not a rich one—perhaps we would find some support and a way to see this gem brought into the light. By this time, Mike was leading worship and regularly introducing his own music. I was singing on the team as well, so the congregation was familiar with our musical abilities. They knew of our background and training in the arts. We figured, who knows? Just as the beginnings of *Toymaker's Dream* originated in a humble Tulsa fellowship, so too might our show be birthed out of this unassuming little band of believers.

I asked Mike if he would mind if I took a stab at writing the script. He had tons of work yet to do on the score, so he was all for it. I started pumping the foot pedals to fire up my old 80s Apple computer with its ginormous eight-inch screen (kinda like writing on an iPhone nowadays—but not really), and set to work on the script.

Mike immersed himself in writing and arranging the score on his new Korg music workstation (a beautiful keyboard which had been given to him as a birthday gift by some of our church friends).

Late one evening, from within the confines of our tiny bedroom where Mike had been sequestered every night for the last several weeks, long strings of symbols came bursting out from his lair.

"Oh NOOOOO! Oh noooooo! Awwww God! *^$$#%&@@son of a #$^@$&#!!!" In those days, we cussed mostly in dollar signs, exclamation points, ampersands, and the like, and usually only when something really bad happened.

"What? What?" I squawked. It was a miniscule bedroom, not much room for injury in there; a stubbed toe maybe? I dreaded what his reply was going to be.

"I've lost it all!! All of it!!" I think he may have been crying.

Easily fifty hours of work gone, with the push of a button. No retrieving any of it. Oh the heartbreak. He went to bed, sad, tired, and determined to start again.

And start again he did. It took him the better part of a year, but what he produced was Broadway worthy. We were pleased with the script, but knew that it needed to be workshopped and refined. In theatre-speak, this meant it needed to be played with by a bunch of actors in an informal setting to see what needs to be changed, added, cut, and so forth. Unfortunately, as was our seeming lot, we had zero resources—neither human nor monetary—to work with.

Then, Mike got laid off from his job.

Okay, so fine. We flirted with the hope that perhaps this was the sign we'd been waiting for. Was God getting ready to launch us into the full-time ministry? We knew mounting a production of this size and scope would take huge amounts of labor, intense focus, fundraising, and time. Time being one thing that Mike had little of when he was working full-time. We reasoned that in order to make this thing happen, he would need to be freed up from regular work in order to put his full energy and attention toward making this production a reality. We were going to need a strong support system in place underpinned by a group of people who wholeheartedly believed in *The Project*. Our church had been quite supportive of us to this point, and Mike had shown himself as a faithful and gifted leader. Surely everyone would see it as clearly as we did. But how to pitch the vision?

I always say, when you're not sure what to do, write a letter. This seemed to be a theme with me. You'd think we would have taken a closer look at the track record of our past missives. Nonetheless I convinced Mike that we should compose a "missionary" support letter about *The Project*. We asked our church family to consider funding us as *artist missionaries*. Their sponsorship would allow us to keep our time freed up in order to produce this powerful vehicle for the Gospel. The invitation was heartfelt, well articulated, and compelling. We were petrified, but we sent the letter out anyway.

"Chirp, chirp, chirp . . ." went the crickets.

Well, we did get one response: it basically said, "Keep your day job."

Only problem was, Mike didn't have one. We weren't totally surprised, but we were still very disappointed. I had this crazy fantasy that maybe, just maybe, this time, the people of the Church would catch our vision and that our own version of what Impact Productions had done so successfully in Oklahoma would finally be born here. This was Los Angeles, for Pete's sake, the land of every arts resource we could possibly need. All we required now was a strong group of like-minded believers to stand with us. We had a powerful original piece of theater that had the potential to touch hearts for Christ. A high-class vehicle, but no passengers and no gas.

As before, we found ourselves feeling like we had this calling and no way to fulfill it. We were either lost in the crowd of the Mega-Church, or dead in the water at our sleepy little neighborhood fellowship. And so, *The Project* was shelved yet again.

Our sails deflated and our boat stalled, we began to search the horizon once again for the Promised Land, our place in the Kingdom that would make room for our very big ideas.

After years of going around the same mountain, we both began to question whether God was calling us at all. Perhaps our desires were just selfish ambitions that we were selling to ourselves as ministry.

We were growing tired of the never-ending struggle to make ends meet, flitting from one unfulfilling day job to another, never choosing the traditional *career path* in the absolute certainty that one day we would be released to pursue our passions full-time.

Restlessness began setting in. For me, a sense of isolation, suffocation, and lost-ness was increasing and I started feeling again like I wanted out of Los Angeles. With all the noise raging in my noggin, the added clamor of the frantic city energy only compounded my scattered thought processes. I spent nearly every waking hour with diametrically opposed desires: to be an actress/singer/dancer/director and somehow serve the Lord therewith, while just as desperately wanting to be living somewhere beautiful, quiet, and safe for my kids, with my sanity intact and some degree of joy. I wanted my cake, and ice cream, and to eat it *all*.

I could find no satisfaction, and the older our kids got the more sure I was that I didn't want to have them grow up in a place where I was afraid to let them play alone in the front yard. The grass was always greener, everywhere else.

We sit in the living room reading late one evening. It's been a long week of classified scouring and resume dropping for Mike. We're both pooped. The kids are somehow able to sleep despite the heat and the party our Armenian neighbors are having. I think if I hear "Macarena" one more time, I may go mad and pull out all of my eyelashes.

Mike's reading *The Stand*. I haven't read a novel—a secular one anyway—in at least ten years. Stephen King used to be one of my favorites. Right now, I'm in *John* chapter five. I've read verse twenty-eight at least a dozen times . . . *for a time is coming when all who are in their graves will hear His voice and come out*—"Ahhhhhh Macarena!" I snap the cover shut.

Mike sets his book down in his lap. "Maybe I should go back to school." His statement sounds much more like a resignation than an excited declaration.

"To do what?" I ask, incredulous, so as to not reveal my secret hope that he's serious.

In actuality, my heart is totally divided between wanting with all my being for us to have the financial stability that Mike choosing a conventional career would bring, while loathing the thought of him laying aside his dreams and his massive talent for a better paycheck.

"Teach," he says.

"You are an amazing teacher."

"Well, if I had to choose any other career besides music and acting, I guess it would be teaching. And it looks like it's time to choose."

Something like relief bursts inside my chest. And sadness. Were we giving up? I had to admit; a clear direction and a predictable income would be a welcome thing indeed. Not to mention bennies and retirement. Bennies—a term I learned from Matt and Cheryl. We'd never had those before.

"But I don't know if I want to teach *here*," he says.

"Or raise our kids here," I add.

"I don't know. Sometimes I just want to go someplace quiet and clean and beautiful. Get close to the mountains," he says, echoing my many pages of journal entries.

"Where?"

"I don't know. Maybe Montana. Or maybe back north again, closer to family."

"Yeah, they already know we're crazy and seem to love us anyway." My heart feels light for the first time in a while.

"Let's pray about it."

So, we prayed about many nutty possibilities: Montana, where Mike's childhood buddy and partner in many slightly illegal acts—who was now saved—lived; Ohio, where Claude and Lilly were happily basking in rolling fields of green grass and whimsical stands of magical forest groves; back up North, where there was always Mike's family who would take us in, despite our apparent insanity; and finally, the mountains of the far North where my mom, brother, and sister had circled the wagons to live out their days in the unspoiled wilderness.

So many options. So little cash.

We imagined a new life for our family in a place of sanctuary, far from the noise and confusion of too many humans in close proximity to one another. A place where things were simpler, where a person could breathe, and one's soul could heal. In the end, we opted to move to where the air was clean, the mountains soared to meet the sky, and the rivers ran wild over the granite. Nope, not Montana, but dern near as stunning.

My mom and my brother were endeavoring to go into the resort business together. My brother, a contractor (and incidentally, now a Christian), had purchased a pristine 80 acres of land with a 360-degree view of mile upon mile of misty ranges and jagged alps. He had already begun improving the property (how do you improve paradise?) in preparation for building a lodge.

"Wanna help?" they asked.

"Let us check our schedule—YES!" we replied.

So once again, we packed up our stuff, loaded up the truck, and we moved to . . . Shangrileeeee.

"What about teaching?" I hear you yelling. "What of sanity?" I hear you cry. Patience, my young Padawans, there's more to this story.

BORN AGAIN
(PART III)

BORN AGAIN (PART III)

PARADISE FOUND

NOT THAT WE ARE PEOPLE OF EXTREMES or anything—okay, so we are, I'll give you that—but moving from a population of well over eight million, to a sleepy little lake town was somewhat of a shock.

As the twists and turns of the winding black and yellow ribbon dividing the trees finally ease up, we slow and turn off the highway at the Rushing Creek Center sign. Pop. 243—yep, read that right. Just beyond it, stands a towering Sasquatch, carved by chainsaw from the trunk of a huge Douglas fir tree. His rough-hewn features are chunked into a warm smile that welcomes us to our new home.

In a half-block distance, we pass four of the eight amenities of this pock-sized community, all situated on adjacent corners: a diner (Big Foot's twin brother apparently owns it—he waits out front beckoning us in, one massive arm held up in a slack wave), a general store with gas pumps and a tire hut, a burger shack with picnic tables and umbrellas, and a brand new sparkling community church building. One block more and around a bend is a tiny post office and the elementary school; a block in the opposite direction is a long-closed resort property and a small private airstrip. Then the lake.

Tucked snugly into ridge upon ridge of wilderness, the whole of Rushing Creek Center spans a whopping four miles. The bulk of the town's inhabitants reside within a four-block radius of the town hub. A number of the original Gold Rush era houses and buildings still remain, now surrounded by additional dwellings built in the 1960s. Many of these stand empty during the snowy winters, fishing boats and hunting gear stowed in leaning sheds and under crumbling blue tarps, awaiting the return of the vacation-ing city dwellers.

We park our whole world in my mom's gravel driveway and feel the earth spin for a few moments as we put our feet on the solid ground and gaze at the next chapter of our lives. Blinking back at us is a charming and weathered little two-story cabin with Swiss cheese for siding and a tin A-line roof. We regard one another like two foreigners, separated by miles of culture and a slightly differing language. We make a silent agreement to give one another a chance.

My mother, having retired a number of years earlier, had made the trek to Rushing Creek Center (following my brother who had come a year or so prior) and snapped up one of the original houses built in the early 1850s. It had fallen into disrepair over the years, but my brother, my mom, and my sister, had all worked together on a complete remodel of the interior. (My sister had also relocated to the area after a rotten divorce.)

Stepping across the threshold of my mom's abode was like passing through some kind of porthole into a DIY magazine spread: the interior of some long-dead miner's cabin now transformed into a fresh and modern layout, all the result of my brother's artistry. The new open and bright main floor was finished with bullnose arches, half-round tile hearth, and white-washed knotty pine paneling. Mom's choice, however, of lush, cream-colored Berber carpeting was the object of many chuckles and knowing smiles from her new neighborhood friends; soon, this last vestige of her city life would be shades of earthy russet, like the ever-encroaching mountains.

I wondered if *this* city girl would be able to make the switch. For me, an adjustment period would indeed be on the agenda. I would most definitely be retiring my heels (pumps were like to gather plenty of cobwebs here) and no potstickers or woodfired pizzas in these parts.

At first, life in this tiny lakeside hamlet felt a little like stepping into a less dangerous version of *Deliverance*. The loveliness of the place was, of course, instantly captivating: the clarity of the air, the closeness of the sur-rounding mountains, and the intense cerulean of the sky were absolutely dizzying. And there was no noise. If you sat still, the silence was almost deafening, pressing in on your eardrums, like being deep underwater. At night it amplified the symphony of the crickets and frogs. During the day, you could hear the towering cedars and firs announce the approach of a breeze moments before it hit your face. If the quiet was ever interrupted, it was only by the distant buzz of a chainsaw or the piercing screech of an osprey or eagle. Being surrounded by so much fierce beauty was intoxicating. I was always walking (and driving) around under the influence. I remember praying, "Lord, please, don't ever let me grow used to this."

Within a day or so of our arrival, a swarm of old mud-caked four-wheel drive vehicles rumble into the yard and park at odd angles in the dirt and pine needles (we soon learned that local trucks were referred to as *rigs*, most of which were *beaters*, meaning covered in dents and duct tape). Out hop my brother's posse, our first introduction to the deep fibers of this course and rugged alpine fabric. The standard dress code appears to be cutoffs or well-worn Carhartts, faded Budweiser and Cal-Trans T-shirts, sweat-rimmed caps bearing the brand names of heavy machinery, and muddy logger boots. Salt of the earth, to be sure.

They introduce themselves with broad smiles and hearty handshakes from calloused paws. Every pair of eyes meets ours with acceptance and kindness. A few of these craggy fellas bear monikers like Injun Joe, Inspector Bob, Billy the Kid, or the Creature; for a couple of this crew, teeth are somewhat of a scarcity.

It isn't long before the ice chests are dragged from the back of one of the rigs, the squeaky lids announcing Miller Time. Impromptu back deck gatherings around cold cheap beer and jovial conversation are a way of life for these colorful and unpretentious highland folk.

My mother's neighbors were equally enchanting, albeit in a much milder way—simple, friendly, down-home people who love their gardens and their cross-stitching. A number of them had lived their entire lives here. Most were retirees from forestry, logging, or county jobs of varying kinds. There were also a small number of young families with kids the same age as ours. With the exception of a handful of middle class retirees and vacationing second-homeowners, the majority of the population lived at or below the national poverty line, which meant for most, keeping life simple was how it was. It made for very real people.

Our kids took to mountain living like bass to the lake. No adjustment period needed. They had grown up in deep adventure, traversing many untamed lands dense with forest, mountain, and stream. Now, they were living where the real wild things were, just a few paces off the back deck. Yep, all three of my kids—Em, Tim, and Mike—resumed their weekly quests into Greenland to fight the evil Empress Dingledork and the Weed Creatures on the shores of the Bay of Tears. Unlike Los Angeles however, *here* the lake and the woods were for real.

Soon Mike and I both had jobs, he at the local school as the maintenance guy, and I as a clerk and bookkeeper at aforementioned general store. We were living our very own Mayberry RFD.

℃℈

The scales of our frantic Los Angeles life began to fall off as we settled into our new adventure. We spent the first year living communally with my mom and working our tails off. During the summer and fall, we were brushing, clearing, burning, sawing trees with chainsaws, and cutting boards on my brother's lumber mill, all the while praising God and keeping a close eye on our appendages.

"This will cut your dick off," my brother warned us at chainsaw school. He laughs heartily with a robust "Praise God" after his often blue jokes, as if Jesus gets a kick out of them too. Not a churchgoer, my brother is a leather-tough mountain man who has his own very personal and unique relationship with the Lord.

The winter months were spent researching the resort and travel industry and creating an extensive business and marketing prospectus complete with 3D models of an amazing octagon-shaped lodge. It was quite an endeavor and though the work was hard, the slower pace of mountain living was providing a healing balm to our battered souls.

For the first few months the blue sky and permeating serenity of the trees were all the church we needed. We found friendship and fellowship with another family who lived just around the corner from my mom. They had four kids; two were Em and Tim's age. They were devout Christians, the couple having turned to Jesus to escape a life of drugs, alcohol, and incarceration.

They held a weekly Bible study in their home with a handful of other young, disenfranchised Christians from the neighborhood. They were a group of interesting misfits who didn't jive with the more conservative (and elderly) congregation at the corner church, but who were most certainly a loving and genuine bunch. They invited us to participate. Being the new city kids, Mike and I were now the oddballs, but they accepted and welcomed us (and Mike's guitar) wholeheartedly.

While we enjoyed the intimacy of the little Bible study, we began to feel like we still wanted to find a *real* church. We did visit the community church once, but quickly found that the atmosphere was far too conservative for the likes of us. You'd think we'd have been happy with this; after all, we wanted to find a church home that was genuine and full of nice people who loved Jesus. But, we just couldn't go back to organs and hymnals. We were spoiled by rock and roll worship and entertaining charismata. We were convinced that there was a right way to do church, and determined to either find it, or create it.

THE LITTLE CHAPEL

Our new friends told us about a church some forty miles down the mountain, in Junction Gulch, a small Gold Rush town of about thirty-six hundred souls. The drive was long and winding, but they said that the pastor was awesome, the worship was sweet, and the Spirit was alive and well.

The Little Chapel met in a funky old two-story movie theatre on Main Street in downtown Junction Gulch, which was the county seat for the region. The theatre was built in 1939 and was still showing the flickers on Friday and Saturday nights.

We heard that on Sunday mornings, at seven a.m., two vans would pull up out front, two burly guys would jump out like a couple of roadies and unload enough musical equipment for a full on rock concert. It looked like The Who had come to town.

We decided to pay them a visit.

When we arrive, we're greeted by folks—many are our age—who're gathered out front; they welcome us with smiles, and hellos, and handshakes.

The cramped, dimly lit lobby offers just enough space to shimmy past the greasy snack counter and through the double doors that lead to the auditorium which, it turns out, is not the cobwebby old haunted movie house I expect. It's laid out much like a traditional live theatre. We pass underneath an overhead balcony as we enter and stand looking down the raked main floor seating to a small, elevated stage in front of the expansive movie screen. I imagine that once upon a time, this might be where cancan girls or a barbershop quartet did their thing at intermission.

For the Sunday service, the theater space has now been transformed into a glorious worship space. A forest of silk ficus trees and sprays of fresh flowers surround the instruments and amp stacks. An army of fifteen-foot tall hanging banners flank the stage: exquisite handmade tapestries depicting an array of scripture verses, lions, lambs, gigantic flames, doves, and anything else you might find in God's throne room. Rich with color, the shimmery fabric swirls with mysterious symbolism; they make me think of the huge standards that were carried out to the battlefield by the armies back in the days of knights and swords.

Every seat is soon filled, all the way up to the rafters.

The music begins. At the keys, a handsome young man is leading the band. A long sleek ponytail flows down his back and a neatly trimmed dark beard frames his well-chiseled jaw. He flashes a dazzling smile at the congregation.

"Praise the Lord!" he calls out, then sings in a deep edgy voice, "Yeah, yeah, yeaaaaahhh . . . Whoaaaaa whoa whoa . . ." Smooth and bluesy. Robert Powell officially loses his place as my Jesus poster child. This guy can sing.

The music continues and blows my expectations out of the water. I mean, we're accustomed to contemporary worship music, but these tunes are new. They're fresh and full of poetry and prophetic language. And the melodies, well, let's just say it's obvious that these songs were written by musicians who made their way into the church scene via the professional music world. They're good. Oh how I long for the whole arts world to be converted!

And the worship band here is handling the music very skillfully. It sits comfortably in my chest, like reconnecting to an old friend.

Down in the front, in the floor space to the side of the stage, a small group of gals are dancing. It's synchronized, but they aren't wearing gold lamé or turtle-necked frocks. Another woman also dances, but it's more freestyle, not unlike my Lilly. My heart swells with cautious optimism.

Behind us, two men stand in the aisles twirling colorful flags in time with the music, kind of like syncopated aircraft flaggers. One of them—who looks like a big burly lumberjack without the beanie—whips two around at once with great dexterity and grace. The fact that these are men doing the twirling gives it a certain warrior-like masculinity that I find appealing. This is new for me, but it is fascinating and beautiful.

The pastor takes the podium. He's around my age, and wearing jeans and a casual pullover. Normal guy. Good sign. I hold my breath to see if the sermon lines up with my buoyant hopes. Pastor Lee's message is full of grace, wisdom, and the Word, and he's funny as hell. Perhaps we *have* finally come home.

❧

Over the next several months, Mike and I both started feeling the pull to be a part of this robust church. Perhaps this might be a place for our calling in the arts to flourish. We were becoming convinced that The Little Chapel was calling us down from the mountain. We started making the trek as many Sundays a month as our cash flow would allow. Lucky for us we didn't have kids who barf on curvy roads. The more time we spent among our new church friends, the more I was falling in love with them. They were an exceptional bunch of people and I was eager for new relationships.

You remember our dear friends Matt and Cheryl, of course. Early on in our involvement at The Little Chapel, a friendly couple approached us and introduced themselves. Turned out Melody and Brian were long-time friends of Matt and Cheryl. What in the heck were the odds of that? They'd been hippies together back in the Jesus-Freak days of the early 70s. Melody and Brian had been roadies for Matt's band when Matt was a rock star drummer. They had their children around the same time, and had remained close for over three decades. They had watched each other's children grow up, visiting each other at least every few years.

We became instant friends. Melody and Brian invited us to their home a number of times, giving us a sense of familiarity in our new surroundings. Who'd have thought we'd find connection to our allies six hundred miles away, in a remote little town, at some obscure little church. Bizarre.

We were welcomed into the fold with warmth and camaraderie, and were soaking in the amazing goodness of God's grace. Pastor Lee's messages were mostly focused on community, loving God, one another, and ourselves. (What?) Yep, home was definitely the word that kept coming to mind. It was good to be here at last.

This too was a charismatic church, meaning the gifts of the Spirit were embraced enthusiastically, and openly employed. However, these guys were not even remotely reminiscent of our Wonderland Gone Wild experience of a few years earlier. Don't get me wrong, the services were buzzing with prophetic and angelic words and plenty of jargon around the charismatic gifts, but at a level that we were accustomed to and comfortable with. It felt free and fun.

What I loved most about the church was that while it was truly a gathering of radical lovers of Jesus who were *sold out for the Kingdom* (translation: genuinely committed to the faith), there was a real down-to-earth feel to all of the gatherings and a strong sense of community abounded. It seemed like everyone loved one another and was deeply committed to the fellowship of the saints (translation: they liked to just hang out with each other).

Groups often gathered after church at the local diner for lunch. They would push all the tables together and basically take the place over, laughing, telling jokes and stories, talking about the day's message, and what God was doing in their lives. Just like a big, happy family. Friendships were genuine and people seemed to support and encourage one another in their daily lives. As you know, this has always been like bee to flower for me.

A LITTLE CHAPEL HISTORY

Thy Kingdom Come, Thy will be done on earth as it is in Heaven.

-Jesus

The Little Chapel was well established by the previous pastor who had been at the helm for nearly twenty years. Pastor John Williamson—let's call him Papa John—was a very charismatic leader who forever lived to see revival. He came from a long line of ministers, and preaching seemed to come as naturally to him as wind in March. Papa John believed mightily in the power of God to heal, the believer's inheritance of that authority, and their calling to exercise it boldly. When it came to the manifestation of the supernatural, he would settle for no less than God's kingdom on earth.

A couple years prior to our arrival, Papa John had accepted an invitation to lead a much larger fellowship (let's call it the Church of Wonders, or COW for brevity's sake), which was some forty miles farther downhill from Junction Gulch, in the nearest large-ish city (let's call it Big Town, for anonymity's sake). After his departure, Papa John's influence still lingered in a decidedly potent way at the Little Chapel (in keeping with our theme here, let's call it TLC for short). He was still highly regarded as the Church Father and TLC looked to him as such for oversight, guidance, and wisdom.

When he left, Papa John appointed his young protégé, Pastor Lee, to take over the helm as senior pastor of The Little Chapel. In his short but effective time in charge thus far, Pastor Lee had brought a world'a healing to a bunch of people in a world'a hurt. It seems that while Papa John was a formidable preacher and wielder of the superpowers of God, he kinda lost sight of the sheep. As they invariably will when left on their own, those little critters had become somewhat unruly, nipping and kicking at one another. They were in need of the gentle touch of a shepherd.

Pastor Lee was just the man for that job. He was highly gifted in helping the poor bleaters sort out their relational issues and learn to be nice. He had a way of calming the flighty creatures down and focusing their attention on more productive activities like loving and serving one another, and being a blessing to the community. He wholeheartedly believed in allowing people to flourish in their gifts. He understood that in doing so, folks could be more of who God created them to be, and in turn the Church, all it was intended to be in the world.

Now, under Pastor Lee's adept hand, much of that snarkiness had been transformed into action that resulted in vibrant ministry. TLC was rife with bustling activity and opportunities to serve. There were homegroups, a number of classes and Bible studies, outreaches, potlucks, church in the park, even an annual weeklong summer family campout at the lake. One radical group met for weekly prayer meetings that often lasted into the wee hours of the morning. Ministry teams visited the jails and prisons, and provided domestic violence awareness classes for abuse victims. There was a thriving youth ministry for both junior and senior high school kids. They had even established a small, Christian elementary school.

The Little Chapel was home for many artistic types as well. They had recently formed the Creative Guild for the Arts, a consortium of artists and performers seeking to use their talent to glorify God.

For such a tiny town, this was an amazingly well put together and flourishing fellowship. Opportunities abounded for all. Possibility was thriving and hope was blooming in all its glory. It's no wonder they had a congregation growing towards three hundred souls—nearly ten percent of the town's population at the time—very impressive, and not a bad ROI.

Meanwhile, a little further south in Big Town, a swirling vortex was amassing ominous clouds and picking up velocity, generating immense suction toward its epicenter. I like to call it Hurricane John. At this point we were blissfully unaware of the destructive nature of this storm. In fact, from our vantage point at the time, it was rather pretty.

HOUSE OF BLUES

Toward the end of our first year of mountain living, Mike and I and my family began to seek funding for the resort. We found it next to impossible to secure the kind of start-up capital we would need; none of us had stellar credit and finding investors was proving to be difficult at best. As a group, we were struggling to come to consensus on what kind of investors we wanted involved anyway.

Tensions were beginning to run a little high. Our quarters were becoming cramped (both the living and the spending kind) and the wind in our sails was waning. Mike and I decided it was coming nigh on time to have our own place again. We needed time and space to regroup, reassess, and reflect on what the heck we were doing before the family business became a family casualty. A rent payment would leave us far below the poverty level at our current wages, but we decided it was necessary to make a go of it.

A short distance up the highway, we found a charming little blue cabin in the woods. As if my mom's little village wasn't isolated enough, this new place was perched on the tip of the outer canopy. It was an enchanting abode, complete with river access, cute little gnome-like footbridge and unending multi-level decks. There were lots of secret little closets and Winchester Mystery Rooms upstairs that the kids soon turned into their own private fairytale bunkers. Whoever built the place had a strong conviction about not wasting any space. Or else they were a little bonkers.

While living at the edge of the grid was a somewhat romantic existence, this little-bit-city girl soon became lonely for a broader stroke of the humanity brush. As much as we all loved the place, I wasn't at all sure how long I could do this degree of seclusion.

☙

The sun filters through the trees casting a dark forest onto the walls of Mike's tiny makeshift music studio in the enclosed sun-porch. The surrounding woods lean in to have a look through the foggy glass at the human who is engaged in what seems to be a rather serious phone conversation. Mike is unaware of their eavesdropping, being otherwise fully engaged.

His last couple of conversations with Angel had been very difficult. His illness had advanced aggressively and he'd gone back home to Puerto Rico to be with his family. After we'd left LA, there was no one there for him and he didn't want to die alone. Mike called Angel from time to time to check in and see how he was doing. Angel's outlook had become increasingly dark and depressed. He was completely immersed in his anger toward, well, just about everything. It was distressing for Mike to be able to offer no solace, but Angel was always glad to hear from him anyway. Mike decided to talk to him about trying to find a way to get to Puerto Rico to see him, pray for him, and just to be there for him.

Angel's mother answers the phone. She speaks very little English, so when Mike asks for Angel, she tells him to wait. A moment later a man comes on the line.

"I am sorry. Angel passed last week." Angel's tio delivers the sad news.

Mike can hear Angel's mother in the background saying something. Tio translates for her.

"Maria says to tell you, thank you for being a friend to Angel. He loved you and your family and always spoke kindly of you."

Mike puts his hand over the receiver and relays the message to me. I think of Angel's shiny curls, the deep dimple on his cheek when he smiled, his buttery laugh. Loss catches in my throat.

"We loved Angel too. I'm so sorry we couldn't be there with him. Please give our love to the family." Mike hangs up the phone. We cry and pray.

It was inexcusable that this kind, generous, creative, and loving young man had been so damaged by his experience with the church. And that we had played a part in that. What a tragedy that he died with his heart heavy,

274

with the bitterness and disappointment of rejection. We took some comfort knowing that he passed away surrounded by family who loved and accepted him for who he was.

ꮯꮲ

We loved our little blue hideaway. Our time there, though short, was a peculiar and mysterious mix of adventure, tranquility, adversity, and an intense longing for more of God's Kingdom. At the same time, though, we found we were in a strange holding pattern. Wanting with all our hearts to serve Jesus through The Little Chapel, yet stuck in isolation at the edge of civilization. What to do, what to do? Pray about it and wait upon the Lord.

We invited Pastor Lee, his wife Shelly, and their family up to have a day at the lake with us. They had three kids: a teenage daughter and two sons, the youngest close to Tim's age. We had a barbeque at the lake and our kids swam and had a great time together. Pastor Lee kept us in belly laughs with his hilarious stories. I was a little intimidated by Shelly at first. She reminded me of the tough girls I'd known in high school; broad shouldered and tall, Shelly had a fierce energy that suggested an ass whooping wasn't beyond possibility if you rubbed her the wrong way. I was soon put at ease, however, by her engaging questions, the way she listened with her eyes, and laughed at my jokes. We opened up about our hopes and dreams for the arts and ministry and for *The Project*. Pastor Lee seemed genuinely excited about our lofty vision and told us he would love to see all of our artistic gifts uncorked for the kingdom.

I was so happy to feel connected to our pastor and his family. The community I so deeply desired was right at our fingertips. As charming as the fairytale life in the woods was, I could feel the pull beginning. I had a feeling we wouldn't be on the fringe for long.

ꮯꮲ

One vivid memory I have of our stay in the little blue cabin is the day we finally abandoned the use of the rod forever.

Pastor Lee gave a teaching about disciplining children. Besides being a pastor, he was also a licensed family counselor, which bore some weight with me. Probably because I was in such deep need of counseling for depression and wackiness, that I was already looking at him as some kind of beacon on the shores of sanity.

Turns out that Pastor Lee was also a badge-carrying expert in a parenting technique called Love and Logic that offered some interesting alternatives to spanking that we were eager to put into action. This technique offered the simple concept that when your kid exhibits maddening, err, ehem, I mean challenging behavior, you can help them learn to make healthy decisions by offering choices that are win-win for everyone, thereby producing responsible and productive contributors to society, instead of people you want to strangle with their own shirt.

"You can stay out here and make cookies with me, or you can continue to scream like a banshee, but that'll have to be in your room. As soon as you can be fun to be with, you can be out here with me."

I remember so vividly the moment I just thought, *screw it, I'm not doing this rod thing anymore.* Well, I probably didn't think *screw*, but maybe *the heck with it.* Nah, it was probably screw.

ANYWAY, Em had done some thing that I somehow deemed worthy of corporal punishment, although now I can't even imagine what that could have been; she was a great kid. Likely, I was just swimming in PMS hormones and imagined a roll of the eyes or something. I told her to bring the rod and meet me in my room.

I sit on the bed, looking at my sweet nine-year-old standing in front of me, face to face, in her purple corduroy overalls. She looks me squarely in the eye. Not challenging me, just questioning me with calm exasperation floating just under her utter confidence.

My heart melts and I look down at our old instrument of pain and control. The lettering is beginning to rub thin on the contact side. It looks like it says: *rain up a child in the way he should go, and in the end he will not depart from i—*

I just can't do it. Deep breath. "Em, we've been talking about it, and dad and I have decided that we're not going to use the rod anymore."

Blink, blink. "Okay." Blink, blink.

"Please go to your room until I can be more fun to be with."

Mike and I had discussed it from time to time, but never officially declared an end to the insanity. This day, the end finally came. It was a liberating day. For my kids yes, and also for me.

Mike was in total agreement, even though he had secretly stopped using it ages ago. Again I say, cheater.

So now we could throw that ol' wooden spoon in the fire pit. We would have repurposed it for stirring cookie dough, but it was engraved with all kinda disturbing reminders about spanking, and well, we had used it on our kids' butts and that would just be gross.

⁕

Winter was coming.

Our increasingly frequent trekking down to church was making life a little difficult; the gas expense was killing us and the miles were killing Ol' Bessie.

Ol' Bessie was our rig, and she was a beater: an early eighties model Ford Econoline van the size of a small ocean liner. Our car had died, leaving us completely stranded, but in classic good Christian neighborly fashion, one of the folks from the church in my mom's neighborhood had procured the monstrous vehicle for us from the back forty of his parents' ranch. She was held together with naught but bailing wire and chewing gum and she was bedecked to the nines in her vanilla pudding paint and chocolate pin striping, accessorized with hay straw in every crevice, and a hand carved *Twisted Sister* logo scratched into her dashboard.

Ol' Bessie had a wagonload of character. She especially liked showin' off when we would give some poor unsuspecting passenger a ride some-where, by dropping off a body part when you slammed the door (which was necessary to shut the doors all the way). But she came to us free of charge and full of laughs, and hey, she got us from A to B for a while. Besides, our old beater also gave us loads of practice in humility.

I was all for humble. Poor, on the other hand, I was not into at all. Poverty was very tiring to me. We were living with only the tips of our noses above the bills that were piling up when I was laid off my seasonal second job. I'd been cleaning rooms at a local Bed and Breakfast. Mike's second job—handyman at a local ranch—trickled to just a few hours a week. Like everyone in those parts, we were piecing it together, but the gaps were getting too wide for us to straddle.

The word must have gotten out at TLC that our jobs had dried up and that we were not making ends meet, because a number of people approached us with money saying that the Lord had told them they were to give it to us. One precious couple gave us a generous check and someone else bought an expensive part for Ol' Bessie, who had been ailing of late.

It was humbling to accept so much charity, but we took it as God's faithful blessing. We had a strong conviction that God was our provider and in the face of our bleak financial status, He was lavishing provision on us. This manifestation of His grace and trustworthiness pricked our consciences and inspired us to once again commit ourselves to tithing.

Broke, on unemployment, and mired in debt, we not only pledged to give ten percent of anything we earned or otherwise received, but we also pledged to give a sizeable monthly amount toward the church building fund. We would trust the Lord for that as well.

In the mountains, everything just kinda curls up and snoozes for the winter. The temperatures dropped into the realm of bone chilling and the winter snow would soon be upon us. This would bring all lumber milling and property improvement for the resort to a screeching halt. It had become obvious that the resort was more in the realm of the five to ten-year plan (if even still in the possibility sphere at all), and we were praying about our continued involvement in the venture.

At least seasonal work qualified us for unemployment benefits (a means of subsistence for many in this area) otherwise we'd have to foist ourselves on my poor mom again. We had pretty much determined in our hearts that we didn't want to go back to big city living, but we just weren't going to survive without some serious upgrades in employment.

As each day passed it was becoming clear that if we were to continue with this mountain living and being involved with TLC, we were going to have to come *down* the mountain. In Junction Gulch, the air would still be crystalline and the trees still close, but there were also real jobs, real groceries, and the possibility of a real future.

We were now in deep at church, forging new and exciting friendships with a number of people, including Pastor Lee and his family. Our place in the Body of Christ was coming into focus. Home was calling to us.

And so, after our brief adventure in the blue hideaway, the rumblings of another move came rolling toward us, urging us downward, toward new beginnings. And new endings.

MOUNTAIN FOLK

LITTLE BLUE CABIN

OL' BESSIE

WE ACTUALLY LIVE HERE.

SETTLING IN

We moved to Junction Gulch in the dead of winter. We had neither jobs nor house—just the kindness of one of the Chapel's single brothers who opened his home to our family for a few months until we could get on our feet and find an abode to call our own.

Christopher was as gentle and kind a Christian soul as you could ever meet. If you asked for his shirt, he would give you his coat as well; he went the extra mile as a natural matter of course. Pure salt. He had a fairly large home and opened it freely to folks who were just passing through or who were in need of a resting place between jail or rehab and regular life. He graciously gave us two rooms, including his own master bedroom for the time that we sojourned with him. Being the 'good cooker' that I am, I gladly prepared killer meals in an attempt at some recompense for his immense kindness and generosity.

Within a few months, we had finally saved enough money to be able to move out on our own. We found an affordable house to rent and somehow qualified despite the fact that our only source of income thus far was welfare and food stamps. Mike was busting his butt trying to find work; the only steady thing he'd been able to find was part-time subbing as a teacher's aide. He was hopeful that this might eventually land him something full-time at the high school.

The kids were settling into the elementary school (tuition for the Christian school was out of the question for us). They'd left behind a few close buddies, but we were hopeful that they would quickly make new ones.

We were beginning to feel fully grafted in and part of the family of God again. I felt an immense sense of relief to have found a healthy, thriving fellowship that was chock full 'o nutty, radical, lovable, creative, Jesus lovers. They were crazy, but not too crazy, if you get my meaning. It was an exciting time and our hearts were full of hopeful expectation as we settled in and looked eagerly forward to what the Lord had in store for our family and His Little Chapel.

෬෨

It was not long before our involvement in TLC increased exponentially. The creatives in the congregation had, of course, quickly spotted us and we were beginning to forge some friendships. We artists do tend to flock.

One of the more colorful of the group was a gal I'll call Starwalker. She was a crazy bird, who liked to hang out on the fringe. She was a poet and an Imagineer of the highest degree. She loved more than anything to play. Especially with words and ideas. We became bosom friends.

Starwalker and her hubby Ritchie were among the Elders. If Starwalker was the live wire, Ritchie was the ground; they made a perfect couple. Starwalker was the architect and facilitator of a ministry for the arts known as the League of Extraordinary Artisans. The League was going to be making a presentation to the congregation at a Sunday service to rally enthusiasm and support. Pieces were to be performed and/or displayed. Starwalker, having wheedled out of us the details of our secret theatre project, asked Mike and I to present a synopsis and an excerpt from the music. You remember *The Project*, the one packed in bubble wrap and tucked safely in that stack of boxes over there. Yes, that one—the one that's gyrating and hopping up and down like there's something alive inside scratching to get out. Starwalker was wholeheartedly behind the idea of having the show produced through TLC and became one of our champions. We got out the box cutter and readied ourselves to set that thing free.

Pastor Lee (most people just called him Lee) was an enthusiastic supporter of the arts. He loved to see people flourishing in their gifts and seemed to be open to letting folks find a way to express them. I was feeling hopeful that *The Project* had found a home too.

We spent a couple months in the early fall preparing for a reader's theatre version of the show to be presented at a local coffee bar. A number of folks from the Artisan's League graciously and enthusiastically volunteered to read and sing parts. We met a few times to do some read-throughs and rehearse flow and execution. The day of our performance, the tiny venue was packed wall-to-wall with eager faces. It was a bit awkward to deliver the intensity of this piece to an audience that we were practically touching knees with; this show begged a full-size stage. But our makeshift ensemble, all seated on stools, performed with full-voiced gusto. The audience roared in the end, which as you know, is what I live for.

We started plans for a dinner theatre fundraiser for the following year that would include another more polished mini-version: a real cast, costume and set concepts, and themed décor and food. One very committed supporter took it upon herself to go door-to-door to local businesses to seek donations toward this event and recording studio time to make a demo of the music. She raised a fair amount of cash for us.

It was wonderful indeed to see our vision of so many years unfolding at last. What a blessing to get such positive and enthusiastic feedback and support. It had been a long road to get there, but now it seemed like it would finally take flight.

A PROPHET'S REWARD

Eli was a prophet. He also owned a local machine shop. During the week he fixed stuff. Sundays, he read people's mail (delivered prophetic messages). It was agreed that Eli and his wife had been touched in a big way by the power of God. They were brimming with prophetic gifting and passion. Eli even started his own mini prophet school at TLC where he trained up regular folk to flourish in the art of hearing God's voice and speaking it to the people. This was highly prized by Papa John and Pastor Lee and the rest of the church. While I felt squeamish about the title Prophet, I liked Eli. He was a nice guy and an entertaining speaker. When he got up to preach, he made us all want to practice using our individual prophetic voices so we could help people draw nearer to God.

By the time we moved down the mountain, Eli had already been sucked into the hurricane that swirled above the COW down yonder in Big Town. It had been foretold that this would happen, just as it had been foretold that Eli would be a Father to Prophets. He was destined to go; Junction Gulch was just too tiny for the likes of that scale of calling. Now he was down at the COW running a full-sized prophet school, which boasted hundreds of students.

Lucky us, Eli still doted on our Little Chapel and Pastor Lee, and he came up from time to time to minister and *love on us*.

One Sunday, not too long after Mike and the kids and I had moved into our new home, Eli paid TLC a visit. It was fun to see him. For someone with such magical powers, he was, after all, just a regular guy.

He was the speaker for that Sunday and we all listened and wrote our notes on the blank page provided in the Sunday bulletin. I felt a touch of relief knowing that we were in obedience in the very area the Prophet was there to speak about: tithing. I felt confident and a little proud that we'd been so faithful in our giving. Afterward, as expected, Eli had a few Words to deliver to some of the congregation.

When a Prophet stood up front and said they had a Word for some of us, it was always a mixture of excited expectation and nervous apprehension for me. Would he dazzle us with his uncanny knowing? Would he deliver a Word of Correction? When he called out our name that Sunday, my heart was more full of titillation than trepidation.

"Mike and Kathy, I feel like the Lord has great things for you. He's faithful and He's seen your faithfulness. He sees your hearts and knows that they are bent toward Him and his Kingdom. He has bestowed great gifts upon you for the gathering in of the lost. He's not forgotten this. As you are faithful with your resources, He is faithful to bless and return them a hundred fold."

As he speaks, Eli makes his way down into the congregation. He stands right next to us and addresses us as if we were neighbors chatting over the fence. When he finishes, he pulls out his wallet.

"How much money do you guys need to make in order to meet your monthly needs?"

Huh? My brain is trying to catch up and figure out where he's going with this. My heart, likewise is doing the hippity-hop. All eyes are on us.

"Uh, er, uh . . ." My mental calculator clickity-clacks on the keys trying to come up with the right amount—don't want to get this one wrong, it might cost us.

"Uh, about . . ." I name a figure.

Eli opens his wallet and pulls out a twenty and pushes it into my hand. "Here's a down payment on the blessing the Lord is going to pour out on you. God is going to far surpass that in the days to come."

Eli is now looking around at the crowd (and it's a full house), "Ok. I want all of you to add to the Martens' down payment, and to your own. Come on down. Dig deep and bless the Martens."

Whaaaat is happening?! My neurons are misfiring and my mind is tweaking as people get up from their seats and begin filing past us, shoving money into our hands. I open up my purse and just hold it there like a street mime taking her collection. People stuff in crumpled up singles and neatly folded wads. They drop handfuls of change that jingle joyfully to the bottom. Soon my purse is overflowing into my lap, and Mike has to tamp down the mass of cash that's blooming over the top.

My cheeks flush crimson; I burst into tears, and bury my face in my hands. A flood of gratitude, humility, and something like relief rushes through my veins. I have no words. No frame of reference for such an act of kindness. It seems to perpetuate itself like a wave moving through the entire room. Mike, likewise, sits there in shock and awe, dumbly grinning and thanking people who wear similar grins, as they stuff, and jingle, and joyfully bless the Martens.

It was an experience I will never forget.

Later, at home, we poured out the booty on the kitchen table. Our kids had witnessed and taken careful note of this unbelievable spectacle. With squeals of "Whoa!" and "Wow!" they eagerly jumped in to assist with sorting and stacking the bills and coins.

It almost felt wrong to count it. I felt like Fagan un-crumpling the day's take from my faithful band of pickpockets. "Now, now, mah' diahs, easy wiv'a goods! An keeps yer'ands wehs oi can sees 'em!"

Eight hundred sixty-two bucks . . . and twenty-nine cents. Not a bad take for a Sunday.

Seriously though, this blew us away. Such a wacky act of generosity. I just didn't know what to make of it.

In retrospect, I can't be sure if the act was born completely out of love for the Martens—although I have no doubt that was true of some of the folks who gave—or out of obedience to the Prophet. At the time it was simply accepted as a welcome gesture of genuine helpfulness and community that enabled us to make ends meet for a few more months. And of course, we took it as a sure sign of God's unfailing love, provision, and faithfulness.

ON SPIRITUAL WARFARE

For our struggle is not against flesh and blood, but against the rulers,
against the authorities, against the powers of this dark world and
against the spiritual forces of evil in the heavenly realms.

~Ephesians 6:20

If you've never ventured into the world of Christian Charismania, you may be unfamiliar with the notion of spiritual warfare. The verse in Ephesians is often used to remind us that we're living in a great spiritual war. We're taught that part of our calling as believers is to stand victorious over said powers of darkness. We are to put on the Full Armor of God; take up the Sword of the Spirit, which is God's Word (the Bible); and to pray. Pray like heck. In doing so, we are meeting the Enemy (anything that sets itself up against God) head on and doing damage. The weapons of our warfare are prayers and worship.

Spiritual warfare I was familiar with, but had mostly understood in the context of prayer. Much like ALCF, TLC took this mighty seriously, but in addition to intercessory prayer, they looked at worship as one of the Church's most dangerous weapons indeed. The musicians, the dancers, the flaggers, the monolithic banners, all were considered powerful artillery to be used against the Enemy.

I was intrigued by the concept of worship as warfare. I had fun with the imagery of armor and swords and shields. Okay I admit it; I'm a Lord of the Rings and Braveheart nerd. Not so much a fan of the real deal, but like so many, I'm guilty of the Hollywood driven romanticizing of war. I'm not so keen on movie violence either—I watch most of it with my eyes closed—but badasses walking away from an explosion in slow-mo gets me kinda riled up inside. So fantasizing about my alter ego with her big-ass broadsword kicking some Devil butt in the spiritual realm was a frequent occurrence for me during worship.

TLC's worship leader (let's call him Morrie, shall we?) was friendly, charismatic, and funny, and he looked like Jesus (long flowing hair, neatly trimmed beard). Morrie was big into the warring songs. He invited Mike and I to come and join a few worship team practices; he wanted to see what kinda stuff we were made of. I guess we passed, 'cause not long after, we were asked to sing and play guitar at a special service they were having on the church property.

Oh, did I mention that the church had a property? Yep, they owned a good-sized parcel in town and now The Little Chapel was finally preparing to become a Big Chapel. Pastor Lee and the Elders determined that the time had come for a leap of faith. In preparation for the launch of the building project, they were spending lots of time in intense prayer and also having special worship services right at the building site to *lay the foundation*, as it were. I felt honored to be called to be a part of the team that would *do battle in the Heavenly Realm.* Our worship would be warfare and we would clear the way for the next advancement of this little Kingdom Army.

You can imagine my glee on that Sunday evening at the church property, when a group of about ten women dressed in full camo came walking in slow-mo up the dirt driveway to the beat of the war drums. No wall of fire behind them, but we were sure something else was on fire in the realm of the spirits. They danced with their tambourines and flags, rockin' the Heavenlies and takin' no prisoners.

Got pesky drug dealers in the neighborhood? Sing to the Lord a new song, and see them ousted. Got a filthy strip club on the corner? Pray and watch as they go into foreclosure. Got corrupt leaders in government? Dance a dance of freedom and see them overthrown. Got a witch hanging out at the church back door? Wave the flag of peace and witness her salvation. Wherever the Enemy is holding ground, we are the armor clad Army of God, ever ready to go in yelling, "Fire in the hole!" For this was our mission: establishing God's Kingdom on Earth as it is in Heaven.

KATHY GETS A SOLO FOR EASTER. THAT'S OUR GIRL, EM, SINGIN' BACKUPS.

෬

Sozo is a Greek word used more than one hundred times in the New Testament. It means to be saved, healed, and delivered. There was this guy—I guess he was a pastor—who travelled around the country training ministry teams in a method for bringing people into a greater freedom in Christ, (meaning in this context: emotional well-being through inner healing and demonic deliverance). His definition of Sozo was: "To be saved out from under the devil's power, and restored into the wholeness of God's order and well-being by the power of God's Spirit." This was spiritual warfare on a personal level.

This technique was being used very enthusiastically down at Papa John's church (the COW). They had teams of Sozo prayer warriors with whom one could schedule an appointment for a *Sozo Time*, an extended guided, inner exploration and *soaking* prayer session (or sessions if your demons were particularly sticky). Lee and the elders enthusiastically gathered a group of about twenty-five people to go through the Sozo training series, and they became the new Sozo Ministry Team of TLC.

According to Pastor Lee, the gist of the team's goal was this: "We all know Christians—some of us *are* these Christians—who struggle throughout life with recurring themes of sin. Many struggle to the point of giving up because of the fruitless and discouraging results of *trying harder*. The Sozo Ministry brings to light the key areas in the believer's life where the Devil has *an easement onto their property*. By locating these places of access, believers can take authority over the Oppressor and get free."

The Sozo Team's motto: "Be nice, pray hard, use breath mints."

This sounded okay to me, being an ardent wrestler of fruitless and discouraging results myself. The revolving door of my mind taking me from exultant praise, to doubt and unbelief, to deep unworthiness, to abject self-hatred, was my one-stop-shop to recurring themes of sin. My ongoing struggle with depression was a source of deep shame for me. I looked at these thought patterns as loathsome sin and I desired, more than anything else, to be free from them.

Perhaps Sozo would be my ticket to freedom. I contacted one of the leaders on the team. We got together and chatted over lunch at a local cafe.

Naomi's countenance is sweet and gentle; she looks directly and softly into my eyes. I don't know her well, but for some reason I unreservedly open up to her.

"I love Jesus with all my heart. I'm committed to serving him and pouring out my life for him. I love the lost and have devoted myself to using my life and all of my gifts to see them saved and discipled. I love the family of God and want so much to be a vital contributing member." I vomit my resume all over Naomi's tuna on rye.

"So what seems to be the trouble?" She asks; her kind smile draws me out.

"I'm also a lowly worm. A ship tossed on the waves of doubt, fear, and unbelief. I disappoint the Lord on a regular basis with my depression, despair, and hopelessness."

"Wow. That sounds like a bummer. How's that working for you?" she asks. I've heard these precise words come out of Pastor Lee's very astute mouth. Because I trust Pastor Lee, I feel at once at ease. I can trust this lady; she's obviously been trained by the best.

"Not so well." I sigh and push my sandwich to the side.

"I've even been on Prozac for the last six years. It helps me to not yell so much at my kids, but now I feel like I can't feel much of anything. I rarely laugh anymore and I can't seem to get out of this rut that runs in circles in my head."

Revealing my use of psychotropic medications is risky. Trusting antidepressants over God's power to heal is a semi-unspoken taboo in church circles. I search her face for her verdict.

"Hmmm." She chews thoughtfully. She looks in my eyes and smiles. "I'm thinking that a Sozo time would be a good thing for you. Let's pray about it for a few days and see what the Lord shows us, then maybe we can schedule one."

We finished our lunch, chatted and laughed, and I felt that this indeed might be just the prescription. Our conversation gave me a hunch she had struggles of her own, which made me feel connected and heard. I was relieved to have found someone who felt safe enough that I could let them in on some of my secret darkness.

❧

We met for my Sozo time in the living room of one of the Elder couples. Naomi was there and her ministry partner for our session was Charlotte. Charlotte was an Elder, but she was not old. She was, however, older than *I*, and seemingly wise, gentle, and caring—all good qualities for an Elder to possess. Also, Charlotte was a close friend of Starwalker and a little wacky and fun. Besides, she knew how to play the spoons (she demonstrated for us), and that was just too awesome to take lightly.

Their home is lovely and inviting with big overstuffed chairs and tastefully appointed décor. I settle into the embrace of a fat, cozy recliner.

"Zo, vhat zeemz to be ze pggggrrrrablem?" Dr. Sozo inquires, touching the point of her pencil to the tip of her tongue.

We chat about my thoughts and feelings around my bouts with depression and anxiety. We talk about childhood issues like feelings of abandonment and having grown up with people who drank and argued and all the usual stuff that many of my generation went through.

Charlotte sits on my right, her hand on my shoulder. Naomi is on my left, mirroring Charlotte. She prays in tongues for a bit, is quiet for a few moments, then says, "I feel the Holy Spirit is saying you've given the Enemy access through areas of un-forgiveness toward your parents."

"K. I don't feel angry though. I've got a pretty good relationship with my parents. I've never really thought about needing to forgive them."

"We can tend to hold on to things without even knowing it. It becomes a point of access. A gateway. I feel like this is a good direction to start."

So the two prayer warriors went to work, showering me with love and blessings and blanketing me with the sweet presence of the Holy Spirit. They rebuked the Enemy, used their giant God Scissors to cut any slimy strings that Satan might have tied onto my soul (Charlotte was keen on acting things out metaphorically), and proclaimed me free indeed. I also prayed, asking forgiveness for my un-forgiveness. I blessed my parents and promised to be a good girl and eat all my peas.

And that was about it. Simple. They were nice and they prayed hard. I don't recall breath mints, but I don't recollect bad breath either, so they were probably good on that front too.

Apparently, I got off easy. My friend Starwalker recently recalled an experience she went through with the *expert* Sozo Team that had come up from the COW to hold a training to teach the TLC team how to do it *right*.

As part of the training, each member of the TLC team was to have a Sozo time with a pair from the COW team.

Starwalker and her hubby had arrived at the training after a rough morning and a gnarly disagreement. Starwalker sported a lovely wet pink nose and very suspicious puffy, red-rimmed eyeballs. Of course, the headmaster proclaimed that they would be starting the first round of ministry time with the poor snuffling sod in the front row (Starwalker was sure they thought she had started her morning with a boilermaker and a doobie, and that's why they picked her first).

She was sequestered away with two total strangers into a separate room where they sat her in the hot seat as they prayed in tongues and circled her like carrion crows. One of the gals stopped abruptly, pointing a bony finger in Starwalker's face and shouted.

"You! Have a spirit of rebellion upon you!" She continued wagging her accusing digit in front of Starwalker's chaffed sniffer.

"Yes! A spirit of haughtiness!" Number Two mirrored Number One's indicting finger jab as if she were a partner in some kind of absurdly melodramatic cheerleading routine.

This tirade went on for a bit and afterward, they asked her what her last name was. Puzzled, she told them her married name and her maiden name, which identified her as being from good German stock. They mmmhmmmed and aha'd and went on to explain that their intuitions were obviously dead on and were clearly promptings from the Holy Spirit about her German heritage. What?! What the hell did that mean? Of course, if I had heard about this encounter before *my* Sozo, I probably would have run the other way. I have since read on the interwebs (it's disconcerting how many recovery groups exist for former members of these types of church movements) a number of disturbing accounts of disastrous fallout from these practices. I count myself fortunate that I was in much less aggressive hands with our own gentle and kind TLC ladies.

A few days after our prayer time, I probed Naomi for her guidance regarding my Mother's Little Helpers.

"So what are your thoughts about me still being on meds?" I asked.

Naomi was thoughtful. "I don't know, Kath. That's gonna be your call. I felt like your Sozo went well. What do you think?"

I felt okay about my ministry time. I trusted God for my complete deliverance. But I was scared. My emotional state was so mercurial, even on meds. I didn't know if I wanted to risk a return to the really dark places. Or to the rage. Oh my. This decision felt like a very big stretch. I decided to pray about it.

"That's awesome Kath. I know this is a biggie. I also know that the Lord is faithful to hold you tight and is able to fully deliver you, but you gotta be in a place of utter trust."

I took a few days to pray and seek God's peace in the matter. I discussed it with Mike. He was hesitant (he had experienced the roller coaster), but supportive in whatever decision I felt the Lord was leading me to.

I called Naomi. "So I'm thinking that if I'm to really trust in God and his power to fully save, heal, and deliver me, I guess I need to step out in obedience and go off the meds."

"Praise God." Naomi's exaltation was quiet and unadorned. "He'll hold you firm Kath. And I'm here for you. Do you have a plan?"

"Well, I figured I'd taper the meds over a couple weeks and see how it goes."

"Well, like I said, I'm here for you. If you need to talk, please, call me."

Naomi's voice was confident, strong, and committed. I felt that I wouldn't be in this thing alone if it didn't go well. So I set my face toward heaven and took the free-fall.

(Five weeks in after stopping meds) *Today is a rough day so far. Fierce agitation/anger. Jesus.*

(further in) *Lord, thank you for your faithfulness! I know that you have delivered me from depression—you have called me out of darkness to walk in your glorious light . . .*

(further in still) *Jesus, help! My head is so full—I can't seem to find myself in here—or you either. Please help me, God.*

(a number of weeks beyond that) *Very hard day today Lord. I am struggling to see the point of my life . . . why does my heart still hurt so much? Is it unbelief? Is it demonic? Jesus, I am crying out to you! Like David, my bones are turning to dust inside of me . . .*

. . . inside I'm just dying, empty, confused. Where is the joy, peace, freedom, hope? Where is my salvation? If my life here makes no difference, then WHAT IS THE POINT?

. . . Please, relief Lord. How many times must I come to this place? I must not be all the way dead yet, because I'm still feeling pain and grief. Oh, Lord. I love you so . . .

Hide the Vodka, the children, and the rod. The roller coaster ride has begun. What was the deal? Was my Sozo only so-so? Was my emotional imbalance incurable, or was I just incurably sinful? But nothing was going to shake my faith in God's goodness. It had to be my badness. I knew if I hung in there, He was going to see me through to the end—even if it was one that was completely unthinkable to me at the time.

STUTTERING FORWARD

Our first year in Junction Gulch had been a big adjustment for our family, lots of transitioning and disquieting upheaval, and now like a slow-mo crash dummy, I was hitting the Prozac wall. I had way too much time on my hands in which to spiral into my very unhappy place, and I was going there more and more frequently. My head was spinning with alternating anxiety and depression over just about every area of my life.

I finally swallowed my pride and scheduled counseling time with Pastor Lee. He was comforting and kind, but he was a ninja with the mirror. He just didn't let people off the hook when it came to taking personal responsibility for their own suffering.

He basically told me that my problem was that I was seeking my identity in being a human doing, rather than in being a human being. In other words, I needed to understand that my self-worth didn't come from what I did, only from who I was: a Child of God.

I got this reasoning as clear as day when I was in my right mind. Unfortunately, I was of two minds, and the left one didn't always look at things the same way as the right.

Besides, I was becoming confused about what exactly a child of God looked like, at least as defined by the Great Lexicon of the Church of the Holy Charismata. The profile was like one of those little holographic pictures that you pull out of a box of Cracker Jacks. You know, the little pictures that look like a princess when you hold it one way, and a wicked old hag when you turn it ever so slightly the other.

I took home some worksheets and a book recommendation. I did the first couple of exercises and then did a slow slide into a zone that I have (thankfully) only visited a handful of times in my life. It was deep, and dark, and disturbing. This visit lasted for a number of months. I did get out of bed, but only because I had kids and I didn't want to scare them.

The adjustment period for our kids was proving to be somewhat difficult as well, but in a different way. They had already gone from schools in LA with populations upwards of eight hundred, to the school near my mom's house that boasted an enrollment of about fifty, then to the school up the road by the little blue cabin where they topped out at a whopping twelve or so kids.

Now they were back in civilization, with zero school chums, entering in the middle of the term, into a crowd of four hundred. Luckily they were very resilient. It seemed a little tougher on our boy though. Kids can be just plain mean (as can their parents), and though he wasn't a sissy, Tim had a heart the size of Texas, and tender as a lamb. We had many a night that first year at tuck-in time, with tears and anguish over the mean boys at school.

I am happy to report, however, that while retaining that heart of gold, our little Timmy grew up to tower over most of those jerks and could kick their *dad's* asses. He also developed a razor wit and a brilliant mind that leaves most of those turds in the dust. But no bias here.

Em, of course, walked in there with an intellect and a vocabulary that pretty much blew her teachers minds right out of the gate. She and her brother had grown up with very little TV and ginormous imaginations, which made her a dream for her English teacher.

Most of the kids her age just didn't know what to do with the likes of her—scary smart and totally secure in herself. Luckily, for the time being, she was content to disappear into her books and her story writing. She eventually found a few others that came from the same planet as she had, but it took a couple years.

Turns out, our family was not the only one going through transition. We hit Junction Gulch as The Little Chapel was entering into a time of great revolution as well. It was happening gradually, so we didn't notice it for some time. Truth is, the shift had begun upon Papa John's departure and would be churning out change after change for the next twelve years or so. We just happened to hook in at the vanguard of a couple of biggies.

It was announced that Morrie would be leaving to take a position with another church overseas. This left two giant holes in the church staff roster: Worship Leader and Youth Pastor.

Mike was working, but not nearly enough hours for us to make ends meet. He was eager about the opportunities that could possibly be opening for him with Morrie leaving. He would obviously be great in either or both positions.

Mike loved working with teenagers (he was very good at it) and hoped he would be considered as a replacement for Morrie as youth pastor. He was also leading on the worship team once a month at least, so he was anticipating that Lee might see that he was a natural fit for the gaps that Morrie was leaving. Mike went in to talk to Lee and make his heart known.

"Duly noted," was about the extent of Lee's response.

A few weeks later it was announced that a new couple was moving up from the COW to join the TLC pastoral team as Youth Pastors. It was Papa John's son and daughter-in-law, Seth and Rachel. Soon after, a similar announcement was made about the worship team leader. There had been two 'lay leaders' while Morrie was there, Mike and one other musician. The other musician was chosen as the new team leader. It was hard to not be disappointed.

Once we met the new couple that was to lead the youth group, however, it was clear why they had been chosen. Aside from the obvious reason, Seth and Rachel were also a sweet, dynamic, and gifted young couple, full of passion and big, cutting edge ideas. They both were closer to teenage than not, and of course, Seth was cut from the same cloth as his papa: destined for great things.

✑

Probably the best thing that happened for me that year was Mike kicking my booty out of the house.

"Go get a job, woman!"

I felt so overwhelmed with my emotional state that I didn't know if I could handle getting a job. Mike, being the ever wise man that he is, knew that I had too much time to sit around and wallow in my misery. He also knew that if I didn't start adding to the income soon, he might have to turn gigolo, and he didn't want to have to explain that to the kids, or the church.

So, I pulled myself up by the bra straps and I got a part-time clerical position at an insurance agency. This was probably the best therapy I could have chosen. It forced me to not think, just do. Mike has always been my Yoda.

The initial few weeks of work were exhausting for me. I was using different parts of my brain for the first time in quite a while. I felt like I could lie down and sleep for a month every time I took a nap. I finally acclimated and found that my energy was starting to increase. Apparently it takes a lot less brain cells to do insurance than to wallow in the pit of despair.

A number of months later, I began to be reacquainted with my old friend Creativity, and felt ready to pick up the ball on *the Project* again. We dusted off the script and set our sights toward the dinner theatre fundraiser.

TWO LADIES

It came from somewhere behind us, in the back of the room. The worship service was in full swing. The music was sublime and the presence of the Holy Spirit was thick in the air, wrapping us all in a transcendent blanket of bliss.

From among the chorus of voices praising God's goodness, came a great sonorous wail. The single voice rose on its harmonious note to a crescendo that would threaten to shatter all the windows in the auditorium, if there had been any. She sang on, like the lone soloist in a black church choir, raising the hair on my neck and making my heart take flight.

I wasn't exactly sure what to make of it. I loved the sound; it was brazen, edgy, soulful, but I could feel the energy around me tense up a bit. I wanted desperately to look behind me and see from whom this powerful song was emanating. Who was this voice in our midst that could sing God's praises with such power and abandon? It was ridiculous, and fun, and a little bit dangerous and out of control. It brought me such delight, but the rest of the room, I don't know. I could feel people pull themselves in, stiffen. It was almost like they just hoped it might go away soon.

Later, I looked around, but apparently she had gone. I asked someone about her.

"Oh, that's Rose."

"Wow! What a voice."

"Well, yes. We see her from time to time. She always does that. I think she's an actor or something. She's got some issues."

My heart hitched just a little. I was talking to someone who was considered an elder (as opposed to an Elder), and this didn't feel so much like love. I filed it away.

At the time I didn't identify it, but my antennae popped up out of my head a quarter inch or so. They were still below the surface of my hair, so I don't think she, or even I for that matter, noticed.

I still wanted to meet this wailing worshipper. It wasn't like she was retching, or flailing, or even out of order (we were all singing, for God's sake). She was just . . . different. And she stood out. Waaaaay out.

ℰℐ

Jillian danced like a goddess. She was beautiful and voluptuous like a Marilyn, but moved like a Grace. A Venus, only with lots more clothes on. She was not a part of the dance team, but she also wasn't merely one of the occasional ladies who made their way to the dance area to bust a few moves for Jesus. Jillian was one of the magical creatures. When she moved onto the floor, the space around her enlarged and the atmosphere expanded.

Sometimes, with a nod from the worship leader, she would step up and dance on the stage. She occasionally would bring a sheer and shimmery shawl or scarf to accompany her as her partner: a flowing, waving, undulating manifestation of the Spirit, winding above and around her body like the gentle caresses of a lover.

Jillian was obviously trained in dance, and her skill, displayed so elegantly before the Master, was a thing of beauty. I didn't know Jillian yet. We'd not been introduced, although the same *elder* who filled me in on Rose did feel the need to let me know that Jillian "had issues" when I commented on how lovely her dancing was. Whatever. I loved it when Jillian danced. She made me want to dance too. And so I did.

I waited for a Sunday that she wasn't dancing. I didn't want to presume to invade her space. When I could stand the apprehension no longer, I buoyed my courage and moved into the aisle and down to the front. The familiar tingle of my armpits announced the arrival of the sweat. My heart moved into its alternate position in my throat. It'd been many years since I had danced publicly, but somehow, the Spirit was propelling my feet forward.

I danced, and it was like embracing an old, dear friend. Oh how my muscles had longed for their connection with the music. It's an ache that never goes away. I felt the eyes of the people on me, and I struggled to keep my focus on the Lord's presence. I didn't want to be in danger of performing, but I confess that this was a fine line for me. Nevertheless, it was a sublime feeling to dance again, and later, people thanked me. That, of course, is like throwing gasoline on a flame.

A few Sundays after my first act of bravery, Jillian was on the floor again, along with a few other ladies. I felt my heart tug: *join them* it urged. I figured it was an invitation from the Holy Spirit.

That would be rather presumptuous of me, wouldn't it Lord? I prayed.

"Don't be an ass. Get down there and shake it, girl!"

I'd worn my black combat boots just for the occasion. So with my inner cudgel beating my ribs to a pulp, I moved once again to the floor, but this time it was *her* territory.

I stepped off the carpet and onto the black. Space opened up for me. I closed my eyes and took a deep breath. I let go of my thoughts and let the Spirit lead my body. Soon I found that I was dancing right next to Jillian. The music changed, and we were into a much faster more driving, upbeat tune. Jillian smiled at me. She winked and said, "Follow me."

She jammed into a series of hip-hoppy kind of steps, then froze. I repeated her movements and froze. She moved again and stopped. I repeated. Then without thinking, on my next turn, I did something completely different from her and she followed my lead. This went on for a few more measures until we switched again. Then at some point, we continued alternating between moving and still, but instead of repeating one another, we would do completely different moves from each other—move, stop, move, stop— moving in, around and through each other's very tight body space. It was an amazing experience. No thought. No choreography. Just pure, in-the-moment movement. When the song finished, we were soaked to the skin. I was huffing and puffing and vibrating from head to toe. It was so exhilarating and liberating and powerful. We were one and we were two. Actually, we were three. We could feel the Lord's pleasure as we danced together. We complemented one another well—a sinewy beanpole and a curvaceous va-va-voom—tearing it up for Jesus. We were good together and I was hooked.

THEATRE: THE NEW PROZAC

Giving myself permission to dance opened up a deep well for me. My muscle memory quickly nudged and awakened my theatre muse. What a profound itch that thing is for some of us. Hydrocortisone won't touch it. No amount of nailing it to the cross can kill it utterly, only for so long. That damn thing is so prone to resurrection.

Enter: The Rose.

You remember Rose, the back-row wailer. She stayed after church one Sunday and I finally had the pleasure of making her acquaintance. I was instantly smitten.

Not long after, I found myself at her home one morning for coffee.

I'm welcomed at the door by an Orca whale masquerading as a dog. He is the size of a small car and full of massive effervescence as he takes my entire right arm into his mouth in greeting.

"Okay, okay, Mr. Bubbles," Rose says, using her full body weight to pull her pup back.

I brush my slobber-coated arm on the front of my sweatshirt as I scan the place for the nearest sink. The room is an open floor plan with living room, dining room, and kitchen all adjoining. A large orange cat is curled up on the dining room table; another, a calico, sits on the counter watching us.

"Come on in," Rose says, smiling widely. Her mouth takes up a great deal of her face, with teeth like large pearls surrounded by thick ruby lips. Her eyes are lined with black inside the lash line; her black hair streaked with shocks of white at the temples. Everything about her emanates a kind of vastness. She's not overweight by any means, but she is somehow large, fills up the room with herself. Her clothes are flowy and brightly colored.

"May I wash my hands?" I say. Dogs and cats sometimes make my eyes itch.

"Of course. Coffee?"

"Oh yes," I say.

She runs beans through a grinder, adding a pinch of salt to the filter.

"Mellows the flavor," she says. I later find out that she's a chef, trained in Italy.

Dishes are piled on the drainer along with many empty beer and wine bottles. A large pot simmers on the stove with the aroma of food from heaven curling up from under the lid.

"Lamb stew," she says.

Rose gives me a tour of their backyard. Fall has taken most of what were abundant flowers, but she is proud of the eclectic if not disturbing yard art her husband has tucked around here and there: a fat, smiling be-jeweled elephant Buddha statue; a bird bath of mosaic tile with a Barbie doll perched provocatively on the rim; another doll, this one a baby, planted feet up among red hot pokers. Mixed era furniture and other stuff (which she calls *chachka*, my first exposure to this word) is arranged on a gravel area surrounded by ankle-high grass. My husband likes things wild, she tells me, laughing. She nods toward a crucifix hanging on a tall oak tree; a suffering Jesus turns his eyes skyward.

"Walter loves to chide me for my faith. He calls it my 'Judeo Christian guilt trip.' He's a cantankerous old Jew, but I adore him," she says, looking at her hands. The fingernail of her left ring-finger is painted fire engine red. (I later find out that Walter's is too. "To remind us that marriage must be tended to," she told me.)

We sit at her kitchen table sipping our coffee. The orange cat takes in-termittent sips of Rose's glass of water. She tells me about her life, which has been hard.

"If they made a movie about my mother, it would be called The Devil Wears Culottes," she says.

We laugh a lot. And pray together. Her world feels so foreign to me; she seems so untamed. And genuinely kind.

"My motto," she says: "Love is better."

Rose and I bonded quickly. She was as loony as everyone said. She knew it and made no apologies. She was a wounded, tender, zany, kind-hearted oddball. She was mysterious and strange, open and raw. She was a gargantuan talent: an actress to be reckoned with and a sultry singer with a Merman twist. She also loved Jesus with all her being.

And she had *issues*. Who the hell doesn't? I didn't care. We were kindred spirits in many ways—especially the ways of theatre—and when it came to *the craft* . . . she got it.

Rose wasn't a native of the area, she was a transplant from more than a decade before Mike and I. She'd been all over the world. She was a professional actress, and had, over the years, graced the local community theatre group with her ferocious artistry.

She was getting ready to direct an upcoming production of Neil Simon's *God's Favorite*. She approached me about playing one of leads in the show, a plucky, Jersey-mouthed Angel of God. Of course I was all over that.

The show was irreverent and a little bawdy which, for the love of the game, I could easily compartmentalize. We enjoyed glowing reviews in the local paper and effusive praise in the guest book. Lots of people were filled with the healing balm of laugh-induced endorphins. This, to me, was ministry. Oh how I loved the laughter. And the applause, well, let's just say my alter ego was mightily stroked and the longing was awakened once again.

Rose and I had an utter blast working together. We spoke the same language, shared a similar twisted sense of humor, and enjoyed some good belly laughs. We were a couple of Jesus loving theatre junkies and after the show closed, we were already plotting and scheming for more.

Of course, as my relationship with the Rose grew, TLC's trusty Character Barometer—the elder—made sure that I was properly warned about getting *too* close. She had me over for tea and a special chat.

"I've been praying about it and I feel like the Lord wanted me to caution you about your involvement with Rose."

Blink, blink.

"You need to know she's got some issues, some strongholds of the Enemy, and I'm just a little concerned that you might be opening yourself up to something that you don't really want to get on you."

Blink, blink. Heart beat increasing, pits tingling, mind racing.

"You just may want to be careful how much you let her in. Be praying for her, but be cautious with your involvement. You have a calling on your life. I wouldn't want to see it get waylaid by dangerous associations."

This truly pissed me off. But this person was in the high regard of the leadership (both at TLC and with Papa John) and in a position of prominence. Familiar and unsettling feelings began to percolate from places that I thought had been thoroughly purged. I understood that Rose had her "issues" and that she was different and did not necessarily submit herself to the "authority" of church leadership. She respected the pastors (both Lee and John), but she didn't feel beholden to do or be anything other than what she felt God asked of her personally. She walked her walk in her own matchless way.

"Well, thanks for your concern, I'll pray about it."

I left with the hot shame of not having come to the defense of my friend. I folded under old patterns of spiritual manipulation and control that I thought I had put behind me. What the hell? I was being put in a terrible position of playing some kind of *us and them* game again. *Us* being: people without issues (ain't that a laugh), and *them* being: those who don't look the way *us* thinks they should. Yes, this was going to take some serious prayer.

I spent days agonizing, praying and journaling about the situation. I found it deeply disturbing and frankly infuriating. I armed myself with a bunch of Scripture verses about love and gossip, and we met again to chat.

I hate confrontation more than just about anything. Even throwing up, which I loathe, but kinda feel like doing when I have to confront someone. I sat with my guts churning and I launched into my spiel.

"I've been thinking and praying a lot about what you said to me the other day. I've been feeling pretty uncomfortable with it. It felt an awful lot like gossip to me."

"Well, I certainly wouldn't want you to feel I was gossiping about Rose, but I can sense when people have got demonic attachments or influence going on. I've been called as a 'watchman' of sorts. I'm not saying that Rose is possessed or anything like that. I'm just saying she has some strongholds in her life that may be giving the Enemy some access. Since you're a part of the worship team, I felt it was important that I make you aware of it."

"Well, it didn't feel loving to me or like you were at all concerned with Rose as a fellow believer. It just felt like gossip. Rose is a person of good character and deep commitment to the Lord. A little out there? Maybe. Different? Definitely. But I don't really get anything like *demonic attachment* at all."

We continued our discussion, trying to make ourselves clear to one another, neither one really persuading the other to the intended revelation. The conversation was amiable in the end, but the whole thing made my craw all scratchy and inflamed. It felt so out of character from the things we were all being taught about love and compassion. I just wasn't sure what to do with the feelings that this exchange was bringing up, so I did what I always did, stuffed them deep so I could go on loving my church.

❦

Little by little, we'd been putting together some pieces from *The Project* in preparation for the fundraising dinner. Activity around it was sporadic, since Mike and I were both now working more and busy with many other church activities, theatre, our kiddos, and life.

I enlisted the help of a gifted young artist to draw some costume concepts. I did some set sketches and we had some preliminary rehearsals with the cast to start working on music. It was a rush to hear all of the voices singing the chorus parts. It felt like our long held dream was becoming a reality.

We were also excited because Em was finally old enough to play one of the lead characters, a little girl that gets healed by the metaphorical Jesus. Her character had a solo and a reprise and it would be an emotionally challenging role. Em was already showing amazing vocal abilities and was the perfect age for the part. Tim was all set to play the Little Blind Boy. Okay, so it was a walk-on that Mike invented for him, but what the heck can a seven-year-old expect. Buck up kid, gotta pay your dues just like everyone else.

I hold one music rehearsal in particular as a fond memory. We had cast Rose in the role of The Prostitute. (Every allegory about Jesus must have someone to stone, right?) She was the only trained actor in the bunch besides Mike and me.

We stood in a circle in our living room. There was an ensemble number that included a repeating solo verse from Rose's character. Everyone had only kinda learned their parts and was feeling their way through it for the first time. When her solo came up, Rose—Method as she was—slithered down onto her belly on the floor and then reclined provocatively as she sang her slow and languid phrase: "Come, abandon your cares to my hire. Tryst with the flames of desire. If only for one single hour."

She stayed there, lying on the floor, like Mae West on her chaise, invitingly primping and undulating quietly until her next solo. When it came 'round again, she turned up the heat again, slowly shimmying her shoulders and rolling her head, like the whore that she was (playing). The men in the room—hell everyone in the room—sucked in their sphincter muscles and sang on, pretending not to notice. When the song was finished, she jumped up, laughing and joking, confident as a peacock, while everyone else let out a collective sigh of relief and a few of the dudes checked their flies.

Oh glory-be! It was one of the most uncomfortable and breath-held-in moments in church musical history. It was marvelous. I was at once mortified for Rose and wanted to sit at her feet and learn of this wondrous thumbing of the nose at decorum. *We were actors, for Christ's sake!* We should be free to *act* like it! Mhm. I know. Issues. Whatever.

We set the fundraising dinner date for Christmastime. I secured a venue to hold the event, and wrangled a full staff of youth group teenagers to serve and help at the dinner. One of the couples in the group who owned a local café was set to cook some mean gourmet vittles designed around the theme of the show. We had the décor all planned out. The only thing left was ticket sales. Being a fundraiser and all, we set the price fairly high. Not too high, but really-nice-dinner-out high.

We sent out a letter to the church mailing list. A familiar refrain then played for *The Project* (and for us): "Chirp, chirp, chirp."

I think we sold like eighteen tickets. Okay, that may be dramatizing it a little. It was more like twenty. When we were a couple weeks out, we issued refunds. We would barely cover our costs, let alone get any exposure or have any working capital to move forward.

Disappointed? Yep. It was so weird. Everyone had been so enthusiastic about it. We'd been totally convinced that people were fully behind us and were taking the show under their wing as a project of TLC.

There is something to be said for timing though, I will concede to that. Building fund pledges, twenty-five different conferences coming up, Christmas looming, outreach trips being saved for; it was totally understandable. There were many things vying for people's attention and dollars. Why should our thing be given priority? We got it. It still stung.

Mike bucked up and turned his attention to the recording of the music. At least if he could produce a decent demo, perhaps we could seek additional support from other churches, maybe even down the hill, from Papa John. Mike pulled some of the funds that had been donated for the dinner theatre, bought some studio time down in the big city, and went to work. We recorded a number of the songs from the show, but it was slow going.

Like so many other dreams, this one finally just stalled and got put into mothballs. Over time, the remaining money that had been raised for *The*

Project got sucked up into the church fund labeled General. Some time later, when Mike approached them, the Elders wouldn't release any of the money for him to do the final mix, so the demo was never completed.

I think I might be able to find a copy of a dog-eared script in the closet somewhere along with some rough recordings of the music, if you know a guy who knows a guy who's brother-in-law might be interested in a really cool Christian theatre piece.

THROUGH THE RABBIT-GLASS: WONDERLAND REVISITED

All in the golden afternoon
Full leisurely we glide;
For both our oars, with little skill,
By little hands are plied,
While little hands make vain pretense
Our wanderings to guide.

~Lewis Carroll, from *Alice's Adventures in Wonderland*

When I heard Connor Roberts was coming up to visit TLC, my tummy did a slow roll. Connor Roberts was a Prophet. A Big Gun from back in our ALCF days who often traveled preaching and giving prophetic words to churches.

I hadn't met him, but he was quite famous, in certain circles. I had heard him preach on a couple of cassette tapes that Luanne had shared with me back in the day. His messages, like our old pastor Len's, were weird and full of bizarre imagery and obscure Old Testament Scripture references. It was typical of all prophetic words delivered to the church, proclaiming that something really big was just around the corner. With his slow southern drawl, he sounded like a nice ol' corncob-pipe-whittling grampa from the backwoods.

This guy was connected with the whole Blessing Movement that spawned the crazy condition Pastors Jim and Len had contracted back in Wonderland that had driven their people completely mad. I'd heard some scuttlebutt about a number of way-out and inaccurate prophetic words that had been given by Connor Roberts, but since I needed to believe that my new leadership had their heads screwed on right, I decided that I would let the rumors go. These prophetic types could get a little carried away; I knew that.

Brother Roberts was going to be a headliner at a huge four-day prophetic conference being held down at the COW. Since TLC was an adopted sibling, we would reap the benefits of him being in town.

Upon hearing someone announce that we were privileged to be having a visit from one of "our Prophetic Fathers" I put one finger on each antenna and pushed them down deep. I loved my Little Chapel and I didn't want to believe that we were circling back around into affiliations with strange and distant cousins. I chose to trust that Pastor Lee (and ultimately Papa John) were not going to steer us into any doo-doo that we then would have to scrape off our boots and out of our hearts.

The service and the message were the usual fare, for a Man of God. Of course, the sense of excitement and anticipation of having such a celebrity visit our humble little congregation created a charge in the air and added a little extra oomph to the worship time.

Connor spoke of mules and farmers, ticks and fleas, eagles and eaglets, raindrops on roses and whiskers on kittens. He reminded us that we were no longer guilty of our past sins and should forget them, just as God had. *If only I could forget.* He exhorted us to repent of believing the lies of our Enemy. He cautioned us to not remain stuck in the pain of our past sins thereby missing the Prophetic Anointing that God wanted to release upon us. Pretty standard stuff told through a different set of metaphors.

The people were pretty jacked up by the presence of the Power Wielding Papa. "We must respond to the call of the Father to enter into our greatness!" was the shout out of the day.

But I knew this would be the case, it always was after compelling speakers with tons of ethos. This led to lots of talk and newsletter articles and subsequent sermons, but I didn't fully notice where it was going . . . yet.

On the contrary, I found *myself* stirred by the call to greatness, though this should be no surprise; I was prone to the allure of the prophetic gifts. It's also true that I'm easily aroused by a noble theme and cry at the opening strains of Star Wars.

In the end, Brother Roberts seemed to be pretty much about helping the people to understand their inheritance in Christ. I was okay with that. For the moment, TLC still seemed to look like our Little Chapel. I bristled a bit at the bestowing of title and position upon Roberts—after all, he was just a regular guy who poops and farts like the rest of us—but what the heck did I know?

૯૦

The turning of the millennium was a bellows on the Spirit's fire, stirring up a mighty wind in the church. We all wondered what Y2K might bring. For the faithful, it promised to be the turning of the tide toward Kingdom Come. Although some beans and rice were bought in bulk, mostly the talk was of unprecedented outpourings of the Holy Spirit and great waves of Revival.

We began hearing murmurs of a new movement that was being birthed. To ring in the New Year, a call was going out across the land heralding a nation-wide forty-day fast for the youth of America, and none other than our old ALCF friend, Pastor Len, was leading the charge. He was finally hitting the Big Time, just as it had been foretold. This was no surprise to Mike and I. Fasting and praying was Len's brand, as it were, and we always knew that his fiery message was too big to be contained in one locale. It was oddly disquieting however, to find out that he was to be the guest speaker at a big youth conference that was scheduled down at the COW. This meant, of course, that he would also be venturing up the hill to speak at The Little Chapel.

I was weirdly divided about this. I hated that such a close brush with old Wonderland ties was headed our way, but I really had liked Len, crazy coot that he was. Len and his wife had been a source of comfort and encouragement to me when I was just a wee babe in the faith.

Of course, I knew that he would be his typical goofy self, ranting, rocking, stirring up (and spraying) the crowd with his infectious zeal and his disarming punch lines. I'm embarrassed to admit that I carried a secret little pride at being able to say that we were friends. But somewhere deep in my motherboard, all kinda lights were flashing, and my inner Robot hollered, "Danger Will Robinson! Danger!" I soothed my vigilant gatekeeper saying, *Shhhhhhh, it'll be fine. It's just Len.*

So Len showed up. His message hadn't changed much, except that it was now being aimed specifically at the young people. He was putting out the call to the youth of America to join the Army of God and commit to a life of fasting and prayer.

He gave some background on how he had come on to this path. Of course, this included sharing his affiliation with Pastor Jim and how The Harvest

307

(their church) had started down south. Old hauntings stirred and rose into the forefront of my memories. A little hive popped out on the back of my neck.

Happily, he quickly moved on to share that the Lord had called him to a new ministry. He said God told him that the outcome of this call to the youth would birth a prayer movement that would change the destiny of our nation. He was ramping up for a huge rally to be gathered in Washington DC to pray and fast for our country to turn back to God.

As predicted, he wowed the crowd. If you'd been there listening as an unbeliever, you'd have said he was off his bloody nut. If you were born again and of the Charismatic persuasion, you'd have said he was an anointed Prophet and that he was totally awesome. Same old Len.

After the service, he greets us with genuine joy and affection.

"Mike and Kathy Martens," he says.

Hugs all 'round.

"So great to see you. How are you guys? Aw, I'm so sorry Susan isn't here. She'd love to see you. How're your kids? How are Emily and . . . and . . ."

"Tim," I say.

"Yeah! Tim! Tim."

"They're awesome," Mike says.

Len looks exactly the same—forehead perhaps expanding its real estate a smidge—but otherwise he's hardly aged a day. He's still buzzing from his message, rocking a bit as he talks, a little spit bubbling at the corner of his broad grin.

"That's great, that's great. So you two're living way the heck up here, huh? You must love it. It's beautiful. God's doing some mighty things up here."

"We love our Little Chapel," I say.

"So glad you two are plugged into such an awesome church. You guys coming down to the conference at the Church of Wonders?"

"Not this time. Sorry to miss you," Mike says.

"Hey, that's fine, that's fine." We stand around smiling at each other for a few moments. The space in the conversation becomes wide and gaping.

"So, great to see you guys," he says.

"Yeah! Yeah . . ."

The crowd begins to press in. We have another round of hugs; he promises to give our love to his wife and family; then Mike and I step aside to let him receive his fans.

Afterward Mike and I talk about it.

"Weird to have him show up all the way up here," Mike says.

"Yeah, weird."

"You'd think we'd moved far enough away," Mike says, laughing and shaking his head.

"Well, it's just Len. I didn't see anyone convulsing or barfing," I say, comforting myself.

"Yeah. Well, who knows, maybe they've moved past that stuff," Mike says with little conviction.

"Hmmmm. On to bigger and better things."

"Well, bigger, anyway," Mike says.

That was a scary thought. I started wondering where this all could be going. We'd been unplugged from the scene for so long, I didn't know what was going on back in our old stomping grounds. Given that these men never acknowledged the damage done by their manipulative leadership practices, it was a bit worrisome to think that they were continuing to grow in influence and power. I wasn't yet couching my foreboding in such terms in my mind, but my knower was still buzzing faintly with warning bells and panic lights.

I figured that whatever the deal was, we were probably pretty safe up here in our special Little Chapel in the mountains. Likely these incidences of comingling would be few and far between. Or at least, in the midst of these visitations, we would keep our eyes on what it seemed Pastor Lee was trying to build: a church family of loving people who were passionate about Jesus, compassionate toward the lost and hurting, and an asset to the community.

TO LIVE AND DIE IN JUNCTION GULCH

Mike was getting restless. We were both so tired of the proverbial running out of money before running out of month way of life. He just wasn't seeing any light at the end of the search for full-time work. He was dead in the water as far as hopes of any kind of paid ministry positions with TLC. Lee had mumbled a few words about a possible position with the Christian School, but that too failed to manifest. Try as he might to stay positive and hopeful, Mike was feeling that his future in this small town was looking dim.

He began entertaining the thought of expanding his search to other areas. He put together his resume and started searching for youth pastor openings. He even broadened his consideration outside the state. His childhood buddy was living in Montana, and he was putting out the word for Mike up in his little neck of the Big Sky. It was breaking my heart to think of leaving, but it seemed like financial (and other) doors were shutting for us rather than opening.

We invited Pastor Lee over so we could share our concerns and plans with him and get his input.

Lee had this weird way of comforting people. I can only describe it as: *spankouragement*. That's Greek for lovingly administering a talkin'to while letting you know how awesome you are.

"You guys are so precious to us. You bring a tremendous amount of gifting to our body." His voice was always so soft and his words almost slurry, like he'd had a quick hit of Jack before coming. It always made me a little sleepy.

"You've become an important part of who we are. You told me that you were committing yourselves to The Little Chapel and to this community. What happened to that commitment?" Pastor Lee was big on covenant commitment and had preached on it a number of times.

"Well, uh, blah, blah, blah, want to trust God, but . . . blah, blah, need a job . . . mumble, mumble, blah, blah." We tried to explain ourselves in logical terms, but somehow logic seemed to vaporize into the air and leave us with what sounded more like excuses for running away when times got tough.

"You know, my family and I have had to struggle through some lean times to be here. But we made a commitment to Papa John to take care of God's house here. We've let our roots go deep. We're gonna live and die in Junction Gulch."

Now, I'm sure this looks like we were simply biting on a slightly different version of the same ol' worm from years gone by. You'd think we would recognize the putrefied, petrified, fosilified old thing, but I'm telling you, Lee was a magical disarming ninja who could slice you up with loving words and leave you with a brand new perspective and a repentant heart.

"We love you guys and would hate to see you go. I think God's got great things for you here, if I could ever uncork the two of you. Pray about it. Now give me a hug."

And with that, he was gone, leaving just a wisp of black smoke. There we sat, feeling like Lee couldn't do without us and like we would be letting God down if we didn't keep our commitment to living out our lives with TLC.

We prayed and asked God for his blessing to enable us to stay.

Within a month, Mike landed a permanent full-time position as a teacher's aide at the high school. Spooky.

ℭℌ

It felt good and right to stay and invest ourselves in our little mountain community and our Little Chapel. The next year or so kept us busy as we both became increasingly involved with church. We were asked to take a series of classes for people in leadership positions. I guess that was considered a promotion of sorts.

Regular paychecks were a boon, like winning the lotto. And yet, as grateful as we were to have jobs and to be able to go off of the welfare dole, we were pretty much living at the poverty line. Still, we remained faithful with our tithe and somehow managed to squeak out our building fund pledge each month. I guess we were becoming real life grownups. Again the idea of Mike going back to school to become a teacher started poking its head in at the fringes of the radar.

He continued to lead worship a few times a month, introducing some of his songs on Sunday mornings. It was a fun rush to hear the congregation singing Mike's words and music. He was also leading worship at some outreach events at other churches and some retreats and kid's camps.

Em was enjoying the Junior High youth group, singing on the youth group worship team, hanging out with a few chums, eating cookies, and playing games. I was happy that she was getting involved; our vision for our kids had always been that they would grow in their participation in church, discover their callings, and choose to serve the Lord with their lives.

Someone anonymously gifted a junior drum set to Tim, so he quickly wheedled his way into getting to attend the Jr. High group as well. He was technically too young, but he came with bennies, having his own kit and all.

Jillian and I continued to dance and conspire on ways to build a dance team that focused on our funky freestyle. Starwalker and I were collaborating on writing, producing, and performing some sketches that we presented occasionally at Sunday services.

I continued to alternate between hope and despair; my old pal Depression was never too far away. I must say that having a creative outlet did help, but I was stuck in the mind rut of wanting what we did to be more professional and wanting it to be my full-time career. As was my seeming lot, however, we lacked the skilled resources to pull off what I had in my mind. Every creative idea had a Step One that read: *Start holding classes in*—fill in the blank—*to train people so we can*—fill in the blank. Nevertheless, it felt like we had somewhat of a green light from Lee on just about anything we wanted to do, and being active was a balm to my fragile psyche.

THE GATHERING STORM

TLC continued to be visited from time to time by the overflow from the COW of Prophetic Fathers, Evangelists, missionary leaders and other celebs that frequented there. A number of our herd were regularly trekking to Big Town to take advantage of the many conferences, classes, and Schools of the Supernatural that were now being hosted by Papa John and Eli.

Those who were paying visits down the hill were bringing back with them strange and mysterious stories that I found increasingly disturbing, like outbreaks of *holy laughter* and *drunkenness in the Spirit*, both of which were catch phrases from our past that gave me the heebie-jeebies. Visions of Pastor Jim and Len's Carnival of the Weird flitted up from my deeply buried nightmares. There were reports of feathers falling from out of nowhere and people having gold fillings mysteriously appear in their teeth. Names associated with that whole bizarre movement were beginning to float around various conversations far too often.

All the hubbub swirling around Papa John drew some of our number so strongly, they up and moved down to Big Town to get closer to the eye of the storm.

One of the first to go was the lovely Charlotte (Dr. Sozo, Player of Spoons) and her quietly sweet hubby, Chuck. They had gotten a taste of something they wanted more of. Chuck had come back with reports of having received some Heavenly dentistry work himself, but later had to recant because Charlotte remembered him having that gold filling done years prior. Oh well. All that fun was calling, so off went one of our favorite couples—pillars of the Little Chapel—leaving that corner of her lovely frame sagging a bit from the loss. I'm sure the TLC ledgers also felt the pinch. Charlotte and Chuck were, without doubt, significant givers. I somehow kind of understood and accepted their choice. Luckily Charlotte had only just grazed the surface of my heart.

TLC was bustling with activity. I too was plenty busy with work, kids, dance, worship team, assisting with the Jr. High youth group, and cavorting in the creative with Starwalker. I turned a blind eye to the weather and kept myself distracted doing what I did best: tap dancing for the crowd.

If I'd been looking more closely and hadn't kept poking my antennae back down, I probably would have noticed the fleeting glimmer of the ship that was hovering above the dark and broiling cloud mass just down the hill from us.

೮౩

Alice laughed. "There's no use trying," she said: "one can't believe impossible things."
"I daresay you haven't had much practice," said the Queen. "When I was your age, I always did it for half-an-hour a day. Why, sometimes I've believed as many as six impossible things before breakfast."
-Through the Looking-Glass

Starwalker and Charlotte were partners in many kooky antics and creative pranks, buddies from a ways back, before I rolled into town. They had a bit of a broader take on God and Heaven and most things spiritual, and shared some kind of magical knowledge that didn't make it into the Elder's meetings.

One night, I had the opportunity to hang out with these two way-out wayfarers and get a little first-hand taste of their playfulness. A group of about five of us TLC ladies bundled into Starwalker's SUV to head down to the COW for a special evening service. Charlotte was now living in Big Town and was to meet us there for an evening of fun and possible mayhem.

The special guest speaker was Brother Luke. He was a missionary with a huge ministry in Mexico. He'd been preaching in the remotest villages in the far-off jungle for some thirty years. Brother Luke was known for his boldness, his deeply challenging messages to the complacent American church, and his cowboy swagger. Not an altogether unusual résumé for the Charismatic Church. Oh, and he had purportedly raised several hundred people from the dead and regularly experienced crazy miracles like broken limbs being spontaneously healed, people getting new brains, and lepers being cleansed.

Of course you know I had my doubts. This kind of stuff still made me super nervous, but I pushed past it, because hey, I didn't get out much. Plus, my chums were a fun group whom I trusted and heck, ya' never know . . . something could happen.

We were all slaphappy and a little giddy because, well, number 1) this was a silly group of woo-woo girls anyway, and number 2) it was gals' night out and time to partaaaay. We sang and laughed and joked all the way down the long and winding road to the funny farm.

When we arrive, Charlotte meets us in the parking lot.

"Hey ladies! Ready for some fun?" she says.

A chorus of hoots and hollers from the group.

"Wait. I brought something," Starwalker says. She narrows her eyes at Charlotte and grins.

What? A flask? Some weed? With these two wackies I'm starting to expect just about anything. Starwalker rummages in her big Mary Poppins bag.

"Voila!"

With a flourish, she pulls out a long, thin wand. It's clear and has Technicolor fiber optic filaments running up the handle and erupting out of the end like a plume of sparking rainbows. It blinks and twinkles its flamboyant lightshow as Starwalker waves it over Charlotte's head like an enchanted and perhaps slightly crocked fairy godmother.

"I encircle thee with the splendiferous light of Silliopolis and Spiritus Sancto. All the angels of the Cosmos will be drawn to your Maxima Cum Laude and will dance above you tonight. Rejoice!" She flips her arms up like an orchestra conductor, then taps Charlotte on each shoulder with her wand. "I knight thee Five-Star General of the Royal Army of the Raucous Realm. Arise and go forth!"

Starwalker brandishes her wand over each of us, continuing her playful incantations. My stomach tightens a little and I become suddenly aware of the entire parking lot. The vast church grounds. The universe itself. What if someone sees us here, casting spells?

Nothing to be alarmed about. Just some harmless, goofy fun. And it's Starwalker and Company. We're good. You have to get creative when alcohol is not permitted.

"I have brought the anointing pot," says Charlotte. "In honor of this Galactic Occasion."

She produces a tiny pot of glitter and proceeds to anoint each of us with stardust upon our noses, foreheads, and cheeks. We shimmer and glimmer like angels from on high.

Soon we titter and giggle and wimble-wamble our way through the miles of parked cars toward the great belly of the COW. The strains of backbeat and electric guitars are already blasting their way out of every udder and teat.

The worship band at the COW makes it a practice to crank their stacks up to ear-splitting decibels. And although they're exceptional musicians and the music is great, every drumbeat and bassline is a breaker of driving sound, pounding directly into your chest cavity and curling itself around your heart. I later learned that this was a carefully calculated mathematical equation divined from the secret government annals of the Great Dr. Mesmer and the lost journals of The Amazing Kreskin. It had a way of hypnotizing you and then bludgeoning your neurosensory system into submission.

The house is packed—probably six or seven hundred people. It'll be standing room only tonight. Worship is already in full swing.

"I had Chuck save us some seats," Charlotte yells. She grabs Starwalker's hand and we form a linked line like a gaggle of kindergartners on a fieldtrip. Bypassing the bleachers, she winds us through the swarming and sweaty bodies, right into the heart of the main floor seats.

Papa John's youngest son is the worship leader tonight. He and his young wife have beautiful voices. They sing of Jesus' sweet love. I close my eyes and take a deep centering breath, focusing my attention on connecting with the presence of God.

One last rousing number has everyone up and out of their seats, dancing in the aisles; flags and shimmery streamers flutter in arcs through the air. Celebration. Unbridled joy.

As people settle back into their chairs or their places on the floor, Papa John takes the podium. He moves and speaks with a relaxed, unhurried flow. He often takes long pauses, seems thoughtful about the next words he will allow. He takes time to look at the faces of his flock, smiling at them, sometimes chuckling. This is always met with their chuckling with him, like: *We all know something special, isn't this fun?*

Papa John leans casually on the podium. A good neighbor.

"I'm hungry," he says. "You?"

The room cheers and hoots.

"So hungry for the things of God. So happy to be here. So excited. Can't wait to see what Jesus is gonna do. Ya know, after so many years you get to know when you're seeing the real deal. When someone is walking in deep integrity and purity and they back it up with a real demonstration of power. I can honestly say that Brother Luke is a real hero of mine, and the impact of his ministry resonates around the globe. Raising the dead, healing the sick, driving out devils . . . On earth as it is in Heaven." More cheering. He looks down at the front row, "We're so, so glad to have you here brother. You guys, let's let Brother Luke know how much we love him."

The room jumps up. Applause. Cheers.

Brother Luke hippity-hops up the expansive steps to the stage. He dances a little jig in his snakeskin cowboy boots and blue jeans topped with a broad western buckle. A red bandana hangs from his back pocket like a floppy tail. He's like a Texas Leprechaun, but without the ten-gallon hat. He hoots like he's at a rodeo.

"Holy Ghost! Glory! JEEEEESUUUUSSS!!" he hollers, arms up, pacing and hopping from foot to foot like Rocky at the top of the stairs. "Wooooooooohooooo!"

"JEEEEEESUUUUSSS!!" the crowd echoes.

Here we go.

"Thank ya'll. Thanks. Wow. Holy Ghost. Alright." Brother Luke spreads out his Bible and several notebooks and steno pads across the podium. He leafs through some of the pages of each, waiting for the crowd to simmer down. He looks up at us. Smiles. His eyes are huge behind thick, wide glasses. Grey hair cropped to the scalp, long gray and black striped goatee cascading off his chin about six inches, fanning out wide and then chopped straight across the bottom like a whisk broom.

"Ya'll settled down now?" He smiles warmly.

Laughter.

"Got yer Bibles ready? You better. Yer gonna need 'em." He leafs through his Bible. Swish, swish: the familiar sound of tissue paper pages.

"So y'all'r wantin' to raise the dead, heal the sick, and cast out demons."
The crowd erupts again like a stadium full of football fans.

"Well I hope so, 'cause that's what I come here ta' teach ya' ta' do."

More cheering and hooting. The excitement in the air is electric. It doesn't take much to set off the ovations. My antennae are extended full-on; they're in danger of putting someone's eye out. Nevertheless, I find myself strangely reactive to the joyous anticipation. I'm kinda hoping that we're in for something special here tonight: a change. I still cling to a thread of hope for the miraculous.

"Well, some of you may not know, I'm from Mexico." He pronounces it "Messico." "We've been ministering down there for the last thirty-some years—"

"Gloria a Dios!" someone shouts. More cheering.

"Ah!" Brother Luke says, and then rambles off something in Spanish, but I miss it.

"And the Devil, well, he ain't too happy with us. This is a war folks."
Applause.

"But that's nothin' new. Bible says so." He pauses, paces. The house is quiet, but expectation thunders around us.

"We're up over three hundred dead raisings now." Brother Luke hollers like a buckaroo, "Wooooo hoo!" dances another jig, then is suddenly solemn.

"We need you to pray for us. Pray for Messico." Brother Luke's brow bunches up. He flips through the pages of his Bible. Scowls. Paces. He's quiet for several moments again.

"So I might have to get a little cantankerous with ya'll. That alright?" Titters from the crowd, but he's not smiling.

"Ya'll say you want the power. You wanna heal the sick. Raise the dead. But you don't wanna fast and pray. You don't wanna study your Bible. You wanna stay in your comfortable church . . . drive your comfortable car, drink your comfortable Caramel Macchiato."

"Amen, Brother!" "Preach!" "Bring it!" pop up here and there from among the crowd.

"This is not a Starbucks. This is not time to be cute. You can't order God up like your cappuccino. You got to obey him. We're in a war." He stops and looks sideways at us, holds the serious pose, then smiles.

"Can you handle that?" he says, then bursts into a deep belly laugh. His voice is rough and roiling, like rocks and sand in a tumbler mixed with so many years of public hollering. The people laugh too, but it's become a little shy.

"Look, I'm in this. I'm not gonna quit. I'm not afraid. But you are. Look people. It's Jesus. It's submission to Jesus. We preach the Gospel. And we toe the line, in the Holy Ghost. That's what we do. And we see the dead get up and walk. JEEESUSSS!" He raises his arms again and prances around the stage.

"We was in a village, way up in the mountains," Brother Luke shifts gears with dizzying speed. His voice has modulated up a half-step; he's now light, jovial. "Waaaay up, so far yonder that we had to walk in the last five miles. Word had come down to one of our little churches in the valley— we've planted over a hundred churches in Messico now—word had come down that leprosy had gotten a foothold in there. That ol' Devil. He don't like it when churches start growin'. Anyway they sent word to get me on up there to heal 'em. Well, it ain't me doin' the healin'. Glory! Holy Ghost! But look, when I touch people, things change . . ."

Brother Luke went on to tell the most amazing story of how he and his team went up into that little village where a hundred or so people were shut up in this big quarantine hut.

"We could smell 'em as soon as we entered the village. 'Brother Luke,' the pastor says to me, 'you're too late brother. Most have died already. But I know Jesus is mighty and will do a great work because you are here.' So in I went. I almost lost my lunch from the smell. The smell of rot and death. Row after row of bodies layin' on mats, wrapped up in oozing rags, most of em' with half their faces gone. Holy Ghost! . . . "

"I proceeded to lay down on top of each one . . . forehead to forehead, I stretched out on each one."

Groans and gasps emanate from the audience.

"*Shaaata Cataaaaarrrra* . . . and I began to pray and call on the Holy Ghost; FIRE! HOLY FIRE I called out."

"Man, I'm tellin' you, it was gross. I was head to toe goo and stink." He whoops again like a bull rider. "I like this stuff," he says, grinning.

The audience laughs, looks around at each other, murmuring and chatting under their breath.

"I walked out of that hut after three hours of layin' and prayin.' I go wash up and the pastor's wife brings me a big bowl of atole y frijoles y tortillas. She always takes good care of me. Them pastors wives know how to take care of me. I finish up and I hear shoutin' comin' from the middle of the village. My brothers from the valley come running, 'Viven! Viven! Gloria a Dios! Jesus alabanza!' They gather round me and we head over for the hut and there comin' out, are those I had laid upon. They was walkin' and clean and raised up! A hundred and nine souls raised up from the dead, and another twenty cleansed of their leprosy!"

Pandemonium ensues. *Am I buying this?* My heart pounds. My stomach hurts and I have that feeling of sinking. I want to believe. Papa John, all the other pastors, the whole room is ecstatic. What's my problem?

"Look. I got somethin' inside of me. What I know that you possess, if you know Jesus. I know something about you. There's a freight train in you that wants to be let out. It wants out. I'm telling you, everyone in this room has a freight train in 'em. If you love Jesus. And it really likes exposing itself. Especially to unbelievers. So let it out! Holy Ghost! FIRE!"

The crowd applauds and whistles.

Brother Luke nods to Papa John. One of the other pastors picks up a mic from one of the musician's stands and instructs the congregation to assemble in front for prayer. Brother Luke steps down among the crowd. I watch as people brave the press to get close to the Man of God.

"Whatever it is you're up here for, whatever it is you want, it'd be good if you's specific. Last year I prayed for a gal who told me—she had about shoulder length blond hair—and she told me she wanted to be a brunette. I laid hands on her, and she came back the next day and she was sportin' a head full'a long brown hair."

He makes his way along the first few rows stopping in front of each person. One by one he either bops them on the top of the head or blows on their hands or forehead, like he's blowing out a candle. A few he embraces. Some wobble and weave. Some hit the deck like swooning Southern Bells. Some are laughing and doing a herky-jerky bowing thing—like they are being punched repeatedly in the gut.

I stay firmly planted and just observe. My head swims. Yes, I want to know and encounter God's power. Yes, I want to believe that God heals the sick, even raises the dead. But I'm thinking, if this guy has raised the dead, where the heck is the news media? How come this stuff isn't in the headlines for all to see?

". . . blessed are those who have not seen and yet have believed."

~John 20:29

Brother Luke's ministry time wraps up, and the crowd begins to thin. The musicians keep playing for the remaining people who are still praying. I go down to where my girlfriends have inhabited some open floor space. They've formed their own little prayer enclave. I join them to just stand in the quiet and try to refocus my attention on the real main attraction: God.

The musicians play a soft tune that lulls my heart and mind into an attitude of stillness and devotion. The mayhem of the previous hour and a half begins to recede from my addlepated mind. I stand with my arms up, reaching for God's presence, just letting my inner vision float around in the halls of God's great throne room. I begin to weep. Is it frustration? Sadness? Annoyance? Relief? I'm not entirely sure.

The words it is *finished* come into my mind. *What? What is finished?* I wait to see if God has anything else to say. I turn it over in my head. What have I been asking for? I decide to dare to hope that the words are referring to depression. Perhaps this was to be the end of my endless battle.

A moment later, a man comes by, muttering something in tongues and puts his hand on my forehead. I know it's not Brother Luke; he's already headed out to Marie Calendar's with the pastoral team. Just being touched while in this emotional state brings fresh waterworks. I hazard a peek from behind my tear-laced lashes—it's just some random prayer team member. Of course, the guy assumes that my gushing is due to him possessing some mighty anointing that has the power to evoke such emotion with just a touch of his hand. He pushes harder on my head and steps up the intensity of his prayers.

"Shambala shambala sholeo bada guda! Bless her Lord! Get her!" he commands as he pushes me toward the floor.

I continue to cry and allow myself to be gently but firmly shoved to the carpet. My communing with God now abruptly severed by this presumptuous act, all I can think is: *What the hell? You jerk! Fine I'll lie down just to get you to go away, but in my heart I'm standing up!*

I lay on the carpet for a moment trying hard not to sit up and yell at this idiot when from just above my face I hear his voice again.

"We've got gold here! Gold dust here!" he booms, too close for my comfort.

"And here! Here too . . ." Mr. Power Prayer hollers as he steps to the side of me where Charlotte is also lying on the floor, similarly bedecked in stardust.

He moves along our group, peering at our glitter-speckled faces, all of us strewn on the floor like a pile of rag dolls. I don't know if my buddies have all been likewise helped to the ground, they're regular inhabitants thereof anyway, but at the moment it matters not. What's fun is, we just lay here, in our sparkly glory, and let this guy believe we're covered in gold.

Next to me on the floor I hear Charlotte begin to giggle. It wiggles its way into my throat, then Starwalker's, and then into the rest of our shimmering imposter posse, until we're all celebrating our secret with our own private guffaw-fest. Those around us interpret this of course, as an outpouring of the Spirit. Fine with me. I hate the idea of being labeled as a *Hard to Receive* (yes, this was an actual label), so let them think whatever they will. I'm just glad to have a belly laugh in the middle of the desert. And hey, maybe, just maybe, this would be the day of my deliverance.

Just so happens, it was a turning point after all.

A CORDIAL INVITATION TO A SPECIAL MEETING OF THE PEOPLE OF THE INNER SANCTUM

Our worship team was invited to play at Papa John's for an evening service. Mike led worship that night; I sang on the team too. There was a group of folks from TLC who came down to cheer for our team. After the service, Lee requested that Mike and I join him and a small number of others for a late dinner at a local diner.

We gather in the intimate banquet room in the back. The party is small—a dozen or so—and consists of worship team leaders and a few other lay-leaders like myself. Eli and his wife join us as well. We order our coffees, teas, and diet Cokes; the conversation pops with light conviviality.

Soon Flo delivers our burgers, sausage and eggs, chicken fried steaks, and our side salads with beets and garbanzo beans. We eat our food while both Lee and Eli keep us entertained with their lively stories and infectious laughter.

As the dishes are being cleared, the atmosphere in the room shifts just slightly.

"Well, I'm so glad it worked out that you guys were all able to be here tonight. Shelly and I have some news that we want to share with you." Lee's demeanor slowly morphs from stand-up comedian to spiritual father.

"You know, Jesus was often surrounded by a crowd of folks that he was teaching and ministering to. But he also had those closest to him that he counted as his inner circle, those that he shared with on a more personal level. Shelly and I think of you guys as part of our inner circle. We wanted to get together with you to let you know about some exciting changes coming to The Little Chapel, before any public announcements are made."

My figure-outer is ticking away in the background, flipping through all the data files trying to surmise what Lee could possibly be preparing to reveal to us.

"We've actually known for some time, but Papa John asked me to wait to share until all the pieces were in place and the timing was right."

The room has his full attention. The walls have moved in close and I'm feeling a vague sense of unease; Lee is uncharacteristically solemn; his cheeks flushed.

"Papa John has asked me to come on staff at the Church of Wonders. Shelly and I and the kids will be moving to Big Town." He chokes slightly on his last few words.

Stunned silence fills the air as his announcement slowly runs over us like cold cod liver oil—enveloping us, but not being absorbed.

Lee clears his throat and continues, "I know this seems out of left field. I never ever thought I would ever leave Junction Gulch or The Little Chapel." Lee's voice cracks again and his eyes begin to well.

"If Papa John were not the one asking this of me, it would never happen." Lee weeps as he shares; this starts the flow of tears in many of the inner circle.

"When?" Someone manages to croak.

"Pastor Craig and Valerie are relocating to Junction Gulch and he'll be taking over as senior pastor of TLC next month. Papa John has need of my particular giftings in family-life counseling and I've just got to be obedient to my spiritual father." Lee wipes his eyes and nose with his crumpled napkin. He seems relieved to have unloaded this burden.

My heart has constricted into a tight ball in my chest. Even after just finishing a meal, a deep hollow has formed in the pit of my stomach.

My mind is reeling, but now I'm putting the pieces together. Pastor Craig is from a church in a neighboring state. Lee and other members of the leadership team have been making periodic trips to minister at Craig's church. Likewise, Craig and his wife have visited and spoken at TLC a number of times over the past year. For the last few months, Lee has been preaching and teaching about change and how important it is for believers to be flexible and able to adapt to changes brought by the moving of the Holy Spirit.

Lee is talking again, ". . . going to be announcing it to the congregation next Sunday at church. I'd appreciate it if you would hold this in confidence until then."

The meeting somehow is over. Dazed and dumbfounded, we stand, push back our chairs, and gather our belongings in the dim light of the inner sanctum. More tears flow as we each in turn make our way to encourage and embrace Lee, not willing to utter the word *goodbye* just yet.

The ride home is painful and quiet. Mike is not so surprised. I am devastated.

It was weird. Lee was just a guy, and yet he was also a force of nature. He'd hooked us all and found a way to wind his engaging personality and earthy kindness around everyone's hearts—mine being no exception. That's not to say that this was necessarily a conscious or devious act. I don't know what's in a person's heart. It was just that his words from a year before kept floating into my consciousness:

"We made a commitment-mitment-mitment-mitment . . . we're gonna live and die in Junction Gulch-ulch-ulch-ulch-ch-ch."

This was happening, and it had been sanctioned from on high. I had to keep pushing my pain and disappointment away. I should have seen it coming. For a year before the bomb was dropped, there'd been signs. Sermons preached. Articles written. More and more emphasis was being placed on the power and authority of Papa John, the badge *Apostle* being pinned to his chest.

Once again, I was being told to trust the wisdom of my leaders and their ability to hear and obey the will of God. Part of my heart was again screaming, "Warning: You're in too deep. You've seen this stuff before. It's happening again!"

I was getting a momentary glimpse of what was troubling my heart about the gathering storm above the Church of Wonders. And that evasive glint that kept flashing from above the swirling cloud mass, it was registering ever so faintly on my radar now: The Mother Ship Reloaded, hovering and preparing for touchdown and occupation.

PRESSING IN AND MOVING ON

Once the big announcement was made to the congregation, there was no time wasted in the transition. Craig and his wife Valerie relocated to Junction Gulch and they dove right in as senior pastors.

After a period of mourning, I stuffed my feelings of betrayal down deep and turned my attention back to my own participation in what was left of my church world and whatever I thought God was calling me to do with my life.

I began to feel a sense of excitement over the new church building. God's new house promised to be a glorious space. And since *house* for me always carried the secret connotation of theatre, my vision for the possibilities was given a little shot in the arm. Imagine the kinds of productions we could undertake when we had our own building. It gave me somewhere to focus my attention other than my pain over our recent loss.

Meanwhile, Mike had a vision for *our* house, and he knew it wasn't going to happen on a teacher's aide salary. So, in addition to his forty-hour workweek, he took on a fast track degree program and jumped onto the two and a half year road to his Bachelor's degree and teaching credential. I increased my hours at the insurance office and life got even busier, if that were possible. This was probably a good thing indeed; movement is beneficial for people who tend to get stuck in ruts.

Speaking of new house, we bought one of those shortly thereafter as well. Talk about growing up. Just two years earlier, Eli had prophesied over these two poor church mice that God would far surpass our needs in the area of provision, and now we were doing things like buying houses.

෨

The glory of this latter house shall be greater than the former.
~Haggai 2:9

The walls of the new building were up, the freshly hung drywall our canvas. We took up our Sharpie's and tattooed our new house of praise with blessings in ink. Over every inch of exposed sheetrock we wrote our words of dedication, consecration, and sanctification. Verses and verse, prophetic poems and praise-filled prose became the adornment of our chapel, calling in the lost sheep and lifting up the Most High. We were christening our ship, declaring her glorious destiny.

Singing songs of worship and warfare, we marched around the walls thirteen times, praising, and praying, and proclaiming our victory over darkness. Then we stopped and raised a shout—not to bring down the walls of our new building—but rather to raise up a standard against the Enemy in Junction Gulch.

Then we made ready the paint, rollers, and brushes and we sealed the promises of God into the very fabric of His sanctuary. This was to be a place of refuge. A beacon in the night. A rare and precious jewel crowning the region with righteousness and power. TLC: The Sequel.

Within weeks we took occupation of our new building. The transformation from empty cavernous warehouse space to fully dressed sanctuary was a joyous wonder. The walls yet bare, our massive banners that would adorn them were being carefully saved for the great dedication service to be held several weeks hence.

The roadie crew got to sleep in on Sundays now. No more transporting and setting up equipment, the TLC sound system now had a permanent home. No more rent payment either. Oh yeah, well, the mortgage, there was that.

For the dedication of the sanctuary, there was a festive occasion planned; all the church fathers (including our recently pilfered one) were to be there for the big celebration.

Jillian and I had created an elaborate pageanty kind of thing, which culminated in a dance number to be performed to a new song that Mike had written. We worked on it for weeks in preparation. It was rather spectacle-like and included poetry (read by my daughter), a little drama piece (starring my son), a processional marching in of the banners into their new home, and a big dance number. In honor of unity and diversity, we included a whole section of the dance to be choreographed and executed by the other dance team.

Jillian and I waited in the wings, hearts pounding. (The wings were a side storage closet crammed with sawhorses, spare wire, chunks of two-by-fours, and glops of drywall mud that had yet to be scraped up from the cold cement floor.) We put on our makeup using the tiny mirror in Jillian's compact. I love the smell of grease paint—and wall paint, and sawdust, and sweat—in the morning; it smells like . . . *showtime, folks!*

So far the welcome and opening speeches had gone swimmingly. Now our big number was up.

The houselights go to black (we had no theatre lights, only a single spot, so we did the best we could with only that). Jillian and I creep to our hiding places at the side of the stage behind a barrier we had set up.

Spotlight up on a lone knight and his small son center stage. The action unfolds to the words of a poem, as the noble father kneels down and carefully dresses his boy in his own miniature sized helmet and breastplate. He hands the young warrior a sword, takes up his own, and the two raise their weapons to the heavens and then kneel together in prayer. Light out.

In the dark, a driving syncopated drumbeat begins. The only lighting effect we could manage is to bring up the houselights in sections, moving from the back of the house forward, as the tambourine and flag girls come chasseing up the aisles in their prettiest dresses. The only trouble is, the drumbeat is totally wrong.

The drummer has decided to spice the song up with a new and snazzy rhythm. He is a young whippersnapper and a star drummer who is sowing some oats of his own. Nevertheless, it is going to throw our entire end dance number off. And since Jillian's and my dance is with broadswords, this is going to be a problem—precision is like, critical.

Standing behind his keyboard, Mike stops the band (cool as the new "alternative" beat is, he knows Jillian and I are screwed). The dancers crash to a confusing stop at the back of the room, looking around at each other like: *what the ?* The audience obviously shares their sentiments, but stare straight ahead with that dread in their eyes that says, *awwwww dang, this thing is going to suck.* The dancing girls move back to their starting positions.

Mike counts off. The drummer starts again. The girls come in again. Same damn beat! ARRRRRGH! I'm crapping my pants. I want to run on stage screaming and ranting, like the diva I am; but the big reveal is

Jillian and I in Braveheart style blue-faced makeup and chainmail shirts with DAMN SWORDS FOR CHRIST'S SAKE! We don't want to give that away just yet!

Mike stops the band again. Girls back to starting. The audience squirms in their skin. Mike goes to the drummer. Takes his sticks. Shows him the beat. Mike goes back to his keyboard. Meanwhile, Kathy silently has a freaking coronary behind the barrier.

At this point it's too damn late to turn all the stupid lights off again, so we just start. This time the drummer gets it right.

The tambourine and flag girls, heads held high, come chasseing up the aisles. They arrange themselves in front of the stage area, where they dance in unison and make way for the banner procession.

Now come the standard bearers, flying the mighty colors of God. The huge banners fill the sky as they float up the aisle, hoisted on fifteen-foot poles carried with strength and grace by their handlers. The multihued tapestries are marched up to the front, their bearers doing a Ziegfeld peel-off as they reach the stage, and then moving to their posts flanking the audience and platform. There they hold their ground—massive patchwork soldiers standing at attention. It is a sight to see.

As the standards come to a stop, Jillian and I step onto the platform, swords at the ready. Our dance is not long, but it is powerful as we move like warriors to the beat, clashing and circling, running and leaping; our movements punctuated with the *shhhhing-crack* of steel on steel. We end as the music crescendos, by running off stage, swords raised in a mighty victory yell. AHHHHHHHHHHHHH I scream, and as I do, the embarrassment I felt transforms into rage that rises up from deep inside my belly—I *am* William Wallace.

The crowd goes fairly wild. They either loved it or are just plain relieved that we finally made it through the damned thing.

Once off stage I look down and notice that I have sliced the palm of my hand open on one of the blade burrs. My palm is covered in blood that streaks up my arm from when I had raised it high. Awesome.

ॐ

Pastor Craig was a good guy. He really was. But I had it in for him from the start. I admit that right out of the gate. I mean I really wanted to hate him, even though the guy was willing to put on a dress and heels to please me.

Let me 'splain.

One of the first big events TLC planned after the relocation was a women's retreat. Starwalker was involved in putting it together and she had the great idea of the two of us making a promo video to drive sales, er, I mean encourage participation. She was always looking for ways to put our creativity to work.

We sat down one afternoon exploring concepts and laughing our asses off, as usual. We came up with a very funny series of short sketches that depicted women in various situations dropping whatever they were doing (getting married, climbing the face of Half-Dome, or killing bad guys) to run (not walk) and sign up for the weekend. I would love to say we included a "coitus interrupt-us" scene; but this was church, folks. We used church talent for our cast and everyone took their roles seriously. Rose, of course was brilliant in the hilarious part of a slovenly couch potato who blows up her TV with a shotgun then goes in her jammies to sign up.

For the long shots that we couldn't create (like one of our actresses climbing Half-Dome) we used stock or "other" footage. One of the scenarios was a re-creation of a scene from the movie *The Matrix*; where Trinity is kicking ass, climbing walls, and running from agents. (That was the "other" footage—not exactly legal—so I'm hoping that I'm not signing books from prison after this gets out.) Starwalker was our Trinity for all of our close-ups. She rocked the shiny black leather and chunky boots.

One of the Matrix shots we used was when Trinity dives through a window, tumbles down a flight of stairs and then upon landing, comes up in a dead aim—laying on her back, a Glock in each hand. OMG, awesome. In our version, we cut to a medium shot of *our* Trinity (Starwalker) just as she landed from her fall. She sat up, both barrels pointed into the camera.

Greatest moment from the whole project: While shooting one of our takes of that scene, Starwalker does her roll into frame, sits up with her two black squirt guns held out, and instead of her line, "Get up Trinity. GET UP!" She farts . . . as if on cue. The whole crew just freezes for a second as she looks at her guns and says with such puzzled grace and style, "Holy Crap! I didn't know they were loaded!"

We fall apart. Oh what I would pay for a blooper reel.

The final scene is a tight dolly shot at ground level, of a colorful variety of shoes on the feet of women standing in line, eagerly waiting to get registered for the retreat. Among them are the feet of our stars: rock-climbing shoes, dirt-stained satin wedding pumps (one with a broken heel from running up the highway to get to the sign up), black combat boots, bunny slippers. When the camera reaches the front of the line, it stops on an enormous pair of pumps. Up, up, up it pans; up a pair of extremely hairy stockinged legs, to the tip-top of an unusually tall "lady." As she turns to look into the camera we reveal: guess who? Yep, pastor Craig himself. Or should I say *herself*? He/she smiles sheepishly: busted. Silly Pastor, ladies only!

When we asked Craig to do the part, we never thought he would go for it. When he agreed to don a skirt and lipstick for our cause, you'da thought that would be enough for me to embrace him as our fearless leader. Unfortunately, I held my heartache at losing Pastor Lee tightly.

It took me years to figure out that Craig was not really the object of my resentment at all. He was just the new guy who was doing his best; and I was just a wee girl, still blinkered by my pain. As far as the dress and heels, Craig *did* have a playful side after all; perhaps we had more in common than I thought.

స్

The video promo was a hit with the congregation, but not long after, one of the Elders pulled me aside to deliver a message from on high.

"If you and Jillian are going to build this dance ministry, the leadership wants *you* to be in charge."

"Ummm," I answered, eyebrows and antennae up.

"She's brought a lot of passion to the dance, but she has some maturing to do. We think it's important for her to come under you for some guidance, especially in the area of appropriate dress."

What?! But this is Jillian's ministry! She started this thing! It's been her vision! Her heart! Besides, she can't help it if she's got huge, sexy ta-tas! She straps them down with duct tape and bailing wire for God's sake! What, do you expect her to wear a freaking tent? A moo-moo to erase all evidence of her feminine form? How about some burlap or camel skin?

"Well, okay," I answered, though my heart was screaming otherwise.

My ego, on the other hand, was being mightily stroked. I was considered mature. I was considered leadership material. I was being promoted.

I was a coward and I should have stood up for her.

The issue here was not Jillian's maturity. It was her D cups and her hot patootie. And possibly the fact that it had been reported that Grampa Ruby (a lil' ol' feller who attended TLC—he was in his nineties but revisiting his childhood) had been seen sitting in the back row with his hand in his trousers during one of our dance interludes.

I guess people figured Ruby was the barometer for all of the men in the room, and the answer to men's unchecked libidos is to cover up the women.

Jillian accepted the leadership's wishes for me to be in charge with grace and graciousness toward me. I told her that as far as I was concerned, we were a team and nothing really needed to change. But change it did. It was subtle, but it did. We never spoke of it, but rather than build steam, our vision for a dance team just kind of withered and died a slow death. We stopped getting together to practice and our impromptu dances during Worship became infrequent. Perhaps this would have happened anyway— we both were busy—but I think having this hierarchy foisted upon such a beautifully organic collaboration was a subtle poison.

LET'S TALK DIRTY

For this is the will of God, your sanctification: that you abstain from sexual immorality; that each one of you know how to control his own body in holiness and honor, not in the passion of lust like the Gentiles who do not know God. ~1 Thessalonians 4:3-5

I love sex. Don't you? It's just so . . . yummy, and juicy and . . . Sorry. I'm back.

As I ponder the topics of sex, sexuality, and especially female sensuality within the context of the Charismatic Christian Church, I realize it's so multi-faceted that I could easily write a separate volume on it. I shall try to resist.

The attitude of the Church toward sex, and especially women's sensuality, was an area of interesting tension for me. There was a prevailing need to paint the female form over with thick layers of modesty. This yanked at my insides.

Somewhere early on in my conversion a seed of shame around human sexuality was planted. It grew in my subconscious like a funky weed. It pushed its filament-like tendrils into my knower and then comingled with and wrapped around my original design. It added a new and amazingly powerful weapon to my arsenal against sin: self-consciousness.

I slowly morphed into this weird hybrid that came stock with this fabulously feminine sensuality, loaded with an exquisite set of jeweled buttons and velvet lined pockets, but then was rewired to think these were somehow dishonorable parts that should be wrapped in brown paper and tucked under the mattress for the High Holy Days. I still loved to get it on, but I was terrified of any outward expression of sexuality being misconstrued as carnal or unspiritual.

For many years I echoed the attitudes of my teachers: hyper-vigilant about modesty and propriety, snuffing out every brilliant sexual quip or frisky innuendo before it could pass my lips, changing the channel if a love scene got too lovely, and hiding my body under long tunics and Bermuda shorts. Luckily for me (or not), I didn't have to work very hard to strap in the dirty pillows (unlike Jillian and Lilly with their Girls of Glory), but I was cautious about covering up the fine job that the Good Lord did on the badonkadonk. I also became a black belt in the sideways hug.

As far as carrying this into the boudoir, well, let's just put it this way: no lap dances or other exotic fare for Mikey. At least not for a very, very, long while. Lucky for him, I eventually became willing to make up for lost time.

"Intimate fellowship" as it was called in our early circles was a territory left unexplored and rarely explained by the preachers. It was as if sexuality was not meant to be an openly acknowledged part of the human experience. Woe to the virgins entering the marriage bed for the first time. If there were any manuals, they were likely only one chapter at best. More likely, a pamphlet. It only takes five words to say, "Ladies lie on your back."

The puritanical slant toward sexuality I had cut my teeth on at ALCF was replaced by a bit more relaxed attitude at TLC. By this I mean that Lee actually preached about it—and more in depth than just "Sex is for married people." In addition to talking about reasons for abstaining from pre-marital sex, he had the cojones to cover such areas of interest as masturbation and pornography. Lee handled these topics with surprising grace, his usual fantastic humor, and some downright common sense. He pretty much followed the "all things are permissible, but not all are beneficial" rule. He always brought his reasoning back to the realm of personal relationship and making loving choices where your partner was concerned. All in all, fairly levelheaded stuff.

Even with this more sensible approach to sex, however, there was still a fair amount of stiffness around female sensuality (the sheer sexiness of the female of the species was something to be minimized) and talking openly about sexuality only happened in the context of a sermon. We had our clothing police, were practiced in the sideways hug, and any and all sexual innuendo or playfulness in everyday conversation was considered sinful. It was simply not a part of the language. These unspoken rules were certainly behind the thinly cloaked attitudes towards the likes of Jillian.

My slow transition into wakefulness was creating some strange cognitive dissonances for me in this area especially. I could see the problem, but my prudish programming was still running in the background. The weed of shame was still tangled up in my intellect.

I wasn't prepared for what this would mean for me as a parent with offspring heading full on into puberty.

Absolute abstinence was still preached to the teenagers, and we, of course, agreed wholeheartedly. Old fashioned as it sounds, I still kinda think abstinence is not a bad choice for kids, but for some much stronger reasons than religious purity. We set the dating age firmly at sixteen. Perhaps a tad extreme, but hey, can anyone say roofies?

Whole programs and ministries were (and are) developed around the mission to keep our teenagers unspoiled. Popular at this time was encouraging kids to get a *purity ring*. Now, I know it sounds like some kind of torture device for the boys (it was torture for some), but it was just a ring—to be worn on the finger. It symbolized the young person's commitment to remaining sexually pure until marriage. Kind of like being a nun, only with the hope of one day actually doing the deed.

When Em was thirteen, and heading into high school, Mike and I started getting the traditional first teenage daughter jitters. I wanted to get her a ring. Mike wanted to get a shotgun. We settled on both. Em was just jazzed to be getting a sparkly piece of *real* jewelry.

We decided to make it a special day, just us two girls taking the long drive down to Big Town together. We'd have a nice leisurely lunch, hit the mall, and find a pretty little gold band that would announce to the boys, "You shall not pass!"

One Ring to rule them all.

Mike and I hadn't had The Talk with either of our kids yet. We somehow arrived at the clichéd conclusion that it was best for the mom to talk to the girl and the dad to talk to the boy. Lucky me: Em was oldest, so I got to go first. I decided that the hour and fifteen minute journey to town would be the perfect time to tackle the subject.

You see, up to this point, our poor little girl had been uncompromisingly sheltered. No movies with a rating over PG and no Sex Ed allowed. We had heard horror stories about the liberal nature of public school sex education. In the view of the church (and us), the promotion of safe sex was equivalent to permissiveness. For Christian kids, the only permissible sex was *none*. With this worldview guiding us, we decided to not allow her to participate in that part of the school health curriculum. I pictured dildos and excerpts from the Kama Sutra being used in class and I was just terrified of having my little girl's innocence annihilated by anyone other than her own parents.

All of my little vines of sexual shame came into full bloom on that drive down the mountain with my very mature, intelligent, and curious young daughter. Here was an opportunity of a lifetime for open, honest, bonding and dialogue. Instead, something like a huge heavy wet blanket of awkward shyness and nerves descended upon me and it was all I could do to even speak at all. It was truly, amazingly, WEIRD.

"Well, my love, I thought this might be a great time for us to talk a little about . . ." My armpits start to tingle and a hot tightness constricts my chest.

"About . . . sex."

"Ok."

"So, is there anything specific you would like to know?" I ask, just barely able to hear my own voice over the roaring of the blood rushing through my ears.

"Yeah, mom," my sweet girl says. "How does it actually work?"

Deep, involuntary intake of breath. Roaring bumps up a notch.

"Well, sex is a very beautiful thing . . . In the context of marriage."

Muffled sounds of car engine, tires on pavement, wind whistling in the just barely open rear passenger window, blood rushing in ears.

"Yeah, but, how does it actually *work*?"

"Well, sex is a very beautiful thing, in the context of marriage." I was like a Stepford wife that had blown a circuit. System error. Please shut down this program and reboot your sex doll.

I don't know how I did it, but I somehow managed to completely change the subject and that was the end of that. It was truly surreal. And it left my poor child completely hanging there, in the dark about sex. Well, except that it was a beautiful thing.

Lucky for me, Em found the copy of *How to Talk to Your Kids About Sex* that my old pal Miriam had sent me. I left it sitting on my bedside table. I guess I don't have to tell you that I never read it. I'm sure I was subconsciously hoping Em would find and read it, which she later told me she did. You remember the meaning of Emily's name: Industrious One.

To this day I cannot figure out what the hell was wrong with me. It makes very little sense. Especially considering that I hadn't been raised this way. My mom talked to me about sex when I was prepubescent—I was full of questions and she held back no details. She endured the discomfort out of her respect for my natural curiosity. She didn't make a big deal out of it; she just handled it, simply and without flourish. She stuck to the basic operation of things, which grossed me out enough to keep me in the safe zone until an appropriate age for me to explore further. That was when my sister took over and explained the wonder of The Big O, the magical art of taking care of one's self, and of course, birth control.

And it's not like Mike and I didn't have a sex life. We liked doing it. It was just the explaining of the deed to the kids that somehow brought forth billowing waves of embarrassment and dread over me.

I look back with sadness on having missed out on this once in a lifetime opportunity to share these mysteries with my one and only daughter. We laugh about it now, but I can't help thinking she must feel a little cheated. I can only say I'm glad we had such a self-starter deposited into our care. She figured it all out eventually.

Tim's turn rolled around when he was about twelve. While my mindset on the topic had broadened somewhat by that time, I still loathed the awkwardness of it. We had our suspicions that he'd already figured out most of the nuts and bolts. Well, his own anyway. Mike was much more comfortable in this area, so it was good that he was the designated representative for the man-talk with our son. Afterward, I asked how it went. Mike said, "He already knows."

Of course.

If they gave out life do-overs, this is definitely one area that I would erase and re-imagine. I must admit, however, that I don't know if it would be much easier even now. I'm not at all squeamish about it anymore, but I still find sex a phenomenon that is not easily explained to children. Oh, the whats and hows—no problem. It's the whens and whys that I think would be a challenge. Especially when it involves young pre-adolescents and particularly in these peculiar days, when kids are having sex in like, fourth grade. I'm no prude, but that just doesn't feel right to me.

As I said, that is a whole 'nother book, not likely one I will write.

THROUGH THE (LOOKING) GLASS DARKLY

Our new church venue brought a fairly steady stream of our own special guest stars to grace the platform. Even Lee made the line-up. He visited somewhat frequently for a while (easing the flock through the transition, I guess), which always brought a mixture of joy and pain for me. I gobbled up his messages like getting a thimbleful of water in the Sahara, but alas, seeing him and Shelly left me feeling sad and trapped in my disillusionment.

As far as the other guests: apostles, prophets, evangelists, pastors, and teachers; we had 'em all. Each one put their unique spin on the same old topics. Each one with their passion driving an urgent need for us to heed the message and take action.

"Build the church!" exhorted the Apostle.

"Fast and pray!" cried the Prophet.

"Save the lost!" spurred the Evangelist.

"Love the sheep!" encouraged the Pastor.

"Examine the Scriptures!" urged the Teacher.

As if my to-do list wasn't long enough. Let me just roll out my scroll and add those to the top.

The problem: every one of those bullet points came with sub-lists that went three levels deep. Every category carried the potential for some new program to be born and another meeting to be scheduled.

"But which one shall I do first?"

"Do them all first!"

"But I thought I was supposed be working on being a human being, not a human doing."

"Never mind that, just get to work!"

In addition, we started hearing familiar names popping up more and more frequently. Strange associations were being forged. Pastor Jim and Len's names were swirling up to the surface of the hubbub. The more Mike and I heard people talking about them, the more concerned we became. I wondered how it could be that we walked away from this stuff down south, moved six-hundred miles to the other end of the state, sank our tap roots into this remote place, and now here's the same specter. How is this happening?

Somewhere about that time, Mike and I had a visit from our old pals, Matt and Cheryl.

ᏮᎧ

She tried to fancy what the flame of a candle is like after the candle is blown out, for she could not remember ever having seen such a thing.
~Alice's Adventures in Wonderland

Matt and Cheryl came up to spend a week with their friends—you remember—their life-long pals, Melody and Brian. They were all camping together at a nearby campground. Matt and Cheryl invited Mike and I up to hang out with the ol' gang in their woodland abode at the water's edge. There, we worshiped God among the soaring firs.

The afternoon air is cooler under the trees. We sit in our webbed beach chairs, Matt and Mike strumming their guitars, our voices floating through the canopy and on up to the heavens. It's sweet. Our love songs and prayers are tender and quiet. Boy have I missed our old pals.

When we finish, the air around us is pulsing gently with the fragrant presence of the Holy Spirit. A breeze whispers through the high needles of the dense forest, approaching like the far-off whoosh of cars speeding along the highway—no engine sound, just tires brushing pavement, soft and constant. We sit in the sublime stillness for a bit.

"So how's it going at The Little Chapel," Matt asks, his voice soft with concern, like he somehow knows something's up.

I share some of the things about TLC, the COW, and Papa John that have been bugging Mike and I.

After listing my grievances I say, "I hate to sound like I'm grumbling about leadership and stuff, but it all just sometimes feels like Wonderland, ya know?"

"A lot like," Mike says.

"Yep." Cheryl's eyes are closed. Her mouth is a straight line.

"We've known Papa John for many years," Melody says. "He's a man of high integrity and he really loves the Lord."

Brian and Melody aren't the grumbling sort. They usually see the sunny side of things.

Brian says, "Papa John's a true Man of God. He walks in the office of Apostle with a lot of power. People get healed in his services all the time. He prayed for my bad knee, and it hardly ever bothers me now."

"Well, it's Jesus who does the healing," Cheryl says, her pistol drawn at the hip, "and the Man of God is soaking up the glory for it."

"Down girl," Matt says. He looks at her, eyes playful, his mouth turned up at one corner.

"Well, it pisses me off. These guys and their big ministries, jerking people around and making millions. They just use their platforms to get famous and control people. In the end, the sheep get slaughtered and the church looks like a bunch of idiots to the world. Same old crap." She blows the smoke from the nose of her Colt.

"Now come on Cheryl," Mike says. "You're holding back. Tell us how you really feel."

"I'm sorry you guys. You know how I feel about this kind of stuff. These guys are all a part of the same big club—John Williamson, Pastor Jim, Len, and a slew of others—they induct each other into their elite ranks, and slap the titles of *Apostle* and *Prophet* on each other—as if they have the authority to do so—I don't see that anywhere in the Bible—then they drive their Beemers and stand on their pedestals, while the sheep pour their tithes into the bucket. It stinks of pride and arrogance to me. Sorry, just saying."

I don't always agree with Cheryl's both barrels approach, but what she's saying is ringing the bell of truth. As always, I admire her balls.

Brian stretches and yawns. "Well, I guess we'll just have to agree to disagree. I'm ready for a nap."

Melody's brow has tightened into a zigzag under her silvery highlighted bangs. She purses her lips and looks at her friend. She rubs Cheryl's arm and says, "Love you."

"Love you too, Mel," Cheryl says.

We all stand and hug and say our goodbyes. I've got some processing to do. I feel that Old Man Guilt rising up in my chest. Am I entertaining gossip? Part of me wants to dismiss Cheryl's raw words with a flippant *well, maybe Mel and Brian are right; she doesn't know Papa John or Lee or any of our people*. But something sharp hangs in the air and it keeps cutting into my heart. I can't tell if it's some conditioned inner defense of my leaders, or my knower telling me she's struck verity. Again.

We have a lot invested. Again.

Must breathe. Must seek God. Must journal. And journal. And journal some more.

From that time forward, the recurring cry of my heart was two-fold: "Lord, give me wisdom and understanding" and "Make me real." This prayer was the beginning of the end for me. The realer I became, the more surreal church became.

THE END OF THE (FIRE) TUNNEL

Oh God, how I hated fire tunnels. This had become a common and popular practice at the COW, and it wasn't long before Papa John and his ministry team brought the concept up to TLC. A Fire Tunnel is like the Charismatic version of The Stroll. It looks like this: Two long lines of pray-ers stand facing each other, much like they did in the fifties, only boys and girls are allowed to mix. The participants (the pray-ees) pass through the *tunnel* in a long line as the people on the sides pray for and lay hands on them. They come out the other end totally schnockered on the Holy Spirit. Well, if you were to ask anyone, the goal wasn't to get *drunk*, it was simply to have a deep encounter with God as you passed through the line. No pressure. The *unspoken* expectation, however, was for some kind of manifestation to show up, and that usually looked ever so much like what we had witnessed back in Wonderland. The usual fair was laughing, stumbling around like a drunk, body jerking like you've been punched in the gut, twitching like you're channeling Joe Cocker, and finally falling over and needing to be carried off to the side. Tons of pressure! Pressure to participate, and pressure to manifest some kind of sign that the Spirit was touching you. This seemed to always lead to pandemonium. You felt kinda stupid if you just walked through quietly. I felt stupid either way.

Once folks got hooked into the hype around it, fire tunnels became the norm for many services. Just about every single guest speaker from the COW called for this ritual. I always wanted to make a fast break for the door when they did so. Mike was often stuck on stage playing music (lucky dog), so didn't have to appear like a non-participator as I did. He abhorred the damn thing too, but he often had his excuse strapped around his neck.

I tried it a couple times and despised the compulsion to try to work up some emotive state or some *experience* as I went through. I guess I would have been considered a *Hard to Receive*. Oh boy, those labels burned my biscuits.

After my second (or fifth) go around, and yet another encounter with: nothing, I made sure I was seated in deep meditative prayer while the lines were forming. I kept my eyes shut hard and tried with all my might to just focus on Jesus, but in fact, mostly found myself mad that everyone continued to insist on this being the be-all and end-all new way to experience God. Outwardly, I was a picture of holy contemplation; inside, I had my arms folded in consternation and my chin on my chest like a perturbed little kid. This was another area where I found myself digging in my heels, and it probably didn't go wholly unnoticed. My church was slowly morphing into something that was beginning to look way too much like the COW. Like Wonderland. I could feel my TLC slipping away from me and growing to feel more and more like a stranger.

(September 3) *I have asked You, over the course of this year for two things: Wisdom and understanding, and to make me real . . .*

. . . Sometimes when I read Your Word and then look around at what the Church has become I don't see any comparison. We are something else—a big, noisy, over-active anomaly—a corporation, a business, a three-ring circus, a carnival. A pseudo-community.

. . . We create and worship "super star" Christian leaders. We value "drunkenness" over a fresh word. We lay weights on people's shoulders and call it personal growth. We idolize gold dust, gold fillings,

feathers, angels, falling down, drunkenness, and whatever else—be it from You or not. We look up to men with huge platforms and despise our own community, job, family, circumstances.

. . . The most magnificent times I have ever had in my walk with You have been in the simplest moments. Rarely in the loud, worked up, feverish frenzies. It's when I begin to see You in the everyday, not some distant glorious 'destiny,' that I truly know that I'm born again.

Becoming real.

❧

Our final visit to the COW brought all of these ruminations and misgivings into laser focus. You remember ol' Brother Roberts? Our backwoodsy brother who was also a Prophetic Father? Well, once again, Connor Roberts was headlining at a COW prophetic conference. I still scratch my head now when I think about it, but for some reason Mike and I went. I guess you could say we were entering into the realm of morbid curiosity.

It was the typical scenario: packed house, highly charged atmosphere of expectation, exuberant worship time, effusive praise of the special speaker. I'll spare you the repetition of the details and get to the fun.

This time, Brother Roberts preached about the prophetic gift and how it is bestowed through the passing on of an anointing or *mantle* from one prophet to his *spiritual sons.* Toward the end of his message, he called Eli up. Connor said that God wanted him to pass his mantle as a Prophetic Father on to Eli.

After laying his hands on him and praying, Connor draped his sweater over Eli's shoulders. (While you may think that Connor's sweater was being used metaphorically here, in actuality it was believed that objects could be imbued with supernatural power and therefore he was literally placing his prophetic powers, contained in his sweater, on Eli's shoulders.) Eli's knees buckled and he began laughing and staggering around like he was totally tanked.

Most of this was old hat for us. What happened the rest of the service, however, was like watching an episode of *The Twilight Zone.*

Connor waved his arm over the congregation yelling for God's fire to come upon us. The first several rows jumped to their feet, arms in the air trying to *catch* the anointing as he tossed it out to the crowd. With no invitation from Connor, and seemingly as one big mass, the congregation began rushing the stage. People literally mobbed him, pressing in, stretching their arms and straining to touch the hem of the Holy Man's garment.

Mike and I had a back-of-the-room vantage point, as we had made sure we were close to the exit. I was sure if I could see their faces, they would have all had little crazy cartoon spirals where their eyes were supposed to be. Connor did his best to reach out and touch the people, but they were out of control, like a hoard of zombies after fresh meat, practically dragging him to the ground.

We'd seen a lot of bizarre behavior at church, much of it emotionally dramatic, but this went beyond my ability to tolerate. I didn't want to be around if they decided to eat him.

"You had enough?" Mike asked.

"Hold my hand, I'm scared."

We made our exit and headed for home.

❦

Looking back, there were a number of things that I now consider signposts on our path out of Wonderland. Of course, Matt and Cheryl's misgivings were a signal flare, and obviously the church's growing emphasis on Papa John and the Church of Wonders, fire tunnels, and outward physical manifestations, were all signs that we were, without a doubt, retracing our steps on the other side of the looking glass.

Another—and perhaps the brightest—beacon that caught our attention, was the rejection of church by both of our children.

You're like, "No shit Sherlock, beat 'em with a doctrine stick and scare the Bejeezuz out of 'em with stories of hellfire and demons; that's the sure way to lead them in the way they should go—right on out the back door!"

Em was the first to go, then Tim a bit later.

Up to this point, Emily's involvement at church had been mostly limited to attending the Jr. High youth group and also serving as a camp counselor at a kid's prophetic summer camp. She spent time doing crafts with the kids, and practicing her prophesying skills at a few of the meetings. She seemed open to prayer and the supernatural and even occasionally danced during worship service.

I remember clearly one Sunday when Em prayed for a young man who had only one leg. She must have been around maybe ten or eleven. Papa

John was visiting. He preached on the power of the believer to heal the sick. After the sermon, during the ministry time, a young man was sitting up front in his wheelchair, waiting for prayer; he was missing one of his legs. No one was praying for him yet (who the hell is gonna tackle that one). Em made her way up front without being prompted by anyone and just stood next to him and put her hand on his shoulder. She stood for a long time with her eyes closed. When she finished (I assumed she was praying), she opened her eyes to check and see what happened. The young man touched her arm and thanked her. She came back and sat down. We never discussed the occasion, but I was so touched by her innocent faith, and sad that she didn't get to see that young man stand up on two legs.

Once high school hit, however, she lost any innocent fire she may have been nurturing. The high school youth group consisted mostly of a Goth/skater crowd, not remotely her peer group. Safety pins and black nail polish: not her gig. The few times she attended, she felt isolated and unwelcome. Except for Pastor Lee's daughter, no one paid any attention to her at all. She found the blasting music disturbing and the counter-culture too far outside her comfort zone.

More and more frequently she was coming up with reasons why she couldn't go to the service either, and by the time fifteen rolled around, she requested that she be released from having to go at all. As much as we had hoped and prayed that she would choose to follow Jesus, we could see that her heart was not in church and that the high school youth group was definitely not her cup of tea.

We said yes. What else could we do? Force her to go even though she didn't have any friends there; make her embrace all kinds of stuff that made her super uncomfortable; expect her to pretend to be something she wasn't? Funny that we made ourselves go.

"But why do I have to go if she doesn't!" Tim of course played the injustice card. He was twelve and had no compelling argument.

"Ok, you can stay home too, but you'll have to get up, read ten chapters in your book, and write a book report on it."

"Never mind. I'll go."

Poor Tim. It's tough being the youngest. He was forced to endure just a little bit longer. It was no big deal; he invariably slept through church anyway.

We continued to attend church regularly (sans daughter), but being there just felt strange. I felt isolated, like I no longer fit in. I still had my old confidant in Starwalker; she let me bitch and moan about the state of the church, was always patient and kind as I ranted, and never wagged the bony finger of judgment in my face.

Starwalker is, I believe, from a different planet altogether. In fact the longer I'm privileged to know her, the more I know this is likely true. She seems to be much more familiar with walking among quasars and sifting stardust through her toes than the average earthling. She has a Saganesque love affair with the cosmos that inspires the divine imagination of the open-minded seeker and scares the hell out of the narrow-minded believer.

She was a source of great grounding and comfort for me during that time, even though most of her counsel came from outer space. She too saw what I was seeing, and was on her own top-secret spiritual quest that was drawing her out of the darkness and onto the strange shores of Niburu and Sirius C. We would sit out on my sunny back deck postulating on wide and wonderful imagination-bending ideas. We were our own secret little club of spiritual subversives.

Starwalker had a theory that God was ever so much bigger than the box religion tried to stuff him/her/it into. She rambled on about the vastness of the Universe and how huge the field of quantum possibility was. She talked about theories involving extra-terrestrials and the Annunaki and the Sumerian tablets. What if the God of the Old Testament had actually been a feisty alien overlord dominating the human race as a slave species, and they all subsequently left, leaving us hairy creatures with a big Book full of stories to perpetuate the God-as-Overlord myth?

Wow. Hm. That's pretty out there Starwalker, but . . . *What if?* It might certainly explain blood sacrifice and the miles and miles of rules.

The Evil What If. This exploration of ideas felt so dangerous. A stretching of the paradigm. Of the possibilities. Nah. Crazy. But, what if?

Along with my therapy sessions with Starwalker, I found my sanity mostly in my love for my family and in my involvement in a number of local theatre productions and in some deeply satisfying acting work with Rose. Like King Saul, who was only able to keep his demons at bay through the soothing harp of young David, *my* Prozac truly was the theatre. Alas, Rose and her hubby eventually pulled up stakes and headed east to seek better fortunes. He had retired from teaching and she had no ties with the new Wonderland and certainly no love lost in leaving it.

Over the next few years, our family began a slow slide down the slippery slope. That is not to say that we struggled as a family; we have always been held together with some kinda powerful Crazy Glue. It was more like, together, we entered into a birth canal of sorts—a place of intense squeezing—that would emerge on the other side of church. But, as I said, it was a slow process, subtle and nearly unnoticed by most. Mike and I noticed; we were still deeply in love with Jesus, but deeply disturbed as we watched our little Chapel being systematically drained of her lifeblood and replaced by a three-ring circus.

In keeping with our track record of wise decision making, somewhere in the middle of all the unrest, Mike and I had the brilliant idea of selling our first home, buying a piece of property, and building a new house. Impetuous? Us? I don't know what you are talking about.

We were in the center of a glorious real estate bubble and found that the value of our home had nearly doubled. What a boon!

"Let's sell it and sink every last penny into a never-ending building project that will nearly kill us!"

"That sounds like a great plan! Let's do that!" Well, everyone else was doing it.

And do it we did. Because dumb things are what people do when they are in the midst of emotional death.

The next nearly three years of spiritual turmoil were undergone while working full time, swinging hammers the rest of the time, living in trailers with an outhouse for a potty, moving into other people's houses when the snow hit—two winters in a row—and nearly running out of building capital before we could move in to the damn thing. Deep breath.

It was also during this little side adventure that we finally had our awakening.

✂

All of the tumult in my head about church along with the amazing stress of building a house (with not enough money and snow always on the horizon) began to take its toll. Depression was always lurking just outside my back door, and I was starting to experience various odd and random aches and pains. For a long time, I felt like I had some kind of collar clamped around the base of my throat. I called it The Chokey Thing. It was with me night and day. So were about a million questions surrounding my religion.

> (July 27) . . . *I can do all the stuff. I can do the list. I can do the tricks, say the words, dance the dance, and all of a sudden, I'm lost. Lost in my religion. I don't like that. I don't like who I am when I'm religious. And I still carry the bags. I'm still addicted to religious thoughts and attitudes. I'm afraid—like most of the Church—of Amazing Grace. It's so very messy and out of order. And it smells weird.*

I started doing something that I had always been cautioned against by most of my Christian mentors. I started reading. Books. Books from outside the approved author list.

A number of years earlier I had taken a risk and dug into a book by M. Scott Peck about community building and empathetic communication. It kind of blew my mind. I was so excited about the concept of consensus decision-making within community that I could hardly contain myself. When I tried to have a discussion with Lee about it, he basically dismissed my fervent spiel with a soft and slurry, "M. Scott Peck, huh? That guy's pretty far out there." I hadn't dared read anything by anyone outside the Church for like, ever. It was so refreshing to hear another perspective, but since I so valued Lee's opinions, I just put Mr. Peck away, and didn't venture into much else besides the Scriptures for a long time.

Now, I was reading books about the Emergent Church movement, written by Christians who question the way things are done inside the mainstream church. These were baking my noodle and stirring up the hornet's nest of indignation I still held over the commandeering of my Little Chapel. I was clinging like a tick to the idea that church could and should be all that I thought it ought to be: a place where people meet to love God with all their heart, and love their neighbor and themselves. A place where decisions were made by consensus and questions were welcomed and humbly considered; where God was experienced through contemplation and conversation rather than indoctrination.

The more I read, the more urgent the situation became in my mind. I was losing my church and something needed to be done. I was apparently born with my shoes nailed to a soapbox and a nasty allergy to injustice (real or perceived). I was so desperate for an ally, someone who might understand, someone who had the power to change things. Someone who would give me a hug and tell me how awesome I was and that of course I was a seer of truth and let's join together to save the church and the world.

So, what was the obvious next step? Schedule a meeting with pastor Lee, of course. I was due for a good dose of spankouragement. But maybe, just maybe this time he would hear me.

I drove down to Big Town, all excited and a little scared to meet with my old friend and mentor. I was nervous, first of all, because it just plain hurt every time I saw the guy. Secondly, I never knew which way he was gonna go, whose court he was gonna be in. I decided I would do something a little crazy. I decided I would read him some of my journal. It said it all, why not? So I read him the long passage from when I asked God to make me real and then went on to blast the Church. I'm sure that put him into a very receptive place.

I cried as I read, so I know that he understood I was in pain, but I'm not sure I was altogether prepared for his response. He allowed me to finish my lengthy opening monologue; then he put on his therapastor's hat.

"Kaaaathy." My name oozes out of Lee's mouth like warm drizzly honey. "Bless your heart."

Sniff. Sniff. Honk. (My response)

"Boy. That journal entry is loaded with lots of feelings." He lets the quiet build for a moment.

"What is it that you need from Pastor Craig?" he asks gently.

I babble a lot of words.

"Ok, so you need to feel loved."

Sniff, sniff, "Uhuh" sniff . . .

He thinks for a moment, looking toward the ceiling, as if my words had jumped from my journal pages and are still hanging there in the air and he's sifting through them for nuggets.

"You also need to feel respected. Safe. Known."

Well who the hell doesn't need that? That's not really what I said, but go on . . .

"You have a great capacity for love," he slurs.

I know this.

"But you are so afraid. You've been afraid as long as I've known you, since when you first came to The Little Chapel."

I'm not sure, but I can feel a little spank possibly coming . . .

"Fear is the opposite of love. Love casts out fear. So if fear is present, where is the love?"

"Well, what I was really trying to communicate were my feelings of concern and frustration over the direction the church seems to be going." I try to redirect the conversation back to the facts, ma'am.

"But how can you see truth when you have this great big thing sticking out of your eye," he asks, his head and eyebrow cocked in genuine inquiry.

"Buh . . . buh . . . I, uh . . . Whu?"

"Well it sounds to me like what you've been doing is building a case against Pastor Craig. All this hurt and disappointment has created a logjam, right in your eye. How can you possibly see clearly?" Spank, spank, goes Lee.

"I uh, uhhhhh . . ." Sniff.

"And all the other stuff, well, that sounds like maybe you might be co-operating with a spirit of witchcraft. A Jezebel spirit."

Sound of needle scratching across record—*A whose-its now?*

"Ohhhhhhkaaaay. Wow. Well, gosh. Jezebel. Witchcraft? Really? Hmmmm." I can hear the hounds a'comin' for me. I quote his own slogan to him: "I just thought I was trying to keep the main thing the main thing, is all. The main thing being love." *I'm not trying to run the damn nation or anything.* A little ire has popped up like a gerbil; it's nibbling at my craw.

"Look Kathy, bless your heart, I have a suggestion for you, if you're interested."

"K."

Ever so gently he says, "Start by working on your own love, and see if that doesn't just dissolve that big board you have sticking out of your face. Then see what the Lord shows you. Now give me a hug."

I stand obediently and give him a sideways hug.

"You are awesome! God's got some great plans for you," he says, slathering a little proverbial Myrrh on my owie.

And with that, our meeting is adjourned. Ugh—and I still love the guy.

The sun bathes the back of my head with warmth as I make my way through the COW parking lot to my car. My pride also feels a similar but more stinging kind of heat from the spankouragement it has just received. *Sigh.* Let the roller coaster ride continue.

(May 16) . . . *Lord You are awesome. Thank You so much for setting me on this journey. I'm taking your word for it that I'm not lost. That You're with me. That You've got the map and You're tracing the route with your finger and talking me through it. Take me to Love, Lord. Deliver me from fear. . . . And so, I will talk to my brother Craig.*

Ten days later I was scheduled for a meeting with Craig.

(May 26) *Ok Lord, I've got thirty minutes 'til I meet with Craig. I'm feeling a little nervous, a little spacey, a little scared. I just pray Lord, for your peace and Your presence. Please help me to come into balance and a place of rest. Please help me to get my thoughts and feelings together. Father, I know Your desire is for my heart to be soft and pliable and full of love. Love for my brother. I know I need to let go of my hurt, and my mistrust, and my judgments. Oh, I so long to have your heart in this matter. I know You will reveal that to me. By Your grace I will obey You Father. Whatever You want from me. Your ways are so much higher than mine.*

Here is how our conversation went:

ME: "J'ai des choses qui me tracasse vraiment au sujet de l'église en général, mais je les enveloppant dans un petit paquet commode appelé *vous*." ("I have some things that are really bothering me about the church in general, but I'm wrapping them in a convenient little package called *you*.")

CRAIG: "Sate, watashi wa kyōkai no nagadeari, watashi wa kami ga nozoma reru mono ga hoshī nodesu." ("Well I am the head of the church and I want what God wants.")

ME: "Eh bien, je suis le gros orteil de l'église, et je peux l'aider à équilibrer." ("Well, I'm the big toe of the church, and I can help it balance.")

CRAIG: "Naze anata wa watashi no o shiri no son'nani ōkina itamidearu nodesu ka?" ("Why are you being such a big pain in my ass?")

ME: "Pourquoi tu ne peux pas être Lee?" ("Why can't you be Lee?")

CRAIG: "Ugh. Anata o tasukeru tame ni watashi ga dekiru koto wa hontōni nani mo arimasen. Chūmon ga arimasu." ("Ugh. There is really nothing I can do to help you. I have my orders.")

After my meeting with Craig, nothing changed. And everything changed.

Our badass kids.

Homework break.

Did I mention that we had to tear down an existing two-bedroom house in order to build the new one? Yep, did that.

Our tent city.

LIKE BASS TO THE LAKE, OUR KIDS IN THE MOUNTAINS.

WE DON'T TALK ABOUT THIS.

BORN AGAIN, AGAIN

BORN AGAIN, AGAIN

And here's some breaking news: Another six families have been reported missing since the touchdown of Hurricane John. Details at eleven.

~The Wonderland News

ON LEAVING THE CHURCH

THE PAST FEW YEARS HAD BROUGHT an exodus of sorts to TLC. More and more families (almost all of whom Mike and I had considered friends) were sucked into the vortex and relocated to Big Town. I can only imagine the damage this did to the budget; they took their tithe with them, after all.

Starwalker and her hubby moved to Big Town too, but only because Ritchie needed to be there for his job. They spent a few Sundays at Papa John's, but they quickly found they had lost their taste for COW. They too were becoming lactose intolerant, and so they gave up drinking from the udders and took to other more magical potions to slake their spiritual thirst.

It was hard to let Starwalker go. She was my sole ally and confidant. At least Big Town was only an hour away.

Jillian and her family also became scarce at church and eventually moved out of the area for better employment and for more opportunities for their kids.

I redubbed our Little Chapel, Church of the Revolving Door. New faces replaced the departed. Even pastor Craig and his wife eventually succumbed to the suction, but that was a few years after we went MIA. Looking back, I can see that TLC was clearly just a stepping-stone for them anyway—a farm team.

Like John the Baptist, our beloved chapel diminished, so that the Church of Wonders could increase. And increase he did. The hurricane continues to grow, spawning weather patterns that have reached global proportions. Storm systems are converging across the planet as Papa John, Eli, pastor Jim, Len, and hundreds of other charismatic leaders are coalescing their agenda. And the song remains the same: World Domination. It's all good though. I ask you, who wouldn't want the whole world to be completely run by the charismatic church? It would be a beautiful thing. Wouldn't it?

☙

For our family, our life became singularly focused on the quest for home. We were utterly consumed with simply trying to survive the building project.

When my dear friend Miriam heard that we were camping out and building a house, she threw her tool belt, her tent, her sleeping bag, her bowie knife, her rifle, her grappling hook, her mosquito net, her hand grenades, her MREs, her wind-up flashlight, a spare pair of undies, and her toothbrush into her little hatchback, and thirteen hours later, landed on our doorstep (or where our doorstep would eventually be).

She spent a total of six weeks with us, swinging a hammer and cutting up road kill while sleeping on the hard ground surrounded by mountain lions and various biting insects. She helped us turn a little garden shed into a cook shack with an outdoor shower on the back end, which we dubbed: Little Bangkok. (Who'da thought there was so much you can do with a recycled bathtub, kitchen sink, corrugated plastic, old roofing, and bungee cords). Talk about a MacGyver. And a trooper, and a true friend. She made the first leg of what became an unending wilderness saga a true kick in the pants. I definitely choose her for our team in the zombie apocalypse.

During that summer, Tim made it known that he was done with church. He was of age now (the apparent age of consent for rejecting church is fifteen), and he had no interest whatsoever in being a part of the high school youth group. He had also slept through most of the services for the last several years. We knew this day was coming and that it was silly to require him to go when his heart was not there at all.

Summer quickly passed and winter loomed with just the bones of a house standing and the threat of snow crawling over mountain ridges.

Winter in a trailer? Please, God, no. As the first flakes began to fly, one of the remaining precious families from church graciously opened their home to us for temporary shelter. For two months, while they were away helping at an orphanage in Mexico, our family cuddled up to the fire in their very homey home and thanked God to be out of our snow covered tin cans. Though the she of the couple knew of our struggles, we had long since stopped discussing it; it was too difficult a conversation. Nevertheless, being the salt of the earth that they were, they came to our rescue and I'll be forever grateful to them for that.

In spring, when we started up work at the building site again, missing Sunday services increased in frequency. Our involvement dwindled to Mike only occasionally leading worship. We were still in sporadic relationship with a few families, people we'd been in homegroup with and such, but as I said, I increasingly felt myself withdrawing, an old familiar feeling. Shades of Wonderland in the last days. Life in the trailers was taking its toll. Stress upon stress leads to a mess; and I often felt like one.

(April 10) *Well, I had my first (and hopefully only) all out panic attack at about 2 a.m. night before last. Not good. What a rotten, scary, yucky, unacceptable feeling. It was such an unreasonable, exhausting, unnerving experience. I really don't want to go through that again. I especially didn't like the crawling out of my skin part; it was like having some kind of massive drug withdrawal. Maybe I am having withdrawals from normal life.*

It did give me enough of a scare and lack of sleep to take the next day off work—go to the river with Em—drink coffee, talk, journal, watch the river, listen to birds and conversations, doze. But not to cry. Still stuck there. Not good. Must cry.

Our second winter was upon us, and the house was still uninhabitable.

(November 29) *Sitting at the Laundromat. Drying clothes. Washed them yesterday and left them sitting in plastic bags outside last night. This morning they were frozen stiff. I was a little concerned that I might break the legs off Mike's pants. Then he'd have shorts . . . it's too cold for shorts. Anyway, kinda fun, putting frozen clothes into the dryer. They stay in a perfectly formed wad and go "clank" when you toss them in. You can see little flat patches of ice just on the surface of each clump of shirts or undies. Well, they are now in a nice cozy drum—relieved to be thawing and spreading out after a very cramped night in a very cold plastic bag.*

I never dreamt that we would be seeking alternate housing again. It was just too freaking cold to attempt to hibernate in our tin cans, so we rented a house. My relief was akin to a chunk of frozen laundry enjoying the liberating warmth of a tumbling dryer drum.

Unfortunately, we took the risk of renting a house that was on the market, and gol-dern if it didn't sell three weeks later, forcing us to move out four days before Christmas. Luckily, we weren't so far outside of church that we couldn't reach out to TLC friends who were now COW friends. Ronnie and Sue, a retired couple who had always been friendly with us still had their house in Junction Gulch. It was on the market too, but they were willing to take it off for the winter and rent it to us at a decent price. We knew that they likely had heard through the grapevine that we had gone missing from church, but they didn't bring it up and we were fine with that.

Two years into the building project, four months to occupancy, a breath away from home.

(January 17) . . . The house shapes up more each week. I actually experienced feelings of hope yesterday. Looking at the house and actually liking it—imagining myself living in it. Whether or not we will be able to afford it in the end is the $325,000 question. A feeling of potential financial doom hovers at the end of it all. I try to just keep pushing that back. I'm trying to trust that God hasn't left us and still intends good for our family.

I keep asking myself how long a person can flirt alternately with hope and depression so intensely and still stay sane. I asked my friend at work, "Is running off screaming into the night an option?" She said, "No." I asked her, "How long can I go on?" She said, "Longer."

And so I do. Somehow.

This had been a long, tough road and we were so, so tired. We'd been through too much disappointment, too many changes, too much loss. There was nothing holding us there any longer, so Mike and I began having discussions about leaving the church for good.

Revisiting this territory was momentous. I could feel the tectonic plates shifting beneath me when we talked about leaving. But there was nothing for it; we were sitting in the middle of the ocean with no wind and neither of us had the strength to paddle. Occupying our Sunday seats, pretending all was well was just no longer possible. So we simply stopped going. No big blow-up, no big exposé, no announcements, just an empty spot where the Martens used to sit.

Our exhaustion gobbled up the few extra hours of sleep on Sunday mornings, and we quickly relished these reclaimed hours. It felt so good to just simply let go and once again let God serve us breakfast in bed.

ON THE OUTSIDE LOOKING IN

"But it's no use now," thought poor Alice, "to pretend to be two people!
Why, there's hardly enough of me left to make one respectable person!"
~Alice, Alice's Adventures in Wonderland

Winter in the mountains can be a lonely stretch. People hole up and wait it out. This was when I started feeling the loss of friendships.

It's funny, but I was divided about the fact that people seemed to simply ignore that we were no longer coming to church. I didn't want to discuss it with anyone anyway; what would be the point? Yet, I felt sad that no one bothered to ask either. Not one phone call. Not even from the pastoral team.

We occasionally ran into people in town and they would initially greet us with the normal "How ya doin!" enthusiasm, but then we would watch their faces darken as they would say, "Hey, haven't seen you at church lately. . ." to which we finally started replying, "Yeah, we're not doing the church thing right now."

They invariably took a little step back. Awkward silence. I hated that part, but Mike got a kick out of watching people squirm. "Oh. Well, nice to see you!" they would quickly say, and be on their way. Many folks would look the other way and steer a wide path if we passed at the Post Office or the grocery. Not *all* of them did; some continued to allow a strained hug and displayed what felt like genuine if stiff affection. But there was always that crazy hollow moment, when time would stand still as they wriggled against the questions that screamed in their mind, *Why are you not coming to church? Are you heathens now? How can you still be happy, or married, or okay?*

Being in such a small town made outings a little hard for me for a while. For twenty-plus years now, most of our closest relationships had been within the church, to the exclusion and neglect of nearly all our pre-conversion friendships. Going through a second divorce (of the churchy kind) carried the potential for great loneliness. I survived by stuffing my feelings of loss down deep.

Fortunately, during our second foray into Wonderland, we'd managed to establish some friendships outside of church. Through our involvement in theatre and at work, we knew a number of people who were not religious in the least. Some were Christians, in the typical mainstream sense; some were agnostic; a few were full on atheists.

I found a sudden awakening to what an excellent bunch of people I had in my community who were not a part of the church culture at all. This was a source of not only comfort, but also revelation: folks could be unbelievers and still be amazingly good people. People who would give you their coat and walk that extra mile with you. Real. Friends.

༄

In the spring of 2007, after a building project of nearly three years, we finally moved into our (nearly) completed home. One chilly evening not long after, our family was hanging out together in the spaciousness of our freshly painted great-room, the surrounding woods peering in at us through the massive wall of south-facing windows.

A roaring fire dances and pops in the woodstove, the autumnal flames visible through the smoky glass doors. This is our only heat source, a temple of sorts. A neatly split and stacked pile of firewood stands at the ready on the stone covered hearth. Mike laid every piece of that slate, creating a lovely mosaic band around the edges of the hand-hewn posts and mantel. A chunky basket full of newspaper squats next to the wrought iron fireplace arsenal. But there's one odd piece to this Still Life with Fire that doesn't fit with the rustic ambiance of the scene: an old Nike shoebox.

"What's in there?" Tim asks, momentarily distracted from his Gameboy.

"Oh just a bunch of our old canceled checks." I've been putting my office back together—organizing, filing, purging. "You wanna feed some of those to the fire?"

Being somewhat pyromaniacal, he of course jumps at the chance to burn stuff.

The flames reassert themselves as Tim opens the stove doors. I settle back into my reading as he goes on with his task.

A minute later he hollers, "Hey! Holy crap, there are like, a whole bunch of checks to the church in here. Holy crap!"

I look up; he holds a fist-full of checks, fanned out, like a poker hand. He's only made his way through the first few inches, and the box is packed tight.

"Hey, what, are you the IRS?" I say.

"I was just looking. I saw one and it was for, like three hundred dollars. Then I saw another one!"

Em jumps up, goes over to where he sits, and plucks a stack of checks from the box. She shuffles through and finds two more of our old tithe checks.

"Holy crap!" She echoes her brother's incredulity, as she pulls out another check. "You could've paid for my college education with all the money you guys gave to the church."

Oh, the knife sinks in deep. Oooh OUCH. Ohhh, yikes. A heavy rock materializes in the pit of my stomach. I don't even need to do the math. A moment of truth hangs heavy in the air.

"Yep. That we could've, my love. That we could've."

Such a loaded scene—philosophically, psychologically, theologically, pathologically—so many possible discussions could be had. I have no explanation at this moment to offer my kids that can indemnify our choices. They just were what they were.

"Yeah, guys," Mike says with a sigh. "You hold in your hands a representation of many inexplicable decisions we've made. Hopefully we're getting smarter."

Tim tosses the entire box in and we watch it be engulfed by the blaze.

"I think I'm gonna start my own religion," Tim says thoughtfully, his eyes softly fixed on the small inferno.

He could so do it too. He had already succeeded in business at age six, sitting on the walkway out in front of the general store up in Rushing Creek Center, selling rocks to the locals. He always sold them all.

HUNGRY

*"But if I'm not the same, the next question is, 'Who in the world am
I?' Ah, that's the great puzzle!"*

~Alice, Alice's Adventures in Wonderland

Settling into our home after our long journey was like a long, deep,
heavy sigh. Finally, time to breathe. And reflect. I sat, looking back at the
past twenty-plus years of my timeline, tasting the bitter regret of having
given such a huge chunk of my life to the church. I was experiencing what
I could not fathom before: standing on the outside looking in. I turned and
set my face toward the horizon, but I was a stranger in my own homeland.
A stranger to myself.

I walked away from church dragging my tattered religion behind me.
When I would sit down to rest, all I could see were the holes that were opening up in my tired belief system. I picked at the loose threads and soon the
entire sweater began to unravel. This was one of the reasons questioning was
such a dangerous no-no in Wonderland. Questions beget questions.

One area of cognitive incompatibility that I explored more intensely
during this time of deep digging was around the Fundamentalist Christian
view of women, their roles as wives, mothers, and members of society. You
know, the *husband is the head and the leader of the household; a woman's place
is in the home, caring for the children and submitted to her husband's authority*
thing. The men were the church leaders; the women were the helpers, the
lady's group facilitators, and children's ministry workers. Not to say that
these weren't important roles, but they certainly were viewed as subordinate
to the place of the male.

Much of the Church at large still held these same limiting paradigms. I
was now free to consciously reject the narrow view of women they espoused,
and more than that, the patriarchal nature of the scriptures themselves.

Why in the name of all that is Good would God invent such a wondrous, magical, powerful, sagacious, loving, and sexy creature, and then
assign her a seat in coach?

This makes no sense to me, and certainly does not speak of God's supposed
unconditional love and infinite wisdom. This prejudice—held so tightly by
the church fathers for oh-so-long—was one of numerous absurdities that

continued to beg the question: What else were they mistaken about?

I was finding that this kind of God was one I could no longer believe in. Whoever he/she/it was, the architect of the universe had to be bigger than this impossibly thin slice of stale bread.

Tasting hope gave me a ravenous appetite for information. I continued to dive into reading like an eager alien on a mission to find out all there is to know about this odd and wonderful species.

I was forty-three years old and just waking up from the longest sleep. At age twenty I had pushed the pause button on the search for knowledge and then forgot to unpause. Like a baby duck, I had latched on to the first thing I laid eyes on. Then, for twenty-some years, I held tightly to what I thought was *The Truth*—one that could only be conjectured about—while completely setting aside my intellect and curiosity about the wide world around me. I had so much catching up to do.

THAT GIRL'S GOTTA LOTTA NERVANA

THAT GIRL'S GOTTA LOTTA NERVANA
(A FEW CONCLUSIONS)

"Whooooo are you?" Said the caterpillar.
"Why, I am quite myself now sir," Kathy replied. "And more and more
so every day."

~From Kathy's Adventures In Wonderland

I'M A REAL GIRL!

So who was that girl that spent nearly half her life winding through the tunnels of Wonderland? How was it possible to become so estranged from myself that I forgot who I was?

Perhaps I never really forgot. Perhaps it was just a temporary sort of amnesia that allowed me to remain in a strange otherworld long enough to learn whatever lessons I needed to learn.

My whole life I've been addicted to the need to know *the Truth*. I've bristled at mysteries and been anxious about ambiguity. One thing I brought back from my years of sojourning in the land of dogmas and opinions is the understanding that we don't know anything for absolutely positively sure.

I'm finally okay with that. And for me, this is huge.

The only thing that we can count on for sure is that everything is ever-changing. There is new information every day, and it brings with it the potential for growth. Learning to lean into the unknown has been part of my healing.

Not long ago, my very wise son said to me, "Mom, I don't regret all that we've gone through. I wouldn't change it; it made me who I am."

Turning the corner on regret has been a slow process for me. Leaving the church did not mean leaving my demons. It meant facing them—and embracing them. Hitting the trail into the Desert of the Real brought me face to face with myself.

Digging back into this story unearthed a lot of dross for me to sift through and sit with. Some of it looked like blackened old tubers ready for the compost heap: unworthiness, self-disdain, regret, guilt, embarrassment, anger, neediness, loss. But I'm finding that even these have their roots wrapped around hidden gems that can shine when brought up into light. They're homely, rough and uncut—but potentially priceless when polished into questions. I'm learning that so much is a matter of perspective, and I can choose how I will respond to these feelings and whether or not I'll grow from my choices and their outcomes.

I can own my part of the drama and let go of the rest. Much forgiveness has had to take place, toward myself and toward my fellow travelers. *Forgive us, for we know not what we do.* We humans seem to require heaps of this, because we seem to do a lot of dumb-ass stuff on our way to waking up.

I have no explanation for Wonderland. It was what it was and is what it is. I only know that we were not natives and home was calling us.

Mike and I ran into Eli while we were shopping in Big Town a couple years after our departure from the Church. Our encounter was amiable enough, if somewhat strained. The standard inquiry was made:

"So where are you guys going to church?"

Mike gives his standard response, "Oh, we're not doing the church thing anymore."

Standard moment of silence.

Eli says, "Really. Wow. Ya know, you just couldn't convince me to ever leave the church. It's been my whole life for like, ever. I just have too much invested." My own words were coming out of Eli's mouth.

There was a time when I couldn't imagine it either. I suppose if I had a worldwide ministry with thousands of adoring fans and fifteen books in print, I'd be hard pressed to conceive of any other life either. I can't help but wonder if the all the roadblocks and delayed fulfillment of our dreams was for that very reason.

Our destiny lies along a different path.

HITCHHIKING ON THE GURU HIGHWAY

"Have you lost your marbles, girl?" The Queen bellowed with incredulity.
"If you would have the truth, madam, I have finally found them,"
Kathy replied with quiet confidence.
~From Kathy's Adventures in Wonderland

A few years out of Wonderland I came to the conclusion that I was just damn tired of being on an emotional rollercoaster, and I went on a quest for my sanity. I felt strongly that I wanted to accomplish this as naturally as possible. Retreating back into the shelter of my little Prozac helper was not the road I wanted to take. I wasn't interested in being devoid of emotions (the state I found myself in when on meds); I just didn't want to be bullied and dominated by them.

Of course, this became a second spiritual journey of sorts. I shouldered my information backpack and hopped on the Guru Highway in search of Happy. I explored the wide world of Personal Growth and New Thought. As wild and wacky as the Church could be, there was equal opportunity outside of it for diving into new Dogma and Certainty about the nature of all that is.

My antennae fully extended, I chewed on lots of ideas and concepts. Some of them were craw-stickers, best rolled between my thumb and forefinger and flicked out the sunroof. But some, I can honestly say, have been significantly instrumental in helping me to find my marbles.

For starters, yoga has become a non-negotiable for me. Moving my body, challenging my muscles, and training my mind to stay with the process has been absolute gold. And I don't freak out anymore at the sound of sitars and bansuri—seriously, they used to make me feel like I was opening the door to all manner of evil spirits.

This naturally led to further exploration of meditation. Here, I began to learn how to free my mind.

Thinking: I've always done far too much of it. Forever trying to figure life out. My left-brain a constant whirring figure-outer. Mike claims he can hear the gears grinding and whooshing from across the room. All of the marinating in mind chatter, I believe, was a springboard into my lifelong struggle with depression and anxiety.

Contemplation is one thing, but obsessing is something quite different. It's easy to mistake the two when you're addicted to the noise. Thoughts lead to feelings, feelings to stories, stories to conclusions, conclusions to feelings, feelings to stories, and the spiral goes on. Down and down and down, right into sickness. My antidote: not religion, but practicing presence, now there's a boon. Thinking is not all it's cracked up to be. Some people speak of practicing *mindfulness*. My mind is full enough, thank you. I prefer to call it: mind-less-ness.

When I discovered there was a way to unplug the chatterbox, it was like some kind of crazy-ass drug—but without all the side effects. I can use it a zillion times a day and I won't get all pocky or scabby or lose any of my teeth. It is, however, rather addictive.

Being present. Right here. Right now. What a concept. I can live with that. *Really* live. And all that newly acquired spaciousness leaves ever so much more room for inspiration.

Being more intentional about what I put in my body has also been immensely helpful. Love my java, but five cups a day? Not the best idea (as Paul said, all things are permissible, not all are profitable). Lots of green leafy stuff (talking food here—though I'm open to other green leafy options) and a handful of supplements that help balance my brain chemistry. Simple and revolutionary.

Lastly, finding a gifted counselor gave me a safe place to process all the stuff that rattles around upstairs. I've named and made friends with many of my skeletons; they love me for letting them out of the closet. Counseling also gave Mike a break from the broken record and provided me with tools to actually turn the thing off and get some new and improved tunes.

I guess I won't say that I've wholly left depression behind. But I have reframed how I look at it. I'm learning how to identify the needs behind the feelings and the beliefs underpinning the resulting stories I tell myself. It really is all in my head—and lucky me I get to be the boss of my head. Not always easy. I have an amazingly potent brain. Sometimes it gets the better of me. For a minute. But we're learning to tango and the partnership is growing in hopeful ways.

TWICE BITTEN, THRICE SHY: RECONNECTING WITH AN OLD FRIEND

As far as God is concerned, the jury is still kinda out. For a while, we weren't on speaking terms. I needed some distance. God seemed cool with that; I didn't spontaneously combust, my head didn't spin around, and I didn't start levitating or barfing pea soup.

But several years ago, I started to miss him. Her. It. I missed that feeling of intimate relationship with something greater than myself, that feeling of being in the presence of Love.

I decided to just check in and see how God was doing. I hazarded a little prayer.

"Okay God. I don't really know who you are, what you are, or *if* you are—or if you're even a *you* at all. I don't know if you are a *he*, a *she*, a *we*, an *it*, or a *me*. But whatever. Just being real here. So, here I am; I'm open, if you wanna hang out or something."

No big revelations came forth. No thunder. No still small voice. Just okay-ness. And bigness. And more awakeness.

I started noticing beauty in the most unexpected and simple things. Nature itself started singing new songs to me. Colors and textures got a bit richer. Purple dusky clouds and golden morning light began evoking tears. I started loving people a little bit more.

Even so, when I try to pray, I feel a bit of a strange awkwardness. Like an adolescent on a first date, or like trying to get an acquaintance's name right, only it's hard to get it right because they go by so many damn names.

More and more, though, when I'm simply quiet and still, when I loosen my grip on old concepts, I touch this otherness that is oh so familiar, yet oh so much more than lil' ol' me. Something that feels good and right. Something that I can relax into. Something that convinces me that there is a vast picture in the Technicolor Mosaic, and the pieces are all connected. And Jesus? Well, I acknowledge that he lived. And died. And was attributed with saying some amazingly insightful things. I consider myself an ongoing student of many of his precepts. If I've made an eternally egregious error in this, I'm open; he's welcome at any time to pop in and let me know. I am acutely aware that this will bristle some of you, and I'm sorry for that. I mean no offense; I honor your choice to hold with your views too.

Funny, at one time I couldn't have conceived of entertaining such thoughts, or uttering such words. In fact, if you had said those things to me, I would have been scared for you and considered you utterly lost. I would have prayed for you to be found, to be free from your deception. While I do sometimes feel a little lost in this crazy old world, I don't feel at all afraid for the condition of my soul. I feel like Someone's still got my back and home is inside of me, just in *here*, where my heart is.

EPILOGUE

EPILOGUE
(OR, ALL ENDINGS ARE BEGINNINGS)

So now, having finally given voice to my demons, I can fold up these dusty old journals and feed another fire. I can begin my next adventure with my head on a tad straighter, my imagination restored to its former glory, and hope burning under this fine little fanny.

And what of my lifelong desire to grace the silver screen or trod the boards? What of my desperate love affair with the craft of acting, the art of the storyteller? They still live in the heart of my solar plexus, resting sweetly there: the exquisite pain of unrequited love, and the irresistible invitation, "Know thyself."

I flirt with the frenetic conditioning that goads me to figure out what this should look like. Now that I'm free. And, I rest in the joyful knowing that every day is a winding road and that it's all about the journey. I can be okay with only knowing the steps that are illuminated just a few paces ahead of today. I can pretend that maybe The Great Aha's crazy-ass plan is for my greatest good, for me to enjoy my life to the fullest.

Feet on the ground, eyes straight ahead, I take a running start and leap into the vast unknown . . .

WITH ALL MY HEART, THANK YOU

FIRST AND FOREMOST TO MY VERY best friend and partner of thirty-six years, for continually reminding me of who I am; I will forever treasure your unconditional love and Herculean patience. We're gonna make it through this. To our amazing kids, for showing me what it means to be comfortable in one's own skin and for refusing to conform to the preconceptions of others; you have taught me much. To my lifelong pals Starwalker and Miriam, for being wellsprings of grace in the deserts of Wonderland. To my sister, my hubby, and my daughter for your excellent insight and feedback on that first messy, messy draft; you gave me the courage and confidence to take this book seriously. To Gabriele Kohlmeyer for challenging me to dive deeper and teaching me that there is always a better way to write a cliché. Wait. Dive deeper? Ugh. To my readers of subsequent messy drafts: Diana, Matt, Carolyn, Dianne, Debra, Gail, and Kevin for your willingness, kindness, and encouragement. To Erin Robinsong for your professional editing prowess; you elevated everything to the next level. To Sarah Selecky for teaching me what it is to write with curiosity and courage. To the Great Aha, the Thing Itself, the Keeper of the Big Magic—to Love—for being so committed to my continued edification.

And to you my dear, sweet mom, I dedicate this book. Any questions that *you* may have had are now undoubtedly answered—unless, of course— the next leg only leads to more questions. Surely at least a few have been satisfied. See you on the other side . . . I hope.

> *Child of the pure unclouded brow*
> *And dreaming eyes of wonder!*
> *Though time be fleet, and I and thou*
> *Are half a life asunder,*
> *Thy loving smile will surely hail*
> *The love-gift of a fairy-tale.*
>
> ~Lewis Carroll, Through the Looking Glass

AUTHOR BIO

KATHY MARTENS IS A WRITER OF memoir and short fiction. She is a graduate of the American Academy of Dramatic Arts, Los Angeles, and the Sarah Selecky Writing School. She lives where the mountains soar to meet the blue in the Far Northern Hinterlands of California, where she spends her time writing, hanging out with her bff (aka Mike), being routinely gobsmacked by the beauty of nature, and trying to imagine a kinder, more just world. Her musings can be found online at: **www.kathymartens.com**.

NOTE FROM THE AUTHOR

THANK YOU, DEAR READER, *for reading my story. It took all of my courage to open my heart and share, but I think it was important for me to do so. Because using our voice, sharing our stories, daring to be vulnerable, are crucial to our growth as humans. The bedrock for creating a kinder, more compassionate world.*

It is my sincere hope that my story touched you in some way. Gave you courage on your own journey. If so, please help others to find these pages. Share them with a friend. Reviews on Amazon are incredibly helpful as well. If you feel inclined, you can do so on the Born Again, Again book page; it would be much appreciated.

Thanks again for hanging out with me for awhile.

Printed in Great Britain
by Amazon

24156176R00218